Fiery Dust

Childe Harold's Pilgrimage II, stanza 73 (reproduced with permission of The Beinecke Rare Book and Manuscript Library, Yale University)

Fiery Dust
Byron's Poetic Development

JEROME J. McGANN

The University of Chicago Press

CHICAGO AND LONDON

Library of Congress Catalog Card Number: 68-55392

THE UNIVERSITY OF CHICAGO PRESS, CHICAGO 60637
The University of Chicago Press, Ltd., London, W.C. 1

© *1968 by The University of Chicago. All rights reserved*
Published 1968. Printed in the United States of America

For Cecil

And I more pleasure in your praise

Preface

Like most critical studies this book has a number of different aims. Initially it was conceived as a shorter work, and one which was to have been organized as a strictly connected argument about the different kinds and stages of self-expression that are to be found in Byron's poetry and how they develop into each other. The present work remains a study of the development of Byron's poetry. Moreover, the phenomenon of Byronic self-expression is still the central focus of the book. Egoistic imperatives are both a stylistic and a thematic issue in Byron's poetry—in my opinion, the central issue—and this series of essays is intended to examine the operations and significances of those imperatives.

But my analysis of these factors in the present book is not carried out by logically connected argumentation. While working on Byron I became interested in a number of related matters—the MSS of *Childe Harold's Pilgrimage*, for example—and decided to include this material in the present study. An examination of the composition of *Childe Harold's Pilgrimage* could scarcely be included in a closely knit argument about Byron's stylistic and thematic development, but such an examination seemed to impinge so crucially upon the central issue that I decided to incorporate the material and alter the form of the book. Further, I noticed that a number of Byron's important works (like *Sardanapalus*) had rarely been given the critical attention they so clearly merit; and I found myself either disagreeing with certain traditional attitudes to some works, or feeling impelled to add further comments to others. As a result, the book is now a collection of essays, each of which centers on one or two specific works. Sometimes these essays are primarily acts of literary explication—as in the case of *Marino Faliero* and *The Two Foscari*—and sometimes they involve more complicated matters; the essay on *Cain* and *Heaven and Earth* ranges through a number of central Byronic ideas. In every case, however, each essay is intended to contribute information to the total picture of Byron's development as an artist while at the same time offering a more or less complete "reading" of the work(s) under discussion.

I have deliberately cultivated a variety of critical approaches in these chapters in order to keep the book as lively as possible. Generally the overall purpose of the book has dictated the specific type of analysis in each essay. The analysis of *Sardanapalus,* for example, asks the reader to consider the autobiographical elements which are written into the play. By this means I have tried to keep the reader aware that Byron's self-expressive habits did not disappear even when he wrote in "impersonal" poetic forms.

As to the arrangement of the essays, the central, and much the longest, section of the book deals with *Childe Harold's Pilgrimage.* I have chosen to work with this poem rather than with Byron's masterpiece, first, because it spans the crucial years in Byron's development; second, because Byron composed the poem as a running record of his own life and thought in that period; and third, because it is one of the most neglected of the great works of the Romantic Age. In a sense it is Byron's most important work: no other poem contains more information about himself and his ideas, not even *Don Juan.* Moreover, because its composition stretches over so many years, it becomes a convenient norm by which one can measure the changes that take place in the rest of the poetry. I have used *Childe Harold's Pilgrimage* in this normative fashion throughout the book. For example, the fourth canto of *Childe Harold's Pilgrimage* is contemporaneous with *Beppo.* Different as the two poems are, they show a number of similarities which serve to underline the natural development of Byron's poetry from *Childe Harold's Pilgrimage* to *Don Juan.*

Thus the first two sections and the final section of the book define certain crucial events in the development of Byron's art, and the second section in particular provides a sustained analysis of poetic development in the case of a single, and fundamental, work—*Childe Harold's Pilgrimage.* Sections three and four are developmental studies of Byron's tales and plays. These sections contain analyses of certain basic themes in Byron's work, with an emphasis upon the relation of the particular works to the corpus as a whole. The two sections parallel each other insofar as they each carry the analysis of Byron's fundamental ideas well into his *Don Juan* period. In this way they supplement the study of *Childe Harold's Pilgrimage* and prepare even more particularly for the concluding essay on *Beppo* and Byron's *Don Juan* manner. To have included a separate, comprehensive study of *Don Juan* would have necessitated a radical expansion of the book. In any case, my concern is primarily with the development of Byron's styles and themes, and with presenting studies of a number of particular works and crucial ideas which have been somewhat neglected. For my purposes, the concluding chapter defines the limits of Byron's development, since what it says in detail about *Beppo* applies as well to *Don Juan*.

A word about the arrangement of the three final essays on *Childe Harold's Pilgrimage* (Part II, Chapters 3, 4, and 5). Each chapter is a critical analysis executed within the framework of Byron's MS revisions. In the first essay I have laid out all the MS details and biographical evidence that impinge in any way upon the critical analysis. By thus defining in detail the method underlying all three essays, the chapter on Cantos I–II frees the two succeeding ones from a commitment to the close discussion of primary evidence. Consequently, the statistical evidence for my critical discussions of Cantos III and IV has been placed in appendices.

As a final substantive matter I must mention Robert F. Gleckner's *Byron and the Ruins of Paradise* (Baltimore, 1968), which was published too late to be taken into account in this study. While I admire much in Mr. Gleckner's book, particularly the commentary on the Oriental Tales, I cannot agree with his controlling idea that Byron's is a poetry of radical despair. His poetry is indeed built upon a vision of the world's horror and absurdity, and while he never for a moment forgets this vision, his later poetry frequently advances alternative insights and possibilities. I cannot argue the point here, of course, but I trust the essays that follow, especially the later ones, will corroborate my view.

This book was begun six years ago when I was studying with Cecil Lang and it would not have been completed without his constant help. It is not possible for me to mark out the limits of his influence upon myself or my work. The first two sections are a revised version of a dissertation done for Yale University under Maynard Mack. He and Leslie Marchand have also generously assisted me in gaining access to certain essential materials. In this respect I have especially to thank the late Sir John Murray who allowed me to work with the wonderful collection of Byron material at 50 Albemarle Street, and who gave me permission to print certain unpublished material. Indeed, everyone at John Murray Ltd. has been extremely kind and helpful to me. Thanks are also due to Marjorie Wynn and the Beinecke Rare Book Library at Yale University for allowing me to reproduce a manuscript fragment as frontispiece.

The first two parts of the book were written with the help of research grants from the Fulbright Commission and the Fels Fund of Philadelphia. The University of Chicago, thanks largely to the kind efforts of Gwin Kolb and Wayne Booth, also provided me with financial assistance for which I am very grateful.

I want particularly to thank Stuart Tave, who read my manuscript with great care and who saved me from numerous blunders. Through it all my wife Anne, far in the unapparent, has been a constant and infinitely various help. Michael Murrin has read and discussed most of the book with me and I am grateful for his criticisms and suggestions. His ideas have influenced much that I consider best in this study. John Gerber, Susan Morgan, Harold Bloom, E. Talbot Donaldson, and Virgil Burnett have all contributed to my thought and this book in ways too general and intimate to define here.

Four chapters of the book have already been published and I wish to thank Dorothy Hewlett, editor of the *Keats-Shelley Memorial Bulletin;* David Erdman, editor of the *Bulletin of the New York Public Library;* and Arthur Friedman, editor of *Modern Philology*, for permission to reprint them here in slightly altered form.

The title of Part III, Chapter 2 was suggested by a phrase in Robert Adams' *Nil: Episodes in the Literary Conquest of Void During the Nineteenth Century*. I have taken the title of Part IV, Chapter 1 from a phrase which Paul Goodman has applied to contemporary American culture.

Contents

V. *Fulfillment*

Abbreviations and Short Titles

The following works are cited by their short titles. I have used the abbreviations *CHP* and *DJ* throughout to designate *Childe Harold's Pilgrimage* and *Don Juan*.

Biography	Leslie A. Marchand. *Byron: A Biography*. 3 vols. New York, 1957.
BSP	Peter Quennell, ed. *Byron: A Self Portrait*. 2 vols. London, 1950.
Borst	William A. Borst. *Lord Byron's First Pilgrimage*. New Haven, 1948.
Calvert	William Calvert. *Byron: Romantic Paradox*. Chapel Hill, 1935.
Correspondence	John Murray, ed. *Lord Byron's Correspondence*. 2 vols. London, 1922.
Essays	Paul West, ed. *Byron: A Collection of Critical Essays*. Englewood Cliffs, N.J., 1963.
HVSV	Ernest J. Lovell, Jr., ed. *His Very Self and Voice*. New York, 1954.
Joseph	M. K. Joseph. *Byron the Poet*. London, 1964.
LBW	Malcolm Elwin. *Lord Byron's Wife*. New York, 1962.
LJ	Rowland E. Prothero, ed. *The Works of Lord Byron: Letters and Journals*. 6 vols. London, 1898–1901.
Marshall	William H. Marshall. *The Structure of Byron's Major Poems*. Philadelphia, 1962.
Medwin	Ernest J. Lovell, Jr., ed. *Medwin's Conversations of Lord Byron*. Princeton, 1966.
Moore	Thomas Moore. *Letters and Journals of Lord Byron: With Notices of his Life*. 2 vols. London, 1830.

P   E. H. Coleridge, ed. *The Works of Lord Byron: Poetry.*
                  7 vols. London, 1898–1904.

Ridenour   George M. Ridenour. *The Style of Don Juan.* New
                  Haven, 1960.

Rutherford   Andrew Rutherford. *Byron: A Critical Study.* Palo Alto,
                  Cal., 1961.

I

The Beginning

Feeling as He Writes:
THE GENESIS OF THE MYTH

Hours of Idleness was published in July, 1807. In that same month the *Monthly Literary Recreations* brought out its thirteenth number, which contained—in addition to an anonymous review of *Hours of Idleness* and a previously unpublished Byron poem—Byron's review of Wordsworth's 1807 *Poems.* Byron had many virtues, but an incisiveness in matters of literary criticism was never one of them. His review of Wordsworth is expectedly dull. The essay is notable only because it gives us one famous poet's generally favorable response to the work of another famous poet, and because in it he articulates a criterion for judging the worth of poetry that was to remain for him a lifelong principle (one of the few he had).

> Though the present work may not equal his former efforts, many of the poems possess a native elegance, natural and un-affected, totally devoid of the tinsel embellishments and abstract hyperboles of several contemporary sonneteers. The last sonnet in the first volume . . . is perhaps the best . . . ; the force and expression is that of a genuine poet, feeling as he writes. . . .[1]

Whenever Byron felt that a living personality was projected by a poem or a book of poems he responded immediately. An author "feeling as he writes" was a man in person, dramatically present and humanly interesting. The attitude that Byron takes in his Wordsworth review is simply a more conventional rendering of his remark in his *Second Letter* on Bowles' *Invariable Principles of Poetry:* "poetry is in itself passion, and does not systematize. It assails, but does not argue; it may be wrong, but it does not assume pretensions to Optimism."[2] Byron hated sys-

[1] *LJ* 1: 341.
[2] *LJ* 5: 582.

tematizing, metaphysical speculation, rational optimism, especially in poetry, so that it was not long after this review before he anathematized William Wordsworth from the ranks of "feeling" poets. To the end of his life he was unable to see that Wordsworth's moral, poetical, and philosophical speculations were not the end of his poetry, but the vehicles by which he brought to light the passionate and radically personal struggles in his own soul.

Byron sought to demonstrate this ideal of heartfelt and sincere poetry in *Hours of Idleness.*

> Oh! how I hate the nerveless, frigid song,
> The ceaseless echo of the rhyming throng;
> Whose labour'd lines, in chilling numbers flow,
> To paint a pang the author ne'er can know.
> The artless Helicon, I boast, is Youth;
> My Lyre, the Heart;—my Muse, the simple Truth.[3]

The unpoetic irony of this passage, however, is that Byron deplores just what his own lines, indeed most of *Hours of Idleness*, so painfully illustrate. Lord Brougham's notorious review of Byron's book has, I suppose, been vindicated in history. Time not only pardons him for writing well; it has judged that his delightfully urbane acidity was, after all, justified. Besides, Brougham may have been as responsible for the eruption of Byron's genius as was the Levant, or Byron's mother. In any case, Brougham pounced upon Byron's naively self-absorbed book and took a malicious delight in exposing the sort of poetry "which neither gods nor men are said to permit";

> It is a sort of privilege of poets to be egotists; but they should "use it as not abusing it:" and particularly one who piques himself (though indeed at the ripe age of nineteen) of being "an infant bard," . . . should either not know, or should seem not to know, so much about his own ancestry. Besides a poem above cited on the family seat of the Byrons, we have another of eleven pages, on the self same subject, introduced with an apology, "he certainly had no intention of publishing it;" but really, "the particular request of some friends," &c. &c. It concludes with five stanzas on himself, "the last and youngest of a noble line." There is a good deal also about his maternal ancestors, in a Poem on Lachin-y-gair, a mountain where he spent part of his youth, and

<hr/>

[3] "Answer to Some Elegant Verses, Sent by a Friend . . . ," in *Hours of Idleness* (Newark, 1807), p. 119. Throughout this chapter quotations from *Hours of Idleness* will be made from the first edition and given in the text.

might have learnt that *pibroch* is not a bagpipe, any more than duet means a fiddle.[4]

Byron was enraged by the withering ad hominem attack, and within a year he published his equally ad hominem rejoinder. Yet Brougham's review is not only an accurate response to the aesthetic merits of Byron's poems, it is equally true to the pervasive temper of Byron's volume, which is cast in a decidedly personal mode throughout. *Hours of Idleness* was organized in such a way as to force upon the reader the presence of the poet—a specific man named George Gordon who could and did choose to define himself in place and time in his poetry by reference to a variety of publicly verifiable facts and situations (ancestry, age, schooling, youthful environment, home, etc.). Further, both the Preface and a majority of the notes scattered throughout the volume are as self-conscious as the verse itself. In truth, Brougham's "egotism" is a good index to the highly subjective quality of *Hours of Idleness*. It is interesting that although a good many of the sixteen original reviews of the book do not attack its puerilities, nearly all direct their remarks—more or less frequently—to the dramatized person of the author.[5] *The Eclectic Review*, for example, begins with the following declaration: "The notice we take of this publication, regards the author rather than the book." Perceiving Byron's "anxious search for notoriety," the reviewer decides to give the young nobleman ("here solemnly pledged to signalize himself") a deal of good advice on how to attain his evident goals ("the magnanimity of a moral hero," "the way to true honour").[6] *The Critical Review* is equally personal in its approach. After quoting at length from "Childish Recollections," a poem singled out for high praise, the critic moves on to these concluding remarks:

> We cannot now follow the poet, as we would gladly do, through the characteristic, but tender, descriptions, of three or four of his most intimate associates, nor to the conclusion of this affecting poem, which does not fall short of the passages we have already quoted. Valuable, as this little collection is, from its intrinsic merit, it is rendered much more so by the mind which produced and pervades it.[7]

[4] *LJ* 1: 347–48.

[5] They are listed in W. S. Ward, "Byron's *Hours of Idleness* and other than Scotch Reviewers," *MLN* 59 (December, 1944): 547–50.

[6] *Eclectic Review* 3 (November, 1807): 989–93.

[7] *Critical Review*, Third Series, 12 (September, 1807): 53.

Byron himself was never able to resist the spell of striking personalities, real or fictional. Poets and poetry were themselves often judged primarily on the basis of the author's personal qualities (or at least those qualities which Byron chose to attribute to him). Tasso, for example, who is treated as a great tragic figure in Byron's poetry, is praised as a great poet in *Childe Harold's Pilgrimage* because of the heroic virtues which Byron saw in him as a man. Similarly, one of Byron's early favorites was the Cambridge poet Henry Kirke White, a minor Romantic now fallen into a curious neglect. White's poetry is nearly always of an intensely personal cast. Byron praises his work because it is "sincere," and defends him against the strictures of Dallas with the ingenuous observation: "I should have been most proud of such an acquaintance."[8] His eulogy of White in *English Bards and Scotch Reviewers*, like nearly all the other artists' portraits therein, is strictly ad hominem.

Byron's reaction to White and his poetry is scarcely more personal than that of Southey in his superb *Life* of the poet prefixed to his 1807 edition of White's *Literary Remains*.

> With regard to his poems . . . I have . . . to the best of my judgment, selected none which does not either mark the state of his mind, or its progress, or discover evident proofs of what he would have been, if it had not been the will of Heaven to remove him so soon. The reader who feels any admiration for Henry will take some interest in these remains because they are his; he who shall feel none must have a blind heart, and therefore a blind understanding. Such poems are to be considered as making up his history.[9]

Southey's ability to see a kind of dramatic wholeness in the corpus of White's poetry represents his attempt to give an aesthetic formulation to the same kind of psychological interest that Byron's responses showed. Both men were inheritors of a literary "cult of personality" that had begun to flourish in the eighteenth century. Histories, biographies, personal letters, diaries, and memoirs were in great demand. Sentimental anatomists like Richardson, Sterne, and Rousseau were also very popular, while the historical and antiquarian craze produced volumes of anonymous and pseudonymous "reliques" which learned minds were investing with historically recreated personalities from their researches into the past. Everyone came to know Ossian, son of Fingal, and continued to find an interest in him even after he was exposed as a

[8] *LJ* 2: 8–9. See also *LJ* 1: 336.
[9] Robert Southey, *The Remains of Henry Kirke White*, with an account of his life (London, 1807), 1: 54.

fraud. So too with Rowley. From a more subjective point of view, in fact, the mythic personalities of Chatterton and Macpherson seem to have been the projections of their lonely imaginations—poetic vehicles by which they could attain a kind of self-definition in their own minds and in the public domain. Further, the popularity of the poetry of Young, Burns, and Cowper, to mention only three, depended to a great extent upon an *advertisements for myself* quality in their work. Cowper's poetic moralizings are interesting not because they provide insights into systematic rational or even theological truths, but because the poet is able to present to us a more or less effective portrait of a human soul —a man generous and unpedantic with an interior wisdom that was obtained and kept only with the greatest difficulty. John Newton's Preface to Cowper's early *Poems* is a curiously interesting document in this regard. Though he professes in it that it "is not designed to commend the Poems to which it is prefixed," he does in fact commend them not on grounds of poetic execution, but on the basis of their author's uniquely lovable personality.[10] For his part, Young professed: "I borrow two golden rules from *ethics*, which are no less golden in *Composition*, than in life. 1. *Know thyself*; 2dly, *Reverence thyself.*"[11] His *Night Thoughts* is a manifest illustration of the theory of composition implied in these remarks. His prefatory note to that weighty poem underlines its subjective quality: "As the occasion of this Poem, was real, not fictitious; so the method pursued in it was rather imposed by what spontaneously arose in the Author's mind on that occasion, than meditated or designed . . . the facts mentioned did naturally pour these moral reflections on the thought of the Writer."[12] Unhappily, Young's poetic personality had a good deal less to recommend it than had Cowper's. Burns is, of course, the classic example of the personal poet among the pre-Romantics. That he wanted the reader to perceive a larger, psychological unity obtaining among his disparate lyrics is clear enough not only from his letters, but from his introductory comments to his poetry. In the Preface to the Kilmarnock edition he declared: "Unacquainted with the necessary requisites for commencing Poet by rule, he [the poet of the volume] sings the sentiments and manners he felt and saw in himself and his rustic compeers around him, in his and their native language."[13] His poetry amounts to one man's observations upon himself and his culture, and

---

10 William Cowper, *Poems* (London, 1782), p. ii.

11 Edward Young, *Conjectures on Original Composition*, ed. Edith J. Morley (London, 1918), p. 24.

12 Edward Young, *The Poetical Works*, ed. Thomas Park (London, 1813), 1: 9.

13 *The Poetry of Robert Burns*, ed. William Ernest Henley and Thomas F. Henderson (Edinburgh, 1901), 1: 1.

achieves a coherence by means of a mythic personality very dear to the nineteenth century—one "bred to the Plough, and . . . independent."[14]

This inclination to treat literature as a vehicle for self-expression was international in scope. Germany in particular produced a number of aestheticians who expounded the concept, especially as it was illustrated in more modern poetry. Even Goethe eventually decided—probably under Schiller's influence—that all his work was no more than a series of "fragments of a great confession,"[15] and he deliberately set out to write *Dichtung und Wahrheit* that the underlying coherence of his work might be made manifest. His autobiography was intended to "present in due order the inner motives, the external influences, and the stages of my progress" as a poet. Thereby the reader would have the key for interpreting his collected works.[16]

Southey's apprehension of a psychological coherence in White's often fragmentary poetry is basically the same conception as Goethe's, except that the latter explicitly relates his core of essential subjective meaning to a play of cosmic forces (very like Wordsworth). Southey and Goethe are at one with the thought of the period in regarding the inner personal truth of poetry as a quality hidden away, something requiring exegesis and explanation: in particular, a biographical frame of reference into which the fragments of the poetic confession could be put. For although poets in the later eighteenth century were already beginning to come forth in their works in an intentionally confessional posture, few seem to have ever published an entire original volume of poetry which was deliberately organized to dramatize the author's character and environment (to "present in due order the inner motives, the external influences, and the stages of [his] progress"). *The Task* is a notable exception. Personal as *Night Thoughts* is, the work exists primarily within a spiritual landscape rather than in a historical milieu: it is, in other words, perhaps closer in mode to *The Temple* than it is to *The Prelude* or *Childe Harold's Pilgrimage*.

II

Hours of Idleness presents the reader with a picture of the young Lord Byron in a framework that is essentially realistic. Byron's generally unremarkable use of certain hackneyed poetic forms and styles tends to obscure this fact. Besides, his most immediate models—Strang-

[14] *Ibid.*, p. 5.
[15] Quoted in Karl Bruel, ed., *Poetry and Truth* (London, 1908), 1: x.
[16] *Ibid.*, 2:56–57.

ford's *Poems, from the Portuguese of Luis de Camoens*, and the early poetry of Thomas Moore—scarcely lie in the mainstream of Romantic expressionism.[17] Nevertheless, I do not think that Byron was only—or even mainly—interested in them because of their anacreontic manner of versifying, though critics have always assumed this to be the case. If we look at Byron's lyric "Stanzas to a Lady, with the Poems of Camoens," published in *Hours of Idleness*, we get a hint of what impressed him in Strangford's little volume. He commends the poems to the Lady because Camoens

> was, in sooth, a genuine bard;
> His was no faint fictitious flame;
> Like his, may love be thy reward;
> But not thy hapless fate the same.   (p. 21)

We discover that Strangford himself makes a particular point of commending Camoens' poems to the reader because the verse contains the record of a real man's love woes, rather than the "fictions of flimsy romance," which Byron (p. 22) urges us to scorn. Camoens' life, Strangford tells us, is a sequence of marvels, rather a kind of poem than anything else.

> It has been frequently observed, that the memoirs of literary men are, in general, so devoid of extraordinary incident, that the relation of them is calculated more to instruct than to amuse. The Life of Camoens forms an exception to this remark. Its vicissitudes were so many and so various, as almost to encourage a belief, that in describing them the deficiencies of fact were sometimes supplied by the pencil of romance.[18]

It is significant that Strangford's book, aside from its "extraordinary" subject, epitomizes the kind of editions of ancient and modern authors that were being offered to the men of Byron's age. The selected lyrics and fragments from Camoens' work are prefaced with an extended essay on his life; but as had increasingly become the case with literary commentators after Dr. Johnson, the poet and his poems are scarcely distinguishable as subjects or values in Strangford's introductory study. The poems are regarded as interesting not simply or even primarily be-

---

[17] *Poems . . . of . . . Camoens*, ed. and trans. Lord Viscount Strangford (London, 1803); *Odes of Anacreon*, ed. and trans. Thomas Moore (London, 1800); [Thomas Moore], *The Poetical Works of the Late Thomas Little, Esq.*, 4th ed. (London, 1803). There are no significant changes between the first and the fourth editions of this volume. I have used the latter for convenience.

[18] Strangford, p. 1.

cause they are well written, but because they are Camoens'. Except that Moore's essay prefixed to his *Odes of Anacreon* keeps to a modest length in relation to the text, its character and point of view differ very little from Strangford's. *Poems from the Portuguese* contained only 159 pages, yet 50 of these were taken up by notes (often biographical), and 33 were devoted to the introductory essay.

An even more important influence upon *Hours of Idleness* was Thomas Moore's *Poetical Works of the Late Thomas Little, Esq.* In 1820 Byron wrote to his friend of his early acquaintance with *Little's Poems*, "which I knew by heart in 1803, being then in my fifteenth summer."[19] He was attracted to the poetry not only because of the elusive tone that was its characteristic note—a subtle mixture of humor and sentimentality that we associate with Prior, Sedley, and the seventeenth-century Cavaliers—but also because of the "personal" appeal that the poetry made. In 1813 he reminisced to Moore about the attraction that *Little's Poems* had for him:

> I remember, when about fifteen, reading your poems . . . which I can repeat almost now,—and asking all kinds of questions about the author, when I heard that he was not dead according to the preface; wondering if I should ever see him—and . . . very much taken, as you may imagine, with that volume.[20]

Once again we see Byron's inclination to read poetry in a biographically dramatic frame of reference. Moore, in fact, deliberately fostered such a response by the strategy he chose in the organization of his volume of *Little's Poems*. The fictitious personage Thomas Little, briefly though cleverly biographed by Moore in his "Preface by the Editor," is the organizational focus of the apparently haphazard group of poems arranged by Moore for his dead "friend."

Little "died in his one-and twentieth year," and consequently the poems in the volume are all the products of his youth. A relatively "unambitious" and "indolent" young man, he wrote only for his own momentary pleasure.

> He thought, with some justice, that what are called Occasional Poems must be always insipid and uninteresting to the greater part of their readers. The particular situations in which they were written, the character of the author and his associates; all these peculiarities must be known and felt before we can enter into the

[19] *LJ* 5: 452.
[20] *LJ* 2: 251.

spirit of such compositions. These considerations would have always, I believe, prevented MR. LITTLE from submitting these trifles of the moment to the eye of dispassionate criticism; and if their posthumous introduction to the world be injustice to his memory . . . the error must be imputed to the injudicious partiality of friendship.[21]

Like many young men, Little had a distinct taste for love dalliance and "gave much of his time to the study of amatory writers." The reader is therefore asked to be indulgent not only of Little's technical errors, but of the "warm" character of most of the poems, and of their frequent tone of "levity."

The reference to the poet's interest in erotic literature elicits from Moore a short discussion of the subject. Little's work is in a venerable and honored tradition, Moore implies. The effect of this is to make us feel that Little's humble opinion of his own poems is only a sign of his naive and unpretentious virtue. He was more interested in his intimate friendships, and affairs, than in the quest for more public achievements. Of course one's actual experience of the eroticism in the poems will highlight Moore's genial irony. The editor's quiet smile at his friend in no way detracts from our estimate of either man, but merely emphasizes how fitting such a friendship must have been: for Little loved to practice his own good-natured irony upon his friends and sweethearts, as his poems so frequently show. He was a simple, open, perfectly unmalicious young man, and Moore's summary of his character is, in the end, definitive.

> His character was well known to all who were acquainted with him, for he had too much vanity to hide its virtues, and not enough of art to conceal its defects.[22]

The reader is invited to believe that Little's social circle, though extremely small, regarded him with a special tenderness and devotion. His "vanity" about his "virtues" suggests his naive honesty ("not enough of art to conceal its defects"), and tends to make us feel that this and his other "defects" could only have been insignificant faults, if they were faults at all. We are, in short, thoroughly charmed with him from the outset.

The opening poem in the volume introduces Little as a man hailed at birth by the spirit of Love as "Passion's warmest child." His entire

21 [Moore], *Little*, pp. v–vi.
22 *Ibid.*, pp. xiv–xv.

life is devoted to women—to give them pleasure and to soothe their cares. Love poem succeeds love poem, and Little's young life gradually unfolds as a truly incredible series of amours. We meet "Julia," "Mrs. —," "the large and beautiful Miss —," "Rosa," "Phillis," and a number of other named and unnamed ladies. He is not absolutely peripatetic, however. Rosa and Julia seem to be favorites. He has, moreover, a decided attraction to one or more married ladies, and it is clear that neither in these nor in any other instances does his love maintain a "respectful distance." And yet neither his adultery, nor his promiscuity, nor his inconstancy seems a serious defect in his character; on the contrary, they become signs of his basic virtue, for they indicate not only the depth of his passion and the sensibility of his soul, but also his apparently boundless capacity to find the specially lovable qualities in every woman he meets. Each one of his loves gets, for the nonce, his whole and undivided attention, and he is so courteous and gallant to all that one cannot but believe that he honors and respects each one in a special and individual way. A delightful little "fragment" entitled "The Catalogue" makes just this point with a good deal of artfulness. As she "reclin'd on my breast," Rosa asks her lover-poet to "repeat me the list/ Of the nymphs you have lov'd and carest." Little promptly obliges by happily singing the praises of four of his earlier lovers. The poem is interrupted in midcareer by the apparent delicacy of the editor armed with the asterisks of propriety. The poem is, however, impeccably gallant in its treatment of the ladies. Rosa herself could hardly be offended, for he tells her she will crown his list; and although she does not get her own stanza owing to the untimely interruption of the poem, Little still manages to praise her briefly in the second stanza as his latest and best love. In all this there is a strain of comic irony that is not to be measured, perhaps, with an absolute exactness. This is so because fantasy is such a strong element in Moore's book. The diction is artificial, the situations are stereotyped, and success depends upon the poet's ability to be extravagant with grace.

Little's dramatized career proves him to be as earnestly solicitous as he suggests in "Morality, A Familiar Epistle," a poem which seems to epitomize the whole volume. In it he rejects the advice offered by those

> Who, in methodic forms advancing,
> Teaching morality like dancing,
> Tell us, for heav'n or money's sake,
> What *steps* we are through life to take. . . .[23]

23 *Ibid.*, p. 169.

He goes on to note that no consensus has ever been reached on "what is pure morality," and that he is, for his own part, convinced

> 'T is like the rainbow's shifting zone,
> And every vision makes its own.

He rejects equally the advice of the stoic and the epicurean, and declares himself the disciple of the god of love. As such he is, like his master, unfettered by any form of action except those that he himself invents from moment to moment. His only restriction is that he be a lover always:

> [And] I in feeling's sweet romance,
> Look on each day-beam as a glance
> From the great eye of Him, above,
> Wak'ning his world with looks of love!

Moore plays with his religious metaphor to the end, naturalizing the God who is Love into the sun, and the children of God into sons of the morning. That Moore was working within the conventions of the anacreontic tradition in no way detracts from the real merit of such poems.

As a volume, then, *Little's Poems* remains true to the character of its putative author. He is an undesigning and good-natured soul who lives for successive moments of love and intimacy, and who is committed to serve faithfully the several objects of his love. Each love poem provides another insight into his catholic devotion and availability. Indeed, the book's overall variety is an important index of Little's character. It underlines the unpredictability of his responses, which are never motivated by a conscious purpose, but rather by his own incalculable needs (he is always being trapped by the beauty of his ladies) and the equally unpredictable needs of the women he meets. He in fact lives a life of constant service to others, never deserting a lover unless another engagement demands his special and immediate attention, and always accepting the transience of love and lovers with equanimity. The key to the form of the book is the most important thing for my present purposes. Everything exists to elucidate and define more clearly a hypothetical character: the volume dramatizes the name and nature of the late Thomas Little, Esq.

III

Hours of Idleness imitated Moore's volume in a number of particulars, but the self-dramatization of its purported author was, as we have

already seen, the one element in the book which most struck Byron.[24]
It is not surprising, then, that Byron's early reviewers should have
singled out the strongly expressivistic quality of *Hours of Idleness*, for
Byron seems to have consciously striven to publicize his character in
this, his first book of poetry intended for general circulation. Byron's
Preface—"revealing much . . . about the author's personality," as William Calvert has said—[25] immediately dictates the highly personal decorum which prevails throughout the volume. The book was really a kind
of debut ("I have hazarded my reputation and feelings in publishing
this volume," p. vi). He tells the reader that he hopes his book will provide some amusement, particularly for younger minds; but the dominant motif in the Preface is "fame." He keeps coming back to the idea,
and while he is extremely tactful in speaking of this motivation for his
work, he does not try to conceal it ("To the dictates of young ambition,
may be ascribed many actions more criminal, and equally absurd," p.
ix). A book of poetry seemed a good way to establish a reputation—a
useful thing for a young lord clearly bent upon some ambitious "pursuits hereafter" (p. ix) in society.

As one reviewer acutely noted, this desire for an approving notoriety
led Byron to present himself as a young lord aspiring to the "magnanimity of a moral hero." He continually alludes to his aristocratic heritage and asserts his longing to continue its heroic traditions. To this end
he publishes a good deal of satire and social criticism, for in it we see
the reflection of his innate moral sense. Withal, he is a young man and
possesses all the virtues and defects of his age. Both are related to those
"fierce emotions of the flowing soul" (p. 199) which are natural to any
healthy and spirited youth, and they find expression in his poems on
love and friendship. He acknowledges that he has sometimes acted with
a passionate imprudence, but while admitting his errors in a poem addressed to the Rev. Thomas Becher, he argues that a man is worthless if
he does not possess a strong and enthusiastic soul. He is careful
throughout the volume to exhibit his passionate character, but equally
careful to show that he is aware of the excesses to which "entusymusy"
can carry one. An ironic strain pervades the volume and is allied to the
attitude of self-possessed objectivity that Byron so frequently puts on.
Thus, "Granta, A Medley" concludes with a facetious abruptness. Or,

---

24 Other studies of the relation between Byron and Moore that treat their early
volumes are: Edgar Dawson, *Byron und Moore* (Leipzig, 1902); and Hoover H. Jordan, "Byron and Moore," *MLQ* 9 (1948): 429–39, esp. 429–31.

25 *Calvert*, p. 74.

when he tries to persuade "Marion," one of his lady acquaintances, out of a black mood, he makes sure that his advice is offered in a good-humored way.

> All I shall, therefore, say, (whate'er
> I think, is neither here nor there,)
> Is that such lips, of looks endearing,
> Were form'd for better things, than sneering.   (p. 45)

Byron will be alternately ironic or serious in his love poems, but when he speaks of his more heroic longings he maintains a severely earnest demeanor. It is just such seriousness that produces his worst and his best verse in this early volume, for he has not yet learned how to manage poetic decorum. "On Leaving Newstead Abbey" is typical of the worst poems in this group. After recounting the wonderful deeds of his ancestors he finds himself at the conclusion faced with a present imperative, and he attempts an identification of himself with the figures of the ancestors he has so romantically recalled.

> Shades of heroes, farewell! your descendant, departing
> From the seat of his ancestors, bids you, adieu!
> Abroad, or at home, your remembrance imparting
> New courage, he'll think upon glory, and you.
>
> Though a tear dim his eye, at this sad separation,
> 'Tis nature, not fear, that excites his regret;
> Far distant he goes, with the same emulation,
> The fame of his fathers he ne'er can forget.
>
> That fame, and that memory, still will he cherish,
> He vows, that he ne'er will disgrace your renown;
> Like you will he live, or like you will he perish;
> When decay'd, may he mingle his dust with your own.   (p. 3)

In these dreadful lines Byron tries to strike an equality between his fathers and himself by casting himself in a heroic role. The whole poem takes the form of a romance hero's farewell speech before his arduous quest. But when, at the end, he has to speak of his specific intentions, the poem suddenly loses all connection with the

> mail-covered Barons, who proudly to battle,
> Led their vassals from Europe to Palestine's plain.   (p. 2)

At the conclusion we move instead in the world of Sir Charles Grandison. "Abroad, or at home" is a linguistic disaster under the circumstances, since it is unlikely to suggest anything more than a thoroughly conventional Grand Tour. Like most of the statements in the three quoted stanzas, the phrase is grotesquely domestic in its overtones; the breach in poetic decorum is manifest if we set it beside such a resounding romantic line as "Near Askalon's towers, John of Horistan slumbers." If Byron had been Laertes, this poem would have served him as an apt reply to his father before he left for his education abroad.

Bad as this poem is, it affords us a good example of the kind of grandiose self-dramatizing which lies behind the whole volume. Filled with a desire for greatness, Byron looks to *fama* as a sign of his election. *Hours of Idleness* is Byron's first mythologized account of his own person, his first attempt to create in poetry, and thereby *be*, "A being more intense" (*CHP* III, 6) and admirable than ordinary men. Most of his early attempts at a sublime style fail completely, but they have a real significance insofar as we perceive their intention. Not all his poems in this mode are failures, however. In "A Fragment" and "Lachin Y. Gair," for example, Byron succeeds in establishing an equality between the mythology of heroic pursuits and the possibilities of his own life. In both cases, however, he has recourse to a nonsocial world of his own past. "Near Lachin Y. Gair I spent the early part of my youth" (p. 129), Byron tells us in a prefatory note to his well-known lyric, and we see that the romantic highlands and the literature about them have fired his imagination as much as had the history of the Byrons. The attempt to make the present a continuation of the heroic past is managed in both poems. In "A Fragment" Byron confidently declares his kinship with his heroic forebears by employing an image of sublimity and grandeur to which both have access: the mountains of Scotland.

> When, to their airy hall, my fathers' voice,
> Shall call my spirit, joyful in their choice;
> When, pois'd upon the gale, my form shall ride,
> Or, dark in mist, descend the mountain's side;
> Oh! may my shade behold no sculptur'd urns,
> To mark the spot, where earth to earth returns:
> No lengthen'd scroll of virtue and renown;
> My epitaph shall be, my name alone:
> If that with honour fail to crown my clay,
> Oh! may no other fame my deeds repay;
> That, only that, shall single out the spot,
> By that remember'd, or with that forgot.   (p. 9)

Despite the verbal ineconomy of the conclusion, this is a creditable poem. That immortal "name," so important to him, seems entirely within reach now, for he can join his fathers imaginatively in their wild and "airy halls" in the mountains which he knew as a boy. Unlike Newstead Abby, these suffer neither decay nor change, so that by becoming part of them he avoids the necessity of seeking after vain worldly achievements. Since his true beginning and end are with the dark mists and powerful storms which perpetually show forth their living strength on the slopes and summits of the mountains, his true life and true nobility are a fact of his *being*, so that his worth and stature are limited only by the scope of his own vision of himself, not by the petty measures of the world.

In "Lachin Y. Gair" the same themes and basic techniques are repeated, only the various relationships between romantic mountain, heroic ancestry, domestic England, and aspiring Lord Byron are made more explicit. The connection between Lachin Y. Gair and his heritage is specified in the second stanza. Though "long perish'd" (p. 130), the chiefs of the Gordons live still in the spirit of the region dominated by the great mountain. As Byron wanders about, he hears of their fame in the traditional stories told "by the natives of dark Loch na Garr" (p. 130). But the presence of the Gordons is an immediate experience when he sees and hears the storms upon the mountain.

> "Shades of the dead! have I not heard your voices
> "Rise on the night-rolling breath of the gale?"
> Surely the soul of the hero rejoices,
> And rides on the wind, o'er his own Highland vale:
> Round Loch na Garr, while the stormy mist gathers,
> Winter presides in his cold icy car;
> Clouds, there, encircle the forms of my Fathers,
> They dwell in the tempests of dark Loch na Garr: (p. 130)

Being a living part of "that high world" of which Byron spoke in a later poem, the Gordons need not be concerned that they died "at Culloden," for their greatness does not depend upon "victory" or "applause." Their essential lives were not lived in human history any more than their achievements can be measured in human terms: they are part of the mythic world whose beginning and end is in "dark Loch na Garr." This is where Byron spent his youth and learned of his kinship with a sublime order of life, and when he dies he too will return to an "earthy slumber" in the bosom of the mountain, "in the caves of Braemar" (p. 131). So in the last stanza he speaks of himself as an exile in England's "tame and domestic" regions, and waits for the time of his return to his real life and real home.

The split in consciousness manifest in these two poems, so typical of the Romantic conflict between "real" and imaginative orders of being, does not develop into a source of anxiety in "A Fragment." At the very beginning and end of "Lachin Y. Gair," however, Byron gives us a glimpse of that Romantic discontent for which he was soon to become the byword. The poem opens with a brief and undistinguished statement of disaffection for "the minions of luxury" who are caught up in the ordinary affairs of the world, and it closes with an allusion to his unfulfilled life in commonplace England. But as a whole *Hours of Idleness* displays a radical division of a similar nature. I have already pointed out how Byron's attitudes in his book tend to polarize around his person insofar as he sees himself as a well-bred young nobleman, or as a sentimentalist and a man of feeling. But the frequency with which these two figures merge in the book suggests that their antithesis is only the sign of a more fundamental split in Byron's perception of himself and his world.

Byron's role as nobleman is itself unintegrated, for on the one hand he can project himself into the sublime and imaginative world of his ancestors, and on the other he is imprisoned by a set of decaying heroic symbols and by a society which is totally out of place in his mythologized existence. The world of the youth of feeling is similarly fractured. He bids a mocking farewell to "sickly Sensibility" in "To Romance" (p. 135), and we have already noticed a number of other poems in which he shows a sardonic or amused consciousness of certain forms of youthful naiveté. But these are set off against a relatively equal number of poems in which Byron's rather conventional version of a Blakean Beulah is regarded as a psychological state of great value—especially when it is contrasted with the values of age and maturity:

> Can Treasures, hoarded for some thankless Son,
> Can Royal Smiles, or Wreaths by slaughter won,
> Can Stars, or Ermine, Man's maturer Toys,
> (For glittering baubles are not left to Boys,)
> Recall one scene, so much belov'd, to view,
> As those, where Youth her garland twin'd for you?
> Ah, no! amidst the gloomy calm of age,
> You turn with faltering hand life's varied page,
> Peruse the record of your days on earth,
> Unsullied only, where it marks your birth.   (p. 167)

In "To E. N. L. Esq." he considers the prospects of a life of responsibility and hopes that he may stay "at heart a child" always (p. 180). The poem lingers over a series of recollected images of an age that is now passing away, and when he escapes the stilted grammar and diction that so often disfigure *Hours of Idleness* he is able to achieve brief moments of fine and simple pathos.

> Ah! though the present brings but pain,
> I think those days may come again.   (p. 179)

The effect of the couplet seems to derive partly from the economy of statement, and partly from the verb "may"—which suggests the speaker's deep-felt *need* of the innocence of youth. He knows "those days" cannot come again in fact, but the value that they represent seems so great to him that he ventures a subjunctive which expresses at once his pain of loss, and his obscure perception that youth and innocence may be recoverable as spiritual values.

A longer passage later in the poem operates with a similar kind of dignified simplicity. He is reminiscing over the end of the fleeting love affairs of his youth.

> Thus faint is every former flame,
> And Passion's self is now a name!
> As when the ebbing flames are low,
> The aid which once improv'd their light,
> And bade them burn with fiercer glow,
> Now quenches all their sparks in night;
> Thus has it been with Passion's fires,
> As many a boy, and girl, remembers,
> While all the force of love expires,
> Extinguish'd with the dying embers.   (p. 182, ll. 77–86)

The pathos in these lines depends to a great extent upon the careful use of rhyme and line rhythm. The image of a dying fire is traditional and appropriate, while the management of the verse movement is quite original. Byron interrupts and delays the fulfillment of the fire/passion comparison in a number of ways, and thus creates an imitation in the verse rhythm itself of a slow and gradual process of extinction. After the quick initial couplet, the periodic structure of lines 79–81 is supported by the slightly delayed rhyme (bcb): line 82, which completes the "c" rhyme, drops into the poem with a finality appropriate to the meaning ("quenches") and to the completion of the extended simile. The dying fire image is not completely used up, however: after the simile is finished, it comes back again in the more subdued form of metaphor. The first feminine ending in the passage (line 84), triumphant over grammar, prepares the whole for its "dying fall" in the final line. The fire and love's passion now only burn as "embers," but they continue for a brief while to preserve a vestige of life, just as the feminine ending delays slightly the completion of the line and the whole passage. The rhyme "remembers/embers" is exactly right from a substantive point of view since it is clear that these loves of Byron's past only continue to burn low in and through his act of reminiscing. He does not want to forget—not entirely, not yet.

This reluctance to forego an innocent world in which there are no false friends or deceitful lovers, and in which the unsullied dreams of love and individual integrity are entirely accordant with one's experience of reality, is one of the three predominant themes in *Hours of Idleness*. The other two we have already discussed: the ironic or satiric exposure of falsity in all its forms and (the paramount idea in the book) the mythology of individual greatness and heroic endeavor. It seems to have been Byron's intention to dramatize himself as a young man just on the threshold of maturity and majority alike, and caught in the pull of forces that seem either to hurry him on to, or hold him back from, involvement in busy and mundane affairs. The world of youthful imaginations is clearly presented as the more attractive, while the values of maturity have only a secondary importance: ironic objectivity and a responsible sense of "realities" possess an indispensable corrective function, but they totally lack any capacity for creative or affirmative gestures. Byron occasionally tries to establish a system of positive values upon a reputable career in the ordinary world (for example, at the end of "On Leaving Newstead Abbey"), but in every case he fails utterly to carry conviction. As in the Preface, the objective and realistic Byron is relegated to the task of ironic comment and self-criticism—lest we think from his book that he does not realize the more absurd aspects of his own sentimentality and dreamy imaginative flights. His poems are "the fruits of the lighter hours of a young man," he tells us, and adds: "As they bear the internal evidence of a boyish mind, this is, perhaps, unnecessary information" (p. v). Thus he hopes to disarm the strictures of older minds by anticipating what he believes will be their principal objection.

IV

The different forms in which these conflicted aspects of Byron's personality are dramatized in *Hours of Idleness* clearly prefigure a basic and well-documented characteristic of his later work: the tension that persists between his visionary and skeptical imaginations. In *Hours of Idleness*, the radical splits in Byron's various conventional postures result from his desire to identify with a heroic order of human life that is at once of this world ("earthy," p. 131) and quite beyond it. Insofar as the attitudes of the youth of sensibility (with his innocence and integrity) and of the young nobleman (with his epic heritage and uncircumscribed field of action) are allied to this larger conception, they are not rejected; but insofar as both of these roles necessarily involve commitments to something else, something less pristine and passionate and grand, they are generally thrust ironically or disdainfully away.

But from the point of view of his poetic development, the simple *fact* that he seeks to dramatize himself to his audience is at least as significant. Nearly all of his poetry is crucially dependent, in form and meaning alike, upon the effectiveness with which he can realize an image of himself in the artifice of his own making. The most significant fact about *Hours of Idleness* is that in it we observe Byron trying to organize a series of disparate lyrics into a coherent self-portrait. *Hours of Idleness* is not a book that comes up to the promise of its own formal intention. It is too blighted, too dull in fact, so that its conception and execution remain sundered. In the first place, Byron was inordinately careful and decorous in announcing himself to his audience. As his ingratiating Preface suggests, one of his principal conscious objects seems to have been to persuade his readers that he was a modest but decent enough gentleman-amateur poet on the one hand, and on the other a spirited, ambitious, and sensitive young lord who seemed destined to distinguish himself in the future. This concern for public recognition as a validating condition of achievement produces a strain in his early poetry that is mindlessly slavish to conventional ideas of action and forms of behavior. For all his irony and self-consciousness even at this early stage of his career, Byron often seems unable to reflect upon, much less to understand, what his motives might be for this or that statement. This failure to bring his self-critical powers to bear on his own characteristic modes of thought produces a depressing quantity of stillborn verse.

Byron, in fact, seems more interested in posturing than in carrying out an experiment in analytic poetic autobiography. He seldom descends to the difficult labor of introspection—a staple in all autobiographical forms—but constantly concerns himself with writing poems that demonstrate the principal characteristics of his person according to the most conventional forms of eighteenth-century psychological thought. We are shown his ambition, his reverence for female beauty and modesty, his love of honesty and truth, his respect for strength of character and sensitivity of soul, etc. It is unnecessary to dwell upon the weakening of the biographical product that results from the uncritical use of such ideas. Nevertheless, with all these faults acknowledged I think the book possesses an interest and a poetic significance that is something greater than the sum of its parts—not because the personality in it is particularly extraordinary (he seems a rather typical example of the divided Romantic soul, while the conflicts in his character are put across, for the most part, in relatively uninteresting ways), but because that personality is offered as a true and authentic self-portrait.

Although Byron's volume does not make its highly personal impact simply because he chooses to remind the reader again and again, in the poetry and the prose notes alike, that the author is a specific and historically definable personality, this insistence upon factual reality in the volume is a crucial one. By defining himself so particularly for the reader, and by insisting on numerous occasions that his Muse is "the simple Truth," Byron forces us to regard his poems as personal statements of his real feelings, not as "mere" exercises in conventional modes. For example, the concluding poem in the volume is a complaint of a forsaken lover. Technically, the poem is just indifferent; printed in an anthology, it would be read and forgotten forever. But because the whole focus of *Hours of Idleness* prevents us from reading the piece as an isolated exercise in the craft of poetic creation (with a possible, but irrelevant, foundation in fact), the reader is likely to react strongly against Byron's design upon him: soliciting approval of the poem because it is a statement of the sad and simple truth, because the detailed experience is part of and has contributed to the development of young Lord Byron's character. Brougham was mightily annoyed with Byron's book for just this reason: that the poet should have so confidently expected that his poetry merited attention and praise because of the character of the author revealed therein. It is evident that Byron's "talents . . . are considerable, and his opportunities . . . great," Brougham says; his verse is, for all that, a wretched thing. Brougham is about 90 per cent correct in his wholesale condemnation of the specific poems in *Hours of Idleness*. But, though the book is a failure, it is a most interesting and instructive one precisely because the reader's consideration is not directed to the poetic value of the individual poem alone. A more comprehensive aesthetic supervenes in the relation of the various poems to each other within the biographical structure of the whole book. In this it illustrates a conception of a use to which poetry might be validly put, and to which Byron did put it, quite brilliantly, in his later work.

But a spectacular element insinuates itself throughout *Hours of Idleness* which lends the volume not so much a self-dramatizing as a self-propagandizing quality. *Hours of Idleness* is not a book that essays sublimity, but the impulse to the grand gesture is distinctly present in it. The dominant of the three main themes in the book is the poet's desire for a heroic identification, and the whole work is offered as a kind of portrait of the hero as a young man. We are asked to laugh with him at his own naive follies (as in "To Romance"), to respect the fervor of his satiric declamations at evil and pettiness (as in "Thoughts Suggested by a College Examination" and "Damaetas"), to smile indulgently with him when he uncovers the follies of others ("Granta, A Medley"), to sympathize with him during his growing pains ("Childish Recollections" and "To E. N. L. Esq."), to appreciate and perhaps indulge him in the harmless love affairs of his youth, to weep with him when he loses his first true love, and, finally, to experience through him intimations of the heroic destiny which is ever calling out to him and drawing him on. His "Imitations and Translations" recapitulate most of these ideas. In all this is an impulse to sensationalize the name of Lord Byron. Brougham quite correctly sensed the giant vanity that lurked behind the modest facade of most of the book and he pilloried Byron for his "egotism."

> Perhaps . . . all that he tells us about his youth, is rather with a view to increase our wonder, than to soften our censures. He possibly means to say, "See how a minor can write! This poem was actually composed by a young man of eighteen, and this by one of only sixteen!" But, alas! we all remember the poetry of Cowley at ten, and of Pope at twelve. . . .

Indeed, Byron's book makes such a conclusion impossible to avoid. His conversational and sometimes insouciant manner in the Preface tends to underplay the aspiration to fame which is so much a part of *Hours of Idleness*; but the very attempt to assume a modest attitude toward a subject which he himself keeps bringing up serves only to underline the importance that he attaches to it.

Hours of Idleness is, then, very like propaganda in several ways: in a bad sense, first of all, because the book suggests that a heroic ordonnance is suitable to the self-dramatized figure of the poet when in fact only the design of the book and a few of its more important poems support this implication. Further, the book seems to be to some extent propaganda in a literal sense—which is to say a bastardization of poetry for wholly unpoetic ends (i.e., the furtherance of Byron's public reputation and the political career which he contemplated at that time). But it is also like propaganda in two senses that are important for an understanding of his later work. First of all, there is the very fact that he should conceive himself (which is to say, conceive his poetic materials) within a frame of reference that suggests heroic potential. A man who could write such a book would have no difficulty trailing his bleeding heart across Europe, for he clearly took the attitude that his subject was a great one, that if fully developed it would yield an experience that was at once universal and sublime. Second, and even more significant, the book resembles propaganda because it offers a dramatized picture of a man which purports to be identical with the real person. Paul West has rightly said that "It is Byron and Byron's idea of himself which hold his work together,"[26] so that if we are to come to grips with his poetry, we must discover some means of elucidating how Byron the man has transfused himself into his work, and what happens to his poetry as a result of this.

Northrop Frye has put the problem very well:

> The main appeal of Byron's poetry is in the fact that it is Byron's.
> . . . He proves what many critics declare to be impossible, that a
> poem can make its primary impact as a historical and biographical
> document. The critical problem here is crucial to our understand-
> ing of not only Byron but literature as a whole.[27]

Frye's treatment of Byron, however, does not get beyond the stage of perceiving that his poetry offers a manifold and crucial problem for the reader. I do not propose to disentangle this confusion of rather fundamental aesthetic difficulties, but merely to reintroduce a method for reading Byron that was proposed by Matthew Arnold, and that seems to offer a satisfactory practical solution to the problem of biography in art. Byron and Wordsworth were, for Arnold, the two greatest poets of the nineteenth century. When Arnold wrote his essay on Byron the latter's reputation had been declining slowly for some time, largely because of a growing reaction against the irregularities of his life, on the one hand, and the evident crudities in much of his poetry on the other. Arnold meets both of these objections head on. He seeks to demonstrate the greatness of the poetry by first admitting that Byron's work, like

---

[26] Introduction to *Essays*, p. 2.
[27] Northrop Frye, "Lord Byron," in *Fables of Identity* (New York, 1963), p. 174.

Wordsworth's, frequently shows unpardonable technical flaws that neither Shelley nor Leopardi would have been capable of. He also admits that as a man Byron left much to be desired. This train of thought is taken up in an admittedly ethical, rather than aesthetic, frame of reference. It is, nevertheless, an important element in Arnold's argument, for after making these two admissions he comes to erect out of Goethe's various observations about Byron's preeminence a third category by which Byron's poetry must be judged: the character of his poetic personality.

> His superiority turns . . . upon the surpassing worth of something which he had and was, after all deductions have been made for his shortcomings. We talk of Byron's *personality*, "a personality in eminence such as has never been yet, and is not likely to come again;" and we say that by this personality Byron is "different from all the rest of English poets, and in the main greater." But can we not be a little more circumstantial, and name that in which the wonderful power of this personality consisted? We can; with the instinct of a poet Mr. Swinburne has seized upon it and named it for us. The power of Byron's personality lies in "the splendid and imperishable excellence which covers all his offences and outweighs all his defects: *the excellence of sincerity and strength.*"[28]

The problem with this declaration, and all the subsequent observations in Arnold's essay, is that we seem to detect in the critic an unwillingness to say specifically whether he is praising the man Byron, or Byron the poet. But this is Arnold's main point: that to read Byron's poetry properly one must become involved in the blazing "personality" which it deliberately seeks to dramatize. The poetry does not reveal Byron the man, but the poetic personality into which he mythologized himself in his work.

> When this theatrical and easily criticized personage took himself to poetry, and when he had fairly warmed to his work, then he became another man; then the theatrical personage passed away; then a higher power took possession of him and filled him; then at last came forth into light that true and puissant personality, with its direct strokes, its ever-welling force, its satire, its energy, its agony. This is the real Byron. . . .[29]

[28] Matthew Arnold, "Byron," in *Essays in Criticism*, Second Series (London, 1921), pp. 192–93.
[29] *Ibid.*, pp. 196–97.

The attitude of Swinburne and Arnold is typical of most nineteenth-century Byron criticism, which never tires of telling us about Byron's "sincerity" and "strength." What "strength" means in such a context is easily enough discerned in the Promethean declamations that characterize much of his work. His "sincerity" is another thing altogether. Arnold himself says that the historic "personage" is an "easily criticized" poseur, while the greatest of all the "sincerity" critics, Thomas Carlyle, dismissed nearly all of Byron's work before *Don Juan* as largely trumped-up attitudinizing. What Carlyle meant was that Byron in reality was not like the Giaour, or Conrad, or Childe Harold, and that consequently these were "insincere" representations of himself—not accordant with the truth of fact. But the problem with this type of criticism is that everyone can quote scripture to his own purpose—that with a complex human being like Byron, different opinions about what he was "really" like are bound to crop up. Thus, the whole history of Byron research shows a constant struggle between those who praise him for his poetic sincerity and those who damn him for his insincerity.

Yet there is a common ground on which both of these evaluative critical positions can meet—one which does not praise or blame Byron for his sincerity or insincerity, but which simply asks that the poetry be accepted, and read, as a self-dramatizing vehicle. In a sense, no product of art can be sincere precisely because it is a thing fabricated, created; it exists in an ideal order of its own, no matter how realistically oriented it may be. By the same token, all achieved art can be called sincere because its own internal harmony will suggest no irregularities in the "poet's vision," no disruptive contradictions. But such absolutely disjunctive significations for the term "sincerity" suggest its fundamental critical uselessness as an evaluative tool. Arnold implicitly praises Byron for his sincerity, and insofar as this is true his remarks are not criticism but appreciation. Arnold, however, also introduces a meaning for the term "sincerity" that *is* useful when he suggests that the poetry be read as the dramatization of the psychic life of a single "personality." What Arnold points to in this case is an *illusion* of sincerity created by art, an illusion that makes the dramatic "personality" of Byron presented in his poetry seem fully and empirically "real." Though this "personality" is a product of art and artifice, it is poetically significant because it is not a "persona" in any useful sense of that term's meaning. Most of Byron's poetry is sincere in this third, and purely descriptive, sense: his poetry dramatizes the life of a specific individual who possesses all the "roundedness" of the living human reality. *Hours of Idleness* sets out to do just this, but it fails because the "personality" of the young peer remains largely an "individual" cliché.

One of Byron's earliest critics, Sir Egerton Brydges, seems to have anticipated Arnold's descriptive use of the term "sincerity" in relation to Byron's poetry. Brydges believed that "the history of [Byron's] life . . . proved that he was in reality what his poetry represented him to be."[30] Nevertheless, Brydges also sees that Byron's "sincerity" is an aesthetic form in his poetry, and can be made the subject of critical analysis:

> when an author comes forward as the relater of his own inventions . . . we try his tale by its probabilities. . . . Such an author deals with his proper subjects when he paints the internal movements of the human heart . . . it is the imagination only to which these are known. The test of the power and virtue of that imagination lies in the degree of *sympathy* which it awakens; while that sympathy much depends upon the faculty of *verisimility*.[31]

It is useless to quibble about terms and say, after the manner of Heine on Rousseau, that the dramatic figure is not the historically "real Lord Byron." Perhaps this is true, but it does not matter, for the "got-up" Byron is all that is left. Like any artist, he refined himself out of existence in order to create an image of life, one that, in this case, would seem to live and breathe. The curious fact is, however, that even the most recent biographical discoveries (and who has been more relentlessly pursued for the last century and a half than Byron?) have not significantly altered the time-honored legend that he himself created, and that has been in the public domain ever since Moore's first codification.

Throughout his life Byron strove to become a "historical figure," and to make that figure identical with the dreams of his own very personal imaginations. These dreams shifted with the years, and some evaporated, but they never altogether ceased to haunt him. Even when we seek the man Byron in the driest historical records we find that a mythological transformation often takes place. The mortal figure constantly tends to assume legendary form even when we know our facts are right. He epitomizes that in human nature which makes metahistory possible. He survives in the valley of his saying, to extend Auden's meaning somewhat.

[30] Egerton Brydges, *Letters on the Character and Poetical Genius of Lord Byron* (London, 1824), p. 135.

[31] *Ibid.*, pp. 253–54.

Perhaps nothing illustrates this so well as a fragment of MS preserved in the Beinecke Rare Book Library at Yale University. I have reproduced it here as a frontispiece. The MS fragment contains a version of stanza 73 of *Childe Harold's Pilgrimage II*. In it Byron asks a series of rhetorical questions about a liberator of Greece. Five times he asks a variant of the question of "who" will finally set Greece free, and five times the answer to that question—not publicly recorded—is dashed across the page in his bold script: "Byron." The scrap of MS is a graphic reminder not only of Byron's heroic pretensions, but of his tendency to refuse the distinction between his life in history and his life in art.[32]

This MS fragment was written sometime before 1812, probably in 1809. It contains a strange prophecy, and one entirely worthy of the man who longed so passionately to be in fact what he dreamed he was. Byron's statue now stands in the Garden of Heroes in Missolonghi, a sign that his prophetic hope had not been in vain. Further, he has the fame he sought—more of it, probably, than any other English poet except Shakespeare. Byron gained his notoriety by the force of his projected personality, and it is an irony he would have appreciated that that very specific personality has now largely become dispersed into a variety of modern myths. Nor does a serious, even scholarly, attempt to remain true to the facts protect us from mythmaking, for Byron will not let us rest content with mere facts but forces us on to seek meanings behind them and patterns within them. He forces us to mythmake, and Keats did not know what an important truth he pointed to when he sneered at Byron for "cutting a figure." Byron refused the distinction between his life and his art, and the result has been, as G. Wilson Knight has always said, that he became a work of art, that the distinction could not be easily, or even usefully, drawn.

[32] Byron sometimes objected when his contemporaries read his tales as disguised autobiography. Given the extravagance of many of these biographical interpretations one can readily sympathize with Byron's reaction. Nevertheless, his own poetry, even his public conduct, could scarcely do anything but foster such attitudes. All of his poetry up to the publication of *The Giaour* was distinctly personal in form, often explicitly autobiographical.

Childe Harold's Pilgrimage

On Reading
Childe Harold's Pilgrimage

The Poet in the Poem

"I write what's uppermost, without delay," Byron declares in *Don Juan* (XIV, 7) and even adds that his "narrative is not meant for narration" in the proper sense at all. As he says a bit later:

> I rattle on exactly as I'd talk
> With anybody in a ride or walk. (XIV, 19)

His great comic work gives the reader a series of loosely connected tales about Juan's adventures, but even more it gives us a graphic revelation of the mind of the poet who creates these stories. *Don Juan* is a "poem written about itself,"[1] as Hazlitt has noted: throughout we seem to be with Byron while he is actually spinning his rhymes. The key device for creating this illusion of the poet's immediate presence is digression. M. K. Joseph has well said that

> the substance of the digression can be related *thematically* to the poem as a whole; but its *dramatic* function in the immediate context is to keep alive our sense of the narrator, interposing him between ourselves and the story.[2]

But "dramatic" is not a term completely appropriate to the presentation of the poet's personality in *Don Juan*: the manifold complications of his psyche are extrapolated in a long series of personal self-exposures, but we are never made to feel that the poem possesses a "dramatic" finality, that the poet acts upon and reacts to a series of experiences which force significant modifications in his character. In a word, *Don Juan* has no plot in which the principal character—the poet

---

[1] William Hazlitt, *The Spirit of the Age*, in *The Complete Works of William Hazlitt*, ed. P. P. Howe, 11 (London, 1930–34): 75.
[2] *Joseph*, p. 199.

31

himself—can be said to participate. Juan may undergo psychological changes during his picaresque adventures, but the personality of the poet does not develop. We are given, rather, a succession of insights into the rich and complicated quality of his mind and heart. Byron's string of related stories permits him the widest possible range of personal commentary (on history, art, contemporary manners and affairs, philosophy, etc.): the reader thus encounters the poet from so many angles and points of view that he seems not only fully present, but fully presented.

Childe Harold's Pilgrimage, on the other hand, is a poem in which the poet is both immediately present to us and involved in a continuity of events in a truly "dramatic" way. He undergoes a succession of psychic changes in the course of the four cantos. At the end of Canto II, for example, he laments that "Time [has] reft whate'er my soul enjoyed" (II, 98), and at the beginning of Canto III he recalls the past in which his "brain became,/In its own eddy boiling and o'erwrought" (III, 7). "Yet am I changed," he adds, and he looks to the future (sts. 4–6) for further and more beneficent changes still. At the end of Canto III he gets a Pisgah sight of Italy (st. 110), and again reviews the past and looks to the future:

> Thus far have I proceeded in a theme
> Renewed with no kind auspices:—to feel
> We are not what we have been, and to deem
> We are not what we should be,—   (III, 111)

Canto IV concludes the story ("My task is done," he says in st. 185) of the poet's geographical and psychological peregrinations, and he leaves the reader to benefit by "the Moral of [the] Strain" (186). Through the course of the entire poem the theme unfolds that

> to the mind
> Which is itself, no changes bring surprise.   (IV, 8)

What the substance of the poet's tale of himself is I will discuss more fully later. For now it is important only that we understand the general dramatic nature of the poem, since it is this which will determine how we read it. For example, *The Prelude* is, like *Childe Harold's Pilgrimage*, an autobiographical poem, but its subject is a sequence of events from Wordsworth's past life (i.e., "past" in relation to the "virtual present" of the narrating poet) while the subject of *Childe Harold's Pilgrimage* is a sequence of events that are contemporaneous with the poet's act of narration. *The Prelude* is to *Childe Harold's Pilgrimage* what a reflective autobiographical essay is to a journal or a series of letters. We "get at" Wordsworth's mind through the continuous and developing record of his "present" interpretation of already completed events. *The Prelude* is the externalization of an imaginative dialectic: it is fundamentally a philosophic poem or, better, a cognitive myth whose full implications are gradually unfolded to the reader and the writing poet alike. With the completion of the ascent of Snowdon in Book XIV, Wordsworth has arrived at his most complete definition of the powers of the human imagination. Thus, *The Prelude* amounts to a growing act of imaginative cognition in which the meanings and relationships of the poem's symbols and images are developed into a complete poetic statement of an important human vision (something akin to the vision of Teilhard de Chardin in our own day).

But while we are interested in the mind of the poet in *The Prelude* (as it is symbolized to us in the mythic configuration which is the issue of the poem), in *Childe Harold's Pilgrimage* we are interested in the poet's existential condition. Byron's poem presents a series of actions and reactions in a natural order that we conveniently refer to as "realistic," whereas Wordsworth gives us a series of perceptions and intuitions within an order of experience that we ordinarily call "cognitive." Our relationship to the poet in *Childe Harold's Pilgrimage* is the same as our relationship to Augie March, or to Herzog: all are involved in a play of circumstances, and we are interested in their reactions. The narrating poet of *The Prelude*, however, is the center of an action in the same way that the participating poet is in the *Vita Nuova:* at bottom both poems are not "actions," but acts of revelation. The narrating poet is the "hero" of *Childe Harold's Pilgrimage*, but we could not call the poet the "hero" of *The Prelude* without wrenching the meaning of that specialized term.

Consequently, because no distinction exists in *Childe Harold's Pilgrimage* between the narrator's virtual present and a past series of events about which he writes, and because the poem describes a sequence of "realistic" events in which the narrating poet participates in an immediate way, *Childe Harold's Pilgrimage* places unique demands upon the reader. Aristotle had no experience of a poem like Byron's, but his discussion of narrators, narrative poetry, and drama provides a useful indication of the kind of problem that *Childe Harold's Pilgrimage* presents:

> . . . the poet may imitate by narration—in which case he can either take another personality as Homer does, or speak in his own

person, unchanged—or he may present all his characters as living
and moving before us.[3]

In terms of Aristotle's categories, Byron's poem exists somewhere between narrative and drama, for while the poet comes forward in propria persona, he also presents himself as "living and moving before us"
in a phenomenal setting. The result is a work whose illusionistic character is pronounced and crucial:

> Is thy face like thy mother's, my fair child!
> Ada! sole daughter of my house and heart?
> When last I saw thy young blue eyes they smiled,
> And then we parted,—not as now we part,
> But with a hope.—
>   Awaking with a start,
> The waters heave around me; and on high
> The winds lift up their voices: I depart,
> Whither I know not; but the hour's gone by,
> When Albion's lessening shores could grieve
>   or glad mine eye.   (III, 1)

This stanza illustrates narrative illusionism pushed to its extreme limit.
The poet's revery in the first four and one-half lines occurs at the same
time as his act of narration. Then, with a familiarly Byronic disregard
of prose grammar, he suddenly awakens to describe his present situation. In effect, the poet not only records his musings at the time of their
actual occurrence, he writes down his sensations immediately upon
coming into a condition of exteriorized consciousness. An artist writing
in the first person could scarcely objectify his "poetic personality" as
a person "living and moving before us" more completely.[4] While the

---

[3] *Aristotle's Poetics*, ed. and trans. S. H. Butcher, in *Aristotle's Theory of Poetry and Fine Art* (London, 1907), p. 13.

[4] Susanne K. Langer's remarks on Illusionism in the literary arts, and the difference between the illusions of "drama" and "literature," suggest how *Childe Harold's Pilgrimage* tends to fall somewhere between the two categories. "Drama is not, in the strict sense, 'literature.' Yet it is a poetic art, because it creates the primary illusion of all poetry—virtual history. . . . It is a fabric of illusory experiences, and that is the essential product of poesis. . . . Literature projects the image of life in the mode of virtual memory; language is its essential material; the sound and meaning of words, the familiar or unusual use and order, even their presentation on the printed page, create the illusion of life as a realm of events—completed, lived, as words formulate them—events that compose a Past. But Drama presents the poetic illusion in a different light: not finished realities, or 'events,' but immediate, visible responses of human beings, make its semblance of life." *Feeling and Form* (New York, 1953), p. 306. Though *Childe Harold's Pilgrimage* cannot but exist in the medium of "virtual memory" which is the printed word, its mode of presentation seeks to persuade us that we are reading the "immediate, visible responses" of a human being: not emotion recollected in tranquillity and filtered through an artistic consciousness, but an unmediated expression of self.

act of poetic illusion here is unmatched in the rest of the poem, it is by no means untypical of the general approach to the material. A little later in the same canto, for example, the poet introduces the Waterloo section in a similarly theatrical way: "Stop!—for thy tread is on an Empire's dust!" (III, 17). In this case not only is the act of narration continuous in time with the experience; the poet addresses us as if we were on the scene with him.

Illusions such as these are staples in the poem, and they exhibit a good deal more daring than any comparable scenes in *The Prelude*. The reasons I have already discussed: Byron's work exists in a realistic continuum while Wordsworth's moves in a world that is not significantly impinged upon by Space, Time, or Circumstance ("that unspiritual God," IV, 125). The past life on which Wordsworth meditates, is, of course, an existential record, but the real meaning of the poem is to be found not in these past events as such, but in the poet's immediate act of recovery. The continuum is mental, timeless, spaceless. But because *Childe Harold's Pilgrimage* is fixed within a realistic environment; and second, because the act of narration and the narrated events occur simultaneously in a virtual present; and finally, because the poem tells the story of the psychological modifications that the narrating poet undergoes during the four cantos, the poem demands that the narrating poet be considered a participant in an action whose future progress he cannot know and whose ultimate issue he is, at all points prior to the climax, only partially aware of.[5] Like a character in a novel or a play, he has neither the author's prevision nor the audience's objectivity, but is immersed in the immediacy of the events he himself recounts. Not only can he not see beyond any particular event; he may be equally unaware of the full significance of an event while it is taking place, or even after it has passed. The audience knows more about Macbeth than the character does himself, at least at the early stages of the play; for that matter, the narrator of *The Aspern Papers* is ignorant of himself and the full meaning of his story from beginning to end. The narrator of *Childe Harold's Pilgrimage* is presented in a similarly dramatic way,

---

[5] The distinction here is between the poet's artistic consciousness of his work and his human consciousness of himself as a man in an environment. The poet who appears as the narrator of *Childe Harold's Pilgrimage* does not possess an artistic consciousness with respect to the work he relates. In this he differs from the "poets" of *Don Juan* and *The Prelude* alike, both of whom make their artistic consciousness part of the substance of their works. Both are, in other words, poems written about themselves, about the act of writing poetry. An interesting discussion of this problem can be found in Robert M. Durling's *The Figure of the Poet in the Renaissance Epic* (Cambridge, Mass., 1965), pp. 2–6. He departs somewhat from Wayne C. Booth's pioneering work on this and related matters in his well-known *Rhetoric of Fiction* (Chicago, 1961).

and the story of himself that he recounts involves him in a series of important self-discoveries before he is able to offer the reader, at the end of Canto IV, a revelation that is at once his interpretation of the meaning of his own history and his vision of man's fate as well.

Canto IV: Its Meaning and Method

Part of the meaning of the poem's great conclusion, which begins at the St. Peter's stanzas in Canto IV, is that the narrating poet has come at last to a complete understanding of what it means to be a pilgrim— for him, what it means to be a man. All along he has been driven by the idea that somewhere, if one searches long enough, a place will be found that will answer to all human aspirations, that will satisfy and complete one's humanity. The poet's first pilgrimage was undertaken out of a disgust of England: "Je haissais ma Patrie," the epigraph from *Le Cosmopolite* states, but after his pilgrimage the poet finds "L'univers est une espèce de livre, dont on n'a lu que la première page quand on n'a vu que son pays. J'en ai feuilleté un assez grand nombre, que J'ai trouvé également mauvaises." In Canto III, the poet's journey to the Swiss Alps is another quest to escape from "the peopled desert" (III, 73) of this world, as well as from his own diseased mind and "degraded form" (III, 74). In stanza 156 of Canto IV he deliberately recalls the conclusion of Canto III:

> Thou movest—but increasing with the advance,
> Like climbing some great Alp, which still doth rise,
> Deceived by its gigantic elegance—
> Vastness which grows, but grows to harmonize—
> All musical in its immensities;
> Rich marbles, richer paintings—shrines where flame
> The lamps of gold—and haughty dome which vies
> In air with Earth's chief structures, though their frame
> Sits on the firm-set ground—and this the clouds must claim.
>
> (IV, 156)

> But let me quit Man's works, again to read
> His Maker's, spread around me, and suspend
> This page, which from my reveries I feed,
> Until it seems prolonging without end.
> The clouds above me to the white Alps tend,
> And I must pierce them, and survey whate'er
> May be permitted, as my steps I bend
> To their most great and growing region, where
> The earth to her embrace compels the powers of air.   (III, 109)

The lines from the third canto echo a number of earlier passages, especially III, 62 where the Alps are called "The Palaces of Nature" (hence the appropriateness of the Alp image with respect to St. Peter's, of which the poet asks rhetorically: "what could be/Of earthly structures, in [God's] honour piled/Of a sublimer aspect?" IV, 154).[6] But in the middle of Canto III the Alps only show the poet "How Earth may pierce to Heaven, yet leave vain man below" (III, 62). At the end of the canto he throws off this earlier sense of ineffectualness and declares that he "must pierce" to the "most great and growing region, where/ The earth to her embrace compels the powers of air." His search for fulfillment is still not concluded, however, for when he gains the summit of the Alp he is given a prophetic view of Italy, which is presented as a kind of Promised Land ("the throne and grave of empires; still/The fount at which the panting Mind assuages/Her thirst of knowledge . . . the eternal source. . . ," III, 110). Later, at St. Peter's, the perception of the union of Nature and Supernature, which he sought and partially achieved on the Alp, is finally given him. But now a further understanding comes: that this yearning to possess and exercise godlike powers, to participate in a divine activity, is not capable of fulfillment if human life is to continue. The true end of such a desire is not satisfaction, but creation, and the condition of its being is constant movement, increase, growth.

This theme, which is repeated in the famous Address to Ocean (a mythic vision of an eternal death/life cycle), is a vindication of the act of pilgrimage. In stanzas 157–58 the poet tells us not only what pilgrimage means, but also what the method of *Childe Harold's Pilgrimage* has entailed.

> Thou seest not all—but piecemeal thou must break,
> To separate contemplation, the great whole;
> And as the Ocean many bays will make
> That ask the eye—so here condense thy soul
> To more immediate objects, and control
> Thy thoughts until thy mind hath got by heart
> Its eloquent proportions, and unroll
> In mighty graduations, part by part,
> The Glory which at once upon thee did not dart,
>
> Not by its fault—but thine: Our outward sense
> Is but of gradual grasp—and as it is

---

[6] The mountain image is the focus of the whole third canto. See, for example, stanzas 14, 40, 67, 72, 91, 96, and 109.

That which we have of feeling most intense
Outstrips our faint expression; even so this
Outshining and o'erwhelming edifice
Fools our fond gaze, and greatest of the great
Defies at first our Nature's littleness,
Till, growing with its growth, we thus dilate
Our Spirits to the size of that they contemplate.   (iv, 157–58)[7]

At St. Peter's the poet gains only an intimation of divine fullness and eternally existing Life; for if he is able, "growing with its growth," to "dilate" his spirit to the size of St. Peter's, still the basilica is only one vast image of the even greater spatial and temporal immensity of Life itself, and his apprehension of the symbolic meaning of the church will pass if he continues simply to live. This is in fact what happens in the poem. Nevertheless, the experience at St. Peter's finally exposes the teleology of the poem and of the life of man as well. The poet is made aware of the necessity of a "piecemeal" apprehension of a life which we never fully comprehend precisely because it involves us in constant passage and possibility. Human life is not something that can be "gained" or "concluded" or "fulfilled," but must simply be "kept" in our experience of consecutive vital particularities. Entering St. Peter's with a highly developed sensitivity to immediate experience, a virtue strengthened by the act of pilgrimage, the poet finds that he is forced to apprehend the basilica moment by moment and item by item. When he does finally gain a sense of the order in the vast disparateness of the church, he is impelled onward to the Vatican Gallery, and eventually, to another mountain prospect from Monte Cavo (sts. 174 ff.). The basilica, it turns out, is not a place of fulfillment, but a symbol of a mode of experience and perception: the endless activity of self-discovery and renewed self-development. By such means the soul is forced into a position where it must constantly reconsider its own conception of itself and recreate itself under the influence of fresh experience.

'Tis to create, and in creating, live
A being more intense that we endow
With form our fancy, gaining as we give
The life we image, even as I do now—
What am I? Nothing: but not so art thou,
Soul of my thought! with whom I traverse earth,
Invisible but gazing, as I glow

---

[7] I have benefited in general from reading George Ridenour's unpublished doctoral thesis "Byron and the Romantic Pilgrimage" (New Haven, 1955). My interpretation of these stanzas in particular is simply an extrapolation of Ridenour's view.

> Mixed with thy spirit, blended with thy birth,
> And feeling still with thee in my crushed feelings' dearth. (III, 6)

We never "gain" definitively the fullness of Life in our imaginatively recreative activities, but are always in the process of gaining anew, of becoming and going somewhere else.

This idea of "piecemeal" apprehension amounts to an analysis of the poetic method in the poem itself. As he contemplates the "immediate objects" at St. Peter's the narrator discovers that his "fond gaze" is "fooled" and "deceived" by his own "gradual" powers, that he has continually to reformulate his understanding of the significance of what he sees. Thus it is in the poem. The poet passes from ignorance to ignorance, but, like the fool who persists in his folly, he eventually comes to see at St. Peter's that comprehension is achieved only in successive, and relatively ignorant, perceptions. To "know oneself" one must submit to immediate and partial acts of perception:

> condense thy soul
> To more immediate objects, and control
> Thy thoughts until thy mind hath got by heart
> Its eloquent proportions . . .
> part by part. . . .

This present understanding is wisdom for the future since pilgrimage never ends ("Roll on, thou deep and dark blue Ocean—roll!"); but the poet is also thinking of what has already been recorded in the poem, is thinking of his past blindnesses and partial insights. We know this because the stanzas allude to important moments in the poetic record of his past life. Stanza 156 calls up again the principal issue of Canto III, and stanzas 157–58 reinterpret the meaning of the attempt made therein to harmonize his human capabilities with his more than human impulsions. The line "Defies at first our Nature's littleness" is surely meant to recall the earlier moments when the poet's sense of his human insufficiency weighed heavily upon him:

> Where are the charms and virtues which we dare
> Conceive in boyhood and pursue as men,
> The unreached Paradise of our despair,
> Which o'er-informs the pencil and the pen,
> And overpowers the page where it would bloom again? (IV, 122)[8]

---

[8] See also III, 62, where the gigantic Alps make the poet painfully aware of his littleness; and IV, 17, where the poet speaks of Venice (the "fairy city of the heart") as one of the "charms" conceived in innocent "boyhood."

The sense of absolute *vanitas vanitatis* is contravened for good at St. Peter's and the Vatican Gallery.[9] The way in which the narrator comes to a complete understanding of St. Peter's—through cumulative acts of limited perception that eventuate in a general sense of comprehension—is the image of the poet's experience in all four cantos. "We but feel our way to err," he says (IV, 81), as he scours the ruins of Rome for an understanding of the causes of her greatness and her collapse. He identifies himself with Italy—he is "A ruin amidst ruins" (25) —so that his search for a means of her resurrection (55) to her rightful preeminence is a search made in his own behalf as well. Just as he stumbles over the remains of Rome's enigmatic greatness, so he gropes blindly and uncertainly along for a kind of self-knowledge that will eventually set free his "Faculty divine" which "Is chain'd and tortured —cabin'd, cribb'd, confined" (IV, 127). But he is fooled continually with premature expectations and false hopes:

> But Rome is as the desert—where we steer
> Stumbling o'er recollections; now we clap
> Our hands, and cry "Eureka!" "it is clear"—
> When but some false Mirage of ruin rises near.   (IV, 81)

Though St. Peter's brings enlightenment, the narrator in the meantime moves along compassed about with darkness, and beset with the constant danger of despair from his own vigorous skepticism.

A Process of Discovery: IV, 128–51

Thus, the narrator does not come before us in the posture of a seer or a prophetic instructor except at certain crucial moments—most notably, at the end of Canto IV. "Mark well my words! they are of your eternal salvation," Blake's poet says at the beginning of *Milton*.[10] Byron's poet does not possess oracular powers like this as part of his being, but seeks after a comparable kind of prophetic insight. Further, because he is dramatically presented to the reader in a succession of virtually present moments, and because he is absolutely divorced from Byron the omniscient artist, his thoughts and actions at particular moments are subject to alteration and revision. The narrator gradually accedes to a prophetic office, but in the meantime he "enlightens" us not as an oracle, but as an exemplum. This fact about the structure of the poem has not been

[9] The poet has more to say on this subject in the stanzas on the Princess Charlotte, where his understanding of human power is modified and sharpened to its final form. I will not go into this matter now since my immediate concern is only with the poem's method, its principle of dramatic presentation.

[10] *Poetry and Prose of William Blake*, ed. Geoffrey Keynes (London, 1961), p. 376.

generally recognized, and the failure to do so has led to some misinter-
pretations of the meanings of certain passages. John Wain, for example,
has a fine analysis of the technical merits and demerits of the "Dying
Gladiator" passage, but his interpretation of the basic meaning of the
lines errs because he does not take into account the sequence of the
narrating poet's thoughts as they develop through the whole meditation
upon the Coliseum beginning at stanza 128. After quoting stanzas
140–41, Wain says:

> The people watching the gladiatorial contest are "inhuman," and
> this is linked with a certain tit-for-tat moralizing, never far away
> in Byron. . . . It is all very fine for the inhuman spectators to shout
> with glee, but we know something that they don't: Rome is going
> to fall, and what is more it is these same Goths who will push it
> over, *so there.* This mechanical (and not very accurate) moral-
> drawing from history is an eighteenth-century taste, and the other
> major poets of Byron's day have hardly a trace of it.[11]

The trouble with this analysis is that Wain takes the two stanzas as
an integral statement when in fact they represent an intermediate stage
in a process of thought that begins in stanza 128. The central event in
the meditation on the Coliseum is the forgiveness-curse sequence
(130–37), which grows out of Byron's initial identification of himself
and his present fortunes with the wrecked and desolated arena
(129–31). After he has cursed his destroyers with his forgiveness, he
conjures up yet another image of man's inhumanity to man—the Roman
gladiatorial spectacle which took place in the Coliseum. The associative
movement of the poet's thought here is rather interesting. He begins
with the sight of the ruined arena and then goes on to consider his own
ruination. This leads him to think how retribution always pursues such
deeds, and he hails "great Nemesis" as his "Avenger."

> And Thou, who never yet of human wrong
> Left the unbalanced scale, great Nemesis!
> Here, where the ancient paid thee homage long—
> Thou, who didst call the Furies from the abyss,
> And round Orestes bade them howl and hiss
> For that unnatural retribution—just,
> Had it but been from hands less near—in this
> Thy former realm, I call thee from the dust!
> Dost thou not hear my heart?—Awake! thou shalt, and must.
>
> (132)

---

[11] John Wain, "The Search for Identity," in *Essays,* pp. 163–64.

After delivering his forgiveness-curse, he considers the destruction of the Gothic gladiator in the Roman circus, and once again he cries out for retributive justice ("Arise! ye Goths, and glut your ire!" 141). In so doing, however, he has altered the significance that the Coliseum originally had for him as an image of his own desolation; it is now the symbol on which Roman brutality is focused.

This associational change in meaning might seem at first to have weakened the poetic structure by breaking the continuity of the poet's thought. Actually, the ambivalent associative value of the Coliseum serves to clarify the whole form of his thoughts on retribution for wrong—ultimately, to clarify the meaning of the forgiveness-curse sequence both for him and for us. The "tit-for-tat moralizing" which seems to be his object in stanzas 140–41 breaks down completely in stanza 142 when he again associates sympathetically with the Coliseum.

> But here, where Murder breathed her bloody stream;—
> And here, where buzzing nations choked the ways,
> And roared or murmured like a mountain stream
> Dashing or winding as its torrent strays;
> Here, where the Roman million's blame or praise
> Was Death or Life—the playthings of a crowd—
> My voice sounds much—and fall the stars' faint rays
> On the arena void—seats crushed—walls bowed—
> And galleries, where my steps seem echoes strangely loud.   (142)

His wish for the destruction of the Roman symbol of oppression has been, in fact, tragically fulfilled. As he gazes around he sees the broken vestiges of once great Rome (143–44), and his "voice"—which called out angrily for retribution—now "sounds much" in an "arena void." The hollow echo of his cry is a mournful image of the effects of "tit-for-tat moralizing."

> Hath it indeed been plundered, or but cleared?
> Alas! developed, opens the decay. . . .   (143)

Now, "When the stars twinkle through the loops of Time" (144), the poet is able to see the entire picture of the "wretched interchange of wrong for wrong" (III, 69) in the story of Rome's decline and fall. He had criticized this process earlier in Canto III in the history of the French Revolution, and even earlier in Cantos I–II in reference to the Peninsular War. Now he presents this cycle of historical vengeance as the ultimate human horror, the activity that brings about a "Ruin past

Redemption's skill" (IV, 145). Elsewhere he calls it the cause of "Man's worst, his second fall" (IV, 97), and in the present context he declares that vengeance of this sort not only brings the oppressor low, but pulls down the whole structure of human values as well (145). The entire world is at present in moral ruins, and the poet uses the Coliseum, destroyed in an act of "just" rage, as the focusing image of man's folly of self-destruction.

This vision of history as an inexorable movement of "tit-for-tat moralizing" is one of the principal themes in all four cantos, just as it is one of the main ideas at the back of Shelley's *Prometheus Unbound*. In *Childe Harold's Pilgrimage* the poet calls it a "base pageant" (IV, 97) of tyranny answering tyranny:

> And thus they plod in sluggish misery,
> Rotting from sire to son, and age to age,
> Proud of their trampled nature, and so die,
> Bequeathing their hereditary rage
> To the new race of inborn slaves, who wage
> War for their chains, and rather than be free,
> Bleed gladiator-like, and still engage
> Within the same Arena where they see
> Their fellows fall before, like leaves of the same tree.   (94)

The reference to the bleeding gladiator is clearly an anticipation of the poet's later meditations at the Coliseum, and stands as a subtle portent of the important associational about-face that takes place in stanza 142.

Thus, the Coliseum sequence begins as an attempt to secure eye-for-an-eye justice. Heated by indignation, the poet inclines to disregard his earlier meditations on the theme of vengeance for wrong. But his desire to right "the unbalanced scale" undergoes a series of modifications beginning in stanza 135 when he unexpectedly calls for a *forgiveness-curse*. The modifications are not completed until the scene at the *Caritas Romana*, when the narrator recounts a story that has important thematic parallels both with his forgiveness-curse and with his version of the causes of Rome's destruction. Briefly, the poet tells the story of how a daughter paid back "the debt of blood" (150) to her father by feeding him from her breast while he was in prison. But the poet must be equivocating with the phrase "debt of blood," for its usual meaning —vengeance for suffered wrong (blood for blood)—is obviously not its first meaning here. Rather, the phrase refers to the fact that the daughter owes her very existence to her father. But Byron has a good reason for using the phrase in this unusual way; he wants to keep the idea of vengeance in our minds, to preserve intact the train of associations from the forgiveness-curse sequence to this point. His purpose in doing so becomes clear in stanza 151:

> The starry fable of the Milky Way
> Has not thy story's purity; it is
> A constellation of a sweeter ray,
> And sacred Nature triumphs more in this
> Reverse of her decree, than in the abyss
> Where sparkle distant worlds:—Oh, holiest Nurse!
> No drop of that clear stream its way shall miss
> To thy Sire's heart, replenishing its source
> With life, as our freed souls rejoin the Universe.

Nature pitilessly hews down men and their "worlds" (like Rome), but "this Reverse of her decree"—in which a young girl preserves the life of an old man—is a greater triumph yet. The stanza reaches back to the forgiveness-curse sequence through a complicated but discernible series of associations. The narrator also "reverses" the decree of Nature by forcing Nemesis to balance the scales of Justice not with vengeance but with forgiveness. We are probably also meant to see in the story a loose parallel to Rome in her later years (the aged father) and the emergent Gauls (the younger daughter). Rome is often presented in the last canto as the parent of all subsequent Western civilization (see stanzas 78–79), and history is pictured as a process in which each age bequeaths to the next its "inborn tyranny," its "hereditary rage." The story of the *Caritas Romana* "reverses" this cyclic movement toward death that operated in Nature and history alike, for the daughter seeks to preserve the life of her parent, to pay back the only "debt of blood" that is important for human life. Further, just as the narrating poet's curse is intended to infuse "love" into the "hearts all rocky now" (137), so the girl in the legend replenishes her "Sire's heart" with new "life." By taking the story of the *Caritas Romana* as a principle for living, the "souls" of men are freed from the bondage of a "contentious world" (III, 69) and can "rejoin the Universe"—can attain that "Freedom" which the narrator has been in pursuit of throughout Canto IV (see, for example, stanzas 89–96).

But the *Caritas Romana* not only completes the process of thought between stanzas 128 and 151 (preparing thereby for the triumphant assertion at St. Peter's and the Vatican Gallery which immediately follows), it clarifies and resolves all the poet's stumbling meditations upon bondage and freedom in the last canto. In stanza 96 he blurts out a desperate question:

> Can tyrants but by tyrants conquered be,
> And Freedom find no champion and no Child
> Such as Columbia saw arise . . .?
>
                      Has Earth no more
> Such seeds within her breast, or Europe no such shore?

He gets intermittent glimpses of such an achievement before the Coliseum sequence, and these partial insights anticipate the idea of a "reversed" decree like the forgiveness-curse and the *Caritas Romana*. The parallel is obvious in the most famous of these stanzas:

> Yet, Freedom! yet thy banner, torn, but flying,
> Streams like the thunder-storm *against* the wind;
> Thy trumpet voice, though broken now and dying,
> The loudest still the Tempest leaves behind;
> Thy tree hath lost its blossoms, and the rind,
> Chopped by the axe, looks rough and little worth,
> But the sap lasts,—and still the seed we find
> Sown deep, even in the bosom of the North;
> So shall a better spring less bitter fruit bring forth.   (98)[12]

Here again he senses the need to oppose the tide of bloody events, but this assertion is subsequently overwhelmed by his perception of the constant operation of a death principle to which men deliberately cling. So, later, he contravenes the vision of Egeria ("The nympholepsy of some fond despair," 115):

> Oh, Love! no habitant of earth thou art—
> An unseen Seraph, we believe in thee,—
> A faith whose martyrs are the broken heart,—
> But never yet hath seen, nor e'er shall see
> The naked eye, thy form, as it should be;
> The mind hath made thee, as it peopled Heaven,
> Even with its own desiring phantasy,

---

[12] Compare stanza 47:

> Yet Italy! through every other land
> Thy wrongs should ring—and shall—from side to side. . . .
> Europe, repentant of her parricide,
> Shall yet redeem thee, and, all backward driven,
> Roll the barbarian tide, and sue to be forgiven.

And to a thought such shape and image given,
As haunts the unquenched soul—parched—wearied—wrung—
and riven.   (121)

Similarly, he declares against his vision of human creativity which he
gained earlier at the Uffizi Gallery (49–52):

Of its own beauty is the mind diseased,
And fevers into false creation:—where,
Where are the forms the sculptor's soul hath seized?
In him alone. Can Nature show so fair?   (122)

As he approaches the crucial events at the Coliseum, his despair at
finding a principle of creative and immortalizing love has reached its
deepest:

Few—none—find what they love or could have loved,
Though accident, blind contact, and the strong
Necessity of loving, have removed
Antipathies—but to recur, ere long,
Envenomed with irrevocable wrong;
And Circumstance, that unspiritual God
And Miscreator, makes and helps along
Our coming evils with a crutch-like rod,
Whose touch turns Hope to dust,—the dust we all have trod.

Our life is a false nature—'tis not in
The harmony of things,—this hard decree,
This uneradicable taint of Sin,
This boundless Upas, this all-blasting tree,
Whose root is Earth. . . .   (125–26)

Though his mind thus continually wanders into mazes of uncertainty
and hopelessness, he declares in the next stanza that he will continue to
"ponder boldly," since the activity of groping thought is, in the end,
"our last and only place/Of refuge." The event proves his hopeless hope
justified, for his perseverance in meditation finally leads to a clear understanding that Love can and must be made a "habitant of earth."

The *Caritas Romana* modifies the forgiveness-curse sequence by presenting it again to us in a moderated tone. The girl offers her "gentle
side" (150) to her father, whereas the poet had earlier "wreaked" the
"deep prophetic fulness" of his curse of love (134) upon the heads of
his enemies. Readers like Peter Thorslev have often found the forgiveness-curse stanzas offensive—"petty and vindictive," Thorslev calls

them.[13] Yet surely this is misplaced Christian sentimentalism (or pre-disposed moralizing on Byron's biography), for as the stanzas appear in the poem the poet is graphically presented as the sufferer of intolerable wrongs.

> And if my voice break forth, 'tis not that now
> I shrink from what is suffered: let him speak
> Who hath beheld decline upon my brow,
> Or seen my mind's convulsion leave it weak;
> But in this page a record will I seek.
> Not in the air shall these my words disperse,
> Though I be ashes; a far hour shall wreak
> The deep prophetic fulness of this verse,
> And pile on human heads the mountain of my curse!
>
> That curse shall be Forgiveness.—Have I not—
> Hear me, my mother Earth! behold it, Heaven!—
> Have I not had to wrestle with my lot?
> Have I not suffered things to be forgiven?
> Have I not had my brain seared, my heart riven,
> Hopes sapped, name blighted, Life's life lied away?
> And only not to desperation driven,
> Because not altogether of such clay
> As rots into the souls of those whom I survey.   (134–35)

The problem with which the poet must deal is a fundamental one, for if the judgment of men upon him is allowed to stand, then "Opinion" becomes an "Omnipotence," and "right/And wrong are accidents" (93) of transient human ethics rather than the absolute points of definition by which an individual must judge his own relation to the Godhead. The poet admits his own guilt:

> It is not that I may not have incurred,
> For my ancestral faults or mine, the wound
> I bleed withal. . . .   (133)

But if once the principle of "wrong for wrong" is allowed, human integrity becomes impossible ("Man's worst, his second fall"). The evil that he has received at the hands of his detractors must be exposed and cast out, for it lies at the root of the "boundless Upas" which has overspread the earth and kept man in a cycle of self-destruction and moral death. He therefore invokes Nemesis to curse with forgiveness, a gesture which at once turns the destructive power of Nemesis against

[13] Peter Thorslev, *The Byronic Hero* (Minneapolis, 1962), p. 140.

herself and "reverses" the very idea of cursing. The prophetic style in which the poet's curse is delivered, as well as the ease with which he associates himself with a sublime order of Reality (e.g., "Hear me, my mother Earth! behold it, Heaven!"), makes it impossible to regard his outburst as either "petty" or "vindictive." The prophetic tone is required by the circumstances, for his is not so much a self-defense as a defense of all contingent and erring humanity. It is an assertion of the sacred worth of the individual soul above everything else on earth, including its own sin and weakness and the judgment of other men. The whole scene appears as a terrible last resort for the vindication of the human person against his own and the world's evil, a Jobean cry wrung from a self-confessed sinner asserting that, despite all his weaknesses and perversions, every man must be able to believe that he is "fit for the society of kings" if he is not to die the death, and that if any other man seek to destroy that belief he has committed a fearful wrong that cries to heaven for judgment.

As Mr. Thorslev has noted, however, the narrator's prophetic style does not succeed in obliterating all subjective and personal elements from his curse. Dramatically considered, this fact has two results. First of all, it is a reliable pledge of the truth of the poet's "suffering" that he is unable entirely to forget himself in his role as prophet. But second, because his curse itself borders dangerously upon an act of vendetta, we may tend to forget (with him) that his lips have been touched with a burning coal, and that he has been called upon in extremis to speak a divine, not a human, truth. The cases of Job, Jeremiah, and especially Jonah indicate how often these two results tend to correlate with each other. It is the function of stanzas 138–51 to take the curse out of the poet's tone of voice: that is, the element of prophetic anathema must stand (the tone of a divine utterance), but when the afflatus leaves him, no trace of cursing must remain in his more intimate tone and more personal attitudes. This process begins at the end of stanza 137 when he looks to a future reconciliation in love, and it is completed in the poet's meditation upon the *Caritas Romana* where pity and gentleness are the predominant motifs.

Stanzas 128–51 present Byron's accession to a more perfect understanding of the good and evil in himself and his world. In addition, they repeat the method of the whole canto, in which the poet rummages about the museum of Italy for a solution to the problem of human evil. He alternates between periods of hopefulness and expectancy (for example, stanza 47) and spells of terrible despair; but even after the climax has been passed—in the last thirty-three stanzas of the poem—he finds that the truth he has discovered is not The Truth, but the way to Truth. Once again we are given a statement of the necessity of constant development and painful growth. In the Coliseum sequence, as elsewhere, the narrator is the prototype of groping, stumbling humanity who is, nevertheless, called to a high and splendid destiny; in the end, by "pondering boldly" and by preserving always a responsiveness to new sensations and attitudes, he is enlightened not to a goal, but to the glory of what he is even now engaged in seeking. Gide's famous remark—"Je ne suis jamais, je deviens"—could not be more appositely applied than to the last canto of *Childe Harold's Pilgrimage.*

Dramatic Action in Cantos I–II

But the first two cantos also dramatize the narrating poet in a process of "becoming," only in this case he portrays himself advancing to a condition of mental anguish and futility. I suspect that most readers who regard Cantos I–II as a versified travel book do so because the narrator is so "impressionable" in them. Unlike the exuberant poet of Cantos III and IV, the narrator of 1812 never influences events himself, but is always acted upon. Even his satirical set pieces and declamatory sequences are not hurled forth from a position of strength; they are responses to an earlier disagreeable impression or stimulus, purely reflex movements. But it is just because this is true that Cantos I–II are primarily personal, not objectively descriptive documents, or satirical, or didactic. John Wilson says they reveal "a mind . . . enslaved to itself,"[14] and in fact we find Byron's self-consciousness and sensitivity are themselves the predominant causes of his perplexities, for they subject him to ambiguous, even contradictory, attitudes in quick succession. Everything is equivocal to him: in Portugal are both natural beauty and abject weakness and corruption; in Albania, vigor and bravery as well as vendetta and blood-lust; in Greece, beauty and a heritage of the world's most noble values, but also complete spiritual enervation. As he passes through these countries and observes their manners he gives us not so much a picture of them as a moving picture of his reactions to them; and it is upon the sequence of the narrator's reactions as they are presented in the poem that the structure of the first two cantos, like the last, is built.

This fact is well illustrated in the stanzas on Spain, which contain an

[14] John Wilson, Review of Lord Byron, "The Fourth Canto of Childe Harold," *Blackwood's Magazine* 3 (May, 1818): 217.

elaborate complex of shifting emotions and attitudes.[15] Byron opens the subject by recalling the history of this "renown'd, romantic land" (I, 35), which turns out to be a record of bloody religious warfare carried out under the banner of Christian Chivalry. Spain is now under the shadow of the "Scourger of the world" (I, 52), however, so that a call to arms might well be a noble call to justice and honest patriotism. But the poet does not choose to consider this aspect of the situation, at least as yet; instead, he piles irony upon irony to expose the horrors of the Peninsular War. "Lovely" Spain could use some of her grand, romantic heroes (st. 35) in this fight with the hosts of Napoleon. The poet assumes briefly the posture of an ardent supporter of the Spanish cause (which Byron in fact was) and calls out hopefully:

> Where are those bloody Banners which of yore
> Waved o'er thy sons, victorious to the gale,
> And drove at last the spoilers to their shore?
> Red gleamed the Cross, and waned the Crescent pale,
> While Afric's echoes thrilled with Moorish matrons' wail.   (35)

But the narrator's is really a mock appeal, for the point he wants to make is that the actual history of Spain is a "bloody" tale of carnage and human grief. The first line of the next stanza enforces the poet's irony: "Teems not each ditty with the glorious tale?" Then the ancient goddess Chivalry herself appears and issues a call to arms ("In every peal she calls, 'Awake! arise!' " 37), but when the narrator then asks, "Say, is her voice more feeble than of yore," we have only to look around, with the poet, at the present state of Spain to know the grim answer to that question:

> Lo! where the Giant on the mountain stands,
> His blood-red tresses deepening in the Sun,
> With death-shot glowing in his fiery hands,
> And eye that scorcheth all it glares upon;

15 William A. Borst, whose *Lord Byron's First Pilgrimage* (New Haven, 1948) is the standard essay on the first two cantos, notes some of the "inconsistencies" (p. 44) in the poet's attitudes and tries to deal with them (pp. 42–49). But he does not see how very pervasive they are, nor does he consider that they might serve the poem in a significant way. In general, he argues that the poet's sympathy for the "plight" of the Spaniards was based on "genuine human feeling" (p. 46), and was therefore the true intention of the poetry; while his skepticism and "spleen" (p. 46) were either the result of "low spirits" (p. 44) or Whig partisanship (pp. 44–45), or more simply, "sophomoric bad taste" (p. 46). Swift's mind operated at a similarly sophomoric level, however. In any case, though Borst notes this as a quality of mind that "Byron never completely outgrew" (p. 46) he fails to examine the structure of the poem itself to see if Byron might not have put his inveterate skepticism and "inconsistencies" to poetic use.

Restless it rolls, now fixed, and now anon
Flashing afar,—and at his iron feet
Destruction cowers, to mark what deeds are done;
For on this morn three potent Nations meet,
To shed before his Shrine the blood he deems most sweet.   (39)

The poet wants to see Spain's "well-asserted right" (90) to freedom from the "curst oppressor" (87) achieved, but throughout the canto he finds himself recoiling at the savagery of the whole spectacle. He admires much in the Spanish character, as his tribute to the Maid of Saragoza shows, but his admiration is constantly being choked off before it has a chance to form itself into a definitive statement. "Fair is proud Seville," he says, and praises the city for "Her strength, her wealth," and her noble heritage (65); but in the next breath he mentions Cadiz which has given itself over to the "Cherub-hydra" of "Vice." Similarly, the vigor of the Spaniards is as admirable as their love for their brutal national sport is grotesque:

The thronged arena shakes with shouts for more;
Yells the mad crowd o'er entrails freshly torn,
Nor shrinks the female eye, nor ev'n affects to mourn.   (68)

In the war itself, the Spanish patriot seems more intent upon exacting vengeance than upon securing his freedom:

Nurtured in blood betimes, his heart delights
In vengeance, gloating on another's pain.   (80)

In a MS note to this stanza the poet observes:

The Spaniards are as revengeful as ever. At Santa Olalla, I heard a young peasant threaten to stab a woman (an old one, to be sure, which mitigates the offence), and was told, on expressing some small surprise, that this ethic was by no means uncommon.[16]

"Here all were noble, save Nobility" (85), the narrator says, because only Spain's "vassals" (86) resolutely oppose the invader. But those same defenders of Spanish "Pride" and "Liberty" are brutal in the extreme. When the poet says of Spanish valor in war:

Pride points the path that leads to Liberty;
Back to the struggle, baffled in the strife,
War, war is still the cry, "War even to the knife!"   (86)

---

[16] Coleridge prints "Santa Otella," but incorrectly. See Philip H. Churchman, "Lord Byron's Experiences in the Spanish Peninsula in 1809," *Bulletin Hispanique* 11 (1909): 128.

he is not bestowing unmixed praise. The cry "War even to the knife!" suggests not only heroic resolution, but also that basic savagery which lies at the heart of the Spaniard, and that is, in fact, the correlative of his greatest virtue: Vitality. The very next stanza clarifies this fact unmistakably.

> Ye, who would more of Spain and Spaniards know,
> Go, read whate'er is writ of bloodiest strife:
> Whate'er keen Vengeance urged on foreign foe
> Can act, is acting there against man's life:
> From flashing scimitar to secret knife,
> War mouldeth there each weapon to his need—
> So may he guard the sister and the wife,
> So may he make each curst oppressor bleed—
> So may such foes deserve the most remorseless deed!

It is in this context that the statement "Here all were noble, save Nobility" achieves its full implications. The last three lines are sharply ironic. In lines 7–8 the narrator assumes the personality of the typical Spanish patriot, and he gives two reasons why "War mouldeth there each weapon to his need." The first is an honorable one, the second (in which the specter of vengeance again appears) less so—and in line 9 the narrator speaks in his own person to suggest that the Spaniard's hatred has blinded him to all considerations of justice in retribution, not even to speak of mercy.[17] "Flows there a tear of Pity for the dead?" the narrator asks in the next stanza, again assuming the role of spokesman for the Spanish patriots. His answer suggests that such sentiments have to be forgone, that the cruelty of the French soldier must be answered in kind. Yet the narrator in his own person sees that

> Not all the blood at Talavera shed,
> Not all the marvels of Barossa's fight,
> Not Albuera lavish of the dead,
> Have won for Spain her well asserted right.   (90)

The reason is plain for all to see: Spain is as much slave to her own worst vices as she is the victim of French tyranny. In Canto III Byron dramatizes a similar situation in the sequence of events in France from the Revolution to the Reign of Terror. There, however, he argues posi-

---

[17] The treatment of the Suliotes in Canto II is similar to that of the Spaniards. Though the Suliotes are "Fierce," they have the concomitant virtues of courage and strength. (II, 65) Ali Pasha, their leader, is also their prototype. He is marked "with a tiger's tooth," and the poet predicts of him: "Blood follows blood, and, through their mortal span,/In bloodier acts conclude those who with blood began" (II, 63).

tively that true liberty will only be achieved when men choose not to exact retribution for wrongs. Only thus can the cycle of vengeance be broken (III, 84).

In Spain, then, the poet's sympathies and antipathies are moved in so many different directions that he is finally unable to adopt a coherent attitude toward the sequence of events that unfolds there. At first he tries to laugh the difficulties away with cynical remarks like:

> By Heaven! it is a splendid sight to see
> (For one who hath no friend, no brother there)
> Their rival scarfs of mixed embroidery. . . .
> What gallant War-hounds rouse them from their lair,
> And gnash their fangs, loud yelling for the prey!   (40)

But this kind of defense against his own shifting sensibilities becomes less and less possible as he continues to observe. War, martial glory, Spain, France, and England all weigh equally (or nearly so) in the balance of his equivocal mind. The situation seems a hopeless tangle of blood, crime, and vengeance, and the poetry is an image of the narrator's growing sense of bafflement and helplessness in the face of it. It is the measure of his ability to perceive difficulties and doubts without limit, and of course without solution as well. As he laments the death of his friend Wingfield during the Spanish hostilities, he tells us that his is a song of "unavailing woe" that spontaneously "bursts from my heart" (91).

The general autobiographical form of *Childe Harold's Pilgrimage*, with its confessional elements and journal-like structure, forces us to seek its design in the narrating poet's attitudes, in the design of his psychology. As we have seen from the stanzas on Spain, his personality in the early cantos is as unstable as his forms of thought are equivocal. We cannot take anything he says as a conclusive statement on any subject because his mind is constantly veering off toward different points of view. But if his thoughts are not engaging as precepts, the movement of his mind is exceedingly interesting and instructive as a psychological exemplum. Without a fixed center of established values and modes of reasoning in which he is willing to put his trust, the poet is moved along by circumstance, his own skepticism, and the habit of associational responsiveness, until by the end of Canto II he has passed through various stages of disenchantment with his environment to an attitude of total alienation. His opinions, as ideas, are strictly of secondary poetic importance; what matters is that they are his, and that in them we can read the temper of his mind. Canto II offers a good brief example of this in the episode between "Sweet Florence" and the poet's "too easy youth," Harold (30).

The comparison of Harold's escape from the lady with the escape of Ulysses and Telemachus from Calypso (29) introduces the scene on a mock-heroic note. In the next stanza the narrator addresses Harold and tells him that if the mythical Calypso no longer lives on Goza, still he must beware this "new Calypso." The epic comparison cannot be seriously maintained, of course, especially in the context of stanza 32; the poet's warning is really mockery of a love convention, and Harold's short farewell speech to Florence is in fact what it seems: high-flown rhetoric.

> Sweet Florence! could another ever share
> This wayward, loveless heart, it would be thine:
> But checked by every tie, I may not dare
> To cast a worthless offering at thy shrine,
> Nor ask so dear a breast to feel one pang for *mine*.   (30)

Harold's attempt to sever the relationship with honor on both sides falls flat, for she is no "shrine" but the caricature of a superficial adventuress, and he is too much the dupe of his own formularized rhetoric to recognize the absurdity of his gesture. The mocking description in stanza 32 of Florence's reactions to Harold's successful self-defense establishes the comic decorum of Harold's "gallant" speech.

> Fair Florence found, in sooth with some amaze,
> One who, 'twas said, still sighed to all he saw,
> Withstand, unmoved, the lustre of her gaze,
> Which others hailed with real or mimic awe,
> Their hope, their doom, their punishment, their law;
> All that gay Beauty from her bondsmen claims:
> And much she marvelled that a youth so raw
> Nor felt, nor feigned at least, the oft-told flames,
> Which though sometimes they frown, yet rarely anger dames.

This same frivolously satiric tone predominates in the next stanza. In stanza 34, however, he allows his point of view to shift slightly but significantly. As he gives us the details of how to conduct a successful liaison with a woman like Florence, the inhuman qualities of a convention of social lovemaking begin to become apparent, and the tone of the lines becomes problematical. The indefinable bitterness that lurks behind his mockery in stanza 34 breaks out nakedly in stanza 35:

'Tis an old lesson—Time approves it true,
And those who know it best, deplore it most;
When all is won that all desire to woo,
The paltry prize is hardly worth the cost:
Youth wasted—Minds degraded—Honour lost—
These are thy fruits, successful Passion! these!
Still to the last it rankles, a disease,
Not to be cured when Love itself forgets to please.

The engaging element in these stanzas is their psychological movement, not their ideational content. What process of thought, what peculiarity of temper, has led the poet from the playful comedy of the opening stanzas to the pained exclamations of the last? To deal adequately with this question we would have to sketch the whole meaning and structure of the first two cantos. For the moment, the important thing is that we should see that this is the paramount critical issue. We can, however, indicate in a brief and general way how this answer will have to be formulated. Social corruption is a universal phenomenon, and the young poet's experience of this fact in Cantos I–II, as well as his early personal losses, gradually inclines his skeptical mind to choose thought associations that inevitably conclude in sullenness or depression.

In the early cantos, then, we see that the mind of the poet is objectified to us in much the same way that it is in the later cantos: we observe him thinking and acting, and frequently perceive significance where he remains without self-knowledge. This is true because a similar process is repeated in all four cantos: the poet tells us his story, but because the telling and the living seem to have occurred simultaneously, the poet in the poem can know nothing about himself beyond the stanza he is immediately writing (the moment he is immediately living). He is thus a prejudiced participant in the action which he himself narrates. This is a matter of art, not chance, for it proceeds from the method in which Byron has chosen to cast his poem. Though the poet *in* the poem is presented to us as the artist *of* the poem, he in fact shows no signs of artistic objectivity. He has to acquire consciousness and self-knowledge in the course of the poem; only Byron the artist, who is refined out of poetic existence, possesses such objectivity, and his consciousness is built into the poem's structure, not into the narrator's character. This really basic fact about the form of the whole poem (why it is "dramatic" in character) can be forgotten only at the risk of fundamental misreading.

Those long-suffering stanzas at the beginning of Canto I (2–13), for example, have often been rather harshly treated by contemporary critics for just this reason. As it is, they have weaknesses enough in basic matters of execution; but we ought not to find fault indiscriminately. The lapses in these early stanzas are the same kind that we encounter throughout the first two cantos: thoughtless rhythm, overly generalized metaphors, functionless verbosity, neglect of diction for the sake of rhyme.

> For he through Sin's long labyrinth had run,
> Nor made atonement when he did amiss,
> Had sighed to many though he loved but one,
> And that loved one, alas! could ne'er be his.
> Ah, happy she! to 'scape from him whose kiss
> Had been pollution unto aught so chaste;
> Who soon had left her charms for vulgar bliss,
> And spoiled her goodly lands to gild his waste,
> Nor calm domestic peace had ever deigned to taste.   (5)

Critics like to attack the opening stanzas for their Spenserian diction, yet this stanza—which is probably the worst in the early group—is entirely free of it, while stanza 2, which is full of such diction, develops a raffish charm by exploiting the antique language for some important comic effects.

> Whilome in Albion's isle there dwelt a youth,
> Who ne in Virtue's ways did take delight;
> But spent his days in riot most uncouth,
> And vexed with mirth the drowsy ear of Night.
> Ah me! in sooth he was a shameless wight,
> Sore given to revel and ungodly glee;
> Few earthly things found favour in his sight
> Save concubines and carnal companie,
> And flaunting wassailers of high and low degree.   (2)

Not only are the faults of the opening stanzas not a function of their Spenserian diction, the general meaning of the lines is specifically related to the way the narrating poet uses it. The antique language helps to reveal the poet's attitudes to the reader.[18]

I will return to the second stanza again in a moment, for we can ap-

[18] Andrew Rutherford states the prevailing objection against the Spenserian diction very well: "Byron cannot justify his archaisms as Beattie does his occasional use of 'old words' in *The Minstrel*, by saying they are appropriate to his subject, for Childe Harold, though referred to as a pilgrim, is a contemporary figure, and there is no point in using pseudo-medieval jargon to describe his actions" (Rutherford, pp. 26–27). One does not have to defend every instance of Byron's use of archaic language to see that it

preciate it more easily once we have elucidated the purpose of the whole introductory passage. We make our first assessment of the narrator's character in stanzas 1–13, and the contrast between this initial picture and those presented at various other significant moments later in the poem is an important index to the overall psychological movement. The poet begins by invoking the blessing of the Muse:

> Oh, thou! in Hellas deemed of heavenly birth,
> Muse! formed or fabled at the Minstrel's will!
> Since shamed full oft by later lyres on earth,
> Mine dares not call thee from thy sacred Hill:
> Yet there I've wandered by thy vaunted rill;
> Yes! sighed o'er Delphi's long deserted shrine,
> Where, save that feeble fountain, all is still;
> Nor mote my shell awake the weary Nine
> To grace so plain a tale—this lowly lay of mine.   (1)

He has already told us in the Preface that most of the poem was written "amidst the scenes which it attempts to describe."[19] The first stanza, however, manifestly belongs to a period subsequent to his visit to Greece (ll. 5–6), which is to say—in terms of the poem's own time sequence—after the conclusion to Canto II. He addresses us first in the approximate present, then, and we find that his melancholy feelings occasioned by the passing of greatness (ll. 6–7) as well as the sense of his own ineffectuality (ll. 4, 8–9) parallel the state of his mind as we see it at the end of Canto II (see especially stanzas 92 and 98). Moreover, the contempt he expresses for the host of "louder Minstrels in these later days" (II, 94) is foreshadowed here in the disdain he feels for the "later lyres on earth" who now shame the Muse's ancient glory. Finally, the poet's gloom is also a function of the general social corruption which is suggested by the symbolism of the stanza: waste and infertility surround Parnassus, the mountain sacred to Apollo and the Muses, and the symbolic apex of literature, art, and culture. At the end of Canto II he also finds himself alone and desolate in a corrupted world (97), left "deserted" by the deaths of all those close to him who gave meaning to his existence (96). The relationship between Greece and the lonely poet is explicitly drawn in II, 92.

---

is often most appropriate to the subject of the poem—to the revelation of the narrator's personality, that is. As I shall try to show in the discussion below, the highly derivative character of this language makes it a focus of the narrator's self-consciousness: a tension is set up in the early stanzas of the poem between the narrator's use of his artificial Spenserian diction and his more normal declamatory-meditative-conversational language.

19 *P* 2: 3.

The parted bosom clings to wonted home,
If aught that's kindred cheer the welcome hearth;
He that is lonely—hither let him roam,
And gaze complacent on congenial earth.
Greece is no lightsome land of social mirth:
But he whom Sadness sootheth may abide,
And scarce regret the region of his birth,
When wandering slow by Delphi's sacred side,
Or gazing o'er the plains where Greek and Persian died.

The allusion to the motto from *Le Cosmopolite* fixes the stanzas as an important statement of what the narrator has learned so far on his pilgrimage with Harold.

When the narrative proper begins in stanza 2, however, there is an abrupt change in the tone of the poet's voice. No reader can miss this *fact*, but generally the reason for it is overlooked. Northrop Frye, for example, finds the poet's "semi-facetious" manner in stanzas 2–13 merely "pointless."[20] I do not think this is accurate. The point is that the poet at the end of the first pilgrimage is "A sadder and a wiser man" than he was at the beginning.[21] The epigraph from *Le Cosmopolite* states this clearly. The theme of Cantos I–II is "Consciousness awaking to her woes" (I, 92), the painful education of the poet into a more sensitive and reliable subjective moral awareness, one that he did not possess at the start. The tonal contrast between stanzas 1 and 2 is the poem's initial forecast of the direction in which the first two cantos will ultimately move (that is, toward the tone of st. 1).

Stanzas 2–13 are about equally divided between sardonic mockery and earnest satire or reflection. One of the many editors of the poem, Andrew J. George, discusses the vein of cynical irresponsibility in this way:

> These . . . stanzas have doubtless deterred many from reading the poem. There is in them something of the *Don Juan*, that spirit of melodrama and affectation which is distinctly Byronic. . . . There is here something of a motiveless malignity which would shock those mortals afflicted with the disease which Dean Hole called piosity. . . .[22]

[20] Northrop Frye, "Lord Byron," in *Fables of Identity* (New York, 1963), p. 182.

[21] Coleridge's *Rime of the Ancient Mariner* was a favorite of Byron's, and may have influenced the form of *Childe Harold's Pilgrimage*. The wanderer motif needs no emphasis, but one might recall that Coleridge's poem also begins with a picture of the principal character after the fact, and that both the mariner and Byron's narrator start their journeys in a certain careless atmosphere. Byron alludes specifically to Coleridge's poem in Harold's "Good Night" lyric, stanza 9, lines 1–2.

[22] *Childe Harold's Pilgrimage*, ed. Andrew J. George (New York, 1907), p. 184.

Yet why should we censure the poetic mockery in a passage like stanza 2? We learn a great deal about the narrator in a very short space, certainly much more than we do about Harold. A few general facts are detailed about Harold's life, but the specific thrust of this stanza is its ironic attack upon the sensibilities of the conventionally moral, as Mr. George has noted. The attack is not "motiveless," however, for "piosity" is a disease (as Byron frequently tells us in *Hours of Idleness*), and the poet suggests here that it is quite as symptomatic of social and moral degeneracy as is "riot most uncouth." But the poet seems disinclined to take the objects of his ridicule very seriously, at least here, so that his tone remains cavalier and almost bantering. His mocking use of syntax and diction robs everything in the stanza of moral significance except his own jocose cynicism. "Virtue's ways," "Concubines and carnal companie," "riot most uncouth," even the "shameless wight" himself are all reduced to a dead level of absurdity. This tendency to complete moral nihilism is characteristic of all the early stanzas. When he alludes to the history of Harold's "vast and venerable" (7) hall he resorts again to his irresponsible humor.

> Monastic dome! condemned to uses vile!
> Where superstition once had made her den
> Now Paphian girls were known to sing and smile;
> And monks might deem their time was come agen,
> If ancient tales say true, nor wrong these holy men.

Stanzas 2–13 display this kind of urbane mockery quite often, and it is a significant characteristic of the narrator's early state of mind. He likes to set himself up as a gadfly to all conventional moral systems and attitudes, attacking or hooting at them for their hypocrisy, or selfishness, or self-righteousness. Thus he gets his joke at the expense of the hypocritical monks of those "ancient tales," and in stanza 2 he mocks the propriety-bound attitudes of conventional British morality. Yet this cynicism into which he retreats is only the reverse of the more serious attitudes toward his society which also appear in these early stanzas. In fact, the opening stanzas display a fairly constant alternation between seriousness and persiflage, and it is this kind of indecisiveness that comes across as the most apparent trait of the narrator's character at this point. Thus, if he is contemptuous of self-righteous piosity, he is equally opposed to the gentlemanly pursuit of dissolute pleasures that is especially characteristic of the upper classes (compare *Hours of Idleness*, "Granta, A Medley," st. 13–16). He attacks them as "The heartless parasites of present cheer" (9), and in this case the line betrays no tone of levity whatever. The glimpse we get into the narrator's mind here recalls several remarks in the first stanza of the canto, just as it foreshadows the loneliness described in the conclusion to Canto II, as well as the declamation in II, 26 on society's "Minions of splendour, shrinking from distress."

Insofar as Harold is the product of a sentimental eighteenth-century education he too is mocked by the narrator. "Sickly sensibility" is, as we have already seen, a persistent object of satire in *Hours of Idleness*. But as in that early volume Byron's own feelings about "the man of feeling" are frequently equivocal, so here:

> And now Childe Harold was sore sick at heart,
> And from his fellow Bacchanals would flee;
> 'Tis said, at times the sullen tear would start,
> But Pride congealed the drop within his ee:
> Apart he stalked in joyless reverie,
> And from his native land resolved to go,
> And visit scorching climes beyond the sea;
> With pleasure drugged, he almost longed for woe,
> And e'en for change of scene would seek the shades below.   (6)

The archaisms in the first four lines tend to deflate Harold's conventionally melancholic pose, but the tone of the stanza undergoes a gradual metamorphosis in the second half. The "semi-facetious" antique style at the beginning is the sign of the narrator's skeptical smile, just as it is in the earlier line "Ah me! in sooth he was a shameless wight." The tone grows more complicated, however, for it is difficult to know just how seriously lines 5–9 are to be taken. A line like the eighth is particularly problematical, for it has no Spenserianisms to mitigate its rather grim signification.

A similar effect is produced in stanza 4:

> Childe Harold basked him in the Noontide sun,
> Disporting there like any other fly;
> Nor deemed before his little day was done
> One blast might chill him into misery.
> But long ere scarce a third of his passed by,
> Worse than Adversity the Childe befell;
> He felt the fulness of Satiety:
> Then loathed he in his native land to dwell,
> Which seemed to him more lone than Eremite's sad cell.

The first line of the stanza echoes a line in a famous speech by Jaques in *As You Like It*, in which the theme of evil Fortune and the ravages of Time is paramount. The poet here apparently wants us to recall the tone and meaning of the whole passage from Shakespeare:

> A fool, a fool! I met a fool i' th' forest,
> A motley fool; a miserable world!
> As I do live by food, I met a fool,
> Who laid him down and basked him in the sun,
> And railed on Lady Fortune in good terms,
> In good set terms, and yet a motley fool.
> "Good morrow, fool," quoth I. "No sir," quoth he,
> "Call me not fool till heaven hath sent me fortune."
> And then he drew a dial from his poke,
> And looking on it with lack-lustre eye,
> Says, very wisely, "It is ten o'clock.
> Thus we may see," quoth he, "how the world wags.
> 'Tis but an hour ago since it was nine;
> And after one hour more, 'twill be eleven;
> And so, from hour to hour, we ripe and ripe,
> And then, from hour to hour, we rot and rot;
> And thereby hangs a tale." When I did hear
> The motley fool thus moral on the time,
> My lungs began to crow like chanticleer
> That fools should be so deep-contemplative. . . . O noble fool!
> A worthy fool! Motley's the only wear.   (II, vii, 12–34)

Jaques, Hamlet, Sterne, and the Byron of *Don Juan* are all famous for their ability to hold mockery and melancholy in a delicate—and significant—equipoise. The allusion here is thus most apposite, for it not only supports the tone of comic reduction on which the stanza opens, but prepares us for the darker moods that flit through the later parts of the passage. After the third line, the tone becomes equivocal, as it did in the middle of stanza 6. The straightforward meaning of the seventh line, for example, conflicts with the ironic tone maintained at the stylistic level. This kind of effect happens frequently in the early stanzas ("something of the *Don Juan*," as A. J. George said), and it serves to convince us that the narrator's character is a complicated mixture of cynical humor and melancholy seriousness. He can laugh at Harold's "Paphian girls," but at the same time he is seriously opposed to Harold's dissolute "flatterers" and repelled by the effects of irresponsible pleasure-seeking; he finds Harold a bit ridiculous and without the capacity for effective

self-examination (Harold does not begin to learn the art of "Meditation" until I, 27, and even then he flees it), but the narrator is likewise
sensible of the Childe's pained and gloomy condition (8). He can, for
example, smile ironically at Harold's "vast and venerable pile" which
was "So old, it seemed only not to fall" (7), and in the very next line
cut across his own humor with a serious qualification: "Yet strength
was pillared in each massy aisle." That the poetry in this case is completely undistinguished does not affect its evident intention. He is also
an adept at self-mockery; we frequently find him deflating his sympathetic responses with a sudden ironic thrust, as in stanza 9:

> And none did love him! though to hall and bower
> He gathered revellers from far and near,
> He knew them flatterers of the festal hour,
> The heartless Parasites of present cheer,
> Yea! none did love him—not his lemans dear—
> But pomp and power alone are Woman's care,
> And where these are light Eros finds a feere;
> Maidens, like moths, are ever caught by glare,
> And Mammon wins his way where Seraphs might despair.

Byron had much trouble with the composition of this stanza, which
originally was completely somber in tone;

> And few could love him, for in hall and bower,
> An evil smile, just bordering on a sneer,
> Curled on his lip een in the festal hour
> As if he deemed no mortal might him cheer—
> To gentle dames still less could he be dear—
> But pomp and power alone are woman's care,
> And where these are let no possessor fear,
> The Sex are slaves to ⎫
> Love shrinks outshone by ⎬ Mammon's dazzling glare
> That Daimon wins his way, where Angels might despair.[23]

Revising the stanza, Byron takes away Harold's "evil smile" in order to
make him appear just sympathetically melancholy. The evil is transferred to the

> flatterers of the festal hour,
> The heartless Parasites of present cheer

[23] This is transcribed from the original MS of the canto in the Murray collection.
Compare with the version printed at *P* 2: 21.

with whom the Childe consorts. But the "gentle dames" in the first form of the stanza are not at all attractive creatures, so Byron decides to tone the narrator's description down. They become "moths" caught (unwittingly) by Mammon's "glare" rather than the willing and even deliberate "slaves" to his enticements. The phrase "light Eros finds a feere," a very late addition,[24] supports the narrator's new tone of indulgent mockery toward the ladies. The new fifth line "Yea! none did love him—not his lemans dear—") was clearly a decisive addition, for in it we observe the narrator making an abrupt effort to sound less concerned, to appear more sardonically disinterested. The original seriousness of the stanza still hovers around the playful satire in the last five lines, and the reader is left uncertain as to just how much bite the narrator's irony has in it. This equivocalness seems to me perfectly functional, however, since it reflects again that basic emotional duality in the narrator's character which we find exemplified throughout the opening stanzas.

Perhaps no commentary on the early stanzas of Canto I reveals so well the precise tone of the poet's voice there as does the following passage in a letter from Byron to Francis Hodgson. The letter is especially interesting because it was written just after Byron had finished the first draft of Cantos I–II. He seems to have had the opening stanzas specifically in his thoughts when he wrote to Hodgson, for not only is the substance of the following passage very close to that in the poem, the tonal quality duplicates stanzas 2–13 nearly perfectly.

> I hope you will find me an altered personage,—I do not mean in body but in manner, for I begin to find out that nothing but virtue will do in this damned world. I am tolerably sick of vice, which I have tried in its agreeable varieties, and mean, on my return, to cut all my dissolute acquaintance, leave off wine and carnal company, and betake myself to politics and decorum. I am very serious and cynical, and a good deal disposed to moralise; but fortunately for you the coming homily is cut off by default of pen and defection of paper.[25]

William Borst found it "hard to say"[26] just how serious Byron's declarations in this letter were, and his equivocal reaction is a sensitive reflection of Byron's own attitude. There is a certain wicked perversity in the

---

[24] It does not appear in the Murray MS, but it does appear in the Dallas transcript made in late July or early August, 1811. See chapter 3 below for details.

[25] Letter to Francis Hodgson, 5 May 1810 (*LJ* 1: 272–73).

[26] *Borst*, p. 114.

trick of the final sentence (which closes the letter) where Byron dex-
terously tiptoes away from taking any responsibility for what he has
just said; for he himself does not know his own mind at this point, and
he refuses to become too deeply involved in his volitional impulses and
emotional responses. At the same time, it is perfectly clear that he has
experienced some sort of psychic reaction against "vice," even if he
as yet has no idea what might or even ought to be done about it. So he
substitutes irony for commitment.

Conclusion

The way we naturally read passages like these from Byron's dramatic
and self-revelatory prose can help us keep our responses true to the self-
dramatizing nature of *Childe Harold's Pilgrimage*. The narrator's style
in the poem—the way he expresses himself, the momentary attitudes
that he reveals—are as much a part of the poem's meaning in Cantos I–
II as they are in III and IV. The Preface of 1812 announces the tonal
fluctuations that we do in fact find throughout the early cantos, and I
think it would be a mistake to assume that Byron did not see how such
a technique would contribute to the realization of the narrator's character in the poem. For his part, Andrew Rutherford acknowledges that
the poet "does succeed in presenting different aspects of his personality"
in the poem, but he goes on to say that Byron

> fails to unite them into a coherent artistic whole—a failure which
> must be attributed in part to careless workmanship and lack of
> planning, but also to his inability at this stage to resolve the con-
> flicts in his nature, to develop a consistent attitude toward life. . . .[27]

We shall see that his argument about lack of planning cannot be maintained in the face of the existing MSS. If Byron failed to present a "coherent artistic whole" it is not because he did not try very hard to do so;
this he said himself in his Preface.[28]

In this chapter I have tried to show how *Childe Harold's Pilgrimage*
gives us the poet's history (Arnold's "real Lord Byron") in the form of
the protagonist's own immediate record of his life; and, further, that
this kind of poetic method ("dramatic") places special demands upon
the way we must read the poem. I have also tried to make some prelimi-
nary suggestions about what sort of person the narrating poet is at different points in the poem, and how his story tends to develop from the

[27] *Rutherford*, p. 33.
[28] *P* 2: 5.

earlier to the later cantos. On the basis of these initial observations, I must dissent from Rutherford's statement that Cantos I–II do not arrange themselves into a "coherent artistic whole." This fairly widespread opinion exerts a strong claim to validity in Rutherford's presentation because (*a*) a good deal of the verse in the early cantos in either mediocre or worse, and (*b*) Rutherford's other point—that the two cantos do not "develop a consistent attitude toward life"—is clearly an accurate description of the specifically ethical development of the cantos. The narrator's sensibility is dislocated, and this condition only becomes more aggravated as the cantos proceed. Yet *Hamlet* is the story of a similar type of mind, nor do the eighteenth and nineteenth centuries show any lack of novels and poems which take such men for their heroes; the literature of our own day abounds in "alienated" personalities. The fact that the poet in the poem does not attain a consistent attitude toward life has nothing whatever to do with the question of the aesthetic "consistency" of these early cantos. The logical conclusion of this view is that which Ernest J. Lovell, Jr. arrived at some time ago: that Byron's poetry is, as a whole, hopelessly crippled by its inability to offer us a "consistent attitude toward life" like Wordsworth's.[29] A critical argument, like this, from moral precept is always hazardous, for it may turn out that the poetry in question espouses a different ethical position altogether. Such is the present case, for Byron, like his beloved Montaigne, deliberately sought to avoid the kind of ethical consistency that Wordsworth sought. In the end, his poetry embraces alienation, skepticism, constant change, as it were by necessity, and attempts to show how man achieves a Godlike sovereignty (or a childlike innocence) even in a "waste and icy clime" (*Don Juan* VII, 2).

Byron did not think ideology of paramount importance for such an achievement. Certain positive concepts remain crucial for him (e.g., love, personal integrity, strength of will), but he almost never treats these programmatically. Works like *Sardanapalus* and *The Island* show a marked commitment to the idea of an earthly paradise, but even in them ideology is sidestepped for dramatic and symbolic presentation. Goethe was right: Byron could not write philosophic poetry, and he rarely tried (his satires, for example, are not interesting because they are arguments but because they are passionate self-dramatizations). We can abstract certain predominant Byronic ideas and themes from his works, but—as readers have always discovered—we must not

[29] Ernest J. Lovell, *Byron: The Record of a Quest* (Austin, Texas, 1949), p. 41, for example.

expect that they will submit to the convenience of programmatic definition. Byron's "coherence," as a whole, becomes realized in the definition of his various, metahistorical character; the coherence of his individual works, on the other hand, depends upon *poiesis*, the symbolic
organization of immediate and dramatic materials. A work like *Childe
Harold's Pilgrimage* illustrates both of these facts about Byron's poetry,
for on the one hand it contains the story (or at least *a* story) of his metahistory, and on the other it presents that metahistory in a dramatic and
symbolic form. Byron-the-narrator tells his own story and in the process
not only discovers what his life means, but finds that its meaning prolif-
erates and develops as the story continues. The poem is a journal that
eventuates in an autobiography, for the overall coherence that the latter
form pretends to and that the former (at least by intention) does not,
becomes realized in the total work within the narrator's own act of self-
discovery. *Our* experience of the work involves the perception of this
self-dramatization and self-discovery in the narrating poet, whose purpose in writing is "to create" himself—"and in creating live/A being
more intense."

The Twofold Life:

HAROLD AND HIS POET

A well-known children's rhyme by Robert Louis Stevenson begins with two statements of fact that can pretty well sum up today's prevailing critical view of the relationship between the poet Byron and his fictive hero Childe Harold.

> I have a little shadow that goes in an out with me,
> And what can be the use of him is more than I can see.

Whether or not Byron saw an artistic reason for Harold's presence, contemporary critics do not, and most would say that Byron did not either.[1] A common argument holds that Harold is in reality the poet Byron prowling about his own poem under an assumed name,[2] and succeeding only in adding further confusion to an already shapeless piece of work. Byron's declarations that he intended no identification between himself and Childe Harold generally fall on deaf ears today. There are many good reasons why this should be so, and Jeffrey's early discussion of the poem isolates the most important ones:

> In Lord Byron, however, the interest of the story, where there happens to be one, which is not always the case, is uniformly postponed to that of the character itself [i.e. Childe Harold]—into which he enters so deeply, and with so extraordinary a fondness, that he generally continues to speak in its language, after it has been dismissed from the stage; and to inculcate on his own au-

---

[1] *Marshall*, pp. 36–38. *Rutherford*, p. 33. Robert Escarpit, however, thinks that Harold sometimes functions as "un élément de stabilisation esthétique": *Lord Byron: un tempérament littéraire* (Paris, 1957), 2: 77. His related discussion has some parallels with my own here.

[2] See, for example, *Calvert*, p. 112.

thority, the same sentiments which had been previously recommended by its example.[3]

Jeffrey's reaction is a paradigm for all the major critical statements of his own day, including those of Scott, Ellis, and Wilson.[4] Each of these men argued that Byron, in propria persona, took upon himself in the course of his poem certain of the traits and attitudes of his titular hero Childe Harold. The presupposition in such a view—as Jeffrey's statement indicates—is that a clear distinction exists between the narrating poet and the pilgrim Harold. Among contemporary critics Andrew Rutherford takes the minority view by agreeing with the early commentators on this point:

> There are . . . two central characters instead of one, and they are for the most part clearly differentiated. . . .[5]

At the same time, however, Rutherford argues that this "clear" distinction counts for little since it serves no useful purpose in the poem.

An examination of the text uncovers some interesting facts about the purely formal separation of narrator from titular hero. In most cases it is possible to distinguish them quite clearly at any particular time. The following outlines represent an attempt to deal with this neglected but basic rhetorical problem. No outline of Canto IV is required, of course, since Harold does not speak at all in that canto (though he does appear in it, and I believe still performs an important role in the psychological drama).

Canto I:

SPEAKER	STANZAS
Poet	1–13
Harold	Lyric: "Adieu, adieu"
Poet	14
Harold	15–26
Poet	27–84
Harold	Lyric: "To Inez"
Poet	85–93

[3] Francis Jeffrey, Review of Lord Byron, *Childe Harold's Pilgrimage, Canto III* and *The Prisoner of Chillon and Other Poems* (London, 1816), *Edinburgh Review* 27 (December, 1816): 281. Jeffrey makes the same point in his earlier review of Cantos I–II: *Edinburgh Review* 19 (June, 1812): 466–67.
[4] Walter Scott, *Quarterly Review* 26 (October, 1816): 174; George Ellis, *Quarterly Review* 7 (March, 1812): 197–98; John Wilson, *Edinburgh Review* 30 (June, 1818): 94.
[5] *Rutherford*, p. 28.

Canto II:

	Poet	1–30, ll., 1–4
	Harold	30, ll., 5–9
	Poet	31–72
		(Suliote Song)
	Poet	73–98
Canto III:		
	Poet	1–46
	Harold	47–51
	Poet	52–55
	Harold	Lyric: "The Castled Crag of Drachenfels"
	Poet	56–118

I have collected the evidence for this outline in an appendix. For now it is important to note that a blurring of the distinction between the narrator and the Childe occurs twice in the poem: first, in stanzas 14–26 of Canto I, and second, in stanzas 47–55 of Canto III. In each case Byron makes it very clear that some distinction is to be drawn, but he does not strike an unmistakably sharp line for the reader. I am not certain whether or not this indeterminateness is a flaw in these passages. An important aspect of the poem depends upon our ability to see both the similarities and differences between the narrator and Harold, and, especially, what happens to each of them during the course of the pilgrimage. Consequently, Byron must make it apparent that their psychological relationship is quite intimate, and the blurring of their individual thoughts on these two occasions (which, as we shall see, are signal moments in the poem) does serve this purpose. Nevertheless, one has the impression that the technical management is crude. Byron uses the Childe as an object-self in a confessional poem that involves, first, a journey of self-discovery, and second, a therapeutic movement toward a better self than the one he was at the outset.[6] But Byron did not have any models to guide him in techniques for handling ego-projections in a first-person confessional form. Had he written the poem one hundred years later he might have managed the problem much more smoothly.

In any case, given the basic rhetorical distinction, we must look more

[6] A recent study, published after this chapter was written, argues much the same point. See Kenneth A. Bruffee, "The Synthetic Hero and the Narrative Structure of *Childe Harold* III," *SEL* 6 (Autumn, 1966): 669–78. Mr. Bruffee and I differ, however, on the type of narration in the canto. He calls it "reflective" because he thinks Byron "is writing from a retreat in the Alps" (673). Both external and internal evidence on this point are clear, however. Written sequentially, the poem is "immediate" not "reflective."

closely at the moral and psychological characteristics of Harold and his poet. Most critics would probably agree that their personalities are at least vaguely distinguished at least some of the time. But I think we ought to press the poem further to find if Byron's method justifies in any way his statement to Dallas that he "would not be such a fellow as I have made my hero for all the world."[7] A canceled MS passage from the Preface to Cantos I–II casts some doubt upon Byron's protest to Dallas.

> My readers will observe that where the author speaks in his own person he assumes a very different tone from that of [Childe Harold], at least till death had deprived him of his nearest connections.[8]

Moreover, Harold's original name "Childe Burun" has justifiably been called to witness against Byron's public statements that he and his hero had nothing in common.[9] Despite the purely rhetorical distinction between Harold and poet outlined above, the poem develops a number of similarities between the two men which no one can fail to notice. Thus, although the poet is not afflicted with Harold's moody loneliness at the beginning of the poem, in the course of the pilgrimage he too falls prey to such feelings—for example, at the end of Canto I, again just before the tour through Albania, and again at the end of Canto II. Furthermore, whenever the poet Byron describes his own state of mind his words will likely as not recall some aspects of Harold's character, or some sentiments which Harold expressed in his own person. In II, 97, for example, the narrating poet's mood and opinions distinctly echo Harold's circumstances before the pilgrimage was undertaken.

> Then must I plunge again into the crowd,
> And follow all that Peace disdains to seek?
> Where Revel calls, and Laughter, vainly loud,
> False to the heart, distorts the hollow cheek,
> To leave the flagging spirit doubly weak;
> Still o'er the features, which perforce they cheer,
> To feign the pleasure or conceal the pique:
> Smiles form the channel of a future tear,
> And raise the writhing lip with ill-dissembled sneer.

Harold's pilgrimage began as a flight from a similar social milieu, and his disgust of life at the beginning of the poem corresponds to the narra-

[7] *LJ* 2: 66.
[8] *P* 2: 4.
[9] *P* 2: 3–4, 5, 323.

tor's melancholy here. At the outset the poet showed himself completely aware of the vacuity of such society, but whereas earlier he was able to mock and burlesque its hypocrisies and vanity, here his equilibrium is shaken, and we find him in a psychological condition similar to Harold's at the beginning of the poem.

The fact is that the narrating poet in Cantos I–II undergoes a gradual change of attitude under the pressure of external events. His ironies become increasingly bitter and sardonic, his disillusionment grows, he becomes more and more introspective and brooding. By the end of the first pilgrimage the poet has appropriated Harold's gloomy malaise to himself. The series of personal losses, lamented in some of the most moving passages of the early cantos, climaxes the poet's education in woe. They establish the appropriateness of his despondency at the end of Cantos I–II. In addition, because these griefs are his especial burden, they emphasize how conclusively he has fixed himself at the center of his poem. The perception of this process naturally inclines one to think that Harold never had a real significance in the poem at all; that because Byron's true subject was himself, he ought not to have let Harold distract us.

I do not think that Harold ever seriously obscures the subjective character of *Childe Harold's Pilgrimage*. More important, the definition of his anxiety at the beginning introduces into the poem right away a sensibility against which we can measure the changes that take place in the narrator, and a moral context in which that sensibility has significance. "Worse than Adversity the Childe befell" (I, 4) because of his disillusionment with his own life and the lives of those around him, and as the pilgrimage strengthens him in his despondency, it gradually draws the poet into a similar, in some ways even more extreme, state of mind. Harold's position in the poem throws the narrator's development into greater relief. As Jeffrey said, "Lord Byron . . . continues . . . to inculcate, on his own authority, the same sentiments which had been previously recommended by [Harold's] example."

From the start of the poem the personalities of Harold and the narrator show several other coincidences and similarities. These serve to suggest the potential Harold in the narrating poet, so to speak, and they foreshadow the latter's subsequent career. We have already discussed at some length the ambiguous elements in the opening thirteen stanzas—the alterations between seriousness and mockery in the poet's tone of voice. In addition, the irresponsible quality of the poet's humor here is an analogue of Harold's restless flight from himself and all moral com-

mitment.[10] If we compare the kind of satire practiced by both men in
Canto I this similarity will be further underlined. I have argued in an
earlier chapter that the poet's reckless and uninhibited exposure of
Spain's corruptions was not satire at all, but the dramatic presentation
of a particular subjective condition and set of attitudes. Similarly, Harold's attack upon Portugal (15–26) is without restraint or direction, and
it tells us more about Harold and his melancholy state of mind than it
does about Portugal or moral imperatives. His response to the natural
beauty surrounding Cintra leads him to rail at the decadence of the
Portuguese:

> Oh, Christ! it is a goodly sight to see
> What Heaven hath done for this delicious land!
> What fruits of fragrance blush on every tree!
> What goodly prospects o'er the hills expand!
> But man would mar them with an impious hand: (15)

> Poor, paltry slaves! yet born midst noblest scenes—
> Why, Nature, waste thy wonders on such men?   (18)

On the other hand, the convent of Nossa Señora de Peña and the peni-
tential practices of Honorius embody a kind of austerity which seems
as contemptuous of the world as does Harold's attitude. Byron's pilgrim ridicules the monastic rule nonetheless.

> Deep in yon cave Honorius long did dwell,
> In hope to merit Heaven by making earth a Hell.   (20)

The contradictions go further yet. If Harold rejects asceticism as degen-
erate, all man's attempts to adorn his life and works with splendor also
seem grotesquely unreasonable. Thus he comments upon the ruin of
Quinta da Monserrate:

> But now, as if a thing unblest by Man,
> Thy fairy dwelling is as lone as Thou!
> Here giant weeds a passage scarce allow
> To Halls deserted, portals gaping wide:
> Fresh lesson to the thinking bosom, how
> Vain are the pleasaunces on earth supplied,
> Swept into wrecks anon by Time's ungentle tide!   (23)

The remainder of his commentary on Portugal is devoted to an attack

---

[10] Canto I, stanzas 27–28.

upon the Convention of Cintra made (ostensibly) from the point of
view of a patriotic Englishman.

> How will Posterity the deed proclaim!
> Will not our own and fellow-nations sneer,
> To view these champions cheated of their fame,
> By foes in fight o'erthrown, yet victors here,
> Where Scorn her finger points through many a coming year?
>
> (26)

But Harold really has as little use for the war and the whole British part
in it as he does for the Convention. Thus, he mocks at British indignation over Cintra:

> Behold the hall where chiefs were late convened!
> Oh! dome displeasing unto British eye!   (24)

and at the government bureaucracy whose job it is to administer England's affairs in Portugal:

> And ever since that martial Synod met,
> Britannia sickens, Cintra! at thy name;
> And folks in office at the mention fret. . . .   (26)

But if the Convention was a military and political blunder, the whole
war is suspect on moral grounds as are any specific military victories—
and not only in respect of Napoleon's unjust invasion.

> Convention is the dwarfish demon styled
> That foiled the knights in Marialva's dome:
> Of brains (if brains they had) he them beguiled,
> And turned a nation's shallow joy to gloom.   (25)

The "joy" that swells in the patriot's heart at his country's conquests in
war is a "shallow" and ignoble emotion in the first place. As we have
seen in our discussion of affairs in Spain, this is an attitude with which
the poet is ready to sympathize. But he can sing of arms and men with
equal sympathy under proper circumstances, whereas Harold is completely skeptical of all military affairs, as the narrator tells us in II, 40.

Thus, Harold's misanthropic commentary on Portugal is a series of
apparently gratuitous shifts of satiric point of view. The fact is that he
stands on no code of principles, but puts forward his own contradictory
self as his only moral point of view and standard of evaluation. If his
disquisition takes up a number of specific ideas, these are kept in a re-

lation to one another only because of the personality of the speaker. This is only to say, however, that ideas are a secondary consideration in "satire" of this sort; primarily the poetry dramatizes the state of mind and passionate attitudes of a specific figure. But Harold's self-dramatizing "satire" is so like the poet's own style and method that if the stanzas had been attributed to him and not to Harold I do not believe that any reader would have felt an aesthetic dissonance in the poem. To say this, however, seems tantamount to saying that Harold and the poet are only nominally distinguished. In many respects this is perfectly true, though as we shall see in a moment the two men differ fundamentally in one crucial characteristic. But even if this difference did not exist, to assert a moral, or psychic, equivalence between Harold and narrator does not necessarily imply that Harold is a useless and irrelevant figure in the poem. In a work that is so obviously a function of the narrating poet, Harold fills the important role of "alter" or "object self."

Byron had said that he would not have been such a man as his gloomy and "unamiable" hero, and, knowing as we do his inclinations to a public career as well as his delight in stimulating social intercourse, we can readily agree with Peter Thorslev that Byron and his hero were, in this respect at least, very different.[11] The poet's irony and humor in Cantos I–II define this difference very well, as we have already seen. But Byron —the man and the poet—had another side to himself that scarcely needs documentation: it has become an unchallenged truism in Byron scholarship that this man was, in propria persona, divided against himself, and that this division is reflected clearly (if too simplistically) in his pessimism, on the one hand, and his mocking humor on the other. Recently John Wain has sharpened our perception of just how deep this division actually went.[12] He argues that the "Romantic" and the "Satiric" aspects of Byron's personality do not really get at the heart of the man's radical doubleness—that these two aspects of his mind are really no more than the obverse and reverse of the same insecure personality. At the beginning of *Childe Harold's Pilgrimage* the poet pushes the anxiety-ridden Harold on stage before us, and although he treats his hero with sympathy because Harold's insecurity springs from his corrupt social milieu, his mockery of the Childe is his implicit declaration of his own (relative) psychological self-assurance. But as the pilgrimage progresses it becomes increasingly evident that the two men are somehow very like each other, despite the poet's periodic smirks at Harold's emotional

11 Peter Thorslev, *The Byronic Hero* (Minneapolis, 1962), p. 131.
12 John Wain, "The Search for Identity," in *Essays*, pp. 157–70.

instability. His insouciant mockery grows more bitter until his whole person gradually assumes the gloomy and brooding qualities which he had earlier attributed to Harold alone.

If, when Byron returned to England, he had not been immediately "shocked with [the] death(s)"[13] which are recorded in his poem, Cantos I–II would probably not have become the somber work that it now is. In its original form the *Childe Harold's Pilgrimage* of 1812 was a poem composed of about equal parts of ironic raillery and sarcasm and of romantic melancholy—with a slight inclination to the latter. It was not a very good poem precisely because of the refusal to adopt a definitive poetic style, or, more accurately, to indicate clearly in the poem itself how these two "satiric" and "romantic" styles mirrored each other. Even in the original poem the reader cannot fail to sense a relationship between them. But the poem does not help to clarify this relationship, nor does it provide the reader with a coherent artistic means of gauging just how alike the poet and Harold are, or what significance this likeness might imply. In short, the two are artistically unrelated at the conclusion of the original poem.

When Byron made his final additions and deletions, however, he transformed what had been an aesthetically inconsistent poem into one that was, for all its imperfections, well organized and artistically consonant—the dramatic presentation of the poet's "Consciousness awaking to her woes." The received form of the poem exposes, rather than obscures, the psychological equivalence between Harold and the poet. Byron does not gain an uncomplicated personal "identity" thereby—a quality that Mr. Wain apparently thinks every artist should have—but he does give his poem a stylistic identity: the underlying similarity between the poet's mocking and melancholic attitudes (largely associated with his subject and object selves, respectively) is forcefully presented. At bottom, then, *Childe Harold's Pilgrimage I–II* does not describe a search for a balanced identity at all, but a search for self-knowledge. This is its substantive issue. From an aesthetic point of view the early cantos narrate the poet's search for a style in which the ambiguities and uncertainties of his personality can be explicitly stated and faced. The poet Byron would not be like Harold, but after his pilgrimage he finds that he can do no other. At the end of Canto II he *is* "The wandering outlaw of his own dark mind" (III, 3), and he does not blink the confession of his anxiety-ridden condition. At the begin-

---

[13] *LJ* 2: 52. The data on the MSS revisions are given in the following chapter along with a fuller analysis of the early cantos.

ning of Canto III he refers to the earlier cantos and his self-characterization therein.

> Yet must I think less wildly:—I *have* thought
> Too long and darkly, till my brain became,
> In its own eddy boiling and o'erwrought,
> A whirling gulf of phantasy and flame:
> And thus, untaught in youth my heart to tame,
> My springs of life were poisoned. 'Tis too late!
> Yet am I changed; though still enough the same
> In strength to bear what Time can not abate,
> And feed on bitter fruits without accusing Fate.   (7)

The stanza is an important one for a number of reasons, one of which is that it helps to establish the relationship between the earlier and the later cantos: having recorded in I–II the origins and progress of his psychological disorder, he now will narrate (III, 2–3) the further stages of his spiritual adventure.

In Cantos I–II, then, Harold performs a crucial role. He is an objective correlative of the poet's own deep uncertainty of mind—even at the earliest moments of the poem. But at the outset of the pilgrimage the dramatic figure of the poet shows no immediate consciousness of his own cynical imbalance, although he is perfectly aware of a similar condition in his object self Harold. By consciously objectifying his own state of desperation in Harold's, he affords himself a means of confessing what he previously could not face about himself, and in the sequence of Cantos I–II presents his access to self-consciousness in a significant form —in a "story" that gives a meaningful "plot" to the detailed facts of his poetic life. From a purely formal point of view Harold is the norm of the poet's development in Cantos I–II. He represents what the poet has it in him to become, but "would not be . . . for all the world." His very existence in so personal a poem as *Childe Harold's Pilgrimage* is an important sign of the narrating poet's inner disquietude. The poet creates him as his alter ego in order that he may be able to objectify certain aspects of himself without immediate self-incrimination. The poet's awareness of his psychic disease expresses itself in the creation of Childe Harold, while the projection of Harold away from himself testifies to his present inability to acknowledge and deal with his own anxieties.

Nevertheless, this truth about the poem's dramatic nature should not be used to hide the clumsiness of Byron's whole approach. It is important to be clear about Harold's function in the poem, but it is equally important to see the awkwardness of the alter-ego device as Byron used it. Still, as so often in Byron, one of his most patent technical flaws turns out to be at the same time a distinct poetic asset. The very obviousness with which he uses the alter ego to protect himself from public judgment intensifies the subjective quality of the poem and heightens our sense of Byron's personal presence in his own work. By doing so, it makes the poem more effective dramatically, more powerful emotionally, even though—paradoxically—this intensifying of the poem's force ultimately depends upon an (apparent) artistic weakness. Byron, of course, could not have planned this effect. It is a very real one nonetheless, as the history of Byron criticism proves: one of the chief delights in reading Byron's poetry has always involved the discovery of the hiding places of his soul, all the half-concealed and half-revealed corners out of which Byron cannot stop peeking. Thus, Byron's very clumsiness here becomes a kind of honesty, and at least partly an artistic virtue. Nor is this the only instance of his gaining a poetic advantage through the conscious or unconscious exploitation of apparent technical flaws. *Don Juan* is full of such effects. Indeed, it seems to be a law in Byron's poetry that anything goes so long as it serves to advance our sense of Byron's immediate and personal presence.

Be that as it may, in Cantos III and IV Harold continues to function as touchstone for the poet's own development and alter to the poet's ego. As I have already noted, however, the direction of the poem changes at the beginning of Canto III from an educational pilgrimage to a therapeutic one. In the earlier cantos, the instability and melancholy of Harold and the poet are the result of their perception of moral ambiguities—of activity and futility, achievement and vanity, pleasure and pain, good and evil, life and death. Since these and similar moral contradictions are inconceivable except in pairs, the self-conscious artist is always aware of a basic conflict in all life, a threatening duality that is the image of his own mind. *Childe Harold's Pilgrimage* does not seek to eliminate or negate this duality but, in a way similar to Schlegel's when he formulated his concept of Romantic Irony, to establish his sense of division as a value rather than a liability. Harold objectifies the disastrous results that such a perception can lead to, and the narrating poet shows that he too is subject to these dangers. The early cantos adumbrate the liabilities of ironic, or double, perception in their presentation of Harold's developing spiritual inertia. "The blight of life—the demon Thought" produces a terrible

> weariness which springs
> From all I meet, or hear, or see:
> To me no pleasure Beauty brings;
> Thine eyes have scarce a charm for me.   ("To Inez," st. 4)

At the beginning of Canto II, for example, Harold's moral sluggishness grows to such an extent that he can no longer be moved by the mournful spectacle of "all that men regret" (16). He even has to be urged along his journey by the narrating poet (at this point still able to muster an ironic smile). His earlier active responses—invective and angry lamentation—are stilled ("But Harold felt not as in other times/And left without a sigh the land of war and crimes"), and he slumps into a carelessness that abrogates the basic moral imperatives of indignation at human evil and concern for human suffering. But the narrating poet only suggests the moral atrophy taking place in Harold. It is not until Canto III that this process is finally exposed in its completed form, when Harold's emotional life becomes nearly completely attenuated by the premature loss of his *cor irrequietum*. At the end of Canto II the narrator also inclines to the despair of absolute indifference, a feeling that has grown steadily upon him as "Grief with grief" (II, 96) continues to accumulate.

> O'er Hearts divided and o'er Hopes destroyed
> Roll on, vain days! full reckless may ye flow,
> Since Time hath reft whate'er my soul enjoyed. . . .   (II, 98)[14]

This Harold-like weariness and inanition which overcome the poet at the end of Cantos I–II is one of the opening motifs of Canto III. Stanzas 1–7 recapitulate the history of the poet, while stanzas 8–16 are given to a description and analysis of Harold's immediate past. The similarities and differences in the two passages establish the crucial distinction between Harold and the poet which will govern the events in the last two cantos. The poet is at once depressed by the struggles of the past and fearful of his prospects for the future (3–4). His sense of hopelessness is related specifically to the "whirling gulf of phantasy and flame" (7) in his mind, a condition which earlier drove him in pursuit of "the weary dream/Of selfish grief or gladness" (4), but which only resulted in a feeling of emotional sterility and spiritual emptiness (3). At the same time, he welcomes the prospect of new activity (2) and announces the therapeutic end of his renewed pilgrimage, to create a

---

[14] I depart from the usual punctuation of the text here by removing the colon after "destroyed."

"being more intense" and then become himself the energetic creature of his imaginative aspirations (6). This exuberant hope alternates with his feelings of uncertainty and trepidation, however, so that the first seven stanzas close on a note of cautious and inconclusive anticipation.

> 'Tis too late!
> Yet am I changed; though still enough the same
> In strength to bear what Time cannot abate,
> And feed on bitter fruits without accusing Fate.   (7)

The problem is that only the thinnest line separates the vitality of the poet's projected "being more intense" from the "boiling and o'er-wrought" confusion of a dark and wandering mind. The latter results only in the sterility and death of "crushed feelings" (6) while the former will, ideally, renew, nourish, and sustain him. A fresh pilgrimage is thus begun under equivocal signs, for although it will bring new adventure, new feelings and sensations, these experiences and emotions can be either a blessing or simply another curse.

The poet undertakes the new journey in a spirit of wary determination. But when we meet "Long absent Harold" (8) again, we find him wholly indifferent to the prospects of renewed pilgrimage ("He of the breast which fain no more would feel"). He leaves because "in Man's dwellings" he has become "Restless and worn, and stern and wearisome"; but—unlike the poet—his longing for the freedom of "the boundless air" (15) is not borne along by the "airy images, and shapes ... unimpaired" (5) which characterize the creative thrust of the poet's mind. "Could he have kept his spirit to that flight" (14) of his imagination "He had been happy." As it is, his actions are all a function of a mind "In its own eddy boiling and o'erwrought":

> Then came his fit again, which to o'ercome,
> As eagerly the barred-up bird will beat
> His breast and beak against his wiry dome
> Till the blood tinge his plumage—so the heat
> Of his impeded Soul would through his bosom eat.   (15)

Thus Harold plunges ahead once again. His hopelessness is a function of his distraught mind, and the poet's comparison of him with those mariners who "would madly meet their doom/With draughts intemperate on the sinking deck" (16) establishes the integrity of the poet's consciousness, which can so analyze and judge his object self Harold.

We approach now the question of the root meaning of the last two cantos, the nature of their restorative influence. I must go into this matter briefly here since it will help to define the distinction in these opening stanzas of Canto III between the "impeded Soul" of Harold, which the poet criticizes through his imagery, and the "chain'd and tortured—cabin'd, cribb'd, confined" (IV, 127) thought of the poet on whose ceaseless energy such a high value is placed—most memorably in the later portions of Canto IV. In a sense they are the same thing since both represent actual states of being of the passionate imagination. Their correlation is further emphasized insofar as Byron the poet is seen to fulfill them both in his own experience. But they are not both realized in the person of Harold, and this fact points to the qualitative difference between them. Harold's "fever at the core" (III, 42), which has its analogue in the life of the narrating poet as well, is like Napoleon's and Rousseau's: it is predominantly ruinous and self-lacerating, and productive only of a deteriorating emotional fluctuation between chaotic frenzy and languid weariness. This is precisely what Byron wants to eliminate from his poetic life, and he does it not by trying to circumscribe or subdue his passionate energies, but by giving them complete freedom to seek their own limit.

> I know not why—but standing thus by thee
> It seems as if I had thine inmate known,
> Thou Tomb! and other days come back on me
> With recollected music, though the tone
> Is changed and solemn, like the cloudy groan
> Of dying thunder on the distant wind;
> Yet could I seat me by this ivied stone
> Till I had bodied forth the heated mind
> Forms from the floating wreck which Ruin leaves behind:
>
> And from the planks, far shattered o'er the rocks
> Built me a little bark of hope, once more
> To battle with the Ocean and the shocks
> Of the loud breakers, and the ceaseless roar
> Which rushes on the solitary shore
> Where all lies foundered that was ever dear:
> But could I gather from the wave-worn store
> Enough for my rude boat, where should I steer?
> There woos no home, nor hope, nor life, save what is here.
>
> Then let the Winds howl on! their harmony
> Shall henceforth be my music, and the Night
> The sound shall temper with the owlets' cry,

As I now hear them, in the fading light
Dim o'er the bird of darkness' native site,
Answering each other on the Palatine,
With their large eyes, all glistening gray and bright,
And sailing pinions.—Upon such a shrine
What are our petty griefs?—let me not number mine. (IV, 104–6)

Here, over the tomb of Cecilia Metella, Byron announces the death of
the old man and the birth of the new, the bill of divorcement from his
earlier domestic situation, the determination to sunder himself permanently from everything which makes him doubt or fear the vital
urgency that drives him on. He has been burning his bridges to the
society that he both loves and hates since the beginning of the poem,
but one by one. Not until now does he begin to realize that all reason
for regret, timidity, and reluctance is irrevocably gone: "There woos
no home, nor hope, nor life, save what is here." So in stanza 106 he
determines to measure his song to the music of the howling sea winds
and the indurated melancholy of the owls that cry to each other across
the desolate Palatine. Both wind and bird raise melodies of isolation,
but the poet finds in their music not that recurrent insecurity, but a
sense of release from the continuous anxiety to which he is prone. The
"harmony" that he perceives in the wild roaring of the wind is the
exemplum for the passionate concord within himself, while the balanc-
ing of the stanza's discordant symbols—the crying of the solitary owls,
the howling of the unchecked winds—is the sign of the poet's own
fearful emotional symmetry. Both wind and bird are alone and self-
sufficient; as such, they are paradigms of Byron's Lucretian view of
Nature.[15] For Byron, Nature is sovereign and wholly autonomous,
so much so that man finds her fearful and threatening. In the end, as
Spenser saw in his vision of Mutability, she demonstrates herself absolutely superior to human culture—those mere works and days of transient humanity, whose years wait upon death and whose span upon

[15] Allusions to and quotations from *De rerum natura* are scattered throughout Byron's works. "If Lucretius had not been spoiled by the Epicurean system, we should
have had a far superior poem than any now in existence. As mere poetry it is the first
of Latin poems" (*LJ* 5: 554–55). Byron did not think that Lucretius' natural determi-
nism was wrong in itself but that it did not allow for the immortality of the spirit, of
which "it appears to me that there can be little doubt, if we attend for a moment to the
action of the Mind. It is in perpetual activity. I used to doubt of it, but reflection has
taught me better" (*LJ* 5: 456–57). For his earlier absolute materialism see *LJ* 2: 18–21.
Significantly enough, as we shall see in later chapters, it was his materialism which led
him to affirm the reality of the spirit, for to Byron the norm of eternity was to be found
in the natural order: "Matter is eternal, always changing, but reproduced, and, as far
as we can comprehend Eternity, eternal. And why not Mind?" (*LJ* 5: 458).

Armageddon. If Nature and her children seem to endure independently of all man's schemes to control his milieu, it is because they are their own reason for being, and derive their character from their existence, not from human reason or understanding. They *are*, therefore they are *what* they are. In stanza 106 Byron strikes out for the same kind of absolute integrity that he finds in Nature's free wind and solitary bird, and he implies that the passions, the aspirations, all the activities of life are exhilarating and valuable just because they are his. Out of what he is Byron resolves to establish the nature of his unique Person. By self-definition as an individual, analogous to Nature in independence and autonomy, he begins to achieve a spiritual freedom that sets him apart from all culture, and from everything he "hates in this degraded form" (III, 74) as well.

Thus the summary of Harold's career at the beginning of Canto III has a twofold purpose. On the one hand, it stresses the similarity between Harold's fictive history and the actual history of the poet himself, as nearly every commentator from the time of the poem's publication has been aware. Both are subject to the same melancholy, dissatisfaction, and restiveness in the society of England's soulless "crowd."

> But soon he knew himself the most unfit
> Of men to herd with Man, with whom he held
> Little in common; untaught to submit
> His thoughts to others, though his soul was quelled
> In youth by his own thoughts; still uncompelled,
> He would not yield dominion of his mind
> To spirits against whom his own rebelled,
> Proud though in desolation—which could find
> A life within itself, to breathe without mankind.   (12)

There is nothing in this portrait to distinguish Harold from his creator. "His soul was quelled in youth by his own thoughts" echoes stanza 7 just as the final line recalls stanza 5.[16]

Other details in the lines correspond to observations about himself

---

[16] See "The Dream," lines 1–26 where the ideas discussed in the first sixteen stanzas of Canto III are repeated. The comparison is interesting because Byron's distinction between Harold and himself, set out in the separate treatment of his hero's past, is paralleled by Byron's respective dream and waking lives. The lyric states precisely the relationship between the two that I am trying to describe.

> Our life is twofold! Sleep hath its own world . . .
> And dreams in their development have breath . . .
> They leave a weight upon our waking thoughts,
> They take a weight from off our waking toils,
> They do divide our being. . . .

that Byron scatters throughout the poem (cf. III, 113, for example): both feel more at home in the solitudes of Nature than "in Man's dwellings" (15), both are self-exiles from their homeland, both are connoisseurs of despair. But Byron lays out in declarative terms for Harold what in the earlier stanzas of Canto III he only suggests about himself through the pervading tone of certain passages. The difference is important, for Harold as a result becomes sharply defined and even delimited as a character, whereas Byron's moral life is left a congeries of contradictory impulses and unfulfilled potentials. Harold has no hope at all left, but Byron is not so simplistic or definitive about himself: his tone in stanzas 3–7 is often "hopeless," but at other times it is energetically resigned (7) or even spontaneously exultant (6). The difference arises from the fact that Byron as a character is still in the condition of becoming, whereas Harold is now fixed and determinate. There is a sharp dissimilarity, for example, between one for whom "all was over on this side the tomb" and one who departs not into a void but into unknown (though *perhaps* fruitless) regions and experiences (1–2). Byron's very indeterminateness gives him a depth and complexity that Harold does not have; it permits him to display with great vigor a variety of passing moods and attitudes, whereas for Harold such contrarieties are impossible. In him nothing is passing or transient, all has come to be. "Years steal Fire from the mind as vigour from the limb" (8), the poet observes at the beginning of his summary of Harold's past, and in the case of his hero the recreative "spark immortal" (14) has been finally extinguished. There remains only that furious and burning fever which destroyed Napoleon and consumed the "self-torturing sophist, wild Rousseau" (III, 77).

The crux upon which Byron balances the possibility of spiritual regeneration is set out in stanza 14. The lines repeat the theme touched earlier in stanzas 5–6, where images of liberation and transcendence are specifically associated with the restorative imagination operating in solitude.

> Like the Chaldean, he could watch the stars,
> Till he had peopled them with beings bright
> As their own beams; and earth, and earth-born jars,
> And human frailties, were forgotten quite:
> Could he have kept his spirit to that flight
> He had been happy; but this clay will sink
> Its spark immortal, envying it the light
> To which it mounts, as if to break the link
> That keeps us from yon heaven which woos us to its brink.

Like the poet, Harold had cultivated his imaginative faculties, and habitually bodied forth from his own mind "beings" as "bright" as the transcendent world suggested to him by the stars. "Who can contemplate Fame through clouds unfold/The star which rises o'er her steep, nor climb?" the poet rhetorically asks (st. 11), once again correlating the poetic Temple of Fame (situated on a mountain which must be climbed) with "The star" that represents the achievement of all human desires for completion. In stanzas 3–7 Byron himself determines to continue upon such a poetic quest in the poem actually under composition, and although the thought that it may be but "a dreary strain" dampens the intensity of his enthusiasm in stanza 4, still it does not deter him from pursuing his poem in a (perhaps blind) effort to give and gain the exalted living image of a "being more intense." "Like the Chaldean," Harold would have been happy could he have kept his spirit bent upon such a quest; as it is, "this clay will sink its spark immortal, envying it the light to which it mounts." In the impersonal grammatical construction of this final clause, Byron asserts on the one hand the reason for Harold's unhappiness (the refusal of the recreative imaginative pilgrimage), and *suggests* on the other that such an eventuality is the lot of all men. A foreboding enters the poetry as a result, for we are led to doubt the ultimate success of the poet's own mission. Unlike Harold, the poet has not yet despaired of the search for imaginative regeneration, but these lines show clearly his own gnawing sense of doubt and dread. His personal resolution will eventually be strengthened by the pristine heroic examples of Marceau ("he had kept the whiteness of his soul," 57), Morat and Marathon ("true Glory's stainless victories," 64) and Julia Alpinula (who, concluding these examples of successful human fulfillment, is explicitly compared with the most important image in the canto, the Alpine summit: "like yonder Alpine snow,/ Imperishably pure," 67).

The emotional complement of Harold's furious anxiety is the state of spiritual weariness and sensational dearth (16) which the poet had also ascribed to himself in stanzas 1–7. This in Harold eventually stabilizes into an equilibrium of nearly total indifference to the phenomenal world, as the Rhine Valley sequence beautifully illustrates. The Waterloo section had depicted the tragedy wrought by those who, like Napoleon, *prey* upon high adventure (42), and the castles of the robber barons along the Rhine repeat the theme:

> In their baronial feuds and single fields,
> What deeds of prowess unrecorded died!

And Love, which lent a blazon to their shields,
With emblems well devised by amorous pride,
Through all the mail of iron hearts would glide;
But still their flame was fierceness, and drew on
Keen contest and destruction near allied,
And many a tower for some fair mischief won,
Saw the discoloured Rhine beneath its ruin run.   (49)

Such thoughts turn Harold even further in upon himself. If they tend to pacify his recklessness, this is not an unequivocal blessing, for he seeks as a result to separate himself even more completely from experience, to encapsulate his emotions and sensations and feed his thoughts on fantasies of innocence and easement alone. He desires an emotional life not completely inert, only absolutely introverted. His inclinations remind us of the dangers that a life of self-subsistent imaginative solitude hold out for him, and of course for the poet through him. The basic issue of the poem—how to remain *in* the world and yet keep free *of* the world, how to wed imagination to objective reality—is thus forcefully recapitulated.

Under the influence of the Rhine Valley Harold begins to pass into a state of near dormancy. His weary despair assumes a languorous, disinterested, and almost timeless character. Harold's last words in the poem reveal something very like a lingering somnolence, in which Memory seems the only principle of life. "Lulled in the countless chambers of [his] brain,"[17] Harold eulogizes over the symbols of Time's unconcerned and deep dominion in the Rhine Valley. The "tenantless" and moldering castles induce a quiet revery upon their past. The flowing river itself is the image of passing time, but though the waters afford the land a "blessing" of fruitfulness, they make Harold recall "the sharp scythe of conflict" and turn his plaintive contemplation into a wish for oblivion ("Even now what wants thy stream?—that it should Lethe be."). But if Memory produces "blighting dream(s)," it also soothes despondency by extinguishing passions (52), by re-awaking an idealizing and tender affection for "The helpless looks of blooming infancy" (54), and most of all by evoking again recollections of a past "pure" love (apparently for the "sister" mentioned in Canto I) to whom Harold addresses "The Castled Crag of Drachenfels." Only the local "peasant girls," delicately romanticized in his fancy, seem to sustain him now in his insulated state:

[17] Samuel Rogers, "The Pleasures of Memory," in *Poems* (London, 1854), p. 15.

> And peasant girls, with deep blue eyes,
> And hands which offer early flowers,
> Walk smiling o'er this Paradise;
> Above, the frequent feudal towers
> Through green leaves lift their walls of gray;
> And many a rock which steeply lowers,
> And noble arch in proud decay,
> Look o'er this vale of vintage-bowers;
> But one thing want these banks of Rhine,—
> Thy gentle hand to clasp in mine!

The anxieties and shocks of contingency seem to have driven Harold to choose a life in a world of his own idealized imaginings, and to disregard altogether the higher though more trying value embodied in a life of change, transience, and self-developing pilgrimage. He presents a wistful and deeply pathetic image in this, his final dramatic appearance in the poem, for his impulses carry him far into another world of tender and soothing childlike fantasies. He is not spiritually wasted, but his whole being has become so ingrown that his communion is now only with the absent and the dead. He seems closer to the wraiths whom Byron found haunting Parnassus than to anything immediately human. Since Harold represents an important aspect of the poet's own personality, and a valuable one, the poet's deep sympathy for him is evident throughout the Rhine Valley sequence; but so is his clearsighted understanding that Harold has unwontedly circumscribed the scope of the very imaginative faculty he seeks to preserve, and has severely limited thereby his capacities for self-fulfillment and liberation. This is graphically shown in Byron's brief but moving summary of Harold's condition. Nothing now stirs in him but a tenderness felt for "The helpless looks of blooming Infancy":

> and though in solitude
> Small power the nipped affections have to grow,
> In him this glowed when all beside had ceased to glow.[18]   (54)

Thus Harold establishes the integrity of his self-created life, but its scope of action is so severely restricted that his achievement is as much an ironic comment upon the poet's earlier unequivocal assertion that "true Wisdom's world will be/Within its own creation" (III, 46).

That Byron clearly recognizes the limited "paradise" that Harold

---

[18] "This" in the final line refers not to "affections" but to Harold's specific love for the young girls mentioned shortly before.

has chosen—a state of being expressing Harold's unwillingness to exert himself any longer upon the vast order of reluctance that reality represents—may be seen in what I take to be his symbolic use of Marceau and Ehrenbreitstein. Marceau's heroic deeds and honored grave contrast with (they do not satirize) Harold's pathetic retreat from action, and the fortress of Ehrenbreitstein—with its history of defeat in peace and victory in the strife of arms—perhaps offers a moral warning about Harold's situation and the peaceful world of the Rhine Valley in general. Nevertheless, Marceau and Ehrenbreitstein do not contradict, but qualify, the value represented by Harold's imaginative solitude and the placid fecundity of the Rhine Valley.

Although "The Castled Crag of Drachenfels" is attributed to Harold in Canto III, its manifest relation to the personal life of the narrating poet emphasizes once again his intimate connection with his creator. In the Morgan Library MS of the lyric the lines are addressed by Byron to his sister, but even without this information no one has failed to see the subjective origin of the poem, as well as of stanza 55. Aesthetically Byron did well to put the lines in Harold's mouth, for they set forth the Childe's wistful passivity, and thus contrast with the poet's gradually increasing commitment to a heroic and perpetual pilgrimage:

> The race of life becomes a hopeless flight
> To those that walk in darkness: on the sea
> The boldest steer but where their ports invite—
> But there are wanderers o'er Eternity,
> Whose bark drives on and on, and anchored ne'er shall be. (III, 70)

Since the narrating poet understands Harold's reluctance to commit himself to the life of heroic imagination symbolized by the endless voyage, he underlines the parallel between himself and his hero at the beginning of the final movement of Canto III, as he explicitly associates his own passive tendencies with the comforting tones of "a Sister's voice."

> Clear, placid Leman! thy contrasted lake,
> With the wild world I dwelt in, is a thing
> Which warns me, with its stillness, to forsake
> Earth's troubled waters for a purer spring.
> This quiet sail is as a noiseless wing
> To waft me from distraction; once I loved
> Torn Ocean's roar, but thy soft murmuring
> Sounds sweet as if a Sister's voice reproved,
> That I with stern delights should e'er have been so moved. (85)

What he does not know when he utters these thoughts is that the stillness of the lake is not an invitation to seek rest and peace, but Nature's announcement of the wild storm whose "wondrous" (92) strength will shortly break out over the lake and mountains. Thus the powerful voice of Nature contradicts his "Sister's voice," and opposes his inclination to give up the dangerous life of uncharted and endless voyaging for more placid and domestic comforts. "If I rest," the poet says, then always

> the far roll
> Of your departing voices, is the knoll
> Of what in me is sleepless.   (III, 96)

In Canto IV the final decision to accept his mission of unceasing and high endeavor is made (105), and again the conflict within himself is set out between domestic and homely values and the attractions of perilous voyaging. In the Rhine Valley Harold represents the negative of this passionate devotion to unending pilgrimage, which turns out to be one of continuous self-development and self-discovery as well.

Thus it is highly appropriate that Harold's last words in the poem should reflect his disinclination to continue the arduous journey. Byron embodies the strength of his own spiritual inertia in the characterization of his hero—just as he had earlier objectified in Harold his deep uncertainty of mind and self-lacerating *Angst*. The device of considering his own pressing spiritual difficulties at a remove that permits sympathy as well as judgment introduces a broader sensibility and perspective than would otherwise be possible. When the poet has to face and resolve these same problems in his own person he is provided in advance with an exemplum that clarifies for the reader, as well as for himself, the significance of the issues: energetic passions have been seen to eventuate in emotional disorder, producing in turn a sense of weariness and inanition, and a longing for peace. The poet sees this as the basic tendency in his own moral life as well, and his chief (psychological) problem in Cantos III and IV is to maintain a high level of passionate self-commitment along with an equivalent control that does not at the same time weaken his energies. The force of the poet's drive for complete fulfillment and self-expression must not produce chaos and turmoil, but instead create a nonrepressive order that answers to the need for unlimited self-development. In the Rhine Valley Harold achieves a control, or at any rate a subsidence, of his passionate energies, but only at the price of a corresponding diminishment of his self-recreative potential ("in solitude/Small power the nipped affections have to grow").

With the substantive problem of Cantos III and IV (anarchy vs. order) thus clearly defined, the narrating poet pursues his personal quest for resolution without making any further reference to Harold until the very end. After the Rhine Valley Harold is no longer needed since his principal function in these cantos has been to mirror (and thus objectify to the subject self of the poet) those qualities in the narrating artist which would vitiate the heroic enterprise. Thenceforward the poet struggles with his own reciprocal tendencies to inertia and frenzy and eventually overcomes the fruitless alternation between these two emotional poles. He does this by discovering that his conflicted psychology is, properly understood, only a reflection of the unending systole and diastole in Nature herself; that "frenzy" and "inertia" would rather be called the active and passive forms of one and the same vital energy by anyone who conceived of life as a successive and not a conclusive thing; and that the creative activity of the artist is itself an image of this progressive dialectic, while the movement of the dialectic is the only sure guarantee that art is forever possible.

At the conclusion of Canto IV Harold reappears, and if Byron's first purpose in thus bringing him back is to ensure a modicum of formal coherence in the poem, it must be granted that he makes his hero serve the occasion in a most brilliant way. Byron in his own person has just concluded his triumphant statement in St. Peter's and the Vatican Gallery when he suddenly recalls the negative image of himself, Harold, to introduce the passage on the death of the Princess Charlotte. These stanzas embody the operation of those adversative forces in life which are the contrary (and complement) of the recreative powers revealed at St. Peter's and the Vatican Gallery.

> His shadow fades away into Destruction's mass,
>
> Which gathers shadow—substance—life, and all
> That we inherit in its mortal shroud—
> And spreads the dim and universal pall
> Through which all things grow phantoms.... (164–65)

It is a stroke of fine technical propriety that Harold, the lost soul of the narrating poet, should introduce the poem's definitive challenge to the imaginative celebration just concluded. Like Demogorgon at the end of *Prometheus Unbound*, Harold now returns to "send us prying into the abyss" (166), and to remind us that the creative thrust of human life is not apocalyptic and does not annihilate the forces of entropy and negativity.

and the cloud
Between us sinks and all which ever glowed,
Till Glory's self is twilight, and displays
A melancholy halo scarce allowed
To hover on the verge of darkness—rays
Sadder than the saddest night. . . .   (165)

Byron's magnificent lament over the Princess Charlotte is really an elegy for a universe which longs to be freed of death and evil, and cannot. "How we did entrust Futurity to her" Byron declares (170), and he explicitly equates her with the Virgin Mary and her stillborn child with Christ:

and, though [Futurity] must
Darken above our bones, yet fondly deemed
Our children should obey her child, and blessed
Her and her hoped-for seed, whose promise seemed
Like stars to shepherd's eyes:—'twas but a meteor beamed. (170)

But if the death of the Princess and her son is the denial of the hope for a cleansed and restored Natural Order, it is not equivalent to an entropic apocalypse as in *The Dunciad* and *The City of Dreadful Night*.

Scion of Chiefs and Monarchs, where art thou?
Fond Hope of many nations, art thou dead?
Could not the Grave forget thee, and lay low
Some less majestic, less beloved head?
In the sad midnight, while thy heart still bled,
The mother of a moment, o'er thy boy,
Death hushed that pang for ever: with thee fled
The present happiness and promised joy
Which filled the Imperial Isles so full it seemed to cloy.   (168)

"Woe unto us—not her—for she sleeps well," Byron says later (171), and the statement highlights the meaning of this wonderful stanza, and of the whole elegiac sequence as well. In the death of the Princess Byron adumbrates the tragedy of men's constant hopes for peace, happiness, salvation through any nonpersonal frame of reference. Here the context is social and political: the death of the Princess becomes the death of all hope ("with thee fled/The . . . promised joy"), and when Byron says that such messianic expectations for the Natural Order filled England to cloying he suggests the danger inherent in them. Later he specifies the tragedy of all like visions and dreams:

> From thy Sire's to his humblest subject's breast
> Is linked the electric chain of that despair,
> Whose shock was as an Earthquake's, and opprest
> The land which loved thee so that none could love thee best. (172)

Not just the King, but an entire country is plunged into despair at her passing; she was made the rainbow of universal Freedom (169), but this dream seems now utterly canceled. Nevertheless, if the death of this woman negates such hopes as these, it does not destroy Hope, but only releases that virtue from man's wishful illusions. After life's fitful fever she sleeps well, and through this reminder Byron urges us toward a perception of an other- (not necessarily an after-) life. His thought is akin to Paul's when he says that we all run, but for no earthly crown. The death of the Princess Charlotte is a source of consolation to anyone not deluded into expecting that the reality of the Natural Order can be made to fit man's univocal visions of beatitude. In her labors to bring forth the infant of promise, Death intervened:

> while thy heart still bled,
> The mother of a moment, o'er thy boy,
> Death hushed that pang for ever.... (168)

All blessedness here is momentary, and won only after great pain. For one who has struggled long with life's evils for such moments, death brings the comfort of peace ("Oh, happier thought! can we be made the same," 96) and ought to be a weeping world's consolation.

> The gulf is thick with phantoms, but the Chief
> Seems royal still, though with her head discrowned,
> And pale, but lovely, with maternal grief. (167)

The heart of the Princess Charlotte, and of all who share the spiritual royalty which she symbolizes, bleeds "With some deep and immedicable wound" (167) which, if it prophesies the triumph of Death, also frees us from slavery to life—not only after death, but now. The consciousness of our utter contingency releases us from our weary dreams of apocalypse and entropy alike; cut loose thus from any conclusive expectations of life, we are forever freed from what Wordsworth called "the anxiety of hope." The immediate experience, for pleasure or pain, thus becomes fully possible. Toward the end of his life Shelley came more and more to rely upon such a view. It is beautifully exemplified in his lyric "To Jane: The Invitation."

Expectation too, be off!
To-day is for itself enough;
Hope, in pity mock not Woe
With smiles, nor follow where I go;
Long having lived on thy sweet food,
At length I find one moment's good
After long pain—with all your love,
This you never told me of.   (ll. 39–46)

The stanzas on St. Peter's and the Vatican Gallery assert a similar theme of dearly bought humanism, except that Byron's grandiose tone of celebration differs as much from Shelley's exquisite delicacy here as it does from his own elegiac strain in the Princess Charlotte passage. The famous conclusion to Canto IV repeats the theme yet again ("Roll on, thou deep and dark blue Ocean—roll!" etc.), thus closing the epic with a solemn but controlled perception that "There is no home, nor hope, nor life, save what is here."

Harold's participation in and contribution to the conclusion of *Childe Harold's Pilgrimage* is demanded by the very theme on which the poem is resolved. As the stanzas on the Princess make clear, it is as much the incapacities and failures of our imaginative hopes and emotional longings that lead us to a vision of human freedom as it is their capabilities and triumphs. From the continuous alternation of joy and pain, hope and despair, and all of life's contraries which so madden and exhaust the spirit, is born the unreluctant consciousness of these ambiguities and conflicts; and it is upon this consciousness that Byron balances the polarities of the poem. *Childe Harold's Pilgrimage* experiments with formulas for human fulfillment, and the negative results which Harold yields do not merely modify the visionary schemes of the poet, but actually force him to essay a resolution in a totally different context. The forms of his entropic and apocalyptic visions are only valuable insofar as they are regarded as the complementary potentials of an imagination which includes them both, and is capable of yet a third, and superior, action: consciousness itself, the power to reflect upon, if necessary qualify, and at all times retain control of the longings and fears of the human imagination.

I began this discussion with some lines from Robert Louis Stevenson. I think it would have pleased Byron if Mother Goose could have helped supply a summary for the kind of answer I have tried to develop here. In that famous book we are told the story of a certain "crooked man," which begins:

> There was a crooked man,
> And he went a crooked mile;
> He found a crooked sixpence
> Against a crooked stile;
> He bought a crooked cat,
> Which caught a crooked mouse. . . .

In *Childe Harold's Pilgrimage* it is through Harold that we come to know Byron's crooked man, and it is by fostering the Harold elements in himself that the narrating poet exposes the twistedness that marks all life. In Mother Goose the story concludes:

> And they all lived together
> In a little crooked house.

Which is approximately the moral of *Childe Harold's Pilgrimage*. If the crookedness at the root of life cannot be removed, it can be made straight in the attitude of the artist's imagination. *Childe Harold's Pilgrimage* takes its evil a good deal more seriously than does the Mother Goose poem, however, and this difference is well defined in a passage from Auden's eulogy for W. B. Yeats. The lines might as well have been applied to Byron, another of Auden's favorite poets.

> Sing of human unsuccess
> In a rapture of distress;
> In the deserts of the heart
> Let the healing fountain start.

Perhaps Auden was thinking as much of Byron as he was of Yeats anyway, for the last two lines distinctly echo a famous verse in Byron's "Stanzas to Augusta": "In the Desert a fountain is springing."

Die Morgenlandfahrt:
BYRON AWAKING

The history of the composition of *Childe Harold's Pilgrimage I–II* was first set forth by Robert Charles Dallas in 1824 and 1825.[1] The Moore and Wright edition of Byron's Life and Works added little new information about that famous event, and it was not until E. H. Coleridge brought out his great edition of the poetry at the turn of the century that our knowledge was significantly advanced. Coleridge collated the two extant MSS of the poem, and in his introduction drew upon all the then available information about Byron's life to present what has since become the definitive exposition of the poem's various stages of composition and revision.[2] Scholars have used that record ever since without question.[3] The fact is, however, that Coleridge's account is incomplete or inaccurate in a variety of more or less important ways.[4] In the present essay, then, my first purpose is to reconsider this whole matter and, by augmenting Coleridge's records with additional evidence from the MSS and the biography, to present a more complete picture of the state of the MSS and the progress of the poem's composition.

At the conclusion of this factual presentation, I will also offer an analysis of the data in relation to the aesthetics of the received poem. Unlike the later cantos, *Childe Harold's Pilgrimage I–II* is not great poetry; it is, however, one of the most important works in modern Western literature. As the first part of the larger composition, its influ-

[1] See Robert Charles Dallas, *Recollections of the Life of Lord Byron* (London, 1824); A. R. C. Dallas, ed., *Correspondence of Lord Byron with a Friend* (Philadelphia, 1825).

[2] *LJ* 2: ix–xxiv.

[3] Marchand's *Biography* added some important refinements to the strictly biographical information.

[4] One of the most noticeable overall omissions was made in the record of variants, of which Coleridge only printed a sampling.

94

ence was enormous—in particular upon the subsequent widespread development of confessional poetry, and (correlatively) of "sincerity" as an aesthetic criterion. The MSS of these early cantos, and the story of the process of their composition, can provide us with some important clues about the nature of this phenomenon; most of all, however, they can help us to understand the significance of the personal and dramatic quality in Byron's own work. He was a man for whom poetry was an immediate experience, and who was wont to measure his own compositions according to whether they were or were not written "in *red-hot* earnest."[5] In fact, "sincerity" was not just a poetic quality or accident for Byron (especially in his lyrics, *Childe Harold's Pilgrimage*, and *Don Juan*): it was the basic substantive issue and the principle of organization—at once the meaning of his poetry (who and what am I?) and the form of its expression (coherent self-dramatization). This fundamental Byronic modality suffuses even the relatively immature early cantos of *Childe Harold's Pilgrimage*, and can be effectively studied by plotting the various stages of the poem's composition and revision. In my analysis of the MSS, then, I want ultimately to show how Byron manipulated his materials for his particular dramatic purposes.

The original MS of the early cantos is in the Murray collection, and the Dallas transcript made from it is preserved in the British Museum (Egerton 2027).[6] Coleridge's description of these MSS is extremely valuable, though he is not always as accurate as we might have wished. Moreover, his method of presentation and his selection of details have left a number of questions unanswered concerning the first form of the poem, its stages of composition, and Byron's original intentions toward his work. Quoting Dallas' published recollections of his receipt of Byron's original MS just after the poet had returned from Greece, Coleridge gives the following description of the meetings between the two men on July 15 and 16, 1811:

> on the 15th Dallas "had the pleasure of shaking hands with [Byron] at Reddish's Hotel, St. James's Street". . . . There was a crowd of visitors, . . . and no time for conversation; but the *Imitation* [i.e., *Hints from Horace*] was placed in his hands. He took it home, read it, and was disappointed . . . the next morning at

[5] This is Byron's description of his "Stanzas to the Po"; from a letter to Hobhouse, 8 June 1820, reprinted in Leslie A. Marchand's "Lord Byron and Count Alborghetti, *PMLA* 64 (December, 1949): 978.

[6] Following Coleridge's notation I will hereafter refer to these as MS M and MS D respectively.

> breakfast Dallas ventured to express some surprise that he had
> written nothing else. An admission or confession followed that
> "he had occasionally written short poems, besides a great many
> stanzas in Spenser's measure, relative to the countries he had vis-
> ited." "They are not," he added, "worth troubling you with, but
> you shall have them all with you if you like." "So," says Dallas,
> "came I by *Childe Harold*."   (*P* 2:ix–x)

But in what condition were Byron's "great many stanzas in Spenser's
"measure" when he gave them to Dallas? Coleridge quotes the following note from MS D of Cantos I–II. It is written in the hand of Dallas'
son Alexander, who inherited the Dallas transcript from his father and
who edited his father's *Recollections* in 1824.

> The first and second cantos of *Childe Harold* were written in sep-
> arate portions by the noble author. They were afterwards ar-
> ranged for publication; and when thus arranged, the whole was
> copied. This copy was placed in Lord Byron's hands, and he made
> various alterations, corrections, and large additions. . . . The manu-
> script thus corrected was sent to the press, and was printed under
> the direction of Robt. Chas. Dallas, Esq., to whom Lord Byron
> had given the copyright of the poem.   (*P* 2:xvi)

Dallas is himself the origin of the still credited story that Byron originally had no inclination to publish his poem. If we follow the Dallas
description of these events in 1811, then, we must conclude that the
arrangement and revision of Cantos I–II took place almost entirely after
Byron returned to England, when Dallas persuaded the reluctant poet
to give his sensational composition to the world.

   It is true that the largest number of Byron's additions and revisions
were made after he had returned to England. On the other hand, the
MS that Byron handed over to Dallas to read was by no means the
heap of *disjecta membra* that Alexander Dallas' words might suggest.
Byron was no Thomas Wolfe, Charles Dallas was no Maxwell Perkins.
Childe Harold's Pilgrimage I–II had been "arranged" into an integral
poetic unit well before Byron returned to England, and had undergone
a series of important revisions and corrections while Byron was in
Turkey and Greece. With the evidence now at our disposal—from
the MSS of the poem as well as from a number of extratextual sources
—it is possible to reconstruct with a good deal of precision the various
stages in the composition of Cantos I–II. Broadly speaking, the two
cantos went through four separate phases of development:

a) the first form, written between October 31, 1809, and March 28, 1810, including the revisions made during this period;

b) the Dallas transcript in its original state, which is a synthesis of (*a*) with a number of additions and deletions made after (*a*) was completed but before Dallas received the poem;

c) the first edition, which corresponds to the Dallas transcript as subsequently revised by Byron;

d) the seventh edition, which incorporates ten new stanzas into Canto II and prefixes "To Ianthe" to the whole composition.

Using this schema as a guide, we can trace the course of Byron's composition in a fairly orderly way.

Byron began writing the first canto of the poem when he was in Janina, October 31, 1809. By December 16 he had composed sixty-one stanzas and was writing the Parnassus digression (*P* 2:92). On December 30 he completed the first canto, which then stood at ninety-one stanzas. He must have begun writing the second canto shortly after he finished the first, for he was writing the twelfth stanza of Canto II on January 3, 1810 (*P* 2:168). The next definite date that we have is for the stanzas on Albania, which were written toward the end of February, 1810.[7] The canto was completed on March 28 and comprised at this time eighty stanzas. It is evident from the numeration of the original MS that Byron did not patch either canto together from separately written fragments—as Tennyson did with *In Memoriam*, for example. In both cases he began at the beginning and wrote each canto in an uninterrupted sequence, numbering the stanzas as he went along. This conforms to his usual practice, which was first to write a complete unit, and afterward to go back over it making the necessary additions and deletions. He follows this procedure regularly in *Don Juan*, for example, as well as in the later cantos of *Childe Harold's Pilgrimage*. The composition of *The Giaour* and *English Bards and Scotch Reviewers* is similarly accretive.

Before Byron returned to England in July, 1811, he made a number of additions to and deletions from both cantos. In only one instance did he graft a major revision into his poem while the first draft was still in process of composition. This was the insertion of stanza [12] 13,[8]

---

[7] John Galt, *The Life of Lord Byron* (London, 1830), pp. 111, 122.

[8] The numeration of the stanzas underwent a number of changes between 1809 and 1814, when the poem finally reached its present form. Except in direct quotations, or where otherwise indicated, I will use the following scheme in my references to stanzas from the MSS and text. (*a*) The number in brackets refers to the number given in the relevant MS; if the MS shows any changes of numeration, the different numbers are

along with the following lyric "Childe Harold's Good Night." During November, 1809, Byron was writing Canto I in sequence. After writing thirty-five stanzas he paused and went back over what he had written (stanzas [1]2—[35/36]33) revising lines and phrases. At this point, besides the insertion of stanza [12]13 and the lyric, Byron decided to make the most famous minor textual revision in the poem— the change of the Childe's name from "Burun" to "Harold." After stanza [35/36]33 the name "Burun" never appears again as a textual variant, and the original title of the inserted lyric in MS M is "Childe Harold's Good Night." Having added stanza [12]13 and the lyric, Byron revised the numeration of his stanzas accordingly.

Four other additions appear on two MS leaves inserted toward the conclusion of the first canto. The first of these is the lyric "To Inez," dated January 25, 1810 (P 2:77). The lyric takes up all of the first leaf and part of the second. Following it on the MS are three discontinuous stanzas for Cantos II: stanzas [52/53]52(53); [14]15, and [79/81] 80(88).[9] We can only be certain of the dating of these three stanzas within broad chronological limits. They must have been added to the poem some time after March 28, 1810, when Canto II was completed, and before July 16, 1811, when Byron gave his MS to Dallas to read. And although "To Inez" was written in January, 1810, it is probable that Byron did not decide to insert it into Canto I until later, at approximately the same time that he inserted into Canto II the three stanzas which appear on the same MS leaf.[10]

Another major revision of MS M may indicate more precisely when all these additions were made. Byron originally wrote the following lines as stanza [21/22] of Canto I (following st. [20/21]22).

> Unhappy Vathek! in an evil hour
> Gainst Nature's voice seduced to deed accurst,
> Once Fortune's minion, now thou feelst her power!

---

given in the order that they were chosen, and each is separated by a virgule. (b) The unenclosed number refers to that which appears in the first edition. This number will correspond to that which appears in the received text in all cases except for stanzas after stanza 26 of Canto II. Ten stanzas were added to Canto II in the seventh edition, the first of which was stanza 27 of the received text. Where necessary, then, a third number will be given: (c) the number in parentheses refers to the number in the received text whenever this differs from the first edition.

[9] The stanzas are respectively headed in MS M: "Stanza 52 for Canto 2nd"; "Stanza 14 for Canto 2nd"; "Stanza 79 for Canto 2nd."

[10] The stanzas appear in proper sequence in MS D but were not written in England before Dallas made his copy of the poem. See discussion below.

Wrath's vials on thy lofty head have burst,—
In wit, in genius, as in wealth the first'
How wondrous bright thy blooming morn arose—
But thou wert smitten with unhallowed thirst
Of nameless crime, and thy sad day must close
To scorn and solitude unsought—the worst of woes.[11]

On February 1, 1811, Byron crossed the stanza out and added a note directing that it not be printed as part of any published version of *Childe Harold's Pilgrimage*.[12] The months January–March, 1811, were taken up with a good deal of literary activity.[13] His thoughts were much occupied with Greece and her moral significance, and we know for certain (*P* 2:192 and 196) that he wrote two long notes on Greece specifically for *Childe Harold's Pilgrimage* while he was living at the Capuchin Convent in Athens (they are dated January 23 and March 17, 1811). It is likely that he was going over all of what he had written of *Childe Harold's Pilgrimage* during this period, and that the deletion of the Vathek stanza was part of a general process of revision then taking place. If "To Inez" was not added at this time, then, the probability is very strong that at least the three Greek stanzas for Canto II were.

The final major revision made in the poem before Byron returned to England was the insertion of stanzas 8 and 9 of Canto I in place of stanzas [7] and [8] (*P* 2:20), which were part of the original sequence of the canto as written in November, 1809. Once again we cannot be absolutely sure when Byron made this alteration, though the condition of the MS strongly suggests that it belongs to the period of the Vathek revision, if not later. The two new stanzas are inserted into the MS in their proper place on two small scraps of paper; they are, however, unnumbered, and the original stanzas [7] and [8] appear uncanceled in the MS. Nonetheless, all we can be certain of is that the stanzas were inserted after Byron changed the Childe's name to Harold and before Dallas copied the poem from MS M.[14]

Some time in late July or early August, 1811, Robert Dallas made

[11] These lines from MS M appear in a slightly different form in *P* 7: 7.
[12] The note in MS M reads: "If ever published I shall have this stanza omitted. Byron. February 1st 1811."
[13] See *Borst*, pp. 143–48, and *Biography* 1: 266–72.
[14] Dallas did not copy them into MS D. We know from his authority that the only revisions made in the poem after Byron returned to England and before MS D was copied were the insertion of stanza 1 for Canto I and the "polishing" of some lines in the text. See discussion below.

his transcript of Byron's corrected first draft.[15] In its original form this transcript incorporated all of the major revisions discussed above, and nearly all of the minor (line, phrase, word) revisions to be seen in MS M. The Dallas transcript shows no significant additions to the poem beyond what can be found on the corrected leaves of MS M. Thus, whereas the two cantos in MS M originally comprised ninety-one and eighty stanzas respectively, in the first form of MS D the two cantos make up ninety and eighty-three stanzas. Between the end of July and the beginning of November, 1811, Byron made a series of crucial additions, revisions, and deletions, so that the final form of MS D—from which *Childe Harold's Pilgrimage* was first published—differs considerably from its first form. The major corrections made in the Dallas transcript are the following. Six stanzas were dropped from Canto I (sts. [24], [26], [27], and [87–89]) and two others were heavily revised (sts. [25/26] 25 and [86] 87); at the same time, Byron added nine entirely new stanzas to the first canto (sts. 1, 43, 85–86, and 88–92). Three stanzas were dropped from Canto II (sts. [8], [15], and [16]), two were heavily revised (sts. [12]13 and [64]63[64]), and eight new stanzas were added (sts. 8, 9, and 83–88[93–98]).[16]

The process of revision began very shortly after Byron gave his MS poem to Dallas on July 16. After he left Byron, Dallas read the poem, and was so pleased with it that he wrote to Byron that same day praising the work as "one of the most delightful poems I have ever read."[17] Dallas and Byron conferred again about the poem when Byron returned to London on July 23 after a brief visit to Harrow. It was at this, the third meeting between the two men since Byron's return, that "the publication of the poem [was] determined upon." Dallas immediately took the MS to the bookseller and publisher William Miller, who, after considering it for "a few days," declined to publish it.[18] Dallas then took it to John Murray who, in Dallas' words,

> took some days to consider, during which time he consulted his literary advisors. . . . We came to this conclusion; that he should print, at his expense, a handsome quarto edition. . . . When I told this to Lord Byron he was highly pleased and promised if the poem went through the edition to give me other poems to annex to Childe Harold.[19]

[15] *Biography* 1: 278–84. See also my discussion below.
[16] See *P* 2: xviii-xx; 38–41; 78–80; 103–9, 140.
[17] A. R. C. Dallas, *Correspondence*, p. 126.
[18] *Ibid*. See especially pp. 146–50.
[19] *Ibid*.

Thus Dallas and Byron must have met yet a fourth time before the month was out, for all of these events took place before Byron left London for Newstead Abbey on August 1.[20] It was probably on July 28 or 29 that Dallas told Byron of Murray's decision to publish.[21] At this same meeting Dallas renewed his earlier appeals for alterations:

> These preliminaries being settled, I persisted in my attacks on the objectionable parts of this delightful work, now formally become mine. He wrote an introductory stanza . . . polished some lines, and became in general far more condescending and compliant than I ever flattered myself I should find him. . . . Finding I could gain nothing with respect to the sceptical stanzas, the conciliatory one I have already mentioned not having been written at this time [i.e., II, 8, "Yet if, as holiest men have deemed, there be"], I drew up a regular *protest* against them, and enclosed it to him in a short letter [dated July 29] just before he left town, which . . . he did . . . very suddenly [on August 1], in consequence of an express from Newstead Abbey, by which he was informed that his mother's life was despaired of. . . .[22]

Since Byron sent his "introductory stanza" to Dallas before he left town, and since the new stanza is not incorporated into the text of the Dallas transcript, appearing in MS D only as an insert in Dallas' hand on a small scrap of paper, the likelihood is that Dallas had completed his transcript before the end of July. In any case, MS D was certainly made at a very early date, for Byron sent it back to Dallas from Newstead Abbey on or shortly after August 15 with a series of major corrections and additions. Among these were the following: the two ele-

[20] Dallas' record here is confirmed by Byron's letter to Murray of 23 August 1811 (*LJ* 2: 1–2).

[21] See *Biography* and A. R. C. Dallas, *Correspondence*. Also *Moore* 1: 260–61, 270–71. In his biography Moore cited Dallas as his authority for the statement that "it was some time before Lord Byron's obstinate repugnance to the idea of publishing Childe Harold could be removed" (1: 260–61). Opposite this passage in his copy of Moore's biography Hobhouse wrote: "So Mr. Dallas says–but I do not believe the fact" (quoted in *Biography* 1: 281, n.5). As it turns out, Hobhouse—who was with Byron when he wrote the poem and ought to have known his mind about it if anyone did—was justified in his skepticism. But Dallas was not the culprit in the affair. In both of Dallas' earlier published accounts of the negotiations during the summer and autumn of 1811 he nowhere says or implies that Byron held out against publication for a substantial length of time. On the contrary, he makes it quite clear that negotiations for publication were well under way before Byron left for Newstead Abbey on August 1. What apparently happened was this. Moore, after reading Dallas' records of those days in 1811, simply used the phrase "it was some time" to suggest the very real reluctance on Byron's part to publish his poem. The phrase ought not to be read as a statement of chronology but as a description of Byron's hesitation.

[22] A. R. C. Dallas, *Correspondence*, pp. 149–50.

giac stanzas on Wingfield (I, 91–92) with their accompanying note; stanza 8 of Canto II; the heavily revised stanza 87 and the new stanzas 88–90 of Canto I; and probably the new stanza 43 for the same canto. We can tell that I, 91–92 and II, 8 were among Byron's "packets" from Dallas' remarks in his letter of acknowledgment dated August 18.[23] Further, the condition of MS D makes it clear that the revised stanza 87 and the new stanzas 88–90 were added to Canto I at the same time that stanzas 91–92 were inserted. The latter two stanzas are written in Byron's hand on the back of the last leaf of MS D; on the front of that leaf between stanzas [89] and [90]93 Byron put in the following note: "Insert here two stanzas from the next page." Having added these two stanzas, Byron then set about revising [86–89] in order that the tone of the whole passage might better conform with the mood of the Wingfield addition.[24] Stanza 43 of Canto I was probably added to the poem at this time as well, though we cannot prove this from the available evidence. Nevertheless the likelihood is strong since the events treated in stanza 43 parallel the substantive concerns of Byron's additions at the end of Canto I.[25] The tonal similarity is also obvious.

Between the middle of August and the end of September Byron did little with his poem beyond adding notes, correcting early proofs, and sending Dallas the motto for the work.[26] He was, he told Dallas, "too much occupied with earthly cares to waste time or trouble upon rhyme." (*LJ*, 2: 38). On September 26, however, he answered a letter from Dallas (not forthcoming) in which the latter evidently pressed once more for the revisions that Byron had promised earlier, but had not yet made. The issue was the Cintra passage in Canto I (sts. [24–27]). Byron agreed to undertake the business, and asked Dallas to point out the offending verses (*LJ*, 2: 47). On October 10 Byron wrote again—

[23] See Byron's letter to Dallas of 25 August (*LJ* 2: 6) and Dallas' letter to Byron of 18 August (A. R. C. Dallas, *Correspondence*, pp. 157–58).

[24] He began by correcting stanza [86] 87 interlinearly, but after adding three new lines to the stanza on MS D in this way he took up a new sheet of paper entirely and composed the whole of the corrected version of the stanza from the beginning. Stanza [87] was then crossed out in the MS, and its replacement, stanza [87] 88, was written on the new leaf below [86] 87. He then crossed out the whole of [88] and wrote a new stanza, [88] 89, between the lines of the canceled one. Stanza 90 is written at the bottom of a new leaf of paper to replace [89], which is crossed out. Byron then tore stanza 90 off the new leaf and placed the scrap of paper over the canceled stanza [89].

[25] Coleridge suggests (*P* 2: 51, n.2) that stanza 43 was added to Canto I some time in October, 1811. He gives that month as the date of publication of Scott's *The Vision of Don Roderick: The Battle of Albuera*, to which Byron seems to allude in the last line of his stanza. Scott's poem was published in July, however.

[26] See his correspondence with Murray and Dallas between 27 August and 26 September (*LJ* 2: 8–47).

rather hurriedly, as he had just returned to Newstead from a trip to Lancashire—to tell Dallas that he had corrected the Cintra passage and sent the revisions along. The day before, Byron received his first news of John Edleston's death the previous May. He must have responded to this intelligence by writing stanza 9 of Canto II almost immediately, for these verses were almost certainly among the "two or three additional stanzas for both '*Fyttes*'" which Byron sent to Dallas with the Cintra alterations.[27] The stanzas he sent for Canto I were probably 85–86, which appear in the folder of MS D on a separate sheet in Dallas' handwriting.[28] The tragic series of deaths which touched Byron so closely continued to influence his revisions for the poem during October. In a letter to Dallas dated October 25 he sent "a conclusion for the whole" (*LJ* 2: 58).

This dispatch contained a group of stanzas to be added at the end of Canto II. There is, however, some question whether Byron sent all of the stanzas for the poem's conclusion at this time—i.e., stanzas 83–88 (93–98)—or only the five stanzas 83–86(93–96) and 88(98). These five stanzas are inserted in MS D as an integral sequence; they are written on a separate sheet of paper in Dallas' hand. But MS D also includes a set of proof sheets of the concluding stanzas of the poem, and here all six stanzas appear in their proper order. The problem is complicated by the existence of another scrap of MS (in the Murray collection) which contains Byron's rough copy of stanzas 85–88 (95–98). These four stanzas are numbered 3–6 on this piece of MS. Evidently the missing stanzas 1–2 were stanzas 83–84(93–94). It seems clear, then, that Byron composed the six concluding stanzas together as a unit sometime before October 25. Afterward one of two things happened. Either Byron did not send stanza 87(97) to Dallas on October 25 with the other five stanzas, but only decided to include it in the poem at some later date, or Dallas for some reason neglected to copy stanza 87(97) when he was transcribing the new group of additions for the printer. Whatever the case, Byron had finished composing his additions by the end of October.

[27] See Byron's letters to Dallas of 9 and 10 October (*LJ* 2: 51–52). Also *Biography* 1: 295–96.

[28] Stanza 43 of Canto I may also have been sent at this time, though the more likely date is the one I have already suggested. We cannot tell for certain when stanzas 15–16 of Canto II were deleted, or when stanzas [12] 13 and [64] 63 (64) were revised. Both sets of alterations were made by Byron on MS D itself and they seem to have been carried out together. It is possible that Byron did them at this time when he was revising the Cintra passage, and when Dallas' "protest" would have been in his mind again. The middle of August is an equally possible date, however.

From the foregoing data a number of more or less significant conclusions can be immediately drawn. Because it is possible to date with some precision the various revisions in the MSS, we can clear up a number of minor points of fact. For example: not only did Dallas have nothing to do with the change of the hero's name from "Burun" to "Harold," but the Vathek stanza was also marked for cancelation before Dallas ever saw it.[29] Further, and more important, the whole story of Byron's unwillingness to publish must be carefully interpreted. He definitely did not hold out for a long time, as Moore's early biography suggested, nor could he have been so indifferent to the prospect of publishing the work as he seems to have made Dallas believe. Since Coleridge's edition it has been generally assumed that the first two cantos of *Childe Harold's Pilgrimage* were not "seriously intended for publication"[30] before Byron returned to England. However, Byron's MS note to the canceled Vathek stanza, as well as the general condition of MS M, shows clearly that he was, at the least, making careful preparations for such an event. The early MS demonstrates Byron's unmistakable concern for the form of his work from its earliest stages of composition to the latest corrections and revisions made before he returned to England. These facts also controvert the related notion that Byron did not trouble himself about matters of form and aesthetic significance while writing (or revising) Cantos I–II.[31]

Thus the MSS of the early cantos help to supply us with a good deal of new information about when and how the poem was written. Besides this, however, the whole story of the poem's composition and revision can give us some fruitful insights into the meaning and poetic structure of the early cantos. Readers have often noted the tonal difference between the MS poem that Byron brought back with him from the Levant, and the actual work that was finally published in 1812. M. K. Joseph, for example, says that in the original MS the comic elements

> were much more obvious, particularly in the first canto, where they made up over a tenth of the text. . . . The substitution of serious and personal matter at the end [of Canto I] has actually changed the tone of the whole canto, and has rather carelessly disguised Byron's original intention. For, seen in its original context, how could the opening description of Harold have been taken literally or seriously?[32]

[29] See *Biography* 1: 288, n.1; *P* 2: 37, n.1.
[30] *Joseph*, p. 23. Coleridge is the source of this notion: see *P* 2: xiv.
[31] *Rutherford*, p. 33.
[32] *Joseph*, p. 21.

Joseph's point about Byron's original comic intentions in Canto I seems to me unexceptionable. Yet he regards Byron's revisions as unsatisfactory since they resulted in the removal of the comic element from nearly every portion of the poem except the very beginning. On the contrary, it seems to me that the revisions changed *Childe Harold's Pilgrimage I–II* from an interesting, at times brilliant, but always highly derivative personal travelogue (with a truly "pointless" titular hero) to the revolutionary confessional poem which so decisively influenced Romantic and post-Romantic art. If the comic element was more pronounced before Byron initiated his final set of revisions, still the poem in its original form was predominantly melancholic in its tonal quality. Canto II was, moreover, distinctly serious throughout (though not always gloomy and woeful). Nevertheless, before Byron made his last corrections Cantos I and II were basically a series of loosely connected descriptive set pieces—each more or less fine in its own way, but the whole comprising little more than an imitation of such things as Thomson's *Liberty* or Goldsmith's *The Traveller*. It was, in fact, something worse than these structurally. The latter possess a formal characteristic peculiar to much eighteenth-century poetry, including not only the work of such pre-Romantics as Chatterton and Collins, but also much of Blake's poetry: a concern for a philosophic or conceptual integrity, a systematic wholeness whose objective validity (whether rational or symbolic or both) overarches and controls the final coherence of the poem. In poetry of this sort the poet is always a persona, or perhaps a prophetic voice, since his personal existence is kept subordinate to an informing principle, or idea. In *Childe Harold's Pilgrimage I–II*, however, the formal element is not conceptual, but unfolds out of the immediate and changing act of the poet's individual self-consciousness. Byron's final revisions served to pull the materials of his relatively disorganized journal into a pattern of significant meaning: *he* would assume the place of first importance in his own poem, and the whole of the work would be made to derive its impact from the relevance of its parts to the dramatized life of the author himself. In the poem's published form, the tonal differences between the opening stanzas of Canto I and the last stanzas of Canto II are the measure of the poem's root meaning: between them is recorded the step-by-step process of Byron's "Consciousness awaking to her woes" (I, 92). With *Cain* and its author in his mind, Blake dedicated his last work "To Lord Byron in the Wilderness." In *Childe Harold's Pilgrimage I–II* Byron gives us a mythologized account of how he came to embody the "lonely, weary, wandering traveler" so prevalent in Western literature.

The actual history of Byron's life during the months that he made his final corrections is well known. A brief summary will suffice here to indicate how the pressure of certain fortuitous events affected the creation of a poem whose historical significance has yet to be measured, and whose influence has yet to wane. Between August and October, 1811, Byron was shocked by the news of the deaths of five of those who were closest to him: his mother, Charles Skinner Matthews, John Wingfield, Hargreaves Hanson, and John Edleston (the last two not mentioned by name in the poem or its notes).[33] Before any of these sad events were known to Byron, Dallas had been trying very hard to get him to alter the "philosophical, free-thinking stanzas, relative to death"[34] that grace the opening of Canto II. If he was unsuccessful in his exhortations before events had cast a pall over Byron's soul, he had not a chance afterward. Dallas sent Byron his formal "protest" about the skeptical stanzas on July 29, and on August 12 Byron answered the letter:

> I received a letter from you, which my late occupations prevented me from duly noticing. . . . I shall be glad to hear from you, on business, on common-place, or any thing, or nothing—but death —I am already too familiar with the dead.   (*LJ* 1:327)

At this time the only significant correction that had been made was the addition of the poem's opening stanza. Within three or four days of this letter, however, Byron was to send the first of his really signal revisions for his poem. Among these was the removal of the stanzas that originally concluded Canto I, and their replacement by stanzas 87–92. The effect of this upon the poem can pass without comment if we but read the original and revised versions of stanza 87.

> Ye! who would more of Spain and Spaniards know
> Sights, Saints, antiques, arts, anecdotes, and war,
> Go hie ye hence to Paternoster Row,
> Are they not written in the book of Carr,
> Green Erin's Knight! and Europe's wandering star!
> Then listen, readers, to the man of ink,
> Hear what he did, and sought, and wrote afar—

---

[33] Wingfield and Hanson were Byron's schoolmates at Harrow. Hanson was the second son of Byron's solicitor John Hanson. Byron numbered Wingfield among his closest associates at Harrow (*Moore* 1: 43). Byron met Matthews at Cambridge and regarded him as "a man of astonishing powers" (*LJ* 1: 338). Edleston was a choirboy at Trinity Chapel for whom Byron developed a strong romantic attachment ("I certainly love him more than any human being," he said in 1807: *LJ* 1: 134).

[34] A. R. C. Dallas, *Correspondence*, p. 147.

All these are cooped within one Quarto's brink
This borrow, steal (or buy) and tell us what you think. (MS D)

Ye! who would more of Spain and Spaniards know,
Go, read whate'er is writ of bloodiest strife:
Whate'er keen Vengeance urged on foreign foe
Can act, is acting there against man's life:
From flashing scimitar to secret knife,
War mouldeth there each weapon to his need—
So may he guard the sister and the wife,
So may he make each curst oppressor bleed—
So may such foes deserve the most remorseless deed! (*P* 2:78–79)

Also among this group of early revisions was the new stanza 8 for Canto II. If Dallas regarded it as a capitulation to his demands for the removal of Byron's atheistical opinions, the substituted stanza was, nevertheless, entirely consonant with Byron's immediate feelings, and in fact aesthetically more appropriate in the poem that was now beginning to emerge. The new stanza 8 not only looks back to I, 91–92, just written, but was soon to become part of a whole series of stanzas added to the poem which concentrate upon the poet's own grievous and strictly personal experiences with sorrow and death.

In the elegiac stanzas sent to Dallas around August 15 Byron speaks of his "Consciousness awaking to her woes"—a phrase I have already quoted as a statement of the essential formal and substantive meaning of Cantos I–II. The note appended to his lament for Wingfield underlines his meaning:

> In the short space of one month I have lost *her* who gave me being, and most of those who made that being tolerable. To me the lines of Young are no fiction—
> > Insatiate archer! could not one suffice?
> > Thy shaft flew thrice, and thrice my peace was slain,
> > And thrice ere thrice yon moon had fill'd her horn.
>
> > > (*P* 2:94–95)

Nevertheless, at this point in his revisions I do not think that Byron had formulated in his mind an intention to make *Childe Harold's Pilgrimage* as a whole an aesthetic dramatization of his own life. As yet he seems to have given no serious thought to major revisions for Canto II—in particular the ending, which is so crucial from a dramatic point of view. The reason for this is, I think, clear enough from Byron's letters of the period. He was badly shaken by the news of the first two deaths, and was only gradually able to take counsel with himself about them, and the others that were soon to follow. It was not till relatively late—October—that he managed to distance himself sufficiently from the series of deaths to be able to make them serve the structure of the poem he was then getting ready to publish. A comparison of three of his letters illustrates this very well. About a week after he learned of his mother's death he wrote to Scrope Berdmore Davies. News of Matthews' drowning in the Cam had only just reached him:

> MY DEAREST DAVIES,—Some curse hangs over me and mine. My mother lies a corpse in this house; one of my best friends drowned in a ditch. What can I say, or think, or do? I received a letter from him yesterday. My dear Scrope, if you can spare a moment, do come down to me—I want a friend. Matthews's letter was written on *Friday*.—on Saturday he was not. . . . Come to me Scrope, I am almost desolate—left almost alone in the world. . . .
>
> (*LJ* 1:324–25)

Later he was to learn that Edleston had fallen victim to consumption in May. On October 11, shortly after receiving this fresh piece of melancholy news, he wrote to Dallas:

> I have been again shocked with a *death*, and have lost one very dear to me in happier times; but "I have almost forgot the taste of grief," and "supped full of horrors" till I have become callous, nor have I a tear left for an event which, five years ago, would have bowed down my head to the earth. It seems as though I were to experience in my youth the greatest misery of age. . . . I have no resource but my own reflections, and they present no prospect here or hereafter, except the selfish satisfaction of surviving my betters.   (*LJ* 2:52)

The spontaneous grief of the first contrasts sharply with the self-conscious and reflective melancholy of the second. Moreover, in the latter he seems to have come to perceive a gloomy significance in the series of deaths. In between these two letters we find him gradually gaining greater control over his frayed emotions. In the middle of August, for example, he still cannot regulate his depressed feelings. He writes to Dallas:

> I feel tolerably miserable, yet I am at the same time subject to a kind of hysterical merriment, or rather laughter without merriment, I can neither account for nor conquer, and yet I do not feel relieved by it; but an indifferent person would think me in excellent spirits.   (*LJ* 1:333)

In October, however, when he worked nearly all of his important additions into Canto II, he seems to have consciously striven to make his personal losses assume a kind of climactic significance in his poem, and to weave them into a meaningful series of relationships. Thus, in stanza 86(96) he deliberately recalls the conclusion to Canto I, and even echoes a line from the Young passage he had quoted in his earlier note. Stanza 84(94) recalls persistent motifs throughout the poem (see the opening stanzas of Canto I, the Parnassus digression, and I, 43, for example), while the stanza added 87(97) deliberately harks back to the issues on which the poem began. He returns to England not as to a home, but only "To be alone on earth, as I am now," 88(98). He is thrust once again into that ultimate solitude so vividly set forth in II, 26. Thus his "flagging spirit" is left "doubly weak" (87[97]), and we begin to see that the canceled passage from his Preface directs our attention to an important fact about the dramatic movement of Byron's cantos: ". . . where the author speaks in his own person, he assumes a very different tone from that of [Childe Harold], at least, till death had deprived him of his nearest connections" (P 2: 4). This excised remark suggests not only how Byron felt about the deaths of his "nearest connections," but also how he regarded their function in the poem he was preparing to publish.

Thus, after Byron decided to introduce into the poem his own reactions to the five deaths, he began to have a care for the requirements of poetic form. He created a dramatic fiction by means of which the deaths appeared in the poem in a gradual succession, culminating in the conclusion of Canto II. This process of manipulating a sequence of events in order to provide a biographical poem with dramatic and psychological significance was carried out on a grand scale by Tennyson in his reconstructive composition of *In Memoriam*. Byron's additions to Cantos I–II, though more modest in scope and number, are no less significant aesthetically. He had a ready and appropriate poetic structure to start with, whereas Tennyson had only a large mass of dramatically unrelated lyric effusions. In Byron's case, then, the new material provided by the tragic events of 1811 had to be worked into the existent structure with some care if a significant dramatic pattern was to emerge from the whole work. I do not think that his success in this venture can be gainsaid. Cantos I–II may be mostly threadbare, but surely the garment was wonderfully conceived. The first shock of personal loss climaxes Canto I; at this point Byron tells us that his poem depicts his "Consciousness awaking to her woes." A second is inserted in the ninth stanza of Canto II, and the composition concludes by recording yet a third, along with a generalized lament for all his lost connections. Since Wingfield had died at Coimbra in May, 1811, only two days before the terrible battle of Albuera, Byron's eulogy at the end of Canto I is most apposite. Moreover, the new conclusion to the canto focuses our attention even more closely upon the narrating poet and his recorded travels. Writing in England in 1811, Byron reflects upon his experiences detailed earlier in the poem, and he notes gloomily that, since his visit to Spain in 1809, his worst fears for that country have begun to materialize. The battles of Barossa (March 5, 1811) and Albuera (May 16, 1811) have been fought, and now "Fresh legions pour adown the Pyrenees" (89). Worse still, Wingfield has perished at Coimbra. The melancholy political events over which he had lamented earlier are now seen to have had an even greater personal relevance than he had ever realized. Stanza 43 of Canto I is therefore also inserted—to anticipate the lament over Wingfield at the conclusion, and thus strengthen the tragic personal drama which the poem finally unfolds.

Although stanza 9 in Canto II probably refers to Edleston, Byron does not indicate in his poem that the lines were written after his return to England; it seems rather an effusion poured forth while Byron was still in Greece, after he had just learned of the death of a recent and unnamed friend. The intimation of accumulating woes remains nevertheless. In this instance Byron's strategy is very like Wordsworth's in *The Prelude*, Book XIV, when he inserted the Mount Snowdon episode immediately following the lines on Salisbury Plain. In all likelihood the two events recorded in the poem did not occur sequentially at all, but were separated by the space of two years. "The date . . . hardly matters," however, as Geoffrey Hartman has said.[35] And the same is true of Byron's poem, for his manipulation of actual events is done to lend poetic coherence and verisimilitude to the psychological drama. The poem grows by degrees more subjective and personally urgent, and the dramatic dispersal of the deaths contributes greatly to this effect. Thus, the lament at the conclusion of Canto II is the appropriate climax to Byron's *Bildungsdichtung*, emphasizing as it does in a final way the poem's fundamentally personal mode of existence. In these stanzas Byron explicitly calls our attention to the fact that his ultimate state of emotional distraction is the result of a cumulative, and as it were, fatal series of events. It is as if some power were bent upon inflicting ever-increasing woes upon him.

35 Geoffrey Hartman, *Wordsworth's Poetry, 1787–1814* (New Haven, 1964), p. 254.

> And grief with grief continuing still to blend,
> Hath snatched the little joy that life had yet to lend.   (st. 86[96])

This is in fact what Byron believed.[36] The extracts from his letters quoted above show this very well, particularly the phrase in his note to Scrope Davies: "Some curse hangs over me and mine." In all of these final additions and deletions, then, we can discern the form of Byron's intentions toward his poem. In the end, *Childe Harold's Pilgrimage I–II* became the first part of Byron's epic chronicle of his own moral development.

[36] See Charles DuBos' fascinating study of this aspect of Byron in his *Byron et le besoin de la fatalité* (Paris, 1929).

Premature and
Mystic Communings

When Byron finished his third canto of *Childe Harold's Pilgrimage* early in July, 1816, three manuscripts of the poem existed: the rough first draft, a fair copy of this in his own hand, and Claire Clairmont's final transcript of the poem from which it was eventually published. Byron sent all three manuscripts to England, separately, but the fair copy was apparently lost on the way.[1] In any case, so far as we know it does not exist today. The two remaining manuscripts are preserved in the Murray collection. E. H. Coleridge did not collate them in his edition, and the result has been that the history of the poem's composition has always remained largely a matter of conjecture.

Even without the lost fair copy, however, one can arrive at a fairly precise account of when Byron began and finished his poem, and how it developed in the interim. This is possible because the rough first draft (MS R), which Coleridge suggested was no more than a collection of manuscript "scraps" containing discontinuous stanzas and stanza sequences that were later organized into a coherent form in the fair copy, is in fact not this at all. The group of manuscript leaves bound up together in MS R comprises, on the one hand, a completed first form of the poem written out as an integral sequence, and on the other a complement of additional stanzas that were later added to the poem.

MS R shows that Byron originally wrote Canto III as a poem of 100 stanzas. This rough draft in the Murray collection does not contain all of the original 100 stanzas of the poem, however, but includes only a sequence numbered consecutively 4–96.[2] Received stanza 67, which

[1] P 2: 211–12. In my discussion of Canto III here and in Appendix C, bracketed stanzas refer to the numeration they were given in the rough first draft.

[2] Byron was apparently undecided about the placing of stanza [96] 109 in the original MS, for he renumbered it twice, first to 95 and finally to 94. This last change in its numeration shifted the stanza to its proper relative position in the text (after st. 108). See Appendix C.

112

would have been stanza 66 in this form of the poem (see Appendix C), is not bound up in MS R, nor does it seem to have been preserved anywhere else. Stanzas 1–3 and 115–18 are to be found in the Berg Collection in The New York Public Library. Each is on a single leaf of manuscript. Stanzas 1–3 are so numbered and are headed with the poem's title, while stanzas 115–18—the conclusion of the canto—are numbered 97–100. MS R itself contains a total of 109 stanzas, 17 of which are not included as part of the original 100-stanza poem. All of these 17 are unnumbered in MS R, and are bound together at the end of the portfolio. Some were written as short integral sequences, some as isolated additions. They include the following: stanzas 33; 92–97; 98; 99–104; 110; and 113–14. Stanza 88 was also an addition to the original 100-stanza poem but the rough draft is not in MS R. Like stanza 67, it has apparently been lost.

Claire Clairmont's transcript (MS C) from the missing fair copy contains all of the stanzas in the received text in their proper sequence. This transcript was originally written out as a poem of 111 stanzas, however, and did not include either stanza 33 or the sequence 99–104. These appear not only in rough form in MS R, but also as Byron's fair copy insertions in MS C.[3] As Byron's note on the first leaf of MS C suggests,[4] stanzas 99–104 were added to MS C before stanza 33. The numeration of the manuscript was then corrected to a total of 117 stanzas. Stanza 33 was the last addition to the poem, as the second and final adjustment of the numeration in MS C shows.

Thus, the third canto passed through three distinct constitutions before it reached its present form. It was originally written as a unit of 100 stanzas. Byron added 11 more stanzas to this poem (88; 92–97; 98; 110; and 113–14), made his own fair copy of the canto which included the new stanzas, and then had Claire Clairmont make a second fair copy of the 111-stanza work. Finally, Byron added 7 more stanzas to MS C (33 and 99–104) and thus brought the completed poem to its present total of 118 stanzas. As in the case of Cantos I–II these revisions made in Canto III had a substantial effect upon its structure and meaning. Indeed, the added stanzas all but reversed the canto's original direction. Since the detailed evidence for dating these additions is irrelevant to

---

[3] Stanza 105 also appears in MS C in Byron's hand, as Coleridge noted (*P* 2: 214). But if the MS is examined carefully one can see that this stanza was also part of Claire Clairmont's original transcription. When adding stanzas 99–104 to MS C Byron pasted one of the leaves containing the inserted stanzas over stanza 105 (originally numbered 98). He then copied the stanza at the end of the inserted sequence. See Appendix C.

[4] *P* 2: 214.

the following critical discussion, I have collected it all in Appendix C, which the reader can consult at will.

Canto III opens with a dramatic presentation of the poet's immediate sense of spiritual desolation. The springs of his life have been poisoned and he finds himself plunged into a kind of death-in-life in which he can find neither love, nor hope, nor meaning. His immediate desire for forgetfulness is allied to his more fundamental need to recover both inner peace and a sense of his own vitality. To these ends he strives to recreate himself according to the longings of his highest imaginations.

> 'Tis to create, and in creating live
> A being more intense that we endow
> With form our fancy, gaining as we give
> The life we image, even as I do now—
> What am I? Nothing: but not so art thou,
> Soul of my thought! with whom I traverse earth,
> Invisible but gazing, as I glow
> Mixed with thy spirit, blended with thy birth,
> And feeling still with thee in my crushed feelings' dearth.   (6)

Byron's desire is to give to his poem, and thereby gain himself, an imaginative life that is at once vital in all respects, yet is not subject to the destructive and self-lacerating tendencies exemplified in Napoleon and Rousseau (tendencies to which he knows himself to be strongly prone). His attempt is carried out in terms of a pervasive series of soaring and mounting images, and in particular of the image of the Alpine summit. Toward this he constantly moves as toward a goal that will bring complete fulfillment of his desire to be free of "what [he] hates in this degraded form" (III, 74) and of his longing to identify with the godlike "powers of air" (109) which seem to dwell in the Alpine regions. The young poet who wrote "Lachin Y. Gair" and "A Fragment" is not very far away from the pilgrim poet of this canto (at least as he presents himself in its earliest form). When Byron finished the 100-stanza poem in early June, he had carried out a fine exercise in imagistic development —though not so fine as it was soon to become with the additions. Images associated with ascents to and perceptions from mountain tops recur through the canto (see for example stanzas 11, 14, 42, 45, 62, 67, 88, 91, 100, 103, 109–10), and are intimately connected with another large group of "soaring," "growing," and "expanding" images not necessarily associated with mountains (stanzas 60–61, 72–73, 83, 90, 96). The key stanzas in this mountain image cluster are 14, 45, 62, and 109, all of which were part of the original 100-stanza poem.

In them we can see the skeleton of the canto's structure. The first three describe the poet's frustrated yearning toward "The Palaces of Nature"—mountains atop which he expects, like the legendary "Chaldean," to penetrate to the heart of the mysteries of Life, indeed, to become himself absorbed into this exalted and powerful Life-energy. In them is symbolized "All that expands the spirit," but his sense of his own littleness and insufficiency ("vain man") forces him also to admit that his "aspirations to be great" (88) are "appalled" by the enormity of the venture (not to speak of the difficulties attendant upon such a quest, stanza 45). Stanza 109 is the statement of the poet's achievement; its last five lines echo stanza 62 where the poet saw that "Earth may pierce to Heaven" but felt man incapable of a similar venture.

But in its first form the canto did not extrapolate as well as it might have done the process by which stanza 109 became poetically possible. The stanzas that were intended to do this were [84–95], which correspond to the following sequence in the received text: stanzas 85–87, 89–91, 105–8, 111–12. Stanza [96] 109 then followed, and the canto closed with the stanzas to Ada ([97–100] 115–18). Stanzas 89–91 describe the growth in the poet of "the feeling infinite" (90), which eventually leads him to associate himself with his Chaldean image of stanza 14 ("the early Persian," 91), and thus puts him in a position where an equality with the sublime Alpine powers seems finally possible. Further, the "Titan-like" examples of Voltaire and Gibbon, who took up residence in the region of Geneva and seemed participants in its "mountain-majesty of Worth" (67), encourage the poet to "bend" his own steps "To their most great and growing region, where/The earth to her embrace compels the powers of air." But in the original sequence so much emphasis is placed upon the transcendental leap of the soul above its contingent existence that the poem is left with only a tenuous statement of the importance of the "earth" in this cosmic wedding of Nature and Supernature. One of Byron's earliest additions to the poem, stanza 88, indicates his sense of this inadequacy in the poetic assertion. The poet apologizes for disregarding the fact of his mortality in his attempt to merge completely with another order of being altogether. Moreover, the first form of the poem did not elucidate adequately why the Alps are a "growing" region, nor did they illustrate the idea of a cosmic "embrace" between the natural and the transcendental orders.

These poetic inadequacies were later done away with when Byron wrote stanzas 97–104 for his poem during his trip with Shelley around

Lake Geneva. The stanzas hark back to the theme of Nature's "coming ripeness" (61) which was adumbrated in the Rhine Valley sequence, and they apotheosize the ideas of love-harmony and self-creativity in the order of Nature itself. Clarens is "the ground where early love his Psyche's zone unbound" (104), and the entire region participates in the power of Love's "tender mystery" (103). In these late stanzas Byron picks up the theme of natural fecundity from his Rhine experience and grafts it to his receptive capacity for "love and reverence" (88) lately perfected in the still evening of Lake Leman. From this fusion he produces at Clarens the ancient image not of passive but of active and recreating "Love." The passage emphasizes throughout the "Undying" (100) quality of the landscape. It is a sacred place, "full of life" (102), and represents the radically generative powers of the naturalized god. Byron asserts that it is every man's duty to learn the meaning of such burgeoning growth: "For 't is his nature to advance or die;/He stands not still, but or decays or grows/Into a boundless blessing" (103). Byron had called the Alps the "Palaces of Nature" in the opening stanza of the Switzerland sequence, but it is not until this moment in the poem that he is able to envision an appropriate monarch for those splendid halls. "Undying Love" embodies a perfection of passive strength and active power, and the natural scene does homage to it: "here the Rhone/Hath spread himself a couch, the Alps have reared a throne" (104). The region's natural elements offer to Byron's mythopoeic sovereign a couch on which to take his ease and a throne from which he can rule the universe—the regal emblems of fruition and authority.

Another and more serious deficiency in the original form of the canto becomes manifest if we examine the stanzas to the poet's daughter with which it is framed (1 and 115–18). The poem opens with a graphic representation of the poet's "crushed feelings" (6) and inner disquiet, a condition which he explicitly relates to his enforced separation from his beloved daughter. "Forgetfulness" and a release from "selfish grief or gladness" (4) are his immediate objects. He hopes to gain these ends by becoming a "being more intense," but also less "o'erwrought" and distracted (6–7). Thus, when in stanza 109 he "gains" his participation in the imaginative "life" which he set out to achieve, the aesthetic of the canto seems to demand a resolution of the emotional problem with which it began. In stanzas 115–18 he tries to act as if a resolution had in fact been achieved, as if the goal sought had been won. His final address to his daughter is an attempt to pass on to his child "born in bitterness, and nurtured in convulsion" (118) the wisdom he has acquired with only great pain and difficulty:

Albeit my brow thou never should'st behold,
My voice shall with thy future visions blend,
And reach into thy heart,—when mine is cold,—
A token and a tone, even from thy father's mould.

To aid thy mind's development,—to watch
Thy dawn of little joys,—to sit and see
Almost thy very growth,—to view thee catch
Knowledge of objects,—wonders yet to thee!
To hold thee lightly on a gentle knee,
And print on thy soft cheek a parent's kiss,—
This, it should seem, was not reserved for me—
Yet this was in my nature:—as it is,
I know not what is there, yet something like to this.   (115–16)

Except for the difference in particular circumstances, the whole thing is the conclusion of "Tintern Abbey" all over again—with the same sense of pathos in the poet's voice that he would like to conceal behind a show of quiet self-assurance. Wordsworth's conclusion is even more deeply and beautifully pathetic than Byron's, however, just because he tries harder to appear untroubled. Byron's mournful anxiety breaks through his assumed mask fairly quickly. Still, his effort to advise his daughter with his own sage counsel is a fine piece of dramatic pathos, for the more he speaks the more evident becomes his own desperate sense of instability, loneliness, and loss. As soon as he mentions "thy mind's development" he begins to lose touch with his role of wise counselor, and he lapses into a deeply affecting fantasy portrayal through which he is momentarily able to imagine himself with her as she grows up. He in fact believed he would never see her again. His poetic dream-wish breaks off after six lines, as if he were suddenly forced to acknowledge the futility of his own verbal imaginings: "This, it should seem, was not reserved for me." The admission leaves him nearly defenseless against his feelings of bitterness and resentment. Stanza 117, which if read by itself would seem mediocre at best, is in fact a fine example of lyrical dramatization. The stylistic restraint belies the poet's underlying sense of misery which, nevertheless, breaks through quite clearly in the manic metaphor of the last four lines.

But the other most important additions to the canto transform these lines from a structural liability to a distinct poetic asset. When Byron departed on his tour of Lake Geneva with Shelley he left his own fair copy of the poem in Claire Clairmont's hands for transcribing. It numbered 111 stanzas, and included stanzas 88, 92–98, and 110 as additions to the first form of the work.[5] Stanza 110 had been written in late May, but Byron had not been able to find a place for it in the canto's first form. In a sense, the process of incorporating this crucial stanza into the poem involved Byron in the resolution of the structural problem of the conclusion. Shortly after he sent the canto back to England with Shelley for publication he went on a tour of the Bernese Alps with Hobhouse. He kept a journal of this tour, and one of the entries illuminates the sense of disquiet that still rankled within him as a result of the "recent and more home desolation" which he experienced at the separation, and which was the occasion ("real" and poetic alike) of the writing of Canto III.

> I am a lover of Nature and an admirer of Beauty. I can bear fatigue and welcome privation, and have seen some of the noblest views in the world. But in all this—the recollections of bitterness, and more especially of recent and more home desolation, which must accompany me through life, have preyed upon me here; and neither the music of the Shepherd, the crashing of the Avalanche, nor the torrent, the mountain, the Glacier, the Forest, nor the Cloud, have for one moment lightened the weight upon my heart, nor enabled me to lose my own wretched identity in the majesty and the power, and the Glory, around, above, and beneath me.
>
> I am past reproaches; and there is a time for all things. I am past the wish of vengeance, and I know of none like for what I have suffered; but the hour will come, when what I feel must be felt, and the—but enough.[6]

The fact that the weight upon his heart was not lightened by his Swiss adventures is effectively dramatized in the stanzas to his daughter at the end of the canto, as we have seen. But this persistence of his emotional disequilibrium is poetically inexplicable in the first form of the poem. The poet struggles to gain a participation in a higher and more intense order of life, and sets out his imaginative achievement in stanza 109; but the achievement seems all for nought since his emotional condition remains relatively unchanged at the end. The problem is not that he has been unable to resolve his psychological unrest, but that the poem fails to indicate any relationship between the apparent success of the "imaginative" quest (for an identity with the Alp image) and the failure of the emotional quest (for a release from his malaise). The two are

[5] These stanzas were respectively numbered 87, 91–97, and 103 in the intermediate version of 111 stanzas.
[6] *LJ* 3: 364–65.

related as goals at the beginning of the canto (sts. 4–6), and this relationship is later emphasized repeatedly in the body of the work. But the conclusion of the poem in its first form ignores the original relationship; worse, the climax of the original 100-stanza version (at sts. [84–96] 85–91, 105–9, 111–12) positively suggests that a pacific state of being has been reached. In stanza [84] 85 he declares:

> Clear, placid Leman! thy contrasted lake,
> With the wild world I dwelt in, is a thing
> Which warns me, with its stillness, to forsake
> Earth's troubled waters for a purer spring.
> This quiet sail is as a noiseless wing
> To waft me from distraction; once I loved
> Torn Ocean's roar, but thy soft murmuring
> Sounds sweet as if a Sister's voice reproved,
> That I with stern delights should e'er have been so moved.

And in stanza [88] 90 he suggests that he has attained this longed-for stillness:

> Then stirs the feeling infinite, so felt
> In solitude, where we are *least* alone;
> A truth, which through our being then doth melt
> And purifies from self. . . .

Unqualified by any other statements, this declaration contradicts not only the sentiments set forth in stanzas [97–100] 115–18, which Byron was soon to compose, but also his later prose statement that he was unable to lose his sense of his "own wretched identity" in his Swiss environment.

The storm sequence (sts. 92–98) was one of Byron's first additions, and its most evident result is to remind us of the poet's persisting sense of inquietude. The storm attracts him for two reasons. The explosive force of its lightnings reminds him of his inability to wipe out the sense of "desolation" which he carries about within himself, and which continues to torment and poison his soul. He longs to "wreak [his] thoughts upon expression" and with "*one* word" of lightning to "embody and unbosom" all his turbulent sorrows and resentments. The longing remains unsatisfied. But the "fierce and far delight" of the storm not only reawakens his latent disquiet, it reanimates his questing impulsions by exposing the "wondrous" and "joyous" aspects of the storm's tempestuous vigor. "Thou wert not sent for slumber," he says, and recognizes that the "departing voices" of the "sleepless" storm call out to the pilgrim spirit in himself, and contravene the reproving "Sister's voice" of stanza 85. The storm thus turns him back to a renewed search for some "goal" that will satisfy the eagle and the tempest spirits within him. The "feeling infinite" which had stirred within him (90) in the stillness before the storm becomes, in the later versions of the canto, only a kind of necessary prelude to further movement. "All is concentrated in a life intense" (89), but this still intensity is not an end in itself, a goal, a fulfillment of self. Thus, if the poet is left at the end of the night storm with a sense of his own incompletion, the event also serves to open him to fresh impulses for renewal. In stanza 98 he can "resume/The march of [his] existence" in an atmosphere of hope that is a reflection of Nature's rejuvenation around him. The storm sequence, then, has two important effects: first, it forshadows the psychological instability of the poet set forth at the end of the canto; second, it raises the question of whether pilgrims can ever find complete rest or conclusive self-realization ("But where of ye, O Tempests! is the goal?"). In Canto IV the poet tells us explicitly that they cannot, but in Canto III he leaves the question unanswered. Nevertheless, through the addition of these stanzas Byron manages to stabilize the conclusion of his poem by changing the meaning of the Alpine image-hunt which had earlier culminated in stanza [96] 109. When Byron added stanzas 92–98 to the canto, he also added the previously written, but unplaced, stanza 110.

> Italia too! Italia! looking on thee,
> Full flashes on the Soul the light of ages,
> Since the fierce Carthaginian almost won thee,
> To the last halo of the Chiefs and Sages
> Who glorify thy consecrated pages:
> Thou wert the throne and grave of empires; still,
> The fount at which the panting Mind assuages
> Her thirst of knowledge, quaffing there her fill,
> Flows from the eternal source of Rome's imperial hill.

The passage changes the meaning of stanza 109 in precisely the same way that the storm sequence changes the meaning of stanzas 89–91. Instead of representing the achievement of a perfected imaginative state of being, the ascent to the summit of the Alps becomes for the poet a prospect of further pilgrimage, and offers the hope of the eventual discovery of a "fount" that will completely satisfy the longings of his pilgrim's heart. In Canto IV Italy does indeed fulfill his expectations, but though she pacifies at last the emotional turmoil in his soul, and though she shows him the way to perfect his own urgent spirit, the means she offers provide no rest from the task of constant self-discovery and self-recreation, nor any promise that suffering and struggle are at an end. A Keatsian parallel suggests itself. Keats would have a life of sensations rather than a life of thought, and Byron holds to a similar view: "the great object of life is sensation—to feel that we exist, even though in pain."[7] I cannot but think that Byron's observation—which explicitly faces an ugly reality that Keats's does not—strikes to a tragic center of meaning which Keats's more famous remark does not reach.

[7] *Ibid.*, p. 400.

Into Something Rich
and Strange:

THE DEVELOPMENT OF CANTO IV

Analyzing the psychology of Byron's act of composition, Paul West
has suggested that we must

> revise our idea of what composition meant to Byron, as distinct
> from what it meant to, say, Keats and Baudelaire. Byron's correc-
> tions are often as hasty as what he first sets down; but *trouvailles*
> are frequent, and he seems to have to put down *anything* in order
> to pull them down out of the air. He expects something to turn
> up . . . keep writing, for the very act will bring out something
> eventually.[1]

For the most part, Mr. West confines himself to a study of short passages, but his remarks are equally pertinent to Byron's approach to the
structuring of poems on a large scale. The method of revising the first
three cantos of *Childe Harold's Pilgrimage* illustrates this very well.
Contrary to what Mr. West implies, however, Byron does seem always to have begun writing a poem with a fairly precise idea of what he
wanted to say. But the completion of the work in its first form also
seems to have had the effect of clarifying the substantive issues and
artistic problems for him, enabling him finally to formulate an aesthetic
unit whose total form and meaning he did not fully comprehend at first
(though in every instance the eventual product can be seen to be implied in certain undeveloped images and ideas that existed in the original
form of the poem). In the case of Cantos I–II this "clarification" had to
wait upon chance events, for Byron was (understandably) reluctant to
adopt so conclusively the role of the woebegone pilgrim. Circumstances ultimately made him, like Wagner's Siegmund, declare of himself:

[1] Paul West, "Byron and the World of Things: An Ingenious Disregard," *KSMB* 11
(1960): 25.

122

d'rum musst' ich mich Wehwalt nennen;
des Wehes waltet ich nur.

Nevertheless, the original form of Cantos I–II inclined toward such an eventuality, so that the later additions resulted in a work that was structurally well wrought. The revisions to Canto III, on the other hand, seem to have been called forth by the incompletely realized work itself, by Byron's own immediate awareness that he had not really said all that he wanted to say. The development of Canto IV manifests this same kind of growth in and through the act of composition.

Although most critics agree that the final canto of the poem is its greatest, a good many regard it as a poorly organized unit, a fault which is usually attributed to Byron's carelessness in the matter of revisions. William Calvert states the textual basis of the argument when he says that "passages are added almost at random"[2] by Byron after the completion of the poem's first form. The sixty additional stanzas (or nearly one-third of the poem in its received form), though frequently allowed to possess high individual merit, are generally regarded as encrustations which would never have troubled the formal organization of the canto were it not for Byron's misplaced esteem for his friend John Cam Hobhouse. The source of this view is to be found in E. H. Coleridge's Introduction to Canto IV in his edition of the poetry. "As it stood" in the first draft, Coleridge argued, the canto

> was complete, and, as a poem, it lost as well as gained by the insertion of additional stanzas and groups of stanzas, "purple patch" on "purple patch," each by itself so attractive and so splendid.

Calvert's statement that "passages are added almost at random" catches exactly the tone of Coleridge's "Byron had no sooner completed 'this fourth and ultimate canto,' than he began to throw off additional stanzas." The good-hearted but dully pedantic Hobhouse is the culprit in the affair: "The first draft was Byron's unaided composition, but the 'additional stanzas' were largely due to Hobhouse's suggestions during the course of conversation, if not to his written 'researches'."[3]

Not all the new stanzas for the poem were made at Hobhouse's suggestion, however. Further, the number of "Hobhouse additions" was not likely to have included many more than one-third of the total num-

[2] *Calvert*, p. 144.
[3] See *P* 2:311–15. For a detailed discussion of these and other textual matters see Appendix D, where I have collected my evidence for dating the composition of the canto.

ber of additions. But however many subjects were on Hobhouse's "list," or however many stanzas have their origin in that list, is of relatively small consequence as far as the ultimate artistic question is concerned; for when we examine Byron's additions to his poem we find not a series of random or haphazard insertions, but a sequence of stanzas that are, for the most part, worked into the existing form of the poem with evident purpose.

A fairly large number of the new stanzas appear to be simple accretions—stanzas which serve the poem primarily in some local way (usually by expanding upon immediate themes and images). In this group I would include the following stanzas: 2, 12–14, 40, 41, 85–86, 109, 131–32, 152, 173–74, 177–78, 181, and 182. To call them "accretive," however, does not necessarily imply that they are more or less irrelevant. As I shall try to show in a moment, for example, stanzas 173–74, 177–78, and 182 are all important additions to the poem's conclusion: without them its meaning would be much less sharply defined. But not all of these accretions are entirely satisfactory. The poem could well do without stanza 40, for example, which is as irrelevant to the context as it is undistinguished for its poetry. On the other hand, stanza 152 illustrates very well how Byron set about incorporating one of Hobhouse's probable subjects into the fabric of his poem. The stanza serves as a needed pause and transition in the poem by providing a single point of contrast both for the coming stanzas on St. Peter's and for the concluding stanzas on the *Caritas Romana*. The ugly bulk of Hadrian's mole represents selfish and mean pride, contrasting on the one hand with the gigantic and justly proud strength of St. Peter's ("Christ's mighty shrine above his martyr's tomb," 153), and on the other with the triumphant selflessness and self-effacement represented by the *Caritas Romana*.

Stanzas 173–74 were also probably added at Hobhouse's suggestion, and their function in the poem is likewise transitional. In this case, however, Byron seems to be trying to recall for us—just before the final section of his poem—the most basic thematic problems with which he had to deal in the last canto.

> Lo, Nemi! navelled in the woody hills
> So far, that the uprooting Wind which tears
> The oak from his foundation, and which spills
> The Ocean o'er its boundary, and bears
> Its foam against the skies, reluctant spares
> The oval mirror of thy glassy lake;

And calm as cherished hate, its surface wears
A deep cold settled aspect nought can shake,
All coiled into itself and round, as sleeps the snake.

And near, Albano's scarce divided waves
Shine from a sister valley;—and afar
The Tiber winds, and the broad Ocean laves
The Latian coast where sprung the Epic war,
"Arms and the Man," whose re-ascending star
Rose o'er an empire:—but beneath thy right
Tully reposed from Rome;—and where yon bar
Of girdling mountains intercepts the sight
The Sabine farm was tilled, the weary Bard's delight.

On the one hand, stanza 173 is a retrospect of the poet's difficult passage through the final canto. In stanza 106 he had welcomed a perilous life on the storm-lashed ocean, just as he had chosen toward the end of Canto III to forsake the "stillness" of "Clear, placid Leman" (III, 85) in order to follow the call of the "far . . . departing" tempests which dwell in the high Alps (III, 96). On the other hand, the crater of the Lago di Nemi recalls the attitude of implacable hatred which the poet attributed to his English "destroyers," and which he himself sought to keep free of. "Calm as cherished hate," the canceled reading of this phrase "calm as speechless hate," and the simile of the coiled snake, all seem fairly obvious references to the forgiveness-curse sequence where the poet finally brings this basic but often sublimated problem into the open in order to vindicate himself, and all men through him. There he cries out against "the subtler venom of the reptile crew" who have learned "to lie with silence" and deal out their viciousness in "speechless obloquy" (136). "A deep cold settled aspect" refers generally to the "hearts all rocky now" (137), but probably has a specific reference to Byron's wife who, he felt, taught herself lessons in indifference that there might be no reconcilement.[4]

In stanza 174 the poet turns away from all this toward the Mediterranean. The scene inevitably recalls the conclusion of Canto III where he also had a mountaintop vision into the future. Now from Monte Cavo

---

[4] It is perhaps gratuitous to mention that the serpent image here is meant to recall Byron's famous description of the Apollo Belvidere in the act of killing the Python. For Byron's feelings about Lady Byron's "obstinacy" and "sternness" see, for example, his letter to Augusta of October 1820: *BSP* 2:528–30. In 1817 he accused her of trying to "sanction the most infamous calumnies by silence" (quoted by Marchand in *Biography* 2:706). He told Moore in 1819 that he felt there was a "fixed hostility" toward himself in England (*Moore* 2:259–60).

he gets a Wordsworthian "vast prospect of the world": in the "Epic war" sung by Virgil is epitomized the life of the heroic pilgrim, whose days are consumed in a continuous struggle to fulfill a sublime destiny; while the rural retreats of Cicero and Horace—who spent most of their lives combatting the political and moral enemies of Rome—seem to represent an ideal of psychological equilibrium (conceived here in a decidedly eighteenth-century way) which the poet of *Childe Harold's Pilgrimage* has been constantly in pursuit of. The mention of Horace recalls the poet's earlier mournful farewell to him (77). At that time he felt he would never attain the calm but strong assurance of the great Augustan. This second encounter with Horace is unexpected (see IV, 74–77), and not without its significance, for it suggests that the poet has adopted something of Horace's mode to himself. Byron betrays no sense of instability or distraction in his verse. On the contrary, the tone remains controlled and self-assured throughout the conclusion. Stanza 174, then, intimates his achievement of everything he has sought for; the promise of the means of heroic self-fulfillment, and the possession of that inner peace and reconcilement which Horace and the stoical Cicero taught.

It is because the poem involves a number of complex interrelationships that we can often look through the accretive stanzas in this way to the larger issues and movements of thought. An isolated addition like stanza 41, for example, has its place in the continuous theme of man's unconquerable mind.

> The lightning rent from Ariosto's bust
> The iron crown of laurel's mimicked leaves;
> Nor was the ominous element unjust,
> For the true laurel-wreath which Glory weaves
> Is of the tree no bolt of thunder cleaves,
> And the false semblance but disgraced his brow;
> Yet still, if fondly Superstition grieves,
> Know, that the lightning sanctifies below
> Whate'er it strikes;—yon head is doubly sacred now.

The passage anticipates stanzas like 127 and 137 where he apotheosizes the mind which, "Though . . . chain'd and tortured—cabin'd, cribb'd, confined" (127), yet remains indomitably triumphant. It also looks back to earlier passages—the disquisition on Tasso, for example (36–39), whose "insulted" but unquelled mind (36) establishes its preeminence over all oppression and oppressors:

He! with a glory round his furrowed brow,
Which emanated then, and dazzles now,
In face of all his foes. . . .   (38)

Stanza 41 seems to have been especially intended to recall this passage
and stanza 24. In the latter, the "lightning of the mind" is described as
having left behind a "blight and blackening" in the suffering and tortured soul. The lines on Ariosto's bust reinterpret this gloomy observation by pointing out that afflictions of this sort are the sign of heaven's
favor, and that the "true laurel-wreath" of poetic achievement is, like
the "glory" around Tasso's head, something which derives not from
men and human institutions, but from the poet's own inherent worth
and force, which is itself a portion of the divine source of all such power
(see stanza 163).

Stanza 2 was probably added fairly late—when Byron was going
through the whole of the poem in December, 1817, making his final
series of additions. Thus, from the simplest point of view, the stanza
seems simply an expansion of the crowned goddess or queen image
which was applied to Venice in stanzas 1 and 11 of the original poem.
But because the stanza offers a picture of Venice as a kind of dream-
fantasy, it touches upon a number of important themes in the canto.

> She looks a sea Cybele, fresh from Ocean,
> Rising with her tiara of proud towers
> At airy distance, with majestic motion,
> A Ruler of the waters and their powers:
> And such she was;—her daughters had their dowers
> From spoils of nations, and the exhaustless East
> Poured in her lap all gems in sparkling showers.
> In purple was she robed, and of her feast
> Monarchs partook, and deemed their dignity increased.

In stanza 18 he says of Venice that he had "loved her from my boyhood
—she to me/Was as a fairy city of the heart." Stanza 2 is a portrayal of
that fairy vision, perhaps the most graphic in the whole section on Venice. Looked at from the point of view of the speaking poet, the stanza
also represents that action of the poet's imagination which he discusses
for us in stanzas 5–7 (compare also III, 5–7):

> The Beings of the Mind are not of clay:
> Essentially immortal, they create
> And multiply in us a brighter ray
> And more beloved existence. . . .

> Such is the refuge of our youth and age. . . .
> Yet there are things whose strong reality
> Outshines our fairy-land; in shape and hues
> More beautiful than our fantastic sky. . . .   (IV, 5–6)

He pronounces such "over-weening phantasies unsound" and looks now to "other voices" and "other sights"—the "strong reality" of the immediate present in all its aspects (7). This decision leads in turn to the main action of the poem: the meditation "amongst decay" by a "ruined" and desolated poet (25). The notion that the visionary ideals of the imagination are "over-weening" is picked up frequently in the later portions of the canto, most memorably in some of the additions. Stanzas 120–24, which were incorporated into the poem fairly early, echo the motifs of youthful imagination, "mortal bondage" (5), and decay.

> Of its own beauty is the mind diseased,
> And fevers into false creation:—where,
> Where are the forms the sculptor's soul hath seized?
> In him alone. Can Nature show so fair?
> Where are the charms and virtues which we dare
> Conceive in boyhood and pursue as men,
> The unreached Paradise of our despair,
> Which o'er-informs the pencil and the pen,
> And overpowers the page where it would bloom again.   (122)

At about the time that Byron added stanza 2, however, he also inserted stanzas 125–27, thus completing the sequence 120–27 which just precedes the forgiveness-curse stanzas and the celebration at St. Peter's. Stanza 127 qualifies the despair of the preceding stanzas by suggesting that the "Faculty divine," which is "bred in darkness," may eventually break through to the light toward which it mounts. The stanza is a prophecy of the poem's climactic movement.

Also added at this time were stanzas 51–52, which complete the famous sequence on the Venus de Medici. "The forms the sculptor's soul hath seized" and "the mind's Ideal shape" of "Worth" and "Beauty" (122–23) seem an "unreached Paradise" in his moments of despair. But deep buried within him is the persistent belief in his imaginative powers:

>   still teems
> My mind with many a form which aptly seems
> Such as I sought for, and at moments found. . . .   (7)

He distrusts these powers at the beginning of the canto, and his reluctance appears periodically later in the poem; but so do his ungovernable imaginative impulses. At Santa Croce, though "the weight of earth recoils upon" him (52) after his visionary flight, he can "let it go" without fear:

> We can recall such visions, and create,
> From what has been, or might be, things which grow
> Into thy statue's form, and look like gods below.   (52)

Despite later moments of fear and hopelessness, this conviction is permanently established at St. Peter's and the Vatican Gallery. At Santa Croce he perceives that

> The Gods become as mortals—and man's fate
> Has moments like their brightest. . . .   (52)

This initial act of imaginative comprehension is set forth in one of the most important small additions to the canto (sts. 51–52). The perception here is later expanded into a comprehensive vision of man's conclusive recreative powers. At St. Peter's he sees that human "hopes of Immortality" (155) are not delusive. Growing with the growth of their highest conceptions, men's "Spirits" expand "to the size of that they contemplate" (158). The imaginative ideals of youthful innocence thereby become realizable in the treacherous world of experience. It does not matter whether men triumph over their natural conditions or are defeated by them: they become as gods merely by their heroic gestures. The action of the artist reveals this permanent truth by imaging the sublime and "Ideal" forms which represent men's passionate efforts not simply to endure, but to prevail. "Each Conception" of the mind that is "maddened" in its visions of greatness is "a heavenly Guest,/A ray of Immortality" (162), and all together (i.e., *Childe Harold's Pilgrimage*) constitute a unified representation of everything that is godlike in men (for, in this reading, the gods too "become as mortals," st. 52). Apollo is the ultimate symbol of this divinity that shapes our ends, but Laocoön is a "ray of Immortality" as well.

Stanza 2 is swept up into this pervasive and basic movement of thought in the last canto. But the theme of the recreative power of art is approached in a variety of ways, not the least of which is political. If we were to dwell on the political implications of Venice and her situation as they are presented in the poem we would also see how the more purely "aesthetic" aspects of the theme of regeneration are related to social conditions. Italy is represented as the fountainhead of all Western culture, and her "ruin" becomes the symbol of a universal decay. In his poem he will "track/Fall'n states and buried greatness" (25) and attempt to find a means of reversing the deathward plunge of his civilization. A large group of Byron's additions illustrate his efforts to represent art and the artist as the spearheads of this movement toward *risorgimento*. Stanzas 16–17, 80–82, and 54–55 are prominent examples. Stanza 16 alludes to a tale out of Plutarch which relates how certain Athenian prisoners gained the love of their captors by singing excerpts from Euripides. "Redemption rose up in the Attic Muse," he says, and he wonders why Venice's "love of Tasso" (see st. 3) has not softened the hearts of her foreign rulers (17). In this case Byron seems to have overreached himself for an illustration of the theme of redemption through art; only word-music, and word-magic, not mere assertion, could identify singing gondoliers with Athenian prisoners of war. Stanzas 80–82 are woven into the canto much more smoothly, but only because they continue the theme of Rome as a "Chaos of ruins" (81) in a most eloquent way. Stanza 82 introduces the idea that "Tully's voice, and Virgil's lay, and Livy's pictured page . . . shall be [Rome's] resurrection," but once again the assertion is relatively weak as far as the overall movement of the poem is concerned, for it is not at all clear from the context in what sense this would be true.

The addition of stanzas 54–55 is quite another matter. Michelangelo, Alfieri, Galileo, and Machiavelli are instanced as

> four minds, which, like the elements,
> Might furnish forth creation:—Italy!
> Time, which hath wronged thee with ten thousand rents
> Of thine imperial garment, shall deny
> And hath denied, to every other sky,
> Spirits which soar from ruin:—thy Decay
> Is still impregnate with divinity,
> Which gilds it with revivifying ray;
> Such as thy great of yore, Canova is to-day.   (55)

The stanza is an effective (if not especially brilliant) poetic statement of the recreative power of art because it suggests a relationship between the past and the present, and tells us precisely what the artist's "mind" will do: refurnish and revitalize a decayed and ruined world. In addition, the relationship between the present condition of Italy and the "wronged" poet of *Childe Harold's Pilgrimage* is implied in the stanza, so that the perception of "Spirits which soar from ruin" has a prophetic significance not only for Italy, but for the poet as well. The passage thus achieves a significant generalization out of its particulars, for the redemption of "creation" in this poem is made to depend upon the redemption of the poet himself. Further, the stanza is well placed to follow the Venus de Medici passage, where the theme of "What Mind can make, when Nature's self would fail" (49) is fully represented.

Stanzas like these connect with the reiterated theme of the artist-as-hero which Georg Roppen has done well to emphasize.[5] Dante, Petrarch, Tasso, and a host of other great figures in the pantheon of Italian history are brought forward to emphasize the idea that the visionary artificer, whose "nympholepsy" (115) inclines him to despair over the world, is in reality its unacknowledged legislator, for it is only through his persevering act of imaginative creation that men are able to remain actively conscious of their powers and worth. Rienzi is introduced in a late addition (sts. 112–14) to emphasize just this point. He is represented as "The friend of Petrarch," the arch-idealist in Italian letters in Byron's view (114). Further, he is called a "new-born Numa" not only to provide the poem with a smooth transition to the section on Egeria which follows, but to emphasize as well his visionary powers. The Italian politician ("with reign, alas! too brief") is the "Redeemer of dark centuries of shame" precisely because of the "poetic" quality of his mind and person, a man whom Shelley would have rejoiced to call "poet" in his *Defence of Poetry*. Stanzas 56–60, another addition, argue the same idea from a different angle. Dante, Petrarch, and Boccaccio are presented as the most exalted of Florence's heroes, but each was a prophet rejected by his own country, according to Byron. Instead of honoring such men and the ideals they represented, the Florentines display the gaudy tombs of the Medici, whom the poet scornfully calls "merchant-dukes" (60).

But Italian *risorgimento* and the great artists of Italy's past and present are only mirrors in which we perceive the struggle of the poet of *Childe Harold's Pilgrimage* to offer a general redemptive vision to mankind at large. He turns his poem, and his mythic history recorded therein, over to the reader at the end (186), and at the opening of the canto he specifically declares that his aspiration is to take his place in

[5] Georg Roppen, "Byron's Pilgrimage," in *Strangers and Pilgrims*, by Georg Roppen and Richard Sommer (Oslo, 1964), pp. 209–83.

the Temple of Fame with the greatest figures of Western cultural history (9–10). The story told in the poem is intended to establish the heroic and exemplary value of his individual self.

> I twine
> My Hopes of being remembered in my line
> With my land's language. . . .   (9)

We must not allow ourselves to be put off by the gigantic egoism implicit in such an assertion, for the entire poem demands that we "remember" the I-speaker. Byron himself has seemed many things to many men, and if we choose to believe that he was in reality just an insecure and self-deceiving man who never outgrew his youthful dreams of greatness, this does not affect how we must read the poetry of *Childe Harold's Pilgrimage*. The narrating poet of this work writes of himself in a sublime style, and treats himself in the poem as if he were, despite all his faults and weaknesses, a man who lived and moved in a realm where heroes, and gods, and the indomitable forces of Nature and History were in constant communion. This is not a "reading" of *Childe Harold's Pilgrimage* but a simple fact of its poetic decorum.

Thus, if Tasso, Virgil, Petrarch, and the other great figures of Italian and Roman history alluded to in the poem carry to us the theme of redemption through the exercise of man's highest powers, the narrating poet is the work's most important exemplary figure. The action of his mind, set forth in the story told by the poem, must demonstrate a recreative and redeeming virtue. But passages like 16–17, 82, and 54–55 are mainly expository and reflective in character. Their primary function is to raise the central theme of the poem for us, not to act out its accomplishment as do the stanzas on the Venus de Medici, St. Peter's and the Vatican Gallery, and the Coliseum meditations.

It is for this reason that stanzas 27–29, 47, 93–98, 135–37, and 167–72 are so significant. Stanzas 135–37 are the only addition to the important Coliseum sequence (which I have discussed at length in an earlier chapter). They do not change the meaning of that sequence; even without them the passage had always exposed the death-principle of vengeance and "hereditary rage" (94) just as it had aways culminated in the *Caritas Romana*. But stanzas 135–37 dramatize the initial moment in the poet's conclusive act of rejecting the "eternal thrall" (97) of the death cycle into which men are seduced. In these stanzas we observe him "reversing" the entropic decrees of Nature (151) and turning the evil power of Nemesis against herself to fruitful ends.

Two other late additions, stanzas 47 and 93–98, are placed in the poem to foreshadow this notion of a creative reversal of the lethal powers of nature and history. Stanza 47 declares that the "barbarian tide" which has accomplished the ruination of Italy will soon be "backward driven," and will "sue to be forgiven" for their parricide. In stanza 98 Freedom is represented as a banner streaming "like the thunderstorm *against* the wind"; and, again, like a trumpet blown into a gale which, though it breaks the sound of the horn, inevitably "leaves behind" the "loudest" tones, so that those who stand behind the bugler can hear the call of the trumpet augmented by the very tempest which opposes it. Even more signficant than these specific images of reversals are the contextual functions of stanzas 47 and 98. Each climaxes a sequence (42–47 and 93–98) in which the poet inclines to embrace despair and accept "desolation" and "tyranny" as the inevitable issue of life. The final stanzas of each sequence reverse the movement of his mind toward hopelessness. His desperation and uncertainty recur, however, for it is not until much later in the poem that he becomes fully conscious of the mind's ability to triumph permanently over defeat and death.

This permanent resolution is not realized in terms of ultimate political redemption, however, for although he accedes to a conviction that freedom and rebirth can never be wholly prevented, he does not present this creative movement as one which will purge Nature and History of their destructive rhythms. Famous stanzas like 47 and 98, and other similar passages in the poem, have often led commentators to treat Canto IV as a kind of song before sunrise, particularly for Italy. Byron's own vigorous involvement in the politics of revolution in Italy and later in Greece have tended to corroborate this view. There is, of course, no question but that Byron wanted to secure the political freedom of Italy and Greece, but in Canto IV man's ultimate freedom and capacity for rebirth are not made to depend upon the Italian political issue. The poet says that a "better spring" shall bring forth "less bitter fruit" (98), but this is hardly a statement of political apocalypse. It is, in fact, curious that so notorious a revolutionary poem should be so lacking in visions of a transformed political order in Italy (or anywhere else). The climactic statement of human creative capabilities set forth at St. Peter's and the Vatican Gallery is totally without political references. Rather, it is the dramatization of the act of an individual consciousness. The poet finds himself able to identify with the most exalted conceptions of his own imagination, and this capacity is presented as the endowment of all men.

Two very early additions to the canto underline the form of the poet's thought on the political aspects of the poem. Stanzas 27–29, which conclude the section on Venice, are the description of a sunset as seen from the banks of the Brenta near Venice. After briefly setting the scene, he introduces his key rainbow image:

> Heaven is free
> From clouds, but of all colours seems to be,—
> Melted to one vast Iris of the West,—
> Where the Day joins the past Eternity. . . .   (27)

The remainder of the passage involves the gradual obliteration of the many-colored "hues" of Iris: at the end

> parting Day
> Dies like the Dolphin, whom each pang imbues
> With a new colour as it gasps away—
> The last still loveliest, till—'tis gone—and all is gray.   (29)

The stanzas are a fine summary of the initial view of Italy given in the poem: that she is a glorious waste, a "ruin graced with an immaculate charm" (26). As a traditional symbol of hope and future promise, this "vast Iris of the West" might serve as a portent of Italy's political resurrection. Here, however, because the rainbow fades before the grayness of oncoming night, such an interpretation is not possible. Iris is presented only as an apparition of beauty in a desolate region, a wonderful but fleeting event.[6]

Stanzas 167–72 reintroduce the image of the rainbow near the conclusion of the poem. The Princess Charlotte is symbolically presented as having been made the repository of all men's political hopes. Over the head of this woman "Freedom . . . Beheld her Iris" (169), so that the death of "Her and her hoped-for seed" becomes the poem's final sign that Life has no permanent paradises to offer her pilgrim children. A world in time and space inevitably plunges individual and collective histories into recurrent birth and death cycles, so that men are forced to recreate the values that they cherish. But so long as existence perdures, life and creativity are possible: the simple fact of recurrence offers chances of new sensations, visions, and self-developments. It does

---

[6] Professor Frederick Pottle once pointed out to me that Byron is not really describing a rainbow here but a rainbow effect produced by the reflection of the setting sun off some cloud banks.

not matter if rainbows of promise are effaced, or if "the weight of
earth recoils upon" (52) the poet and cancels his vatic perceptions.
"We can recall such visions" simply by continuing to live, and can
"multiply" (5) them at will if we choose. The capacity for recreation
persists even in the worst of times and circumstances, and men will
always raise up "Spirits which soar from ruin" (55). Even death cannot
induce a metaphysical despair, for at the end of all is perpetual rest
from the "contentious world" (III, 69) against which man must continually struggle if he is to bring forth renewed life. Thus the Princess
Charlotte "sleeps well" (171), freed at last from the fitful fever of life
which, if it makes possible all human glory and creativity,

> And if it be Prometheus stole from Heaven
> The fire which we endure—it was repaid
> By him to whom the energy was given
> Which this poetic marble hath arrayed
> With an eternal Glory—which, if made
> By human hands, is not of human thought...,   (163)

yet also demands that we pay heavily in pain and effort to secure them
("The fire which we *endure*"). The vision of man's extinction in death
is, therefore, as much a triumph as the vision of his splendid powers in
life. As he prepares for the eulogy of the Princess he looks into the
"abyss" of death and exclaims:

> Oh, happier thought! can we be made the same:—
> It is enough in sooth that *once* we bore
> These fardles of the heart—the heart whose sweat was gore. (166)

But the "*once*" is important, crucial, for the peace of death which all
men who have truly lived devoutly implore is only a value because they
have participated in the exalting trials or pilgrimage, in the continuity
of a life whose goal is not at the end, but along the way.

This idea of an unlimited life-flow, a continuum in which Nature
and History unfold themselves in successive birth and death cycles, is
most forcefully presented in the address to Ocean at the poem's conclusion. Stanza 182 is a particularly functional addition to this famous
series of stanzas.

> Thy shores are empires, changed in all save thee—
> Assyria—Greece—Rome—Carthage—what are they?
> Thy waters washed them power while they were free,
> And many a tyrant since; their shores obey

> The stranger, slave, or savage; their decay
> Has dried up realms to deserts:—not so thou,
> Unchangeable save in thy wild waves' play,
> Time writes no wrinkle on thine azure brow—
> Such as Creation's dawn beheld, thou rollest now.

The political manifestations of human bondage and freedom continually rise and fall, but the Ocean herself remains outside this temporal flux and perfectly superior to it. She appears as a kind of infinitely objective consciousness, able to perceive the ebb and flow of human history with self-possessed equanimity. "Unchangeable save in [her] wild waves' play," she participates in a life of unlimited power and creativity:

> Thou glorious mirror, where the Almighty's form
> Glasses itself in tempests; in all time,
> Calm or convulsed—in breeze, or gale, or storm—
> Icing the Pole, or in the torrid clime
> Dark-heaving—boundless, endless, and sublime—
> The image of Eternity—the throne
> Of the Invisible; even from out thy slime
> The monsters of the deep are made—each Zone
> Obeys thee—thou goest forth, dread, fathomless, alone.   (183)

The Ocean becomes, in fact, the poem's crowning image of the daimonic and eternal source of all life and energy, and the poet presents himself to us as the child of this god and the sharer of his powerful creativity.

> And I have loved thee, Ocean! and my joy
> Of youthful sports was on thy breast to be
> Borne, like thy bubbles, onward: from a boy
> I wantoned with thy breakers—they to me
> Were a delight; and if the freshening sea
> Made them a terror—'twas a pleasing fear,
> For I was as it were a Child of thee,
> And trusted to thy billows far and near,
> And laid my hand upon thy mane—as I do here.   (184)

Here at the end of the canto the poet repossesses the world of his youthful imaginations in the poem's predominant image of the world of painful and trying experience. We have already seen that the issue of the function of imagination, announced at the canto's opening and there specifically related to youth and childhood, is pervasive. At first the poet is caught between his longing to retain the lovely "phantasies" of his youth, and his awareness of the "strong reality" of immediacy in its various and disruptive forms. This reality is a tempestuous and dangerous thing, and in the course of the poem tends to overwhelm "the charms and virtues which we dare/Conceive in boyhood and pursue as men,/The unreached Paradise of our despair" (122). This "Paradise" is "unreached" because life seems a dark and mortifying voyage to nowhere. At the conclusion, however, the threatening Ocean is transformed into an image of paradisal and youthful fulfillment, and an ideal of beautiful and vigorous permanence is born out of the poet's most important symbol of reality's transience and incompleteness.

Further, the emphasis upon the recovery of a youthful strength upon the Ocean of passage recalls the entire opening section of the canto, the stanzas on Venice. Byron had loved that fabulous city from his boyhood, and she is graphically presented as the city of the sea. Built upon the water, she lives a precarious existence, but gains an increase in value by this very exotic quality in her life. Indeed, she is a "fairy city" precisely because of her watery world: the shifting reflections of her buildings are as much a part of her reality as the buildings themselves. She is at once dream and reality, art and life, and she gains this magical value because she is a "sea Cybele." At the canto's ending, then, Byron identifies with his "fairy city of the heart" by also undergoing a sea change and committing himself to the Ocean's vast and powerful unknown. He becomes the pilgrim of eternity and experiences a renewal of deep hope because he accepts a home and a life on the waters. The Ocean survives the decay of all human things and is the source of all new growth. The sons and daughters of Ocean will also survive despite all apparent ruin. When, therefore, Byron speaks of Venice as a "ruin graced/With an immaculate charm which cannot be defaced" (26), he prophesies his own ultimate condition. Even when Venice and Byron are annihilated, both will survive in human dreams and imaginations.

Besides being drawn into a participation in the wondrous creativity and strength of the Ocean, the poet shares its extreme aloneness. It is from this principle of absolute self-possession that he is able to draw his own objectivity toward the sequence of events that constitute Life, and his own life in particular. At the end of his pilgrimage he is freed completely from those self-lacerating passions which are the source of his anxiety and his exhaustion alike. His awareness of the blessedness in the immediate moment, and the prospect of an indefinite future of such self-renewing immediacies, affords him now a complete satisfaction in the enforced transience of a contingent world.

> Upon the blue Symplegades: long years—
> Long, though not very many—since have done
> Their work . . . some suffering and some tears
> Have left us nearly where we had begun:
> Yet not in vain our mortal race hath run—
> We have had our reward—and it is here,—
> That we can yet feel gladdened by the Sun,
> And reap from Earth—Sea—joy. . . .   (176)

The last two stanzas which Byron added to his poem reinforce this pagan ideal. Life is not an accomplishment, but a persistence, and "To mingle with" this "Universe" (178) of Life one must submit to the sequence of experience, to a series of "ennobling" and "exalting" (177) cosmic "interviews" (178). Strung out along the indefinite length of an arduous life, such moments illuminate the meaning of pilgrimage for the man engaged upon it. But knowledge is not the end of Byron's journey, and although death is its limit, it is not its purpose. Knowledge is the end of *The Prelude*, but in *Childe Harold's Pilgrimage* the insights are momentary and partial, and they only serve to help the pilgrim along the way. The ultimate purpose of Byron's journey is not cognitive, illuminating, but existential, trying. Thus the poem properly ends with the address to the Ocean, the symbol of that which, though fated, remains ultimately unknown. The promise held out is not apocalypse but that radically equivocal and human thing—glory. The mood is therefore deeply pathetic, not triumphant, yet even Wordsworth in his most sublime moments has not eclipsed the grand conclusion of Byron's poem, with its comprehensive presentation of the greatness and the littleness, the glory and the insignificance of man, his works, and his days.

III

Four Tales

The Gaze of Wonder
and the Desolate Heart

> We were guilty of loving each other. Yes, her death was
> a good thing, for her blood will inspire heroes and I have
> no weakness left in my heart. Nothing at all: no family, no
> wife, no friends, nothing to make my hand falter on the
> day when I have to take other people's lives or give my
> own.   EMIL ZOLA, *Germinal*

After *Childe Harold's Pilgrimage: A Romaunt* was published, and
despite the immense success of that book, Byron's mind turned away
from the autobiographical form. He dabbled a bit in satire but finally
settled down to a long affair with the verse narrative. The first tale he
attempted after returning to England was called *Il diavolo inamorato*.
It was written in Spenserian stanzas—a fact which apparently led E. H.
Coleridge to surmise it was to be a third canto for *Childe Harold's Pilgrimage*[1]—but was shortly abandoned by Byron and left unfinished.
The world has suffered no great loss as a result, though the fragment
does have a certain scholarly interest. In any case, Byron suggests in
his dedicatory Preface to *The Corsair* that he gave up work on *Il diavolo inamorato* because the Spenserian stanza seemed an inappropriate
form for a verse tale. It is "perhaps too slow and dignified for narrative,"
he says, though he confesses it "the measure most after my own heart"
(*P* 3:224). Even the story of Harold had quickly turned into self-
dramatization and subjective meditation, and he seems to have felt the
need of a different metrical form to achieve a faster pace and more
objective narration. *Il diavolo inamorato*, set in Venice, begins with
and never really escapes from authorial digression. Whatever *Il diavolo
inamorato* was intended ultimately to become, the initial stanzas betray
Byron's difficulty in getting himself as poet out of the way long enough
to tell the story that is on his mind.

His next effort was another story, in two senses. When Byron wrote
the first version of *The Giaour* in May–June, 1813, he switched to the
tetrameter couplet (with frequent variations) and cast the poem into a
form that refined Byron the narrator out of existence almost com-

[1] *P* 2:xii-xiii.

pletely. *The Voyage of Columbus* (1812) furnished Byron with the formal idea for his work, and Rogers' Preface to his experimental poem explains Byron's interest in it.

> The following Poem (or, to speak more properly, what remains of it) has here and there a lyrical turn of thought and expression. It is sudden in its transitions, and full of historical allusions; leaving much to be imagined by the reader. . . .

> Many of the incidents will now be thought extravagant; yet they were once perhaps received with something more than indulgence. It was an age of miracles. . . . Such was the religious enthusiasm of the early writers, that the Author had only to transfuse it into verse; and he appears to have done little more; though some of the circumstances, which he alludes to as well-known, have long ceased to be so. By using the language of that day, he has called up Columbus "in his habit as he lived"; and the authorities, such as exist, are carefully given by the translator.[2]

Like Moore in his Preface to the *Poems of the Late Thomas Little, Esq.*, Rogers pretends that he is not the author of the work but its editor and translator. Like the fictitious editor who supplies the glosses to *The Rime of the Ancient Mariner*, the author belongs to a cultural milieu not far removed from that of Columbus himself—perhaps the next generation[3]—and consequently he composes his story of Columbus' voyage from contemporary legends about that famous event. He does not question the veracity of his sources because he believes in the various marvels that were part of the legends he worked from. In addition, Rogers would have us believe that the poem is incomplete, a series of fragments surviving some original MS. By adopting this procedure Rogers is able to compose a poem in which he need not apologize for the machinery, superstitions, and imagery. They are from another day, one perhaps less "enlightened," but one which is for Rogers highly "poetical." Thus he contrives a way of entering completely into the strange continuum of his poem.

The Giaour uses the device of "fragments" to give a similar kind of cultural authenticity to the events of the story. Supposedly based upon the experiences of a Venetian nobleman some time during the late seventeenth century, Byron's story is not nearly so far removed in time

---

[2] *The Poetical Works of Samuel Rogers*, with a Memoir by Edward Bell (London, 1892), p. 54.
[3] *Ibid.*, p. 57.

from contemporary England as is Rogers', though the gap with respect to mores and beliefs is at least as wide. Also, Byron's story, like Rogers', is a translation, this time of a "Romaic [or] Arnaout" ballad which he heard "by accident recited by one of the coffee-house story tellers who abound in the Levant." Its fragmentary state, Byron says, is the result of a failure of memory.[4] (Were his readers to assume, as each new and augmented edition of his "snake of a poem" came out, that he periodically recalled additional snatches of the original lay?) This adaptation of Rogers' idea provided him with a means of keeping his inclination to self-dramatization in check. Characters speak for themselves, "the poet" is an anonymous and itinerant balladeer from a strange and distant country, and Lord Byron is safely tucked away in "the additions and interpolations by the translator" which are "easily distinguished from the rest, by the want of Eastern imagery."[5]

A number of readers seem to prefer the earliest versions of *The Giaour* precisely because Byron did manage to keep himself out of the poem almost completely, but also because—as M. K. Joseph has noted—the tale drives straight to its point without its later meanderings.[6] The first version of the poem ran to 406 lines and the first published edition to only 685. To each subsequent edition, however, Byron kept adding passages until, by the seventh edition, it reached its completed form of 1,334 lines. Karl Kroeber argues that these additions manifest Byron's storytelling genius, but he disapproves ultimately because he thinks the device of the multiple narrator improper for the sequence of "schematically sensational" events on which the story is based. The final state of the tale is "confusion."[7] Out of this apparent confusion, however, Mr. Kroeber distinguishes four divisions in the poem that correspond to the four different narrators he sees: lines 1–179 (the ballad singer); 180–797 (The Turkish fisherman); 798–970 (dialogue between the ballad singer and a monk); 971–1334 (the Giaour's confession).

Mr. Kroeber's divisions are mostly accurate, except that lines 798–970 do not comprise a dialogue between the balladeer and a monk. Strictly speaking, the only dialogue in this section occurs in lines 787–831, between the Moslem fisherman and the monk. Lines 832–82 and 916–70 are monologues addressed to the audience by the ballad singer,

[4] *P* 3:145.
[5] *Ibid.*
[6] *Joseph*, p. 50.
[7] Karl Kroeber, *Romantic Narrative Art.* (Madison, Wis., 1960), pp. 139–40.

while lines 883–915 are a fragment of a speech by the monk, apparently still addressed to the fisherman. These distinctions are important, for they emphasize the peculiar character of multiple narration in Byron's poem. *The Giaour* really has only one narrator, the ballad singer, who assumes different roles at different moments in his performance but who is himself the source of the work's final consistency precisely because he lets us know that he is assuming roles, that the poem is a virtuoso production.

This point is not simplistically reductive, for we must keep in mind the kind of "edition" and "translation" that Byron was offering his public. *The Voyage of Columbus* is a conscious imitation of a literary ballad; Rogers discusses MS problems in his prose notes and even tries to date the work. In any case, his imitation did not come directly out of an oral tradition. *The Giaour*, on the other hand, is Byron's imitation of an oral narrative which, he says, he heard by chance in one of the many coffee-houses he saw in the East.

Whether *The Giaour* was in fact based upon an oral ballad or not is of no consequence at the moment. During the two years he spent in the East it seems certain that he must have heard oral poetry, perhaps fairly often. Placing the origin of the story in "one of those coffee-houses" is a piece of exact information. Such houses, called *kafana*, were—along with the courts of princes like Ali Pasha—the regular places where true oral poets performed their works. Milman Parry and Albert B. Lord tell us that as late as 1930, these places existed in the regions that Byron traversed, and that in them true oral poets could even then be heard performing their works.[8]

The second section of the poem, which Mr. Kroeber ascribes wholly to the Moslem fisherman, illustrates as well as any the type of narration Byron strove to create. But to read this long passage as if it were the dramatized thoughts and words of the fisherman is to invite confusion. Lines 179–99 narrate the fisherman's sight of and emotional response to the Giaour as he rides swiftly away from Hassan's palace, alone. That event is referred to later in the same section. We are told that on the night of the feast of Ramazan—the night that the fisherman saw the Giaour—Leila disappeared from Hassan's palace. "The tale his Nubians tell" (465) is that she ran away to join her lover, the Giaour,

> But others say, that on that night,
> By pale Phingari's trembling light,

[8] See Albert B. Lord, *The Singer of Tales* (Cambridge, Mass., 1960), chaps. 1-2.

The Giaour upon his jet-black steed
Was seen, but seen alone to speed
With bloody spur along the shore,
Nor maid nor page behind him bore.   (467–72)

Now we cannot conceive these lines in the mouth of the fisherman. Rather, they seem some other observer's after-the-fact comments upon the narrated action. They presuppose an event we have already heard of, that the fisherman saw the Giaour riding along the shore alone, and they expect us to associate the "others" with that fisherman.

A further difficulty in ascribing all of lines 180–797 to the fisherman arises when we consider that the passage supplies us with information from a number of different times and places. The fisherman would have to have been present when Hassan left "to woo a bride" (533), when he and his vassals were ambushed by the Giaour and his men, and when the messenger returned to tell Hassan's mother of her son's death. Further, we would be compelled to think him privy to some intimate details of Hassan's youth, as well as familiar with the inside of the palace.

None of these difficulties arise if we think of the story as the performance of one of those storytellers in one of those coffee-houses "that abound in the Levant." What Byron intends us to apprehend in the poem is its narrated quality. The bard sings his tale and avails himself of the privilege of all oral poets from Homer to the present: to assume as many roles as he needs to tell his story, and to enter into the psychology of his characters and present his tale from their point of view. (Thus, if Byron projects himself into a role in this poem it is not so much into the role of the Giaour or some other character as into the role of poet-singer.) Lines 180–797 are not the narrative of the Moslem fisherman but the narrative of the bard who, in this section, consistently presents the events of his tale from a Turkish point of view. In this passage the Giaour is always an object of deep hatred for he is an outsider, a "false Infidel" (747) and sworn enemy of the Moslem subjects of Hassan and of the whole Turkish culture which the poet for the time assumes as his emotional point of view.

The "narrated" or "sung" quality of the poem is further attested by the frequent appearance of stylistic devices that originate in a ballad tradition. The "fisherman's narrative" at lines 180–287 contains a number of rhetorical tricks which suggest that the lines are delivered not by a fisherman but by a man skilled in the art of oral recitation. The passage opens dramatically.

> Who thundering comes on blackest steed,
> With slacken'd bit and hoof of speed?   (180–81)

This present tense narrative is maintained through line 199, and its rhetorical significance is underlined when the shift to the past tense occurs in lines 200–207. What we witness here is either a fisherman who knows the storyteller's tricks for securing dramatic effect or—which seems to me more clearly the case given the strongly self-conscious form of the poem—a bard who has for the moment assumed the role of one of his characters. The narrative-for-effect is unmistakable again in lines 208–33 when the present tense is again employed. The device is ancient but always effective: the narrator pretends an immediacy with respect to some important event and thereby "images" the event for his audience not only in his isolated words, but in his dramatic tone and posture. The passage concludes in a long past-tense narrative (234–87) which evidences a rather sophisticated moral sensibility. While we are not meant to forget that the bard's general point of view here is that of a Turkish fisherman, we are forced to remain aware that this fisherman is really only the outward form, assumed for the moment, of the skillful coffee-house bard. The poem keeps us aware of the drama and the creation of that drama simultaneously.

   The Giaour is not, of course, an accurate imitation of oral poetry, Eastern or otherwise. Its "literary" character is evident throughout, not least in its employment of an intricate rhymed form. Nevertheless, Byron scatters his poem with formulaic techniques proper to oral poetry, and the result is a work that captures rather well the spirit of a true oral narrative. The epithet "stern" is applied to Hassan three times, the Giaour is variously "faithless" (twice), "accursed" (twice), and the word "fair" is used seven times in the poem, always in relation either to Leila (three times) or to the natural landscape. In this case the epithet serves an important symbolic function, for the connection between Leila and the natural scenery is, as we shall see, an important thematic element in the poem. Many other expressions—like "avenging Monkir's scythe"—cannot be tested for their formulaic character, but they distinctly convey a formulaic impression. This is, in fact, all that Byron wants. He presupposes in his English readers a knowledge that ballad-type poetry (like Ossian's) frequently evidences techniques of this sort and he gains his oral effect by general suggestion.

   Similarly, he often uses formulaic techniques picked up from the many English ballads, true and bogus, which were so well known to his readers. Thus, the departure of Hassan from his palace begins:

Stern Hassan hath a journey ta'en
With twenty vassals in his train. . . .   (519–20)

A scholar would find this rather inappropriate in an Eastern tale, for though it suggests a ballad form, the tradition is that of Sir Patrick Spens. The error is not especially important, however, for Byron frequently works by general suggestion. The cumulative effect of his "Eastern imagery" is meant to keep his reader from being too pedantic. At the same time he keeps evoking the spirit of oral narrative in whatever way he can.[9] The poet's own performance thus becomes an important element in the story: we view the narrated events not directly but at second hand, in the bard's absorption in and response to the people and actions of the story. This fact is perhaps most evident in the large number of lines that are taken up by the poet's own meditations upon the events he sings of.

The subject of *The Giaour* is not, however, the psychology of the poet. The poem is neither *Don Juan* nor *Childe Harold's Pilgrimage*. The singer's presence is not personal but poetic, not existential but aesthetic. The tale is animated in his act of self-expression, in his performance. Nevertheless, the bard here does exhibit certain attitudes which makes him something more than what a Marxian would call a "transmission belt." For example, his use of the word "Tartar" when referring to the Turks corresponds to the whole introductory portion of the poem (1–179). Despite his ability to enter fully into the feelings and attitudes of his Turkish characters, he is himself an "infidel." Even the very earliest versions of the poem make this clear. The introductory passage in the MS and the first edition is only eighteen lines long, but its reference to Themistocles ("When shall such hero live again?" 6) suggests his Western cast of thought. The expansions of this passage in the second, third, and fifth editions only emphasize the poet's Western concern for ideas of personal and political liberty even more.

That Byron chose to make *The Giaour* an imitation of an oral poem bears significantly upon how we read and understand the work. In the following discussion I shall expand upon this point further. I have, however, gone into the matter of oral poetry at some length here because it also has an important relevance to both *Childe Harold's Pilgrimage* and Byron's late *Don Juan* manner. *Childe Harold's Pilgrim-*

[9] I suppose it is not necessary to point out that neither Byron nor anyone else of his day understood the specific character of true oral poetry. They did recognize the distinction between oral and written poetry, however, and their ballad imitations show that they grasped in a general, if somewhat imprecise, way what characterizes an oral poetic.

age is declamatory self-revelation, and Elizabeth Boyd describes the experience of many readers of Byron when she says that we must imagine Byron himself reciting *Don Juan* if we would fully appreciate it.[10] I will return to this matter in a later chapter, but the reader should perhaps be aware now that Byron's interest in oral poetry was neither curious nor a passing thing. In the end he seems to have developed an ingenious skill for using a story as a means of self-dramatization (which is approximately the reverse of the purpose of a true oral poet). He tells a good story in *Don Juan*, true, but more than anything he conveys to us what a clever raconteur he is, and—even more significantly—what a fascinating and vital individual.

II

Byron found it "a relief to the fever of my mind to *write*" stories like *The Giaour*,[11] and the self-expressive attitude in this remark epitomizes a famous and important quality of nearly all his poetry. His experiences in the East seem to have intensified this inclination to self-expression for he confessed that "With those countries, all my really poetic feelings begin and end." (*LJ* 3:274) Thus it is that the fiction of the oral bard, which no one would have taken seriously in any case, is most useful for the kind of poetry Byron likes to write. The fictive singer not only embraces Byron's own liberal ideas and fascination with things Eastern, his self-dramatizing style is the equivalent of Byron's. As we have already seen in relation to *Childe Harold's Pilgrimage*, scenes and events come alive in Byron's works by virtue of his own emotional responses to them. This is why tone is so crucial in his poetry, for we understand his stories by watching, so to speak, various moods and emotions flit across his face as he tells us about different things. He becomes caught in his own act of storytelling, and we in turn become involved in his act of self-expression.

This self-dramatizing direction in his poetry is fully apparent in his "contempt for language," a constant motif in his works. Gazing on the Palatine in Canto IV of *Childe Harold's Pilgrimage* Byron sees "the moral of all human tales" (108) written in the landscape. The significance of the place is diverse, suggesting a variety of positive and negative values ("All . . . that eye or ear,/Heart, soul could seek, tongue ask"). In stanzas 106–7 he lays out a description, but as he moves into the next stanza he gradually turns us away from objective details. To understand such a place we have to *feel* it.

---

10 Elizabeth Boyd, *Don Juan, A Critical Study* (New Brunswick, N.J., 1945), p. 46.
11 *Correspondence* 1:238.

> Away with words! draw near,
>
> Admire—exult—despise—laugh, weep,—for here
> There is such matter for all feeling:—Man!
> Thou pendulum betwixt a smile and tear,
> Ages and Realms are crowded in this span,
> This mountain, whose obliterated plan
> The pyramid of empires pinnacled. . . .
> Where are its golden roofs? Where those who dared to build?

We cannot "draw near" the scene itself, but we can and must look upon the emotional expressions of Byron to understand the meaning of the place. That meaning, written on the landscape by Time and the God of Time, is now written on the face of the poet. Similarly, Byron urges us to "go see/Laocoön's torture dignifying pain" (160) in the Vatican Gallery. Such a sight beggars mere verbal description, so that the only way Byron can intimate the emotional power of the statue is by himself becoming an emotional medium for us. We "go" and "see" him.

The Venus de Medici stanzas (49–52) are similarly managed. Byron looks upon the statue and sees not a marble artifact but the virtue which produced it and of which it is the expression.

> We stand, and in that form and face behold
> What Mind can make when Nature's self would fail;
> And to the fond Idolators of old
> Envy the innate flash which such a Soul could mould.   (49)

Just as the statue before him is the expression of the creative passion which produced it, so Byron's "descriptive" poetry becomes a dramatization of his own vitality.

> Away!—there need no words and terms precise . . .
>   we have eyes:
> Blood—pulse—and breast confirm the Dardan Shepherd's prize.
>   (50)

The statue has not marble but human qualities, and the reason is that Byron's "Blood, pulse, and breast" have confirmed its passionate reality. The "innate flash" which the stone reveals is a power transferred to the gazing poet, and to prove that he shares this vital fire he creates his own artifact in the next stanza.

> Appear'dst thou not to Paris in this guise?
> Or to more deeply blest Anchises? or,
> In all thy perfect goddess-ship, when lies

> Before thee thy own vanquish'd Lord of War?
> And gazing in thy face as toward a star,
> Laid on thy lap, his eyes to thee upturn,
> Feeding on thy sweet cheek; while thy lips are
> With lava kisses melting while they burn,
> Shower'd on his eyelids, brow, and mouth, as from an urn!

The "surmised" picture[12] of Mars and Venus is the perfect exemplum of Byron's self-expressive mode. As a symbol it comes into being through the poet's passionate response to the vitality he perceives in and through the statue (which, incidentally, is never described "objectively"). Second, the details of the symbol recapitulate its origins, for if Mars gets his life by "feeding" on the sight of his beloved, Venus is quickened in Mars' worshipful gaze. Her life and passionate love are the rewards for the completeness of his belief and responsiveness.

This virtuous interchange between a subject perceiver and a perceived subject is a characteristic of nearly all Byron's poetry, and not least in tales like *The Giaour*. In terms of the total work we can distinguish a connected series of relationships between the dramatic characters, the narrating poet, and the audience. The Giaour, who is the prime object of interest to all the people in the story, is dramatized largely through the responses he elicits from those who watch him, like the monk and the Turkish fisherman.[13] Our first encounter with him is typically indirect.

> On—on he hasten'd, and he drew
> My gaze of wonder as he flew. . . .   (200–201)

Gazes of wonder, fear, terror, hatred, and the like rebound from the Giaour, so that he is realized in the emotional reactions which he provokes. In this respect his position is a focal and determining one for other characters, like Hassan and Leila, who function in similar ways at various times.

In scenes where a character responds to the Giaour, Byron will frequently attach a specific epithet to the sensation that is felt (e.g., "wonder" or "loathing"). We must not conclude from this that such responses are either simplified or stereotyped. These epithets are formal devices which fix the reader's attention so that Byron can complicate

---

12 I borrow this term from Geoffrey Hartman, *Wordsworth's Poetry 1787–1814* (New Haven, 1964), pp. 8 ff.

13 Later in the poem, when his character has been more firmly established by indirection, he can be brought before us in an immediate way.

the dramatized emotional nuances in his characters and weave them around a variety of "objective" details about the Giaour. The passage which the previous quotation introduces (200–276), for example, constantly slips from one emotion to another. In this way the fisherman comes to mirror the shifting looks upon the Giaour's own face. The result is that an emotion, say "fear," becomes rather complicated. At the beginning of the passage the fisherman's fear is allied to his sense of wonder, to the strangeness of this rider who has suddenly rushed before him. But his fear become foreboding when he observes the Giaour's stern glance upon the mosque while the feast of Ramazan is in progress. Yet a third time the fear changes, for a certain inner torment becomes noticeable in the Giaour's appearance. This final state of the fear emotion is much more significant and draws from the Turk a kind of pity.

> But in that instant o'er his soul
> Winters of Memory seem'd to roll,
> And gather in that drop of time
> A life of pain, an age of crime.
> O'er him who loves, or hates, or fears,
> Such moment pours the grief of years. . . .   (261–66)

The initial image relates back to the "troubled memory" mentioned at the opening of the passage. The Giaour's appearance, which has throughout the poem an infectious or mesmeric virtue, here insinuates its power into the fisherman. Like the Giaour, the man who catches a glimpse of him in such a revelatory instant is stricken with the sense of a doom that can never be turned aside, with the sense that such a fatality is possible. For the observer, consciousness transforms a fleeting moment of insight into a terrible knowledge, a sympathetic vision into the darkness which the Giaour's own mind has penetrated.

> What felt *he* then, at once opprest
> By all that most distracts the breast?
> That pause, which ponder'd o'er his fate,
> Oh, who its dreary length shall date!
> Though in Time's record nearly nought
> It was Eternity to Thought!
> For infinite as boundless space
> The thought that Conscience must embrace,
> Which in itself can comprehend
> Woe without name, or hope, or end.   (267–76)

What happens to the fisherman here explains the later reluctance of the monk to look upon the Giaour's face. His mere appearance is dangerous because it is self-revelatory, is an emblem of his own power of inner vision. Thus he seduces the observer into a painful sympathy, like the ancient mariner, by drawing a blithe wedding guest to look upon those hidden terrors which have their source and pattern in man's own heart.

But if we recall the narrative technique of the tale we will see that Byron's perspectives for infection are not confined to characters in the story. The oral narrator is also an affected observer, is, in fact, the obvious norm for all patterns of responsiveness. He enters fully into the various narrative acts in the tale and becomes, as it were, each speaker in turn. The following diagram may help to explain the different perspectives in the poem.

> The Giaour ⎫
> ↕   ⎬ ← the poet ← the audience
> Other characters ⎭

The poet's reactions are sometimes made directly to the Giaour and sometimes indirectly through other characters in the story. The procedure is essentially the same as that we observed in the *Childe Harold's Pilgrimage* passages above. As Byron puts it in *Don Juan*, poets "take all colours—like the hands of dyers" (III, 87). The final perspective is the audience's, which directs its attention to the poet as he tells his story and catches the "original" passions and insights by seeing them again in the chameleon poet. The entire procedure is quite Longinian and characteristic of Byron's predominant aesthetic.

> His strain display'd some feeling—right or wrong;
> And feeling, in a poet, is the source
> Of others' feeling. . . .   (*DJ* III, 87)

Longinus' famous dictum that "Sublimity is the echo of a great soul" explains the series of transferences between the Giaour and the audience. Quoting a passage from *Iliad* XX Longinus asks:

> Would you not say that the soul of the writer enters the chariot at the same moment as Phaethon and shares in his dangers and the rapid flight of his steeds?

Such a principle carries an inevitable corollary for the relation between the poet and his audience.

For does not the flute instil certain emotions into its hearers and as it were make them beside themselves and full of frenzy, and supplying a rhythmical movement constrain the listener to move rhythmically in accordance therewith and to conform himself to the melody, although he may be utterly ignorant of music? Yes. . . .[14]

Longinus explains much in Byron's poetic technique, especially if we couple Longinian theory with the Horatian *si vis me flere*. For Byron the poet stands between the tale and the audience and his primary function is to arouse in his audience emotional responses and rhythms that parallel his own. This basic pattern of responsiveness supports the relationship between the characters in the tale itself. A likeness of this sort suggests that Byron's narrative technique in *The Giaour* imitates one of the poem's central thematic concerns. Such is indeed the case, and we will now turn to examine this theme and its related motifs.

III

Like so many of Byron's works, *The Giaour* represents a world charged with sympathetic imagination. Spiritual realities constantly tend to reincarnate themselves in different forms, places, and persons. In *Don Juan* Byron suggests that "there are such things as sympathies/ Without our knowledge or our approbation" that reproduce (in their benevolent aspects) "a soft kind of concatenation,/Like Magnetism or Devilism, or what *You* please" (*DJ* VI, 38). The spirits of Truth, Beauty, and Love all generate themselves by this means, but so do those of Error, Evil, and Hatred. Castlereagh, Romilly, Wordsworth, and Southey are attacked in his great epic because they are men possessed —incarnated avatars of timeless spiritual perversions. Similarly, his Venetian plays dramatize a world in which evil is a positive and self-perpetuating presence.

> for there is that stirring
> Within, above, around, that in this city
> Will make the cemeteries populous
> As e'er they were by pestilence or war. . . .
>
> (*Marino Faliero* ii, i, 505–8)

At other times Byron calls this evil a Briareus or a Hydra to indicate

[14] Longinus, "On the Sublime," in *Criticism*, ed. Mark Schorer *et al*. (New York, 1958), pp. 14, 18, 20–21.

its multiple nature, and in *Don Juan* he repeats the latter image when referring to war as

> A human Hydra, issuing from its fen
> To breathe destruction on its winding way,
> Whose heads were heroes, which cut off in vain
> Immediately in others grew again.   (*DJ* VIII, 2)

Whether we are fortunate enough to meet the spirit of good (incarnated in beings like Ianthe) or fated to encounter the spirit of evil (which possesses the Venetian Council of Ten), the world is inhabited by angels and devils who actively seek out whom they may devour.

The land and seascape of the Piraeus, described immediately at the poem's opening, is the environmental compass of the events narrated in the poem, and it embodies the quality of all life in that region.

> Fair clime! where every season smiles
> Benignant o'er these blessed isles,
> Which, seen from far Colonna's height,
> Make glad the heart which hails the sight,
> And lend to loneliness delight.
> There, mildly dimpling, Ocean's cheek,
> Reflects the tints of many a peak
> Caught by the laughing tides that lave
> These Edens of the eastern wave.   (7–15)

The passage goes on to describe sky, sea, and land all cooperating in an interchange of benevolence which transforms the scene into a natural paradise. The atmosphere and surroundings are vitalized, and the spirit of the place generates itself in every mortal who is responsive to it. Hearing the song of her lover the nightingale, the rose "Blooms" in response and herself "Returns the sweets by Nature given/In softest incense back to heaven." The interaction, or as Byron calls it, "concatenation," is conceived as an endless process (much as in the Clarens stanzas in *Childe Harold's Pilgrimage III*), for heaven in its turn "yields" up the blessedness again to others.

It is at this point that the spirit of evil insinuates itself.

> And many a summer flower is there,
> And many a shade that love might share,
> And many a grotto, meant for rest,
> That holds the pirate for a guest;
> Whose bark in sheltering cove below
> Lurks for the passing peaceful prow,

> Till the gay mariner's guitar
> Is heard, and seen the evening star.
> Then stealing with the muffled oar,
> Far shaded by the rocky shore,
> Rush the night-prowlers on the prey,
> And turn to groans his roundelay.   (34–45)

If some of the lines in this passage are not especially weighty, the tempo of it all is beautifully managed. The character of the description turns unobtrusively at lines 36–37. But the rhyme "rest/guest" conceals for a time the sense of discord that might be suggested by "pirate," and the next few lines continue to retard the coming darkness. "Sheltering" softens the ominous "Lurks" but does not cancel entirely our faint but gradually increasing sense of foreboding. Two more lines pass peacefully by before the sense of something evil returns. This time the sound of the "mariner's guitar" is cut across by the faint noise of a "muffled oar." Still we are given no specific image on which our sense of fear can settle. Line 43 affords another brief pause before the full realization rushes upon us in the concluding couplet of the passage. We will discover later that the shadows which play across the landscape are signs of dread for the Turkish fisherman, natural portents of the evil symbolized by and embodied in the pirates of the region. Indeed, the cove and grotto are themselves frequent points of reference in the allegorical landscape of Byron's early tales. Conrad weighs anchor in this cove, and in this grotto Selim stashes away his material hopes of revolt.

Byron concludes the passage with an explicit definition of the conflict in the region in spiritual terms.

> It is as though the fiends prevail'd
> Against the seraphs they assail'd,
> And, fix'd on heavenly thrones, should dwell
> The freed inheritors of hell. . . .   (62–65)

The transformation of these heavenly regions into a dominion of hell prepares for the following description of Greece infected with a death-in-life. The poet invites us to go with him to see, spread out under the bright Aegean sky, a corpse embalmed upon a table (68–102). Like a recent death, the land everywhere preserves the appearance of life, and it is this life/death duality which determines the quality of human existence everywhere. The country is stricken with the plague of tyranny and conflict and the disease has raged to an epidemic. The

Greek "slave" lies torpid beneath this spiritual death, but *The Giaour* will relate the tale of a man in whom the war between devils and angels played itself out. He too has been infected, but for him a story is at least possible, even if only the narrative of his death throes—his fruitless struggle to attain a paradise in a land ruled by the Prince of Darkness.

Vengeance, or the "Mutual interchange of wrong for wrong" is, in Byron's poetry, the focal Satanic element, and the story of the Giaour is an attempt to explain its nature. Beloved by two men, Leila stands at the center of the action. She is deliberately associated with the natural paradise of the landscape (473–518) and represents that perfection toward which both Hassan and the Giaour are impelled. At the level of the political allegory she represents the land over which the Turks and the Venetians have been fighting for centuries and to which neither can have any complete claim. Like the Italy of *Childe Harold's Pilgrimage IV*, Leila has "The fatal gift of beauty" and becomes as a result the victim of the conflict. She is not a Turk but a Circassian, and has been sent to Hassan as a slave. Circassian women were noted for their beauty, and though earlier converted to Christianity, their people became Moslem in the seventeenth century (the period of Byron's tale) under the pressure of the Turkish authority which then ruled their country. Thus, if Leila's love for the Giaour seems horrifying to a Turkish sensibility ("And, worse than faithless, for a Giaour!" 536), her conduct is perfectly understandable at the level of the political allegory. She seeks freedom from bondage with Hassan, and if she is destroyed as a result, her will to action still remains a moral lesson to the enervated Greeks. More important, however, is the angry vision of several factions striving for mastery over a land that is not theirs.[15]

Both Hassan and the Giaour are mesmerized by Leila's beauty. So must everyone be, the bard (in his Turkish persona) tells us, just as anyone with sensitivity is captivated by the natural loveliness of the region. Landscape and Leila represent beauty and as such they draw all men to them by a kind of magnetism of goodness. But evil has magnetic powers as well. "The half-affrighted Friar" shrinks from the Giaour's gaze: "As if that eye and bitter smile/Transferr'd to others fear and guile" (848–49). The Giaour's evil eye is the legacy passed on to him by the man he has killed.

[15] See, e.g., the Notes to *Childe Harold's Pilgrimage I–II* and the Preface to *The Giaour*.

> His breast with wounds unnumber'd riven,
> His back to earth, his face to heaven,
> Fall'n Hassan lies—his unclosed eye
> Yet lowering on his enemy,
> As if the hour that seal'd his fate
> Surviving left his quenchless hate;
> And o'er him bends that foe with brow
> As dark as his that bled below.   (667–74)

"True foes, once met, are join'd till death" (654), we are told, but the spirit of hate and vengeance is "quenchless" and survives to other generations and men. The "vengeful Giaour" (680) kills the man who killed his love but he gets no satisfaction. Hassan's death curse blooms again in the soul of the living Giaour. "Condemned to meditate and gaze" (993) on his memory and remorse, the Giaour suffers "Beneath avenging Monkir's scythe" (748).[16] The Turk's curse draws him to a life of spiritual agony and—what is worse—insures its hereditary character.

> But first, on earth as Vampire sent,
> Thy corse shall from its tomb be rent:
> Then ghastly haunt thy native place,
> And suck the blood of all thy race;
> There from thy daughter, sister, wife,
> At midnight drain the stream of life;
> Yet loathe the banquet which perforce
> Must feed the livid living corse.
> Thy victims ere they yet expire
> Shall know the demon for their sire,
> And cursing thee, thou cursing them,
> Thy flowers are wither'd on the stem.   (755–66)

The vampire image, like that of the evil eye, focuses the undying nature of these entropic forces.

Byron's view here, consistently maintained throughout his work, is deeply religious: human life cuts athwart two opposed spiritual planes of reality and thus constantly plays out the war in heaven fought between deathless angels and devils. Human lives pass, but not without being swept up into this spiritual maelstrom; and human life, regarded

---

[16] The Giaour's remorse is not out of character, as Professor Kroeber has argued (p. 139). He does not suffer from the thought that he has killed Hassan any more than Hassan is remorseful about killing Leila. The Giaour's inward torment results from the thought that Leila is dead because of his love for her.

generically (and mythically), *is* the manifestation of that spiritual being swept up into this spiritual maelstrom; and human life, regarded struggle. Through it man enjoys "immortal transports" with his Egeria (*CHP* IV, 119) but must suffer as well the martyrdom of his own desires. The whole action is called "The nympholepsy of some fond despair." When Byron examines this theme in his earlier works the emphasis generally falls upon the element of despair; it will not be until some years after *The Giaour* that he will shift his thought in a more positive direction.

Satan, like God, works in mysterious ways. Who would look to find love in the bosom of his mortal enemy; or, finding it there, who would expect to find death in the heart of love? The Giaour discovers both. Leila is Hassan's passion and possession, but she flees this constraint and bestows herself upon the Giaour. Hassan kills the thing he loves because

> The heart once left thus desolate
> Must fly at last for ease—to hate.   (944–45)

Left in its turn empty of love, the heart of the Giaour burns for revenge. Each man remains forever unsatisfied by his revenge, however. Hassan finds no rest until he weds the "fearful bride" (718) of Death, and the Giaour's remaining life is, like Heathcliff's, a convulsion of longing. The "fiery convert of revenge"[17] is at bottom a disciple of Eros whose life is directed, vainly, toward an "unreach'd paradise" and whose love can only be seized beyond the tumult of time. Moreover, Leila is the fundamental source of both life and death. Both Hassan and the Giaour live only for her love, but it is their love for her which makes them both murderers and which, in the end, results in their deaths. As the famous scorpion image suggests, around the love-consumed heart is flame and within it—always—death. Leila teaches Hassan to feel the passion of love, but likewise

> Her spirit pointed well the steel
> Which taught that felon heart to feel.   (677–78)

She it is who directs the sword of the Giaour just as she later beckons him in visions to join her in another place.

It is "not in/The harmony of things" (*CHP* IV, 126) that these conflicts be resolved. Men are compelled by a "strong necessity of loving"

---

[17] This is Carl Lefevre's fine phrase amalgamated from two passages in *The Seige of Corinth*. Cf. "Lord Byron's Fiery Convert of Revenge," *SP* 49 (1952):468–87.

(*CHP* IV, 125) that which is beautiful, but the "fire and motion" of their souls cannot be satisfied with anything less than "the mind's Ideal shape" (*CHP* IV, 123) of perfection. So this Eros passion is "Fatal to him who bears, to all who ever bore" (*CHP* III, 42) since nothing short of everything can satisfy its desires. To be quenched the fire must be consummated, must exhaust that for which, and by virtue of which, it burns. Similarly, the mortal objects of this desire are themselves subject to a doom by virtue of their "fatal" beauty, their "destructive charms" (*CHP* IV, 43). Thus Leila's death allegorizes the Giaour's fate, that mortal existence forbids any absolute fulfillment. Hassan's death, on the other hand, dramatizes the reason for this prohibition. Both Hassan and the Giaour treat Leila as if she *were* mundane, as if she could be possessed the way a pirate possesses a ship or a conqueror a country. Hassan kills her because he cannot hold her in bondage, and the Giaour says that he would have killed her himself if she had been "false" to him.

Revenging her death on Hassan is the Giaour's confession that he thought her subject to death and limitation—his unconscious admission that he does not trust the eternity of his own mind. Leila is the objectified form of the "charms and virtues which we dare/Conceive in boyhood and pursue as men" (*CHP* IV, 122) and she cannot die (as the Christians would say) "the death" unless the fire in the Giaour's own soul has gone out. But this is exactly what has happened, as the killing of Hassan indicates. Nevertheless, his act of revenge does not satisfy him and he discovers the reason later when Leila comes to him in the visions that objectify his unquenched longings. The desire for Leila has returned perhaps stronger than ever. The murderous hatred of Hassan and the Giaour for each other results in the death of Leila, but the allegory makes it clear that the longing for perfection cannot be extinguished. Leila has an "objective" (in the Platonic sense), eternal reality. Hassan and the Giaour killed her in their own hearts by choosing to embrace acts of death and evil, but she—who represents life and beauty—returns to the Giaour and shows thereby the "necessity of loving" in man and his desire for life. Even his worst crimes cannot utterly destroy these longings, nor can they atrophy in the course of the unconsummated quest. This pattern is repeated in the political allegory. Greece lies before us like a corpse, but the poet calls out for a new breed of "fiery souls" (148). Greece is a corpse because men are no longer "worthy of thy clime." A land breeds heroes only if men are themselves fruitful. But Greece is lovely even in death for she is the "Shrine of the Mighty" (106) who lived ages before and who live on in the memory that lingers in the landscape.

So it is that Hassan can pass his curse to the Giaour because he and his enemy are alike. Traitors both to what Leila represents, both become traitors to themselves. When they fight they struggle with their own negative elements, with their spectres (as Blake would say). Once met, true foes are joined till death. Through the curse Hassan stays with the Giaour until the latter's death at the end, but this is only to say that the Turk's curse is the outward sign of the Giaour's own sickness. Their fight mirrors each man's personal struggle. Hassan is killed and goes to paradise; the Giaour survives but, as he thinks, "alone." He discovers soon enough that he is not alone, that his Love (Leila) and his Foe (Hassan) pursue him still. He is joined till death to his frustration and separated until death from his true love. Perfectly correlative, the two conditions define the nature of a death-in-life. Leila continues to approach him, but only in vision, and it is morally just that an observer (the monk) should speak of the Giaour's visionary experiences in the following terms.

> Much in his visions mutters he
> Of maiden whelm'd beneath the sea;
> Of sabres clashing, foemen flying,
> Wrongs avenged, and Moslem dying.
> On cliff he hath been known to stand,
> And rave as to some bloody hand
> Fresh sever'd from its parent limb,
> Invisible to all but him,
> Which beckons onward to his grave,
> And lures to leap into the wave!   (822–31)

The monk speaks of the vision of the bloody hand in ignorance of the fact that the Giaour severed the hand of Hassan in their death struggle. The monk simply wants to emphasize what he saw with a figurative expression, that the stranger raves to the air as if to some invisible yet terrible summons. We are told, however, that Hassan does not come to him in vision, "for he cannot break/From earth" (1304–5), but that Leila (who sleeps unquietly beneath the restless waters) is his visionary companion. Nevertheless, the monk's comparison is most apposite to the moral of the tale, for Leila remains only a visionary gleam to the Giaour while he is alive precisely because a hand has been severed, because he and Hassan have cursed themselves. "Oh Love!

no habitant of earth thou art," Byron says (*CHP* IV, 121), and the
reason is that man has killed his love and cursed his life with the murder.

The Giaour is allegory because the recounted events are made to
bear a weight of general significance. Hassan's curse, for example, takes
on mythic proportions (something like Original Sin). Merely in terms
of particulars, we see a love triangle doomed beyond hope to the issue
that prevails. But there is the point. Given what they are, no one of
the actors could have behaved differently. Hassan behaves the way he
does because his history made him what he is, and the same is true of
Leila and the Giaour. The story, in other words, has a fatality that defines for the audience an existential condition: fallen man cannot live
with his love in this world. This inevitable quality in the tale is beautifully reinforced in the crucial passage where the fight between the
Giaour and Hassan is described. Byron underlines the meaning of their
combat with an extended simile drawn from Nature.

> As rolls the river into ocean,
> In sable torrent wildly streaming;
> As the sea-tide's opposing motion,
> In azure column proudly gleaming,
> Beats back the current many a rood,
> In curling foam and mingling flood,
> While eddying whirl and breaking wave,
> Roused by the blast of water, rave;
> Through sparkling spray, in thundering clash,
> The lightnings of the water flash
> In awful whiteness o'er the shore,
> That shines and shakes beneath the roar;
> Thus—as the stream and ocean greet,
> With waves that madden as they meet—
> Thus join the bands, whom mutual wrong,
> And fate, and fury, drive along.   (620–35)

What could be done to alter such a condition? The answer, obviously,
is "nothing." This fight has persisted from the foundations of the world
and will continue forever. Nature does not, however, define the condition of man; rather, she takes those forms that man has given to her,
for she too is fallen. The simile here is part of the general allegorical
mode of the poem. It illustrates what man has made of himself and his
world. Nature caught by such a radical duality is the proper image of
man's essential life.

IV

Byron's reputation has suffered more from his early tales than from anything else, and it is partly this critical fact which has led me to spend so much time with *The Giaour*. I do not believe that his early narratives deserve their reputation. Like Keats's *Endymion*, they are much inferior to the work that was to appear later. But we study such works mostly for the light they throw on other, more important poems, or to elucidate signal ideas and stylistic tendencies in germinal form. Keats's career as a narrative poet offers an instructive comparison. Keats is noted for being a careful poet and Byron is not, but Byron's early tales contain at least as much fine poetry as *Endymion* does, and a comparable amount of wretched or mediocre verse. More importantly, in their early work it is clear that Byron executes his themes with a formal precision that we will look for in vain in Keats. Keats later gains a firm control over narrative but only in traditional forms. Both *Hyperions*—the loci of his highest ambitions as a poet—defeated his powers. Byron, on the other hand, moved from an early mastery of the form of traditional narrative to an equal success with the highly complex *Don Juan* manner. The story of that achievement is partly to be found in his early poetry, for the corpus of his work evidences certain stylistic consistencies. We will not understand the necessity of *Beppo's* style without first understanding *Childe Harold's Pilgrimage* and the tales, especially a tale like *The Giaour*.

Understanding Byron's characteristic themes is perhaps no less important. *The Bride of Abydos, The Corsair, Lara*, and *Parisina* all deal with the same general motifs that appear in *The Giaour*. Contrary to popular belief, however, the ideas and problems are by no means trivial. The tales are repetitive to a fault, but not so much in the matter of theme as of versification. Byron is still learning the fundamentals of language. They are all notable achievements, and if *The Corsair* and *Lara* contain the most memorable passages, *Parisina* is probably, on the whole, the best tale. Each centers around an exploration of the nature and consequences of a life that is Eros-directed. Each tells a story of frustrated love and the war of repression within a context where time and contingency in general are strongly emphasized.

But Byron's myths of the Eros-motif are not traditional. Anders Nygren's discussion of the usual Platonic concept of Eros points this up very well.

The two worlds, the world of Ideas and the world of the senses
. . . stand admittedly side by side unrelated to one another, but
not—be it noted—on a par with one another. To man, who is
placed between them and has connections with both of them, it
falls as his lot to effect the transition from the one to the other.
Not that his intermediate position means that he should unite the
two worlds in his own person; but, on the contrary, it is his business to cut himself loose from the lower world and ascend to the
higher. . . . This, however, is possible only in virtue of the Eros
that indwells the human soul. The Ideas as such are quite incapable of making any conquests; they are not forces, they exercise
no influence in the sense-world. The relation between the two
worlds is entirely one-sided; the movement is all in one direction,
from below upwards.[18]

As we have already seen, and as we shall see again, no such fundamental
distinction exists between the upper and the lower world in Byron's
view. Unlike the traditional platonist, Byron consistently tries to "unite
the two worlds." Moreover, in Byron's view both worlds exhibit Eros.
"Eternity is in love with the productions of time," Blake says, and
Hölderlin's life work was directed to expressing the longing of the
gods for man and, reciprocally, of men for the gods. The attitude is
characteristically Romantic. "The gods become as mortals, and man's
fate/Has moments like their brightest": thus Byron in *Childe Harold's
Pilgrimage*, and we will see Sardanapalus speak equally to the point.[19]

The upshot of this attitude is the typically dualistic allegories that
constitute Byron's early tales—indeed, all his early poetry. The lyrics
from this period, especially the celebrated "Thyrza cycle," deal with
precisely the same themes as the tales, and in precisely the same tonal
ways (except that they do without the political schemas). A war exists
in heaven between fiends and seraphs and that war is mirrored in the
world of men. Life is fundamentally divine, but, like the life of the
gods, it is tragic. Both worlds are filled with anxiety and the longing
for self-completion, but both are doomed to suffer the Eros-motivated
existence because they look for completion in orders that are themselves incomplete. The gods have what men need and men have what

[18] Anders Nygren, *Agape and Eros*, trans. Philip S. Watson (Philadelphia, 1953),
p. 170.
[19] The Renaissance poets also tried to unite the two worlds. But the Renaissance
Eros differs from the Romantic in that the former would never think of the gods need-
ing men, of the spiritual orders longing toward "lower" orders.

the gods long for. But no marriage is possible, for once imparadised, man (as god) reaches out for that restlessness which he once sought to escape. The process recapitulates itself forever, since time, conceived as indefinite succession, has become a norm.

Death and life thus become ambiguous terms mirroring the ambiguity in existence. For man life seems a kind of death because it forever falls short of complete fulfillment, while death presents itself as the terminus of unfulfillment. On the other hand, man in this Byronic world longs for "rest, but not to feel 'tis rest" (*The Giaour*, 995). Thus death is itself an unfulfillment, for all that we know of life is in the restlessness of incompletion. This ambiguity is repeated in heaven and for the gods and spirits. Eternal life beyond death is for them—as Keats argues in his *Hyperion* fragments—a source of anxiety and sorrow, whereas for us it seems the image of all human needs. The gods long to die into life. They need men, Novalis tells us, and their need is allegorized in the war that exists in the spiritual order. Byron's early tales all narrate this myth of a cosmos which is fated to an eternity of longing, to the tragic polarity which is existence in time (Nature) and out of it (Imagination). Man longs to be freed of nature, but once released to imaginative realms (as "Le Bateau Ivre" shows so well) he needs to involve himself back in time and natural cycle, back in a world where filthy street puddles bear up paper boats. Only in such surroundings can the imagination guarantee itself life. The view is tragic and cyclical, but it is the way Byron saw it and, by and large, it is the Romantic view. Byron always believed in this duality, but he eventually came to find ways of using it, ways of uniting the two worlds. We have already seen how he did this in *Childe Harold's Pilgrimage*. *Sardanapalus*, *Mazeppa*, *The Island*, and his entire *Don Juan* manner represent four more ways of surviving ambiguity. Indeed, in the last two cases he seeks to define a means not merely of survival but of triumph.

The Motionless Pilgrim

When Byron returned to Geneva on July 1, 1816, after his sailing tour around the lake with Shelley, he was carrying two new packets of MSS with him. One was a complete new poem, *The Prisoner of Chillon*, and the other the last group of additional stanzas for *Childe Harold's Pilgrimage III*. The two compositions seem to have little thematic relation to each other. The additional stanzas for the third canto celebrate the natural beauty around Clarens in terms that emphasize burgeoning growth and the vitalizing power of love. *The Prisoner of Chillon*, on the other hand, tells the story of a man whose powers of affective response are shrunken beyond healing by an extended imprisonment. Despite these differences, however, the two pieces of work are as intimately related as is Byron to his anti-self Harold.

To see this more clearly we should recall a few facts about *Childe Harold's Pilgrimage*. Canto III is the first poem that Byron wrote in which he was able completely to subdue his own Harold-spirit. The malaise of Harold at the beginning of Canto I becomes, by the end of Canto II, the condition of the poet's own soul. As we have seen, however, though Byron and his fictive hero begin their journey in Canto III as comrades in wretchedness, a distinction is drawn between the hopelessness and involuted psychology of Harold (sts. 8–16) and Byron's own sense of insecurity and longing (sts. 1–7). Unlike Harold, Byron begins the journey in Canto III with a kind of hopeless hope, for directing all his wanderings is the desire to create himself anew and seek a more intense life. This questing spirit in Byron cannot be killed, nor will it die out, so that the pathos-oriented description of Harold in the Rhine Valley becomes an important measure of the difference

165

between the two men. Blake would have called Harold Byron's Limit of Contraction.

What Harold and Byron see in the Rhine Valley is a place of enormous fruitfulness. At Clarens they encounter another region whose dominant characteristic is the same ("full of life," III, 102). Byron responds in a wholly positive way to the later scene, but he appears there alone. In the Rhine Valley Harold's consciousness of "the sharp scythe of conflict" (50) contracts his affective energies to such a degree that the valley is, for him, only minimally fructifying. He walks about "not insensibly" in the presence of all the beauty and vitality of the place, and this negative definition of his life is characteristic of the entire passage (see st. 52 and 54, for example). Byron's attitude toward Clarens is totally different. Developing through a series of beautiful images of continuous growth, the Clarens passage climaxes when Byron is absorbed into the deathless energies which he sees in the landscape.

> For 't is his nature to advance or die;
> He stands not still, but or decays or grows
> Into a boundless blessing. . . .   (III, 103)

The passage echoes Harold's experience of the "abounding" Rhine whose waters are a "blessing" (50) to the region. But the echo emphasizes the implicit comment which the later passage makes on the earlier. Harold can muster little more than a response of pleased recognition toward the fruitfulness that surrounds and calls out to him. Byron, on the other hand, stands not still that he may not decay, and he rises to a magnificent blessing of the region. Byron's hymn of praise returns the gift that nature had given him. I might note that if Harold is regarded as merely an aspect of Byron our conclusions about the meaning of the two passages will not change. The difference between the kind of response made to the Rhine Valley and the kind made to Clarens is the measure of the psychological advance that Byron has himself undergone.

The Prisoner of Chillon is an independent restatement of Harold's situation in Canto III. Traditionally the poem has sometimes been read as a celebration of man's ability to preserve his spiritual freedom despite the worst privations. Recently, however, at least two commentators have pointed out the error in this view. Far from being a dramatic celebration of the "Eternal Spirit of the chainless Mind," *The Prisoner of Chillon* is a most graphic argument that there are limits to every man's creative integrity, limits beyond which even the strongest cannot be pushed without losing control over his physical circumstances. Bonnivard's "thoughts and life," Andrew Rutherford rightly says, are "narrowed to the dungeon's scope."[1] The first time the poem appeared, in *The Prisoner of Chillon and other poems* (1816), the narrative was printed immediately after the very different "Sonnet on Chillon." Editors have generally followed this procedure ever since. As a result, readers have sometimes been misled to think that the Promethean defiance of the sonnet carries over into the tale. William Marshall, arguing from purely aesthetic criteria, was the first to point out the mistake in such an assumption.[2] Indeed, it is odd that this misreading should have persisted for so long since Byron's general note to the tale indicates quite clearly that the sonnet was composed after the narrative and under very different circumstances.

> When the foregoing poem was composed I was not sufficiently aware of the history of Bonnivard, or I should have endeavored to dignify the subject by an attempt to celebrate his courage and his virtues. Some account of his life will be found in a note appended to the "Sonnet on Chillon," with which I have been furnished by the kindness of a citizen of that republic which is still proud of the memory of a man worthy of the best age of ancient freedom.[3]

Apparently Byron had not heard any stories suggesting that Bonnivard suffered in the cause of liberty until after the tale was written. Thus, the poem does not "celebrate his courage and his virtues" as it would have done had Byron known his "history" beforehand. The "Sonnet on Chillon," and the note containing a long passage on Bonnivard from Jean Senebier's *Histoire Littéraire de Genève* (1786), were added later to rectify the omission. The Murray MS containing the two poems confirms this chronology.

Bonnivard tells his story after he has been freed to the light of a "new day" (41). But, as he points out in the first and last two sections of the poem, his long imprisonment has taken away all taste for freedom and full light. "I/Regain'd my freedom with a sigh," he says at the end, and if he has, like Harold, acquired a laudable meekness from his extended sufferings, he is not destined to inherit the earth. "Rusted with a vile repose" (6), he finds that physical liberty cannot cure his spiritual circumscription. "The goodly earth and air/Are bann'd, and barr'd" (9–

---

[1] *Rutherford*, p. 72.
[2] *Marshall*, p. 82.
[3] *The Prisoner of Chillon and Other Poems* (London, 1816), pp. 59–60.

10) to him since it has become "at length the same to me,/Fetter'd or fetterless to be" (372–73). Thus he looks forward to the time when he will "have done with this new day."

> iron is a cankering thing,
> For in these limbs its teeth remain,
> With marks that will not wear away,
> Till I have done with this new day,
> Which now is painful to these eyes,
> Which have not seen the sun so rise
> For years. . . .   (38–44)

Marked with a sign which "will not wear away" until the daylight is gone (presumably an image of death), Bonnivard has absorbed the death-in-life of his long-accustomed element.

A glance at some of Byron's other poems about imprisonment may help to explain this tale better. *The Lament of Tasso*, written less than a year later, is another dramatic monologue of an imprisoned man. Unlike Bonnivard, Tasso speaks to us from his cell, just after completing his *Gerusalemme Liberata*. The comparison is interesting, for whereas Bonnivard resembles Harold in that his "springs of life" are almost completely dried up, Tasso is the equivalent of the Byron who writes the last two cantos of *Childe Harold's Pilgrimage*. Both Harold and Bonnivard have lost their self-recreative powers, whereas Tasso and Byron have preserved the ability to invigorate their own lives, mainly through the medium of imagination and art. Byron gains as he gives the "intense" life he images, and Tasso has a similar experience. Writing his great poem, Tasso identifies himself with the resurrection theme of his own work (see st. 1). "But this is o'er," he says, and he fears that he will be unable to sustain the life in himself now that the poem is finished. The fear is short-lived.

> Thou too art ended—what is left me now?
> For I have anguish yet to bear—and how?
> I know not that—but in the innate force
> Of my own spirit shall be found resource.   (43–46)

Byron himself speaks of this inner resource when he says that "The beings of the mind" are "essentially immortal" since they can "multiply in us a brighter ray/And more belov'd existence" and hence always produce a "fresher growth" (*CHP* IV, 5). Dante in *The Prophecy of Dante* identifies this inner resource with Beatrice, the sum and symbol of all his farthest longings and deepest loves. Similarly, Tasso turns to Leonora: "My heart can multiply thine image still," he says (58), and thus he determines to create himself anew from the love which he pours out on the image of the most beloved.

Or consider *Childe Harold's Pilgrimage*. At the turning point of the fourth canto Byron has argued himself into his deepest imprisonment. "Of its own beauty is the mind diseased" (122), he declares, recalling Napoleon, Rousseau, and Harold in the earlier cantos. All men have their Egerias and are consequently trapped in "The nympholepsy of some fond despair" (115). But just as he is about to retreat before this despair he looks inward.

> Though from our birth the faculty divine
> Is chain'd and tortured—cabin'd, cribb'd, confined,
> And bred in darkness, lest the truth should shine
> Too brightly on the unpreparèd mind,
> The beam pours in, for time and skill will couch the blind.

The imagistic parallel to *The Prisoner of Chillon*—light pouring into a darkened prison—is exact. The ancient symbol of man's creative force —the fire or light within that is the counterpart of the fructifying sun (in the natural sphere) and the empyrean flame (in the supernatural) —is one of the most pervasive images in Byron's poetry. Byron will often call it an "ignis fatuus of the mind" (*DJ* XI, 27) when he wants to emphasize the painful aspects of this flame, especially the frustration that results from man's pursuit of it.[4] But when he is conscious of the blessing that a time-continuum brings—as he is in the above stanza—he asserts that "time" (as persistence) will provide the opportunity, and skill (as art) will provide the method, for transforming foxfire into "holy beacons always bright" (*DJ* XV, 90).

The light that presides over *The Prisoner of Chillon* is the ignis fatuus and other subdued light forms. The dungeon is pervaded by a "pale and livid light" (52) that suggests the hectic on the cheeks of a consumptive—an image which Byron and many other Romantics were especially fond of. Kaled's cheeks, for example, evidence a "hectic tint of secret care/That for a burning moment fever'd there" (I, 534–35), while in the face of Bonnivard's dying younger brother we see:

> With all the while a cheek whose bloom
> Was as a mockery of the tomb,

[4] The image occurs as early as 1808 ("To a Youthful Friend," 65–68), and continues to appear through *Don Juan*. Meteors and rainbows are variants Byron often uses upon this theme of evanescent light.

> Whose tints as gently sunk away
> As a departing rainbow's ray;
> An eye of most transparent light,
> That almost made the dungeon bright. . . .   (190–95)

Almost, but not quite, for even this "infant love of all his race" (167) cannot withstand the prison environment.

All such lights are associated in Byron's mind with the unnatural and the dead or dying. In his later poems, however—approximately from the time of the fourth canto of *Childe Harold's Pilgrimage*—Byron increasingly uses the image to suggest death and rebirth into a higher order of reality. He finds "Hope upon a death-bed" in Italy (IV, 72) and specifically sees in Cecilia Metella (who is treated in a crucial portion of the poem) a "hectic light, the Hesperus of the dead" (IV, 102). *Mazeppa* and *The Island*, as we shall see, are written from a similar perspective, and so is *Beppo*.

Bonnivard, however, belongs to an earlier period in which nature is the only norm. Thus, he is left a "wreck" (26) after his years of imprisonment and half-life because he cannot respond any longer to the sun. His own fires have dwindled to the size and quality of the light which pervades "Chillon's dungeons deep and old."

> There are seven columns, massy and grey,
> Dim with a dull imprison'd ray,
> A sunbeam which hath lost its way,
> And through the crevice and the cleft
> Of the thick wall is fallen and left;
> Creeping o'er the floor so damp,
> Like a marsh's meteor lamp.   (29–35)

This ignis fatuus, this "imprison'd ray," is thus deliberately set out as the environmental equivalent of Bonnivard himself, who has also lost his way.

With the death of his second brother Bonnivard plunges completely into a state of death-in-life (47). Blake called this state Ulro, but I do not believe he ever described it quite so brilliantly (or succinctly) as Byron did through Bonnivard in stanza IX. Light, air, and finally even darkness itself are completely removed from his experience. No night, no day; no feeling, no thought: "not even the dungeon light" which was previously so hateful to him.

> But vacancy absorbing space
> And fixedness—without a place.   (242–43)

This is palpable negativity, a void so absolute that its emptiness can only be defined by subtraction. Into it, quite unexpectedly, "a light" breaks.

> A light broke in upon my brain,—
> It was the carol of a bird;
> It ceased, and then it came again,
> The sweetest song ear ever heard,
> And mine was thankful till mine eyes
> Ran over with the glad surprise,
> And they that moment could not see
> I was the mate of misery.
> But then by dull degrees came back
> My senses to their wonted track;
> I saw the dungeon walls and floor
> Close slowly round me as before,
> I saw the glimmer of the sun
> Creeping as it before had done,
> But through the crevice where it came
> That bird was perch'd, as fond and tame,
> And tamer than upon the tree;
> A lovely bird, with azure wings,
> And song that said a thousand things,
> And seem'd to say them all for me!   (251–70)

Nature seeks to lead Bonnivard back to life, and at first he responds to the summons. But when this "visitant from Paradise" (284) flies away he is unable to sustain himself from his own inner resources, is unable to become a part of nature's teeming life because he has none of his own to bring to her (unlike Byron at the end of *Childe Harold's Pilgrimage III*). Left, as he says, "doubly lone" (292), he slips back into an existence on the periphery of life. The creeping "glimmer of the sun" becomes a light which he welcomes, just as he welcomes the circumscribed "liberty" of his dungeon limits. More than a modicum of life he is unable to sustain. Thus, when he ventures to climb to his cell window to gaze upon the natural world outside, he finds that, like Harold, he cannot keep "his spirit to that flight." The eagle that Bonnivard sees recalls the eagle images which Byron applies to his own quest for freedom in *Childe Harold's Pilgrimage III*. In the present context, however, Bonnivard is (properly) "troubled" by the sight of the free bird.

> The eagle rode the rising blast,
> Me thought he never flew so fast
> As then to me he seem'd to fly;

> And then new tears came in my eye,
> And I felt troubled and would fain
> I had not left my recent chain.
> And when I did descend again,
> The darkness of my dim abode
> Fell on me as a heavy load;
> It was as is a new-dug grave,
> Closing o'er one we sought to save;
> And yet my glance, too much oppress'd,
> Had almost need of such a rest.   (253–65)

Nature's second bird-minister, the mighty eagle, is also sent in vain. Bonnivard now quite understands that the portion of nature's life which is within every man "sought to save" him by driving him to the window. "Too much oppress'd," however, he also sees that he cannot respond. The lines are a masterful portrayal of Bonnivard's sense of his own tragedy. "The darkness of my dim abode" is now a needful thing, and he has a melancholy awareness of the judgment upon himself that such a need implies. After this last effort toward full life he never again dares to look upon the day, and the self-consciousness that such an act will bring. It is understandable, therefore, that Bonnivard is reluctant to regain his freedom, for by coming to live in the sun he is forced always to see around him the life that he no longer has, and to contemplate the state of soul that he has chosen for himself.

The relationship between Christian and Torquil in *The Island* is similar to that between Bonnivard and his younger brother in this poem. In both cases the younger man is seen as the "hope" of the older,[5] the symbol of life and its power to maintain its highest achievements through its noblest creation, man. In *The Island* this hope is realized. Christian, the Byronic hero, dies, while Torquil moves forward into a kind of natural paradise. In the earlier poem the reverse is true. *The Prisoner of Chillon* dramatizes the theme of the crippled life, which is the basis for all of Byron's descriptions of the career of the Byronic hero. Having lost all hope in the possibilities of a full life after the death of his brothers, Bonnivard determines to live in the suburbs of existence where there are neither great delights nor great dangers. Thus he avoids having to look again into the abyss he once glimpsed—"vacancy absorbing space"—but only at the cost of barring himself forever from

---

[5] Cf. *Prisoner*, 196–230; *The Island* III, vi. Bonnivard's brother is called "The infant love of all his race," and the image anticipates a recurrent theme of "infancy" in *The Island*, where it is used to define the characters and the love relationship of Torquil and Neuha. Cf. II, vii, viii, xii, and IV, xv.

the other plane of existence, the condition of unending creativity. Once again *Childe Harold's Pilgrimage* provides the norm, for at the end of Canto IV Byron chooses to know and share the life that includes both of these elements, both the abyss of death that swallows up all hope and the "Outshining and o'erwhelming edifice" (158) that is the symbol of recurrent power and beauty.

Byron's Gentle Knight

The fate of Bonnivard and Childe Harold represents one possible conclusion to the life of a Byronic hero. Essentially dialectical, Byron's myth asserts that the unregenerate Promethean man is fated to shuttle forever between the poles of spiritual inertia on the one hand:

> some, bow'd and bent,
> Wax gray and ghastly, withering ere their time,
> And perish with the reed on which they leant,   (*CHP* IV, 22)

and "hereditary rage" on the other:

> the new race of inborn slaves, who wage
> War for their chains, and rather than be free,
> Bleed gladiator-like, and still engage
> Within the same arena where they see
> Their fellows fall before, like leaves of the same tree. (*CHP* IV, 94)

Most of Byron's heroes live out their lives in this second state. Ali Pasha, the Giaour, Conrad, Napoleon are all, like Rousseau, apostles of affliction whose lives are "one long war with self-sought foes." A despair of ever attaining the sublime goals toward which they yearn can whirl them back to the opposite pole of the dialectic (like Bonnivard and Harold). Barring this, they ride the storm of their passions without consummation and forever seek out foes in order to justify their own incompleteness to themselves. The pursuit of revenge is thus characteristic of Byronic heroes. "France got drunk with blood to vomit crime," Byron says (*CHP* IV, 97), and his version of the French Revolution (typical among English Romantics) tells of the metamorphosis of the redeemer into the accuser. Thus, man is primarily the victim of himself, for by presuming the right to render evil for evil he sustains the deepest wounds and the worst bondage.

174

Oh, Power that rulest and inspirest! how
Is it that they on earth, whose earthly power
Is likest thine in heaven in outward show,
Least like to thee in attributes divine,
Tread on the universal necks that bow,
And then assure us that their rights are thine?
And how is it that they, the sons of fame . . .
Must pass their days in penury or pain,
Or step to grandeur through the paths of shame,
And wear a deeper brand and gaudier chain. . . .
In their own souls [they] sustain a harder proof,
The inner war of passions deep and fierce.

(*The Prophecy of Dante* IV, 95 ff.)

The early tales, and plays like *The Two Foscari* and *Marino Faliero*, dramatize the translation of revolutionary action into forms of inner or outer slavery. In these works we are told that war with evil threatens the corruption of those who would bring freedom to themselves and their society. "There is *no* freedom, even for *Masters*, in the midst of slaves," Byron says (*LJ* 5:451). The plays in particular argue that when evil becomes embodied in a political structure it is self-propagating, and cannot be removed without the destruction of the social system which it inhabits. In such circumstances freedom is only possible within the individual, who must renounce his connections with society. In the early tales this same problem is explored as a psychological rather than sociopsychological phenomenon. The Giaour is infected with the disease of the man he hates, and finally kills. Similarly, Shelley's Prometheus has cursed Jupiter, and his bondage and suffering result directly from that act. Ali Pasha is doomed to begin and end in blood.

But all these men are driven by "a fire/And motion of the soul" (*CHP* III, 42) like Napoleon, and Byron regards this energy as the fundamental requirement of any vital existence. It is the inability to understand the nature of this force, and thence to govern it properly, that brings disaster. Byron's thought here seems strictly classical. His Napoleon, for example, is a man who carries out the will of the gods by humbling tyrannical kings. His providential mission turns to his own destruction, however, for he becomes himself a tyrant and sins against the gods by worshiping himself and accepting the worship of others (*CHP* III, 37 ff.). Unable to "curb the lust of war," he preys upon adventure in a ceaseless effort to set a proof upon his own authority. In Byron's view, however, Napoleon's public mission is not a human conception but a Divine Plan, just as the fire within is not a human creation but the gift of Life. Napoleon's career could have been the sign of personal greatness had he not tempted fate and the gods by elevating his own will. Man must submit to the destiny that is given him by aiming neither above it nor below it. Analogously, the active pursuit of revenge is the worst of crimes because it involves the personal assumption of unwarranted prerogatives.

> Though, like old Marius from Minturnae's marsh
> And Carthage ruins, my lone breast may burn
> At times with evil feelings hot and harsh,
> And sometimes the last pangs of a vile foe
> Writhe in a dream before me and o'erarch
> My brow with hopes of triumph,—let them go!
> Such are the last infirmities of those
> Who long have suffer'd more than mortal woe,
> And yet, being mortal still, have no repose
> But on the pillow of Revenge—Revenge,
> Who sleeps to dream of blood, and waking glows
> With the oft-baffled, slakeless thirst of change,
> When we shall mount again, and they that trod
> Be trampled on, while Death and Ate range
> O'er humbled heads and sever'd necks.—Great God!
> Take these thoughts from me; to thy hands I yield
> My many wrongs, and thine almighty rod
> Will fall on those who smote me,—be my shield!
> As thou hast been in peril, and in pain,
> In turbulent cities, and the tented field,
> In toil, and many troubles borne in vain
> For Florence. I appeal from her to Thee!
>
> (*The Prophecy of Dante* i, 104–25)

The same attitudes are predominant motifs in *Childe Harold's Pilgrimage IV*, and not only in the forgiveness-curse sequence. Byron holds up Cromwell's career as an apt example that in life it is man's part to perfect and glorify the will of the gods. In a note explaining his verses on Cromwell Byron writes:

> On the third of September, Cromwell gained the victory of Dunbar; a year after he obtained "his crowning mercy" of Worcester; and a few years after, on the same day, which he had ever esteemed the most fortunate for him, died.[1]

[1] P 2:394–95.

Byron's point is that this series of "coincidences" is really fatality, the manifestation of divine governance. "Beneath/His fate the moral lurks of destiny," Byron says (IV, 85), and everything Byron records of him in the poem illustrates that Providence had controlled Cromwell's career.

In *Mazeppa* Byron again explores the problems that arise because of "the fire which we endure." Ever since Voltaire's great study of him, Charles XII had become the byword of the man hopelessly consumed with that characteristic Byronic chimera, "the lust to shine or rule" (*CHP* III, 43). As such, he finds a place in Johnson's "Vanity of Human Wishes" (a favorite poem of Byron's). The *Histoire de Charles XII* argues the personal and political futility of Charles's career and concludes that the program of a beneficent and peaceful monarchy is much preferable to any policy of conquest, no matter how adventurous or daring. Byron's "Sonnet to the Prince Regent," composed while *Mazeppa* was being written, argues approximately the same point. Because Byron's Charles is consciously drawn after the traditional eighteenth-century likeness, he is easily made to embody the characteristic traits of the Byronic hero. Johnson concludes his portrait of Charles with the couplet:

> He left the name, at which the world grew pale,
> To point a moral, or adorn a tale.   (221–22)

The lines have a suggestive affinity with Byron's famous verses on Conrad.

> He left a Corsair's name to other times,
> Link'd with one virtue and a thousand crimes.

Like Napoleon, who has "a fever at the core" (*CHP* III, 42), Charles is driven along by a "fever in his blood" (*Mazeppa*, 37). The parallel with Napoleon is directly conveyed in the opening stanza.

> 'T was after dread Pultowa's day,
> When fortune left the royal Swede,
> Around a slaughter'd army lay,
> No more to combat and to bleed.
> The power and glory of the war,
> Faithless as their vain votaries, men,
> Had pass'd to the triumphant Czar,
> And Moscow's walls were safe again,
> Until a day more dark and drear,

> And a more memorable year,
> Should give to slaughter and to shame
> A mightier host and haughtier name. . . .

All Byronic heroes have to bear the consequences of their overweening appropriation of the gift of the gods. Like all "Conquerors and Kings" (*CHP* III, 48) whom Byron never fails to pillory in his work, Charles is "Stain'd with his own and subjects' blood" (18). This is the accusation which Byron throws at Napoleon, the contemporary avatar of the universal spirit which possessed Charles XII and many others before him.

The King of Sweden properly appears at the opening of *Mazeppa* to point the moral and adorn the tale of the self-possessed Cossack Prince. When Charles, the Byronic man of will, collapses beneath a tree after his flight from the battle, he has forcibly to subdue the "pangs" of a proud but defeated warrior. "Son courage ne pouvant plus suppléer à ses forces épuisées," as Byron notes in his epigraph from Voltaire, Charles has

> To force of cheer a greater show,
> And seem above both wounds and woe.   (95–6)

But the king's self-control is a grand but pathetic illusion produced for the occasion. Charles' lack of inherent self-possession—his need to force some sort of control upon himself—stems from and results in the same problem that Napoleon had: the inability to rest, to submit to the will of *Fortuna*, and of Nature herself. A passage from *The Corsair* analyzes this characteristic flaw in the Byronic hero very well. Medora tells Conrad she is frightened for him because he

> flies from love and languishes for strife—
> How strange that heart, to use so tender still,
> Should war with nature and its better will!   (I, 395–97)

The transformation of epithets in the first line is a brilliant economic expression of the kind of dialectic that imprisons the Byronic hero. It anticipates Charles's moral character exactly, who is set off against Mazeppa and his early mentor John Casimir.

> John Casimir,—I was his page
> Six summers, in my early age,
> A learned monarch, faith! was he,
> And most unlike your majesty:
> He made no wars, and did not gain

> New realms to lose them back again;
> And (save debates in Warsaw's diet)
> He reign'd in most unseemly quiet.
> Not that he had no cares to vex,
> He loved the muses and the sex;
> And sometimes these so forward are,
> They made him wish himself at war. . . .   (129–140)

Charles languishes for strife rather than for love and pleasure, or books. The lines distinctly foreshadow some of Sardanapalus' statements about the kingly life. Like the following passage, they suggest that Charles is "at war with nature and its better will."

> I loved, and was beloved again—
> They tell me, Sire, you never knew
> Those gentle frailties; if 't is true,
> I shorten all my joy or pain;
> To you 't would seem absurd as vain:
> But all men are not born to reign,
> Or o'er their passions, or as you,
> Thus o'er themselves and nations too.   (282–89)

Mazeppa's irony is even sharper here, for the poem's ultimate point is that Charles does not really know how to reign over himself or his kingdom, but Mazeppa does. The Cossack hero's regal bearing is a function equally of his inclination to the "gentle frailities" and his hard lesson on the back of the wild stallion. The first shows his instinctive tendency to natural virtue and the second is his confirmation in a submission to nature and fate, which finally teaches him how to reign over himself and his passions. In the end we are shown that the "sons of pleasure" (736), like Sardanapalus, or Beppo, Laura, and her Count, or Torquil and Neuha, live in a manner that is at once more natural and godlike. In *Mazeppa* that life is not actually described for us. It is hinted at throughout but the tale is written mainly to show how one particular man of action gained supremacy over himself, and another did not.

Charles is thus Mazeppa's foil in the story. The initial picture of the old prince at the bivouac contrasts sharply with what we have seen of the king. Mazeppa does not languish within himself or put on regal appearances, but attends to the necessaries of the moment. First, he carefully grooms and feeds his horse and, after setting his equipment in order, he prepares his own meal and offers to share it with the others (who, imitating their king, have been lying about "sad and mute").

Charles himself tells us that Mazeppa is an intrepid warrior, so that our initial impression of him as both "calm and bold" (56) is established in the opening scenes of the poem. His horse is named after Alexander's and it possesses characteristics equivalent to his master's ("spirited and docile too," 68). Both fight when they must and rest when they can. As Bucephalus follows the spirit of Mazeppa's will, the aged prince exercises his own will within the terms and after the example of a better will than his own. He can and does establish his own integrity upon any given circumstances. Thus he becomes the master of unknown and shifting Fate. Perceiving that "time at last sets all things even" (417)— a predominant theme in all of Byron's poetry after the separation—Mazeppa is never blindly at strife with his blessedness.

Mazeppa's story explains his character. Ostensibly it tells how "he learn'd to ride" (108) so well, but the manifest symbolism of the events —as Graham Hough has pointed out[2]—extends the literal meaning to an illustration of how Mazeppa learned to control his passions and utilize the "fire and motion" within himself. As a youth he was headstrong and passionate, and fell in love with the young wife of a cruel and "proud Count Palatine" (343). When the liaison is discovered Mazeppa is bound to an unbroken Arabian horse and driven out to die upon its back. The description of that wild ride epitomizes the poetic quality of this neglected masterpiece. At that time, Mazeppa tells us, he could not control himself but was ever

> headlong as a wintry stream,
> And wore my feelings out before
> I well could count their causes o'er.   (526–28)

Strapped to the fleeing horse, Mazeppa struggles to free himself but discovers that every effort only increases the uncontrolled fury of the animal (st. XI) as well as his own agony. His lack of self-mastery is dramatized again in the next stanza when he relates how they entered a "wild wood" and began to be tracked by a wolf pack. Mazeppa, struck with fear and a sense of his own ineffectualness, indulges, first, in a wish that he might die fighting the wolves, and second, in feelings of doubt and despair that the horse will be able to outrun their pursuers. Both hope and doubt are "Vain," he points out for us, and compares the "Bewilder'd" frenzy of the horse with the fury of "a favour'd child/ Balk'd of its wish." The parallel between the mad career of the horse

2 Graham Hough, *Image and Experience* (London, 1960), p. 138.

and his own lack of control is thus enforced (his struggles to escape, his foolish hopes, his "Vain doubt").

The next stanza illustrates yet again the fundamental weakness of unmoderated passions and willfulness. "Prolong'd endurance tames the bold," he declares, for a "headlong" nature tends to wear itself out prematurely and succumb to imposed trials precisely because such a man redoubles his agonies by fighting against them with inner fears and anxieties.

> And what with fury, fear, and wrath,
> The tortures which beset my path,
> Cold, hunger, sorrow, shame, distress,
> Thus bound in nature's nakedness
> (Sprung from a race whose rising blood
> When stirr'd beyond its calmer mood,
> And trodden hard upon, is like
> The rattle snake's in act to strike),
> What marvel if this out-worn trunk
> Beneath its woes a moment sunk?   (529–38)[3]

This is the condition into which Bonnivard and Harold fall, and remain, and it is the crisis in Mazeppa's ride. He now undergoes a kind of death (literally, he is fainting) which he vainly struggles against. This last effort of will having been beaten back, he finds himself cast adrift into total "confusion," released from all self-imposed controls "as on a plank at sea." At a similar moment in *Childe Harold's Pilgrimage IV* (st. 105) Byron regains his hold on life, enters a full and more capable existence where he can see that

> there is that within me which shall tire
> Torture and Time, and breathe when I expire;
> Something unearthly which they deem not of....   (137)

This "unearthly" power is the principle of Life itself, "the fire which we endure" and which can only be extinguished by moral suicide. The force is, strictly, neither spiritual nor physical, but that fundamental thing which is human life and which comprises both together. Byron describes this incarnate power in *The Prophecy of Dante* as the

[3] E. H. Coleridge finds the "conclusion . . . at variance with the premiss" in this passage (P 4:223, n. 1). This is, strictly construed, true, but if we recall the dialectic of emotions that is characteristic of the Byronic hero we will see the point of the lines. The passage leaves unexpressed the specific relationship between Byronic rage and Byronic exhaustion.

> body's self turn'd soul with the intense
> Feeling of that which is, and fancy of
> That which should be. . . .   (III, 163–65)[4]

Mazeppa is saved from death when he ceases to struggle against it, when he gives himself up to the governance of the unearthly power he participates in. So, at the beginning of stanza XIV he tells not how *he* regained life, but how "Life reassumed its lingering hold" upon him. The consequence is an access of responsiveness within himself, a new beginning ("My heart began once more to thrill"). He is borne across an "unknown and silent shore" which is both a real place (presumably a river) and a spiritual boundary. Thus, as the horse enters the water Mazeppa is wakened from his trance and "rebaptized." At this point both horse and man acquire a "new-born tameness" (632) as the animal begins his descent into death and Mazeppa his ascent to life. He makes one more "feeble effort" to break free but immediately leaves off such "idle strife." But "The weary brute still stagger'd on" (666), and with a last effort he carries Mazeppa to what Graham Hough has described as "the land of the wild horses—the realm that is to say where the untamed passions are at home."[5] The experience is both visionary and graphically phenomenal, for the horses are in fact a wild herd roaming the reaches of the Ukraine, and a symbolic revelation of what is most vital and most dangerous in man. They represent a part of that which makes man human and all that makes him bestial. At first unable to distinguish Mazeppa from his horse, they whirl around him sniffing the air, attempting to discover his nature. Finally they detect his humanness and "By instinct" (708) flee away. Left alone, Mazeppa arrives at the fullness of understanding.

> And there from morn to twilight bound,
> I felt the heavy hours toil round,
> With just enough of life to see
> My last of suns go down on me,
> In hopeless certainty of mind,
> That makes us feel at length resign'd
> To that which our foreboding years
> Presents the worst and last of fears
> Inevitable—even a boon,

---

[4] The lines suggest Byron's definition of poetry as "the feeling of a Former world and Future." *LJ* 5:189.

[5] Hough, *Image and Experience*, p. 139.

Nor more unkind for coming soon!
Yet shunn'd and dreaded with such care,
As if it only were a snare
That prudence might escape:
At times both wish'd for and implored,
At times sought with self-pointed sword,
Yet still a dark and hideous close
To even intolerable woes,
And welcome in no shape.
And, strange to say, the sons of pleasure,
They who have revell'd beyond measure
In beauty, wassail, wine, and treasure,
Die calm, or calmer oft than he
Whose heritage was misery:
For he who hath in turn run through
All that was beautiful and new,
Hath nought to hope, and nought to leave;
And, save the future (which is view'd
Not quite as men are base or good,
But as their nerves may be endued),
With nought perhaps to grieve:—
The wretch still hopes his woes must end,
And Death, whom he should deem his friend,
Appears, to his distemper'd eyes,
Arrived to rob him of his prize,
The tree of his new Paradise.
To-morrow would have given him all,
Repaid his pangs, repair'd his fall;
To-morrow would have been the first
Of days no more deplored or curst,
But bright, and long, and beckoning years,
Seen dazzling through the mist of tears,
Guerdon of many a painful hour;
To-morrow would have given him power
To rule, to shine, to smite, to save—
And must it dawn upon his grave?   (718–62)

This beautiful passage is a comment both on the restless Charles, who is consumed with a "mad endeavour" toward his personal goals, and the calm but bold Mazeppa, who has learned the lesson of his wild ride and become resigned to the "hopeless certainty" of human life and death. Like Camus's Meursault, Mazeppa has experienced the annihilation of all his personal hopes and schemes—even his desire for revenge is gone—and has discovered that life begins in the discovery of the fact and meaning of death.

This knowledge is the justification of the plot on Mazeppa's life, the reason that he is rescued by "the Cossack maid." Knowing at last how to live, he sees that life is possible for him. He does not lose his old exuberance—even at seventy, he says, love is still a thing of "fierce extremes" in him. What he gains is, first, the wisdom to care for and "ride" his vigorous life (as he does Bucephalus) and not struggle against it with conscious purposiveness. Charles is puritanically self-directed and has given up the "joy or pain" of love and earthly passion for a life of passionate willfulness. Mazeppa, however, has discovered the wise passiveness of the "sons of pleasure." Second, Mazeppa has come to understand the secret of temporal process. The sun can be made neither to stand still nor to run; he keeps his own course, and all things reach their appointed end. "Time at last sets all things even," he says retrospectively, and Mazeppa is eventually able to take his revenge. Byron does not judge him harshly for this, however, for he seems to do it with a calmness and certainty of mind that are quite unlike the fiery converts of revenge in Byron's other stories. Like all of Mazeppa's acts, this one seems to consummate the emotion that brought it about, seems rather the manifestation of the gods' will than a man's. Biographically the poem is another curious example of Byron's habit of compensating through his poetry, for if he turns back the curse with forgiveness in *Childe Harold's Pilgrimage*, here he indulges it by recounting the history of yet another alter ego.

The ending of the poem is something of a puzzle, for while it is clearly meant to satirize the king for his inability to learn an important lesson about life, as Mazeppa had done in his youth, still the old hetman's tale does achieve its most immediate purpose of helping the restless king get some needed sleep. Byron probably meant to leave the poem on just such an equivocal note, for an irony of this sort would have exactly suited his taste for the perverse. Besides, the ending might not be counted a flaw in the poem were one to measure success in terms of immediate effect. The irony does undercut the integrity of the work at one level, but Byron had begun *Don Juan* while this tale was in process and the antisystematic basis which supports that work from the beginning may have carried over to *Mazeppa*. Don Juanesque moods flit in and out of the tale through the first seven stanzas,[6] and the unconven-

---

[6] Leslie Marchand has pointed this out in his *Byron's Poetry: A Critical Introduction* (Boston, 1965), pp. 70–71.

tional ending amounts almost to a convention in *Don Juan*. "Nothing so difficult as a beginning/In poesy," he jocularly confessed, "unless perhaps the end" (*DJ* IV, 1). The observation follows immediately upon the completely arbitrary ending of Canto III. And Byron had done this sort of thing before. "Granta, A Medley," we might recall, was jerked to an end in a rather similar way, as if the business of writing had grown tiresome and he decided simply to break off. *Don Juan* makes this kind of trick a minor leitmotiv, one of the many stylistic habits of his wayward and pleasure-oriented sensibility.

An Olden Tale of Love

The Giaour, Byron's first completed tale, opens with a seascape that intimates an earthly paradise. But man, "enamour'd of distress," violates Nature's intentions by transforming her "fairy land" into a moral "wilderness" (*The Giaour*, 50 ff.). This natural and human tragedy, detailed in a variety of ways in Byron's poetry, remained for him an important concern throughout his career: "the unreached paradise" is man's (and Byron's) "despair" precisely because he can never give over the intimation of and desire for complete human fulfillment. Byron's poetry maps out the pilgrimage of his frustrated longings, and the curious fact arises that the more skeptical he grew the more firmly convinced he became of the value of his wanderings and the reality of his end. Poetry is "The feeling of a Former world and Future," he says in 1821, adding that "if it were not for Hope where would the future be?—in hell" (*LJ* 5: 189–90). Unamuno argues in *The Tragic Sense of Life* that all religious and transcendental experience demands a prior experience of absolute skepticism. Stripped of all humanly definable reasons for hope, man, Unamuno says, cries out that his highest longings must nevertheless be true. *Certum est quia impossibile est.* This attitude erupts with extraordinary vigor in the last four cantos of *Don Juan*, where Byron even quotes from Tertullian's famous assertion (though he misapplies it to Augustine: *DJ* XVI, 5–6); and he keeps playing variations upon this theme and that of the earthly paradise throughout the final cantos. "He who doubts all things nothing can deny," Byron says (*DJ* XV, 88), and adds that though all visionary realities are clearly "false" by realistic standards, nevertheless they "may be rendered also true" by an even more skeptical and realistic mind. The immense fecundity of Nature remains the norm, for in the

186

face of such a wonder all man's supposed knowledge—especially his philosophic systems—comes to a halt of ignorance.

> If from great Nature's or our own abyss
> Of thought we could but snatch a certainty,
> Perhaps mankind might find the path they miss—
> But then 't would spoil much good philosophy.
> One system eats another up, and this
> Much as old Saturn ate his progeny;
> For when his pious consort gave him stones
> In lieu of sons, of these he made no bones.
>
> But System doth reverse the Titan's breakfast,
> And eats her parents, albeit the digestion
> Is difficult. Pray tell me, can you make fast,
> After due search, your faith to any question?
> Look back o'er ages, ere unto the stake fast
> You bind yourself, and call some mode the best one.
> Nothing more true than *not* to trust your senses;
> And yet what are your other evidences?
>
> For me, I know nought; nothing I deny,
> Admit, reject, contemn; and what know *you*,
> Except perhaps that you were born to die?
> And both may after all turn out untrue.
> An age may come, Font of Eternity,
> When nothing shall be either old or new.   (*DJ* xiv, 1–3)

"Perhaps it may turn out that all were right," Byron says later (XV, 90), for he wants to convince us that "great creating Nature" is infinitely capable. "Whatever bar the reason rears" against even the most fantastic human beliefs "there's something stronger still/In its behalf, let those deny who will" (*DJ* XVI, 7). Thus, for Byron, human existence within a natural continuum participates in the transcendent, even defines the equivocal aspect of both the mundane and the supermundane. Life is hell and heaven, paradise and wilderness; it is a "waste and icy clime" and a present fairyland. Indeed, perhaps the most famous trope in *Don Juan* positively suggests that the two are correlatively actual.

> I'll have another figure in a trice:—
> What say you to a bottle of champagne?
> Frozen into a very vinous ice,

Which leaves few drops of that immortal rain,
Yet in the very centre, past all price,
About a liquid glassful will remain;
And this is stronger than the strongest grape
Could e'er express in its expanded shape:

'T is the whole spirit brought to a quintessence;
And thus the chilliest aspects may concentre
A hidden nectar under a cold presence.
And such are many—though I only meant her
From whom I now deduce these moral lessons,
On which the Muse has always sought to enter.
And your cold people are beyond all price,
When once you have broken their confounded ice. (XIII, 37–38)

The sexual aspect of the metaphor is crucial, for it emphasizes—as do many similar images in *Beppo*, for example—the immediate and natural reality of what Byron liked to call the *beau idéal*.

Byron wrote these final cantos of *Don Juan* immediately after completing *The Island*, the last of his verse tales, which was written in January and the beginning of February, 1823. The thematic correspondences between these works are pronounced, though perhaps not immediately noticeable because of the great differences in the materials. Regency England is some distance from Neuha's paradise and the tale certainly argues more conclusively for a natural apocalypse. Nevertheless, the inconclusiveness of the *Don Juan* cantos is structural, not thematic, for in them Byron is quite positive in his paradisal pronouncements. The affirmation is not that paradise is exclusively true but that it is really true, in despite of all entropic forces. Similarly, if the late cantos of *Don Juan* present factors which negative Byron's visionary gleams, *The Island* itself does not overlook these forces. The King's ship represents that ordinary law and disorder which produce the conflicted world of the Byronic hero, and it does not pass out of existence at the end of the tale: it merely goes somewhere else.

Thematically, *The Island* is Byron's final attempt to define the problems he raised in *The Giaour* and the other early tales which treat the doomed struggles of the Byronic hero. Like the Greece of *Childe Harold's Pilgrimage II* and the Italy of Canto IV, the seascape of *The Giaour* preserves its natural beauty despite the moral destructiveness which man brings to it. Neuha's island corresponds to these earlier places—it represents nature in a state of continuously youthful vigor and beauty—but it differs from them in that it has not yet been plundered by civilization.[1] The condition for gaining this land, as in *The Giaour*, is the possession of the woman who represents the spirit of the place. Torquil's fate depends upon whether or not he can establish ties with "The infant of an infant world" (II, vii).

Because the relation between the Byronic hero and his female love-ideal is of some consequence for understanding most of Byron's tales, including *The Island*, I must go into the matter briefly. Leila, Medora, Gulnare, Zuleika, Parisina, and Neuha are all Egeria figures.

> The mind hath made thee, as it peopled heaven,
> Even with its own desiring phantasy,
> And to a thought such shape and image given,
> As haunts the unquench'd soul. . . .   (*CHP* IV, 121)

As the entire Egeria passage in the canto suggests, however, man's love-ideal is a highly equivocal possession. "The mind's ideal shape" of beauty can produce "holy love" and "immortal transports" as well as "the whirlwind" and "irrevocable wrong" (IV, 118–25). The female counterparts of Byron's heroes are similarly various, but in every case they correspond exactly to the state of the hero's soul which they inhabit. They objectify the passionate impulses in the man whose imagination made them what they are. This is as much to say that none of them are truly "persons." Most readers of Byron have recognized this "unrealistic" quality in many of his women, and it has often been regarded as a grave fault. Such a judgment is, in my opinion, mistaken, for these women are allegorical figures set in an allegorical framework. Blake's females are of the same order. Nevertheless, Byron's women are by no means wholly simplistic counters, for their natures correspond to the respective conditions of their heroes' souls.

Bernard Blackstone has pointed out that "Byron has to kill Christian off, for his rebellion is rooted in hatred of tyranny and not love of pleasure: he is the true Byronic hero, and such heroes never survive."[2] Hatred of tyranny is always allied to the longing for pleasure in Byron's poetry, however, for Byron's heroes are nearly always caught in a situation where something prohibits the fulfillment of the Eros-drive. When his heroes become seduced into a conflict with that which opposes their highest longings they are, as Professor Blackstone has said, irrevocably doomed, for in their engagement with their antago-

---

[1] The parallel between *The Island* and *The Giaour* is nicely epitomized in each poem's use of the rose and the nightingale image in reference to the theme of the natural Eden. See *The Island*, II, xv and *The Giaour*, 21–33.

[2] Bernard Blackstone, "Guilt and Retribution in Byron's Sea Poems," *Essays*, p. 36.

nists they acquire some negative qualities. This idea is used by Shelley in *Prometheus Unbound* to explain the initial circumstance of bondage; Blake gets at the same notion in his theory of the Orc Cycle; and Byron repeats his perception of this truth in his frequent pronouncements upon "hereditary rage" (*CHP* IV, 94). The pattern is perhaps most clearly outlined in *The Corsair* and its sequel, *Lara*. Conrad is devoted to Medora, a wholly positive image of love-fulfillment who presides over his nuptial hall. But Conrad's heart is not sufficiently true to Medora, for he is as "enamour'd of distress" as he is of Medora. Like his mortal foe, Seyd, Conrad's "thoughts on love and hate alternate dwell" (III, v). So he goes to destroy his enemy, is captured, but is finally rescued by Gulnare. She has fallen in love with him and, loathing Seyd, she murders her lord and flees the harem with Conrad. The pair are saved an embarrassing encounter with Medora, however, for when they reach Conrad's hideout Medora is discovered dead. Though no explicit reason is produced for this sudden event none is really needed, for the moral allegory of the story is quite plain. Medora's place has been usurped by Gulnare, and rightly so, for Gulnare is the proper image of Conrad's divided spiritual aims. Untrue to the highest possibilities of his own nature, Conrad gains as he gives the life he images forth. For the rest of his life he is tormented by the loss of Medora and followed about by the faithful Gulnare/Kaled.

The Giaour, as we have seen, presents a similar pattern, only in this case the equivocal aspects of the love-ideal are incorporated in the character of Leila. We never see her directly, but it is made perfectly clear that she draws the Giaour on to revenge just as she had, before her death, drawn him on toward a love paradise. The other tales which treat this theme recapitulate the pattern in one way or another. Selim, more interested in revenge and power than in love and pleasure, loses both his life and Zuleika (they are really the same thing). Similarly, Hugo is as much determined to serve Prince Azo a "wrong for wrong" (xiii) as he is to possess the lover who was taken from him. He hates his father but judges (rightly) that his own nature mirrors that of his parent.

> Yet in my lineaments they trace
> Some features of my father's face,
> And in my spirit—all of thee;
> From thee this tamelessness of heart . . .
> From thee in all their vigour came
> My arm of strength, my soul of flame;

> Thou didst not give me life alone,
> But all that made me more thine own. (xiii)

Parisina remains the focus of this conflict. Misplaced alike in marriage and a (de jure) incestuous love affair, she emphasizes the warp in the love relationship between the son and the father, while her madness and death at the end fully objectify the tragedy which has consumed the passions of both men.

All the mutineers on the *Bounty* begin as pilgrims bound by a common longing and for a common goal.

> Young hearts, which languish'd for some sunny isle,
> Where summer years and summer women smile. . . . (I, ii)

Neuha epitomizes that toward which they are all impelled. Foreshadowing the poem's conclusion, Byron compares her to the

> coral reddening through the darken'd wave,
> Which draws the diver to the crimson cave. (II, vii)

She is everywhere associated with the sea in its mildest aspects and, though soft and gentle, she is "full of life" (II, vii). She is, in fact, the epipsyche of the island and represents, like her land, the love feast called *agapé* which is at once the death and the completion of the Eros-longing. This identification is perhaps nowhere more explicitly drawn than in the comparison of Neuha to Venus rising from the sea,

> With all her loves around her on the deep,
> Voluptuous as the first approach of sleep. . . . (II, vii)

If all the mariners sail in search of her, however, only Torquil completes the quest. Christian's character highlights exactly that rebellious aspect of Eros which Professor Blackstone has pointed to and which is the ultimate cause of the failure of the love-quest. As the leader of the mutineers Christian embodies a quality which is common to all his followers, including Torquil (Byron explicitly tells us that, under different circumstances, Neuha's husband might have turned out just another Byronic hero). Torquil, however, is the one least committed to violence. He leaves Neuha and goes to fight with his comrades most reluctantly, as Ben Bunting ironically points out. His heart remains fixed on his new bride ("I am thine whatever intervenes," he tells her: II, xxi).

Torquil's birthplace further emphasizes the difference between himself and his comrades and the propriety of his ultimate union with

Neuha. Born in the Hebrides and "Nursed by the legends of his land's romance" (II, viii), Torquil conceives his place of origin in terms that clearly suggest supermundane values. In this he distinctly recalls the poet of "Lachin Y. Gair" and "A Fragment," and Byron specifies the comparison in II, xii where he refers to his own "infant rapture" when he roamed a young highlander. Further, Torquil's birthplace has made the sea his closest comrade and his truest earthly home.

> Rock'd in his cradle by the roaring wind,
> The tempest-born in body and in mind,
> His young eyes opening on the ocean-foam
> Had from that moment deem'd the deep his home,
> The giant comrade of his pensive moods,
> The sharer of his craggy solitudes,
> The only Mentor of his youth where'er
> His bark was borne; the sport of wave and air;
> A careless thing, who placed his choice in chance,
> Nursed by the legends of his land's romance;
> Eager to hope, but not less firm to bear,
> Acquainted with all feelings save despair.   (II, viii)

"I was, as it were, a child of thee," Byron says in his famous address to the Ocean, and the same is true of Torquil. Unlike his fellow mariners, he can never be fully estranged from his origins so long as he is near the sea. Instead of being a man without a country Torquil is really a man of uncircumscribed possibilities. He gives himself up completely to the ministrations ("chance") of his foster-parent, the Ocean, much as Wordsworth accepts the direction of "Nature," and this submission to Providence affords him the means of the recovery of his Western Islands. In the end we are meant to understand that Torquil's sea and the Hebrides are the same thing seen in different perspectives: the one is Torquil's imaginative ideal conceived in terms of *kinesis*, the other in terms of *stasis*.

These connections highlight the special relation between Torquil and his emanation Neuha. As his proper consort and counterpart, she too is the offspring of an island associated with the sea and embodying spiritual values (II, xii). But in Neuha's southern world the fixed island and the moving waters are everywhere conceived in terms of *passion* (in the philosophical sense); Torquil's northern sea and island, on the other hand, are defined by images that suggest vigorous movement and action. He is "The tempest-born" while she is the "sunflower of the island daughters" (II, x). Their marriage, in other words, recapitulates the fusion of *stasis* and *kinesis* which each one partially realizes alone.

Together, like true platonic lovers, they join the two halves of the separated world. Torquil resembles all Byronic heroes in that he too longs "For rest—but not to feel 't is rest" (*The Giaour*, 995), and his union with Neuha cancels forever "the irksome restlessness of rest" (II, xiii) which he must, to some extent, suffer without her. But Byron's sea never did betray the heart that truly loved her, and Neuha is that sea's last and fulfilling gift to Torquil. She incarnates his deepest desires and he completes himself in her. In Byron, the restlessness (e.g., anxiety) which aims at cessation is intimately connected with that rest (e.g., ennui) which inevitably produces only further restlessness; in this tale Byron dramatizes a solution to that savage dialectic. Torquil's possession of beatitude is imaged in terms of a "rest" that does not "feel" like rest to him.

Poetically *The Island* is something of a mixed bag, but the perfection of the lovers' land-sea paradise is rendered with great beauty and exactness in stanzas xv–xvii of Canto II. The central idea in these sections is that the lovers have pushed beyond the barriers of ordinary space and time. Because their existence is now defined only in terms of love, they do not live in life as man ordinarily conceives it. The true lover, Byron says,

> Lives not in earth, but in his ecstasy;
> Around him days and worlds are heedless driven,
> His soul is gone before his dust to heaven.   (II, xvi)

This heightened life offers an eternity within the borders of time.

> What deem'd they of the future or the past?
> The present, like a tyrant, held them fast.
> Their hour-glass was the sea-sand, and the tide,
> Like her smooth billow, saw their moments glide;
> Their clock the sun, in his unbounded tow'r;
> They reckon'd not, whose day was but an hour.   (II, xv)

Experience has for them no beginning and no ending. Torquil, in fact, finds that he does not have to glance back longingly over his shoulder toward a paradise that has gone, or forward beyond his present condition for one that is yet to arrive. The future and the past meet in his relationship with Neuha.[3] Christian's situation is, by contrast, a serious predicament, for he knows that he cannot expect any present fulfill-

---

[3] This convergence is emphasized by an important verbal repetition. Byron points out that Torquil's sublime origins are "Loved to the last, whatever intervenes" (II, xii), and he later repeats the phrase with reference to Torquil's feelings for Neuha, his latest love (II, xxi).

ment. As a result, the end of his life becomes a struggle to secure at least a future for his desires, and this future is explicitly represented in Torquil. Christian fears for his young friend's life, reproaches himself for having placed it in danger, and hopes that Torquil may be saved even if no one else is. Once again the allegorical pattern is clear.

By their love Torquil and Neuha achieve an instantaneous identity with nature's enormous fruitfulness. Life is measured not by clock-time but within a context of successive ecstasies. Thus, Torquil's love energies are constantly fulfilled, extinguished, and reborn in his passion for Neuha. The process is conceived as a succession of immediacies, and Eros is thereby turned from a movement toward a goal into a possession of that goal. Torquil's longing undergoes a sea-change into a present intensity when the linear form of his love is bent into a circle. The achievement of this heightened existence requires that the lovers "die into life" like Keats's Apollo. "Wrapt in one blaze" of mutually enflaming love (II, xvi), Neuha and Torquil burn off the "fond and false identity" (II, xvi) which is their earthly persona and in their love-death they gain a higher life. They are like martyrs "burning in the new-born fire" and reveling in their consummating death.

> With such devotion in their ecstasy
> That life knows no such rapture as to die:
> And die they do; for earthly life has nought
> Match'd with that burst of nature, even in thought. . . .   (II, vi)

Nothing human dies in this fire, and a fullness is gained when the desire for life, ending at last, becomes wholly translated into the desire for love. This ancient idea—that love is more important than life, indeed, that love alone makes life possible—is crucial to *The Island*, where everything that is human depends upon the felt experience rather than on the conditions of that experience (upon "ecstasy" and the "burst of nature" rather than upon "life" or "days and worlds"). The lover's existence is defined wholly as an emotional-spiritual élan; life as a continuum for such experiences is taken for granted. As Byron observes in *Beppo*, the most vital man (himself, of course) can "see the sun set, sure he'll rise to-morrow" (43) because all concern for tomorrow's sun vanishes in the aggressive enjoyment of today's, and because present and natural beatitude is the highest spiritual value in a world where the sun is God supreme.

Torquil and Neuha also watch a magnificent sunset in II, xv, and the passage focuses most of these central ideas I have been discussing.

The broad sun set, but not with lingering sweep,
As in the north he mellows o'er the deep;
But fiery, full, and fierce, as if he left
The world for ever, earth of light bereft,
Plunged with red forehead down along the wave,
As dives a hero, headlong to his grave.
Then rose they, looking first along the skies,
And then for light into each other's eyes,
Wondering that summer show'd so brief a sun,
And asking if indeed the day were done.

The lines are yet another repetition of the death/resurrection theme which pervades the poem and which reaches its climax in the great passages of the fourth canto. The sun presides over the island and its prototypical lovers, and his setting is at once a figure of their love (which is described as an ecstatic *Liebestod*) and of their eventual triumph. The sun plunges "as if" to his own death and "as if" he would leave the world forever bereft of light. But it is not so. He is sure of his rising, and his certainty is imaged in the flare of his energies, which are diminished neither by his rising nor by his falling. He masters his "death" as he masters his "life," by taking account of neither. His reality is not subject to life or death, day or night, but is itself the value which gives meaning to these poles of natural existence. Nevertheless, the sun's world is divided: he always shines somewhere but he does not shine everywhere, and this limitation of his powers suggests the supremacy of the lovers. They carry the light and fire which he embodies (in the daytime) and symbolizes (in general) into realms where he does not exist. Thus, like Donnian lovers, they represent a consummation of the sun's merely natural capacities since for them the distinction between daylight and nighttime does not exist. The last four lines of the passage anticipate the poem's central meaning, which is yet to be fully unfolded. When the sun has set the lovers are scarcely aware of his passing, for the light of their reciprocal love still burns brightly. The sun is, in fact, only a figure for the lovers. They "wonder" at the brief presence of this summer god because their own divinity is not subject even to the appearance of an alteration of this sort.

Ben Bunting's intrusion upon their love feast is the poem's way of reminding us that Torquil's allegiance to Neuha is not yet complete. He still has reluctant ties to Christian and his comrades and he returns to the world of the Byronic hero for the last time. As is to be expected, the mutineers put up a futile struggle against their retributive antagonists, and after the initial battle only four survive. Christian is especially oppressed by their defeat because it seems to mean the end of his one "hope" (III, vi), Torquil. Once again the nature of the Byronic hero is sharply defined, for Christian knows that it is his fate to perish without ever inhabiting the Promised Land. His hopes "are all before," and Torquil's peril is his last anxiety. In this condition he prays for a canoe to take Torquil away to safety, and his prayer is answered by the sudden appearance of Neuha and some of her countrymen in two canoes. The event is effective melodrama, but it carries as well an important significance for the allegory. Christian is by no means insensitive to his gloomy fate (cf. III, ix), and he envies Torquil because he recognizes the value that Neuha represents. Nevertheless, he has no Neuha and his fate is thereby settled. The gesture he performs at this critical juncture is essentially the same as that which a second generation Byronic hero makes at the end of *A Tale of Two Cities*. His prayer for Torquil's safety is the spell that finally releases the boy from all ties to the destructive Byronic milieu. Only Christian can utter this prayer since he is the Byronic hero fully embodied, whereas Torquil is in the process of losing his spectre (in Blake's sense) and gaining his resurrected self. Christian's prayer for Torquil makes it clear that the spectre is not praying through Christian for its own perpetuity (which would be the equivalent of a prayer for the continuance of what Blake saw as the Orc Cycle), but that Christian is willing the death of his spectre in order that his "hope" may be fulfilled. Were Torquil to utter this prayer the allegory would become clouded (and he, as a realistic character, morally suspect) because we would not be able to tell whether his old or his new self was speaking.

Torquil's absolute commitment to his emanation is not dramatized until the climactic scenes of Canto IV. The representatives of legal retribution demonstrate their antagonism to all true human life by pursuing Neuha and Torquil when the two fleeing boats separate. This is to be expected, however, for guilt and retribution are dialectical correlatives. I have pointed this out already in connection with the virtual identity between the Byronic hero and his enemy. Retribution cannot live without guilt, and its chief evil is not that it punishes well-meaning guilt but that it seeks to transform all innocence into guilt in order that it can secure its own existence. Dickens, Blake, and Kafka devote much of their work to exposing this unhappy fact about legal processes. In any case, Neuha and Torquil separate themselves at last from Christian and flee before their accusers, but Torquil is dismayed when he discovers that she has led him only to a bleak rock jutting out of the water. "Is this a place of safety, or a grave," he asks her (IV, iii). Actually, it is both, for though he plunges after Neuha to his apparent death, he rises with her again into a submarine cave beyond the knowledge and the reach of the world he has left. They die into life and gain thereby "a central realm of earth again" (IV, vi). The different speculations that his pursuers make about his fate underline the death-into-life motif of the passage.

> Some said he had not plunged into the wave,
> But vanish'd like a corpse-light from a grave;
> Others, that something supernatural
> Glared in his figure, more than mortal tall;
> While all agreed that in his cheek and eye
> There was a dead hue of eternity.
> Still as their oars receded from the crag,
> Round every weed a moment they would lag,
> Expectant of some token of their prey;
> But no—he had melted from them like the spray.   (IV, iv)

The corpse-light is another of Byron's variations upon the ignis fatuus image, and by describing it here only in terms of its vanishing he suggests both death and the end of death. The "dead hue of eternity" is similarly equivocal, while the "supernatural" aspect of his figure directs our attention to the idea of resurrection through death. Like the rainbow image, the final image of the sea-spray recurs in the poem and is associated throughout with the paradisal aspect of Neuha's island.

It is important to remember that Torquil's rescue depends upon his attachment to Neuha. His love and faith must be so strong that he would choose to follow her to the realms of the dead rather than survive without her. This is what his dive implies. Cain is asked to choose between love and knowledge but he equivocates and thus becomes the father of all subsequent Byronic heroes. Torquil is asked to choose between love and life, and by choosing love he gains a life beyond the reach of a world doomed to die.

> all within that cave
> Was love, though buried strong as in the grave
> Where Abelard, through twenty years of death,
> When Eloisa's form was lower'd beneath
> Their nuptial vault, his arms outstretched, and press'd
> The kindling ashes to his kindled breast.
> The waves without sang round their couch, their roar

> As much unheeded as if life were o'er;
> Within, their hearts made all their harmony,
> Love's broken murmur and more broken sigh.   (IV, ix)

Again the Christian form of thought recurs, but we cannot fail to see that Byron's context here is, though religious, quite pagan. Death and resurrection are for him metaphors describing a way of living in the natural, human world without being subject to its mastery. Death and resurrection intimate a transformed state of consciousness which enables man fully to possess again his promised human land. Neuha narrates for her lover

> An olden tale of love,—for love is old,
> Old as eternity, but not outworn,
> With each new being born or to be born. . . .   (IV, ix)

The tale is the history of their submarine cave, but it is really the perennial story of everyone "born or to be born." Like Torquil, the "young chief" of the legend chooses love rather than life and he passes his wisdom to his people by dramatizing his choice in a startling public gesture. His act focuses the demand made upon men to choose to be born. By choosing love before everything else, a man is born into a life that has value and meaning, and until he makes that choice he remains unborn (i.e., outside man's estate).

In one sense *The Island* is unique among Byron's works in the way it lays out an unequivocal program for the possession of the earthly paradise. *Beppo* is the only other work which resembles it with respect to absoluteness of assertion, but the earlier tale is descriptive rather than programmatic in form. The other major stories which make an explicit presentation of the possibility of the earthly paradise—*Sardanapalus* and the Haidée episode in *Don Juan*—both end in tragedy. Neither Sardanapalus nor Haidée is able to establish a society redeemed to innocence.

But the imperative to make a conscious choice for the incorruptible value which Neuha represents—to will the forfeit of everything else for this pearl of great price—is the predominant moral of *The Island*, and it suggests why Byron's last narrative is not, as it first seems to be, unique. Sardanapalus fails to restore the Saturnian Age because he wavers slightly in his devotion to his ideal. The manifest form of that ideal, Myrrha, is herself far from the required perfection. Indeed, much of the play is concerned with the king's successful attempt to purify his Ionian lover, but the fact that this must be done, and the time it takes to do it, are correlative factors in his tragedy. Nevertheless, he does at last make an absolute commitment to his Egeria and in his death he finds a way to victory.

Or consider the Haidée episode, which has sometimes been compared to and contrasted with *The Island*. Byron seems not to have intended Haidée's death and life to have been in vain. If *Don Juan* is episodic, it is not absolutely without a line of development: thus, though Haidée dies, the value which she represents remains with Juan for the rest of his life. We glimpse this in his positive responses to Leila and Dudu, and in his negative reactions toward Gulbeyaz, Catharine, and the crowd of English beauties who tempt him to liaisons.

> But Juan was no casuist, nor had pondered
> Upon the moral lessons of mankind:
> Besides, he had not seen of several hundred
> A lady altogether to his mind.
> A little "blàsé"—'t is not to be wondered
> At, that his heart had got a tougher rind:
> And though not vainer from his past success,
> No doubt his sensibilities were less.   (XII, 81)

Indeed, if we look carefully at Juan's sexual career we find that he has always exhibited a high degree of moral discrimination. Lady Adeline attracts him a good deal at first, but her charms lose their potency when Aurora Raby enters the poem and Juan's life. She is, in fact, Haidée's avatar in English society.

> And then there was—but why should I go on,
> Unless the ladies should go off?—there was
> Indeed a certain fair and fairy one,
> Of the best class, and better than her class,—
> Aurora Raby, a young star who shone
> O'er life, too sweet an image for such glass,
> A lovely being, scarcely form'd or moulded,
> A Rose with all its sweetest leaves yet folded;
>
> Rich, noble, but an orphan; left an only
> Child to the care of guardians good and kind;
> But still her aspect had an air so lonely!
> Blood is not water; and where shall we find
> Feelings of youth like those which overthrown lie
> By death, when we are left, alas! behind
> To feel, in friendless palaces, a home
> Is wanting, and our best ties in the tomb?

> Early in years, and yet more infantine
> In figure, she had something of sublime
> In eyes which sadly shone, as seraphs' shine.
> All youth—but with an aspect beyond time;
> Radiant and grave—as pitying man's decline;
> Mournful—but mournful of another's crime,
> She look'd as if she sat by Eden's door,
> And grieved for those who could return no more.   (xv, 43–45)

As regards simple appearances Aurora and Haidée have little in common, as Juan and Byron are apt to note. But when Byron wants to suggest the spiritual value which Aurora embodies he invariably recalls Haidée, and at one point explicitly reaches for the Haidée comparison.

> Juan knew nought of such a character—
> High, yet resembling not his lost Haidée;
> Yet each was radiant in her proper sphere:
> The Island girl, bred up by the lone sea,
> More warm, as lovely, and not less sincere,
> Was Nature's all; Aurora could not be,
> Nor would be thus:—the difference in them
> Was such as lies between a flower and gem.   (xv, 58)

Which is as much to say that the differences have to do with times and circumstances rather than with ultimate values: the symbolisms applied to each are equivalent, though they are drawn from different spheres of reality. Further, it is important to recall that Juan actively pursues Aurora, and that he does so because he recognizes in her that which he was once given, but lost. Haidée is dead, but what she represented has remained impressed upon Juan's character.

Aurora Raby was born into Byron's poetry immediately after Neuha, and the fact that Haidée can be seen as the paradigm for both (though in each case the terms of the comparison differ) suggests the allegorical likeness between the last two important female figures in Byron's poetry. Nevertheless, if Byron had lived to go on with *Don Juan* we can be reasonably certain that Juan and Aurora would not have been able to possess a paradise as Torquil and Neuha do. Byron arranges the forces against them too carefully in the final cantos of his poem. His presentation of Aurora leaves no doubt that she is his latest Egeria figure, but she is fated to join the company of Haidée. Thus, in the early months of 1823 we find Byron still writing on his old theme, but plotting it both in a tragic and a comic framework. This difference ceases to be a crucial one when we recall the imperative to choose for the ultimate values. Juan did not choose Haidée—she was given to him. The choice in the affair, and the tragedy, are Haidée's. After Canto V Juan begins to acquire self-consciousness, a fact perhaps most forcibly dramatized in Petersburg, so that when he reaches England we can see that his sensibility has been modified by his growing moral discrimination. Aurora is only one among many attractive ladies, but she surpasses them all as a value, including Lady Adeline (who is, considered strictly as an artistic creation, a much more compelling character). Juan senses her worth immediately and he gravitates to her. Lady Adeline notices the developing mutual attraction between them and her own growing jealousy is the poem's most obvious evil portent. The tragic issue that is suggested here is, in the end, more characteristically Byronic than the success story allegorized in *The Island*. As Byron says in *Childe Harold's Pilgrimage:*

> Few—none—find what they love or could have loved,
> Though accident, blind contact, and the strong
> Necessity of loving, have removed
> Antipathies. . . .   (IV, 125)

The theme of a thwarted Eros-drive persists as well throughout his lyric poetry. Withal, Byron suggests that, if hope and longing for the *beau idéal* always remain uncompleted, the act of hope and the passionate desire for completion never cease, and that on the way to the "unreach'd paradise" every man gets glimpses of what he strives for.[4] As he points out at the end of *Childe Harold's Pilgrimage*, these temporary consummations sustain man in his difficult passage, and they can be relied upon to repeat themselves successively. *Don Juan* expresses an equivalent attitude throughout, as when Byron observes in Canto II (his humor qualified beautifully by a subsurface tone of pathos): "Love, constant love, has been my constant guest" (209). As an allegory, then, *The Island* should probably be regarded as normative rather than definitive. It describes the term of man's furthest hopes but

---

[4] One of Byron's most delightful pronouncements upon this truth is to be found in his *Detached Thoughts* (no. 55) where he discusses his love of languages. He says that he wanted to learn Armenian and Arabic, but that every time he set about a program of study he was interrupted by some sexual interest or other. One of his masters, the Padre Pasquale Aucher, assured him that the earthly paradise "had certainly been in Armenia." Once again he left his studies: "I went seeking it–God knows where–did I find it? Umph! Now and then, for a minute or two" (*LJ* 5:436).

does not offer—any more than *Prometheus Unbound* does—the picture of a necessary personal or political future. Both poems are prophecies in the basic sense: they delineate a form of human possibility which yet requires the choice that determines accomplishment, a choice, moreover, that must be reaffirmed constantly. The vision of *The Island* is true because it may be true, always.

IV

Five Plays

The Empty Society

More than fifty years ago Samuel C. Chew produced his monograph on Byron's plays in which he argued that they were, despite incidental excellences, "essentially undramatic."[1] *Sardanapalus* and *Manfred* aside, Professor Chew found them deficient in certain accepted standards of plot development: climaxes, for example, are nearly always abnormally placed, or are not present at all. Today Professor Chew's observations would not be especially relevant, perhaps, were it not that nearly all subsequent and even contemporary critics have followed his lead in criticizing the plays. M. K. Joseph paraphrases Chew exactly:

> It is this failure to produce effective climaxes which makes Byron appear "essentially undramatic"; and it is seen particularly in *The Two Foscari*, where the father's loyalty and the son's death are both foregone conclusions, and there is no dramatic tension—it is all catastrophe and no play.[2]

Marino Faliero and *The Two Foscari* have been particularly condemned on these and other grounds ("there is little to redeem" them "in either dramatic force or language," Professor Marchand has suggested in his recent book).[3] The Venetian plays have a number of weaknesses, it is true, but such highly derivative approaches to them have, I think, obscured certain facts about their structure. For example, the plays are disapproved for not dramatizing "the causes of the struggle": both "open with the opposing forces already arrayed."[4] But

---

[1] Samuel C. Chew, *The Dramas of Lord Byron* (reprinted, New York, 1964). See chap. 3 especially.

[2] *Joseph*, p. 110.

[3] Leslie A. Marchand, *Byron's Poetry. A Critical Introduction* (Boston, 1965), p. 102.

[4] Chew, *Dramas of Lord Byron*, pp. 42–43.

205

Byron maintained that his procedure was "studiously Greek,"[5] and if the Venetian plays are to be faulted for opening in this way then so are the works of Aeschylus and Sophocles. The fates of Agamemnon and Oedipus are as certain as those of Byron's dramatic heroes.

This matter of structure is intimately related to the peculiar themes which Byron deals with in his Venetian plays. The *Agamemnon* does not involve a viable struggle against Fate but is concerned with the gradual revelation of the meaning of a particular fatality in terms of a developing and concatenated system of images, symbols, and dramatic confrontations. Though important and functional, characterization is itself subordinate to the religious or symbolic spectacle whose first intention is to unfold meaning, to explore the significance of the central themes. This perspective seems to me remarkably similar to Byron's. His Venetian plays have "action," of course, but not in a Shakespearean sense. As in Aeschylus and Sophocles, action in Byron is not so much "struggle" as it is "spectacle"—dramatically symbolic revelation. Paul West touches on the fact when he says that "the themes of the plays really are worth attention":

> they are exhaustive dossiers on special aspects of the human condition. They give no strikingly evident solutions. . . . Byron . . . thought highly of these plays, and so did Goethe. Perhaps they were right. Life is no mere question-and-answer game. . . . Instead, for those who try to think things out, life becomes a slowly expanding insight into why the questions are unanswerable anyway. Byron's plays make us think, long-winded as they are. . . .[6]

But West rarely finds much intrinsic artistic interest in Byron's work. He seems to grudge what he does find, and the plays—fascinating as they sometimes are—do not bring him to change his mind. One must add, however, that he does not try very hard to show how their poetry works. He cites examples of bad versifying and points out that the plays are frequently too long. But these faults are well known, and Byron himself admitted them.

Since these weaknesses in Byron's plays have been frequently noticed, I want to go on to some other questions which have been neglected by students of drama, Romanticism, and Byron's poetry in particular. Mr. West's acute comment cited above is a useful starting point. Byron said his plays were never meant for the stage. He called

5 *LJ* 5:347.
6 Paul West, *Byron and the Spoiler's Art* (London, 1960), pp. 119–20.

them "mental theatre,"[7] i.e., closet drama intended to be read as one reads poetry. In them we are given "slowly expanding" revelations of a number of significant human themes. Further, the revelations are made by developing the relations between, and thereby the significance of, certain predominant images and symbols.[8] As in Aeschylus, Byron's characters are often the pawns of the poetry in which they are involved. Like Agamemnon or Clytemnestra, they perform acts of their free will, but the continuum in which these acts are caught up is not subject to human manipulation. Something inexorable strides abroad, a fatality, and this Power is captured for our perception in the poetic relations in the plays. Just before his death the Doge Faliero declares:

> And yet I find a comfort in
> The thought that these things are the work of Fate;
> For I would rather yield to gods than men,
> Or cling to any creed of destiny,
> Rather than deem these mortals, most of whom
> I know to be as worthless as the dust,
> And weak as worthless, more than instruments
> Of an o'er-ruling power. . . .   (v, ii, 65–72)

The relation between this fatal power and the free will of individual men is nicely stated earlier, again by the Doge. Israel Bertuccio censures the Doge for his wavering remorse and says, "you act on your free will." The Doge answers:

>   't is true
> And thou dost well to answer that it was
> "My own free will and act," and yet you err,
> For I *will* do this! Doubt not—fear not; I
> Will be your most unmerciful accomplice!
> And yet I act no more on my free will,
> Nor my own feelings—both compel me back;
> But there is *hell* within me and around,
> And like the demon who believes and trembles
> Must I abhor and do.   (iii, ii, 512–21)

These passages contain the fundamental premises on which the play is based. Men act freely against their own will and feelings: they are compelled by a net of events to be cunning in their own overthrow.

---

[7] *LJ* 5:347.

[8] One of the most disappointing aspects of Mr. West's analysis is his failure to see the image and symbol structures in Byron's plays.

The difference between Byron's Doge and Aeschylus' tragic characters must be measured in terms of consciousness: the latter abet their dooms in ignorance, or with only a fearful, semiconscious dread, whereas Byron's Doge goes to his demise with a clear and terrible understanding of his own helplessness. Consciousness does not save life, or, as Manfred puts it in his play, "The Tree of Knowledge is not that of Life" (I, i, 12).

Marino Faliero is, like *The Two Foscari*, a gradually developing revelation of the nature and significance of corruption in Venice, and —more expansively—of human corruption in general. Images of disease and sickness recur through the play, and the aristocracy is made the central infection sapping the life of the city. The Doge says, for example, that Michael Steno's offense against his wife's honor

> Was a mere ebullition of the vice,
> The general corruption generated
> By the foul aristocracy. . . .   (III, ii, 403–5)

The cause of this general infection is traced through another series of images. The aristocracy are judged to have forfeited their humanity in the service of a machine, the State. "These men have no *private* life," the Doge says (III, ii, 382), and Angiolina sees that "the cruelty in their cold eyes" is the manifestation of their heartlessness (V, i, 390). When the conspirators argue about whether the slaughter of the aristocrats should be general or selective, they agree—with some difficulty—that all must die since all have forfeited their human individualities for an inhuman collectivity. "These men, or their fathers, were my friends," the Doge says (III, ii, 307), but in urging their general assassination he points out that they have become "mere machines" (I, ii 302). They have become absorbed by the state and its functions and are equated with their offices—"the present institutes of Venice" (III, ii, 318). The symbolic focus of all these nonhuman images is the mechanical torture apparatus by which the nobles force their will upon the city. Periodically recalled through the play, these instruments are directly identified with the nobles in the trial scene. The Doge contrasts his "heart" with their "engines."

> The torture! you have put me there already,
> Daily since I was Doge; but if you will
> Add the corporeal rack, you may; these limbs
> Will yield with age to crushing iron; but
> There's that within my heart shall strain your engines.
>   (v, i, 300–304)

All this is straightforward enough. More interesting is the way Byron manages to show how the "fatal poison" tends to grow like a cancer. Ultimately it will kill "the springs of life, . . . human ties, and all that's good and dear" (III, ii, 316–17). The aristocracy is a fixed value (or nonvalue) in the play: what most engages our interest is the way its corruption infects even those who would root it out. The conspirators, including the Doge, are fighting for life, health, and freedom, but as the play progresses we see that they are themselves only carrying the city's disease one stage further in its development. This is the tragic issue of the play, and the point of the Doge's prophecy: that the living body cannot be mended, but must be destroyed to effect a true cure for the city. Of all the conspirators only the Doge senses the organic nature of the evil:

> The whole must be extinguish'd;—better that
> They ne'er had been, than drag me on to be
> The thing these arch-oppressors fain would make me.
>
> (I, ii, 321–23)

The tragic irony in the play springs from the fact that neither the conspirators nor the oppressors are masters of their own wills. The aristocracy forces the crisis, and the conspirators are dragged into the growing corruption of Venice by the inertia of the evil system itself. Israel Bertuccio wants to free Venice from her pollution, but his language is an ironic prophecy of the inevitable failure that awaits his virtuous ideals. Close human ties, he tells Calendaro,

>   are not
> For those who are called to the high destinies
> Which purify corrupted commonwealths.
> We must forget all feelings save the one;
> We must resign all passions save our purpose;
> We must behold no object save our country. . . .   (II, ii, 84–89)

Bertuccio expects an immediate apocalypse and does not see what his statements imply. But we—who have been led all along to associate civic corruption with lack of simple human feelings—cannot fail to recognize Bertuccio's unwitting involvement in the operations of the infernal machine. Secrecy, for example, is one of the identifying characteristics of the evil aristocracy, but the conspirators are forced to assume this as their own insignia as well. The Doge lies even to Angiolina, though ashamedly, in order to keep his secrecy, but she is perfectly aware that his heart is sick and troubled, and that his mind is "stagnating" (II, i, 193). The conspirators are all determined to cleanse Venice of the pestilence with a blood sacrifice. "I am tainted," the Doge says, "and must wash away/The plague spots in the healing wave" (III, i, 14–15). Blood—their enemies' or their own—is likewise the charismatic agent of the plebeian conspirators, for if they succeed Venice is purged, and if they fail their "sacrifice" shall "ascend to heaven/ And draw down freedom on her evermore" (II, ii, 91–92). The Doge's dire prophecy, however, underscores the dramatic irony of these words. When Bertuccio declares that

> They never fail who die
> In a great cause: the block may soak their gore;
> Their heads may sodden in the sun; their limbs
> Be strung to city gates and castle walls—
> But still their spirit walks abroad,   (II, ii, 93–97)

we are meant to see the double edge of his remarks from the imagistic context of the whole play. Byron's "Greek" studies, and his fascination with the Furies, are perhaps most evident in passages like these. The Doge suggests later, for example, that blood vengeance is ominously self-perpetuating:

> one stroke struck,
> And the mere instinct of the first-born Cain,
> Which ever lurks somewhere in human hearts
> Though circumstance may keep it in abeyance,
> Will urge the rest on like to wolves; the sight
> Of blood to crowds begets the thirst of more,
> As the first wine cup leads to the long revel. . . .   (iv, ii, 55–61)

The revolutionary spirit that walks abroad is in fact an Orc figure, and one committed to that terrible natural cycle which Blake so vividly set forth. Tyrants are conquered by tyrants, and nonhuman evil perpetuates itself as easily in noble-minded revolutionaries as it does in callous nobles.

We perceive this most clearly in the sequence of beast metaphors which are used to characterize the evil in the city. The aristocracy, possessed by this evil, is called "vampire" and "Hydra," for example, and the images suggest the deathless nature of that which has invaded Venice. The beast is not the aristocracy but that which has informed the aristocracy and turned them from the men whom the Doge knew and loved to the things which they now are. But the conspirators are inexorably driven to recapitulate the evil against which they struggle.

The "blighting venom" that has corrupted Michael Steno's heart is organic and "shall spread itself in general poison" (II, i, 428). The Doge cries out in baffled anguish that

> the very means I am forced
> By these fell tyrants to adopt is such,
> That I abhor them doubly for the deeds
> Which I must do to pay them back for theirs.   (III, i, 114–17)

It is, however, not primarily the fault of the aristocracy, but of the "mere instinct of the first-born Cain," or of what Blake calls the Poison Tree. The Doge sees that something more terrible than the nobles is moving events in the city:

> for there is that stirring
> Within, above, around, that in this city
> Will make the cemeteries populous
> As e'er they were by pestilence or war. . . .   (II, i, 505–8)

"The accursed tyranny . . . rides/The very air in Venice," Bertram declares (IV, i, 237–38), and everyone becomes an unwilling participant in the fatal designs of "this monster . . . this spectre" (III, ii, 165–66). The nobles are "machines" which serve it, the Doge is himself a "mere puppet" of its purposes (II, ii, 32), and the plebeians are the ignorant "accomplices" of all its designs (V, i, 27).

Thus the play gradually unfolds a picture of Venice being consumed by her best and worst elements alike. She is a house divided against herself (IV, i, 277) and the cleansing sacrifice which the conspirators keep referring to is turned into a prophecy of their own destruction, and that of the whole city. "In th' olden time," the Doge says early in the play,

> Some sacrifices ask'd a single victim,
> Great expiations had a hecatomb.   (I, ii, 230–31)

He carries forward this idea of "one hundred deaths" when he refers shortly afterward to "the Briarean sceptre/Which in this hundred-handed senate rules" (I, ii, 368–69). Later Venice is called the city "of our hundred isles" (III, ii, 134) and the reference picks up the "one hundred" association to indicate the general doom which hangs over all. The conspirators intend to kill their enemies but the idea that they are suicides injects an ominous note into the play, and suggests their moral kinship with the aristocracy. When the Doge first confronts the

plebeians they fear the discovery of their secret plot and make to kill
him. But he says:

> Let them advance and strike at their own bosoms,
> Ungrateful suicides! for on our lives
> Depend their own. . . .
> > Oh! noble Courage!
> The eldest born of Fear. . . .   (III, ii, 97–99, 102–3)

Later the Doge makes it clear that he too is not only a self-murderer
("Each stab to them will seem my suicide," III, ii, 402), but that his
designs also make him a participant in the non- or superhuman vengeance which is working Venice's destruction.

> You would but punish Steno, I the senate.
> I cannot pause on individual hate,
> In the absorbing, sweeping, whole revenge
> Which, like the sheeted fire from heaven, must blast
> Without distinction, as it fell of yore
> Where the Dead Sea hath quench'd two cities' ashes.
> > (III, ii, 418–23)

Like the plebeians the Doge seems to want only to purge and free his
city, but all "breathe in a sort of Official atmosphere"[9] and thus participate in the Power that rides the air and that intends general destruction.
Eventually he sees clearly that "there is *hell* within me and around,"
but in the first act he unconsciously dramatizes the same truth. When
he hears that Steno has been let off with a nominal punishment he throws
the ducal cap off his head as a sign that he is no longer a part of the
government which bandies about justice and all human values. But
after he has determined to take his revenge upon the senate he again
takes up the cap, and the soliloquy which follows points the dramatic
significance of his action. He resumes his place in the corrupt state, and
his troubled mind indicates his reluctant kinship with everything "Hollow," "degraded," and "dishonest" in the play (I, ii, 259 ff.). Just before he dies he takes it off again, in triumph, but now he chooses to be
an unwilling agent of his own and his city's destruction. Rather than
invoking an angel of deliverance, he becomes yet another manifestation
of "the destroying Angel" which "hovers o'er Venice" (IV, ii, 133).

---

9 This is Keats's observation on life in England. He goes on to point out that "governors in these days loose [sic] the title of Man in exchange for that of Diplomat and
Minister." *The Letters of John Keats*, ed. Hyder E. Rollins, 2 vols. (Cambridge, Mass.,
1958), 1:396. (Keats wrote "Officinal" for "Official.")

At the end he comes to recognize not only his own guilt but that of all his fellow citizens. "These things are the work of Fate," he says, but only because he eventually sees that such a fatality is the public expression of something hidden within the hearts of all men. We choose to do what we would not do, for "there was that in my spirit ever/ Which shaped out for itself some great reverse" (V, i, 587–88). This is a personal truth that epitomizes a larger human truth, for—as the epigraph suggests—the Doge is "Dux inquieti turbidus Adriae." Troubled minds are a motif in the play, and they are linked with the metaphors of destructive passion as well as the recurrent images of dream and illusion. The Doge, Israel Bertuccio, and all the conspirators are constantly shown as the pursuers of their own distempered dreams. So too the aristocracy. Lioni leaves the party of reveling noblemen with an obscurely troubled soul. Such parties are one of the signs of the aristocracy's corruption and Lioni senses it. As he recalls the people and events at the ball he discerns the emptiness and artificiality: they are people chasing a dream of life, a seductive parody of vitality. Caught in the "dazzling mass of artificial light," they have neither true sight nor real life.

> All the delusion of the dizzy scene,
> Its false and true enchantments—art and nature,
> Which swam before my giddy eyes, that drank
> The sight of beauty as the parch'd pilgrim's
> On Arab sands the false mirage which offers
> A lucid lake to his eluded thirst. . . .   (IV, i, 62–67)

Living a life of illusion, all the people in the play become "spectres" to one degree or another. Lioni's mind is harmonized for a brief moment by his awareness of the natural beauty that surrounds Venice. But when Bertram breaks in upon him he quickly lapses from reality into the world of spectres, and again doffs his human identity for his role as mechanical senator. It happens quite naturally and is not meant to shock, for Lioni has become habituated to this role and to the limited human awareness that goes with it.

Dream images such as these weave into the play the pattern of human ignorance. Men do what they would not do and they shape thereby the spirit of their own fatality. Indeed, the whole play suggests that it is humanly impossible to live a completely real life. Angiolina is the only character who pursues no illusions, but—as her name suggests—she is so completely healthy and self-possessed that she seems herself unreal, a dream image of the true life. She is a character, not a person, and represents that normative ideal of humanity which Shelley described as "forever sought, forever lost." Thus, to be able to understand her worth, as the Doge does, and the worth of what she represents, is no help: "the Tree of Knowledge is not that of Life," and Angiolina lives only in the mind, one of the spiritual poles of human existence. She is Life in Death, her opposite is the Death in Life of Venice, and *Marino Faliero* is both the dramatization of the furious but futile struggle in men like the Doge to resolve the claims of each, and the manifestation of the workings of the death impulse in all men.

When the Doge utters his prophecy of disaster over Venice at the end of the play we are not meant to see it as the last act of a distempered man. Like Count Maddalo he has learned a good deal in suffering, and his knowledge is summarized in this last, terrible song. He speaks "to Time, and to Eternity," and what he foresees is no more than the inevitable extension of the death process whose agents he, and all men, have been. But the conscious defiance of the speech suggests something more; indeed, dramatizes the values which the play upholds despite the maze of its skepticisms. The first, and most important, is consciousness itself, which if it does not save life at least redeems man from its immediate evils and enables him to affirm its larger designs. Secondly, when he denounces the hollow men of Venice we are given our last sight of his outraged humanity, and the expression of that vital passion which has been at once his human doom and his human redemption. Samuel Chew has said that the play demonstrates Byron's sympathies for revolutionary programs and his hatred of aristocratic tyrannies. This is not exactly true, as we have already seen.[10] Byron does sympa-

<hr/>

[10] Byron always championed revolt against oppression, but he was never without a melancholy sense that man was "an unlucky rascal" to have to suffer both (*BSP* 2:559). This feeling is intimately connected with Byron's sense of a natural fatality and the cyclical movement of history. In his *Ravenna Journal* he observed that "the infinite variety of lives conduct but to death, and the infinity of wishes lead but to disappointment ... an Extirpated disease is succeeded by some new pestilence. ... But, *onward!*" he added, for the revolutionary "*ocean* conquers, nevertheless. It overwhelms the Armada, it wears the rock, and ... it has not only destroyed, but made a world" (*BSP* 2:559-60). In his *Dictionary* he speaks of the decline of the Roman Empire in terms that distinctly recall not only the Venetian plays, but his general attitude toward attempts to reform corrupted states: "Had Brutus and Cassius gained the battle at Philippi, it would not have restored the republic—its days ended with the Gracchi, the rest was a mere struggle of parties. You might as well cure a Consumption, restore a broken egg, as revive a state so long a prey to every uppermost Soldier as Rome had long been" (*BSP* 2:605). Politics, even individual human actions, are seen as manifestations of a larger, and fundamentally natural, life force. Vendetta and assassination were common occurrences in Italy, Byron observed, and he frequently mentions these things in his letters and journals as if they were forms of natural calamity rather than moral goods or evils. See, for example, *LJ* 5:85.

thize with the conspirators, but not because their vengeance is objectively more admirable than the aristocrats' murder. The issues are more complicated, for if the conspirators are to be praised it is because

> there are things
> Which make revenge a virtue by reflection,
> And not an impulse of mere anger; though
> The laws sleep, justice wakes, and injured souls
> Oft do a public right with private wrong,
> And justify their deeds unto themselves.—   (IV, ii, 103–8)

But fundamental rightness and wrongness remain in each case what they are. Thus the conspirators incarnate the only ideals that are left for what Paul West calls "the trapped man":[11] doomed from the outset in a world that cannot accommodate life without death, they fight nevertheless to live, and like Lucifer in *Cain*,

> dare look the Omnipotent tyrant in
> His everlasting face, and tell him that
> His evil is not good!   (I, i, 138–40)

The Two Foscari will seem a poor imitation of *Marino Faliero* if we see it only as a warmed-over version of Byron's earlier Venetian play. Samuel Chew has rightly noted that many of the same themes are carried forward:[12] we note particularly those of civic pollution, the vision of governors as slaves to a mysterious and nonhuman force, and the unresolvable conflict between patriotism and personality. But the play does not have the metaphoric thickness of *Marino Faliero*. In the latter, as we have seen, Byron leans heavily upon closely woven image patterns to secure an effect of a developing revelation of meaning. *The Two Foscari* is less single-minded a work, is not exclusively or perhaps even primarily an anatomy of ideas. Rather, it attempts something *Marino Faliero* left untouched except in the case of the Doge: it attempts to dramatize the effect that life in Venice has upon a number of different, and very specific, people. *Marino Faliero* has only one "personality"—the Doge—and two or three fairly interesting "characters" (Bertram, Israel Bertuccio, Angiolina). *The Two Foscari*, on the other hand, has three distinctive personalities—the Doge, Marina, and Loredano—and at least one extremely engaging character—Barbarigo.

Before we consider this aspect of the play, however, we ought to

[11] West, *Byron and the Spoiler's Art*, p. 100.
[12] Chew, *Dramas of Lord Byron*, p. 99.

make some examination of its ideas and imagistic motifs. *Marino Faliero* has at least four potent dramatic symbols: the ducal cap, which represents the illusion of human power; the equestrian statue of the Doge's ancestor (III, i), which is a portent of doom and a sign of its transtemporal dominion; the mask and cloak of the aristocracy which they wear in public as the badges of their secrecy and inhumanity alike; and the bloody sword waved over the people at the end, another sign of death and doom (and one that distinctly recalls Aeschylus). Each of these symbolic props is the locus of one or more image sequences in the play. *The Two Foscari* contains three dramatic symbols of this sort: Loredano's account book, the goblet of Venetian crystal which he gives to the Doge at the end, and the dungeon of the younger Foscari.

Loredano's accounting tablets are made the framing symbol of the play, and they epitomize both the spectacle of Venetian justice and the moral code of all who serve it. Such justice and such a code scrupulously put out of court all human concerns. When Marina bursts in upon her husband's trial in the first act the court immediately adjourns, for she suddenly focuses the tribunal's attention on the inhuman artifice of the law which they serve.

> 'T was a dreadful sight
> When his distracted wife broke through into
> The hall of our tribunal, and beheld
> What we could scarcely look upon, long used
> To such sights.   (I, i, 364–68)

The pattern repeats itself throughout the play: the automatic forms of tradition and law are meant to cast out human consciousness, and they tend to retreat (for a time) when such consciousness is forced aggressively upon them. Loredano is the only one among the senators who does not follow this rule. He is not shamed by his consciousness of the law's brutality, and—unlike his fellow council members—he does not try to suppress his understanding of realities beneath a hypocritical assertion of patriotic duties.

The principal image related to Loredano's tablets is that of the balance, which is used literally and figuratively throughout the play. At the beginning Barbarigo is disturbed by their increasing cruelty as judges. He is Loredano's chief partner in the plan to limit the power of the Foscari, but his conscience has begun to bother him. Not so Loredano, however, who is determined to pursue his "hereditary hate" until his books are "balanced" (I, i, 18 and 54). Barbarigo is a just man, but his soul has been long delivered up to his official duties. Loredano, on the other hand, cares little for the state as such. He uses the state for purely personal ends; in this case, to revenge himself on the man whom he believes to have murdered his father and uncle. But just as double-entry accounting is Loredano's direct inheritance, he also receives a patrimony of attitudes and convictions that make him act the way he does. This is what makes the idea of a balanced account so effective as poetry: it is a hereditary idea, like his hate and his whole mental procedure. Byron suggests that his belief about the Doge's guilt is unfounded in fact, but he also indicates why Loredano can scarcely help believing what he does. Loredano understands the inhuman character of Venice's institutional processes—this is precisely why he can manipulate them so well to his purposes—so that its history of crimes wrought in secrecy, and covered with a legal form, becomes for him the sign of the Doge's guilt and the norm by which he must be judged.

> *Lor.*
>   When the Doge declared that he
>   Should never deem himself a sovereign till
>   The death of Peter Loredano, both
>   The brothers sickened shortly: he *is* sovereign.
> *Bar.*
>   A wretched one.
> *Lor.*
>   What should they be who make
>   Orphans?
> *Bar.*
>   But *did* the Doge make you so?
> *Lor.*
>   Yes.
> *Bar.*
>   What solid proofs?
> *Lor.*
>   When princes set themselves
>   To work in secret, proofs and process are
>   Alike made difficult. ....   (i, i, 35–43)

Loredano knows that the very inhumanity of the legal forms in Venice makes them wonderful instruments of torture, and he acts accordingly. The Doge has been, like Loredano, a power in the state and a manipulator of its laws so that he perceives clearly what Loredano is doing and makes no outcry against him. Near the end of the play the Doge says that he is beyond both good and evil, and when Barbarigo offers a brief word of good will the Doge rebukes him: "I spoke not to *you*, but to Loredano. *He* understands me" (IV, i, 238–39). Marina is passionate in her denunciation of Loredano's and Venice's brutal artifices, but the Doge tells her: "Woman, this clamorous grief of thine, I tell thee,/Is no more in the balance weighed with that/Which —but I pity thee, my poor Marina!" (II, i, 132–34). A gulf separates the standards of public and private life; understanding this, the Doge dutifully renders to Caesar the things that are Caesar's and tries as best he can to preserve the capacity for making purely human responses as well. Loredano preys upon his human feelings by exploiting this split in the Doge's character: he directs the torture of his son in a process over which the Doge is the presiding officer. The scheme is doubly effective just because the Doge strives so hard to maintain an impersonal demeanor and to fulfill the duties of his office to the letter. By serving the state the Doge is forced to destroy and feed upon his own children. Marina reiterates this theme a number of times in the play, in reference to the Doge and Venice at large. Barbarigo is the first to introduce it when, at the opening, he describes the Doge's strict adherence to his civic obligations in a gruesome metaphor: "he,/With more than Roman fortitude, is ever/First at the board in this unhappy process" (I, i, 24–26). But Barbarigo seems only half conscious of the brutal character of the tribunal, for he tells Jacopo Foscari that the law is merciful which permits a father to serve in the council of accusers (I, i, 84–87). The balance image recurs as an ironic sign that Venice and most of her important citizens are imbalanced, and that they are incapable alike of remedying their condition or even clearly understanding its nature: "To balance such a foe, if such there be,/Thy father sits among thy judges" (I, i, 81–82).

The crystal goblet is one of the focusing symbols for the idea that Venice is destructively corrupt both in spite of and because of the forms of justice and honor which she outwardly maintains.

> *Doge.*
>> 'T is said that our Venetian crystal has
>> Such pure antipathy to poisons as
>> To burst, if aught of venom touches it.
>> You bore this goblet, and it is not broken.
>
> *Lor.*
>> Well, sir!

Doge.
>   Then it is false, or you are true.
> For my own part, I credit neither; 't is
> An idle legend.   (v, i, 294–300)

The Doge's last remark is a brilliantly economical revelation of his complete understanding not only of the malice of Loredano, but of the sham purity of "Venetian crystal." Like the Doge Faliero, he goes willingly to his death, for he sees that Venice is no more able to protect herself against the destructive passions of a Loredano than Loredano is able, given his traditions and environment, to redeem himself.[13] Venice, with her secrecy and machine-government, has made Loredano what he is, and thus she is as much the fitting instrument of his purposes as her "pure" crystal is of his death potion.

As in *Marino Faliero*, the state is here conceived as a productive agent, a parent who passes on to its children its own unnatural life. Jacopo cannot take his children into exile with him for, as Loredano says, "they are the state's" (III, i, 387). Marina answers scornfully that "if/They live, they'll make you soldiers, senators,/Slaves, exiles—what *you* will." The state is a self-perpetuating instrument of death, and Marina more than anyone else clarifies this for us. Just after Jacopo dies of his prolonged torture the Doge says to Marina, "Your children live." Her answer summarizes the truth that to serve Venice is to be her victim, as are all the people in the play to one degree or another. It is also one of the crucial speeches in the play's dramatic action, for these are the words which finally release the Doge's austerely controlled emotions and put him beyond both his office and his enemies (which are, in a sense, the same thing).

> My children! true—they live, and I must live
> To bring them up to serve the state, and die
> As died their father. Oh, what best of blessings
> Were barrenness in Venice!   (IV, i, 208–11)

Immediately the Doge falls to embrace his dead son, and in doing so he finally chooses between his person as father and his role as governor. Up to this point he has struggled unsuccessfully to fulfill the claims of both. Now he is resolved. When the deputation from the assembly comes to request his abdication he refuses, not because he is attached to his office but because he will not violate himself in the interests of

[13] See Marina's speech on the corrupt atmosphere in Venice: III, i, 366–82.

the state any longer—he will not break "*my* oath" (V, i, 47; Byron's italics). Twice before he had asked to be relieved of his post in order to live the private life of a citizen. He was refused because the state needed him. Now the state deems his abdication necessary, but he refuses to serve its wishes.

The character of Jacopo Foscari is little short of disastrous, but his dungeon ruminations are an important event in the play. The dungeon itself is an effective dramatic symbol of the city as a whole. The prison is a place of continuous sorrow, despair, and death; as such, it is the true record of Venice's history, which is more "like an epitaph" than anything else (III, i, 20). It is also a place of darkness and deep silence, so that the chronicle of woe graven on the rough cell walls seems unlikely to be read by anyone but "wretches" like Jacopo. But Jacopo insists that "The tyranny of silence is not lasting." "Use and time" have taught him "Familiarity with what was darkness" (III, i, 79 and 60–61), and like his father he comes through suffering to understand (to quote out of context) that "on the shores of darkness there is light." The play's dark truths cannot be kept from men because, as the Doge says just before the prison scene, "we are slaves,/The greatest as the meanest" (II, i, 57–58). The history of Venice is everywhere one of human grief and frustration, so that when Jacopo says "such a chronicle as this only can be read, as writ, by wretches" (III, i, 27–28), we are to understand that it is a truth for all those who would dare acquaint themselves with it.

Thus the prison cell suggests that the glorious and vital appearance which Venice outwardly maintains is really an illusion:

> these walls have been my study,
> More faithful pictures of Venetian story,
> With all their blank, or dismal stains, than is
> The Hall not far from hence, which bears on high
> Hundreds of doges, and their deeds and dates.   (III, i, 117–21)

The true story of Venice is learned in the dungeon chronicles where we see that men are alive and admirable only insofar as they try to become familiar with the darkness in themselves and struggle to oppose its progress. The Venice of apparent glory is both a lie and a misery, but the Venice of her dungeon is, if a misery, at least the truth. The Doge Foscari, like Marino Faliero, gives a trenchant speech on the innate sin and frailty of man. "Mortals," he says to Marina,

who can read them
Save he who made? or, if they can, the few
And gifted spirits, who have studied long
That loathsome volume—man, and pored upon
Those black and bloody leaves, his heart and brain,
But learn a magic which recoils upon
The adept who pursues it. All the sins
We find in others, nature made our own. . . .
              All is low,
And false, and hollow—clay from first to last,
The prince's urn no less than potter's vessel.
Our fame is in men's breath, our lives upon
Less than their breath; our durance upon days,
Our days on seasons; our whole being on
Something which is not *us!*—So, we are slaves,
The greatest as the meanest—nothing rests
Upon our will; the will itself no less
Depends upon a straw than on a storm;
And when we think we lead, we are most led. . . .   (ii, i, 332 ff.)

Such an awareness does not in itself redeem man's fate, but it does represent a sine qua non for the visions of the earthly paradise expressed in *Sardanapalus, Beppo,* and especially *Don Juan.*[14] The active mind prevents "man's worst—his second fall" and thus preserves man human in a world which is—morally speaking—both contingent and cyclically regenerative.[15] This idea of the second fall is Byron's version of the sin against the Holy Spirit. It is the denial of the obligation to self-consciousness, the refusal to see, and represent, the light in the darkness. Besides being preservative, such knowledge ennobles, for it is not easily won. The deepest misery is also the deepest darkness, or that in which the Ten are involved as well as all those who enslave their minds to the "mysterious" illusions of the state.

But unlike *Marino Faliero, The Two Foscari* does not primarily involve an apocalypse of its fundamental themes. A much more "dramatic" work, the later play presents a related sequence of character

[14] This point of view in Byron's poetry, especially the later work, has often been incidentally noted by scholars. E. D. Hirsch, Jr., has done well to reiterate and focus the idea in a brief, generalized form. See his "Byron and the Terrestrial Paradise," in *From Sensibility to Romanticism*, ed. Frederick W. Hilles and Harold Bloom (New York, 1965), pp. 467–86. His essay confines itself almost exclusively to *Don Juan*.

[15] The theme is typically Byronic. See *Childe Harold's Pilgrimage IV*, stanzas 93–98, 179–84, etc., and footnote 8 above.

studies, and its plot hinges upon the moral education of the Doge and Marina. The most obvious example of all this is the Doge, who vacillates for most of three acts between his human and his civic personalities. When he first appears in the play the strain of his office is beginning to wear upon him. He is preoccupied with his son, and fumbles even his most perfunctory civic duty (II, i). His exchanges in Acts II and III, particularly with Marina, illustrate with what difficulty he keeps his feelings under control while he witnesses, and meditates, the torture of his son. He keeps telling Marina to be calm, but his own emotional unrest is as manifest in its taut restraint as is Marina's in her passionate outbursts. He rebukes the compassion offered by the senator too forthrightly (II, i, 25 ff.), and protests too strongly to Marina when she suggests he is to be pitied (II, i, 145 ff.). In fact, when Loredano directs the torture of Jacopo he is aiming more at the father than at the son, as the Doge well knows. Thus Jacopo's vain attempt to maintain his composure under The Question reflects his father's attitude, and suggests that their agonies are as comparable as their determinations to resist. When Jacopo finally dies the Doge says, "He's free" (IV, i, 193), and the event signals the beginning of the Doge's freedom. Moved by Marina's bitter denunciation of Venice's child-murdering, he finally gives expression to his cruelly stretched emotions. At this point he too undergoes a death, and when he rises up from embracing the body of his son to answer the summons of the Ten, he, like Jacopo, is free. "How fare you?" Marina asks Jacopo just before he dies, and his last word—"Well!"—foreshadows the Doge's release. "Sirs, I am ready," he says to Loredano and Barbarigo, for "nothing further/Can touch me more than him thou look'st on there" (IV, i, 228 and 234–35). Before this moment the "stoic of the state" (as Marina scornfully calls him) manifests a control like that of Charles XII in *Mazeppa*, but afterward he shows the self-possession of a Mazeppa.

Loredano is a fine example of Byron's ability to invest a completely villainous character with life, and secure for him strong dramatic sympathy. Byron apotheosized the characters of Satan, Richard III, Iago, and a host of other literary miscreants, not because he thought them good or evil, but because they were themselves in a grand way, because they had a passionate integrity. Loredano is of their number. Barbarigo has all the right sentiments but is Loredano's lackey nonetheless for, as Loredano sees clearly, he is never "fix'd in purpose" (IV, i, 49). Barbarigo represents whatever conscience the Venetian nobles still possess, but he also mirrors their moral irresolution. They live in a kind of hell and have, as Homer would say, "strengthless heads." Thus Loredano rules them like slaves. The Doge respects his conscious malice, Marina hates him for it, but both have only contempt for Barbarigo and the other counselors. Throughout the play Loredano directs a legal process for personal vengeance; unlike Barbarigo and the other nobles, he never rationalizes his cruelty with an appeal to patriotism (his patriotic arguments are always completely cynical), nor does he justify a sense of shame with a show of compassion. In fact, he has no need of shame for he does not serve the illusion of the state, but only himself. This is nicely brought out in the fifth act when the Chief of The Ten asks the Doge if he will abdicate according to the council's wishes. "Your answer, Duke!" the Chief demands, and Loredano immediately demands in turn: "Your answer, Francis Foscari!" (V, i, 177). Loredano has scrupulously maintained the proper civic forms, including forms of address, throughout the play, but now he addresses him as a private citizen to dramatize his moment of triumph. Thus, when Barbarigo says to him:

> You are ingenious, Loredano, in
> Your modes of vengeance, nay, poetical,
> A very Ovid in the art of *hating*. . . .   (v, i, 134–36)

he summarizes the dramatic success of Loredano's passionate evil—to his own shame as well, for Loredano's perverted vitality is morally superior to Barbarigo's good, but ineffectual, intentions.

A superficial reading of the play might lead one to conclude that Barbarigo finally discards his sycophancy when he comes to understand the depth of Loredano's hatred. Through the first four acts he is completely Loredano's tool, but from the opening of the play he shows signs of a troubled conscience. These feelings grow with the play's development, but his will to act is not affected until the end of Act IV. Loredano then proposes to strip the Doge of his office, and Barbarigo "protests." "Are you then thus fix'd?" he asks Loredano, and when Loredano asks in turn, "Why, what should change me?" he answers: "That which changes me" (IV, i, 321–22). When the council meets to decide the matter Barbarigo does indeed fight against Loredano's proposal, and in the following scene he again actively opposes Loredano's wishes (V, i, 151 ff.), but again in vain.

Barbarigo does at last free himself of the dominion of Loredano, but only because he is terrified by the enormous reality of the man's evil, by its "poetical" character. He seeks a safer place, one where his nakedness will not show so clearly, and he finds it in the Ten. At the end he becomes what the aspiring sycophant Memmo so longs to be: "an unit/ Of an united and imperial 'Ten' " (I, i, 194–95). This fact is well dramatized in the great concluding scene of the play. Just before his death the Doge tells the nobles that he will leave the palace in the manner that he came. They are quite upset by this, since his gesture will scandalize their actions before the people. Unlike the Chief of the Ten, Loredano appears unmoved, but he saves the council from public embarrassment by poisoning the Doge. He does not intend to save them but merely to settle his personal account, to balance his books. When the Doge dies the Chief of the Ten and Barbarigo speak:

> *Chief of the Ten.*
>   If it be so, at least his obsequies
>   Shall be such as befits his name and nation,
>   His rank and his devotion to the duties
>   Of the realm, while his age permitted him
>   To do himself and them full justice. Brethren,
>   Say, shall it not be so?
> *Bar.*
>   He has not had
>   The misery to die a subject where
>   He reigned: then let his funeral rites be princely.
> *Chief of the Ten.*
>   We are agreed, then?   (v, i, 310–18)

To the question, as Byron's stage direction puts it, "*All, except* Lor., *answer*, Yes." For all his evil Loredano remains, as always, completely superior to such moral rationalizations.

Marina is quick to expose the poverty of spirit in men who, like Barbarigo and the Chief of the Ten, need to cover their shame with such magnificent gestures.

> Signors, your pardon, this is mockery.
> Juggle no more with that poor remnant, which,
> A moment since . . .
> You banished from his palace and tore down
> From his high place with such relentless coldness;
> And now, when he can neither know these honours,
> Nor would accept them if he could, you, signors,
> Purpose with idle and superfluous pomp
> To make a pageant over what you trampled.
> A princely funeral will be your reproach,
> And not his honour.

"Splendour in hypocrisy" Marina calls this elaborate funeral and the phrase is equally applicable to the men who conceive and agree to such hollow pageants.

In this last scene Marina achieves that complete nobility of person which she did not have before. She rails at Loredano and the Doge throughout the play, but her passion is—as the Doge says—excessive and useless. Marina knows something is radically wrong in Venice, but her grief for Jacopo, her pained bewilderment at the Doge, and her indignation at Loredano all obscure her understanding of herself and of the events around her. More, they obscure the obligation *to* understand which Byron places on all his characters.[16] Marina does not want to understand, however; she wants to save Jacopo (and, later, the Doge). This is why the Doge's speech on innate human frailty and fate in Act II is so important for her. It is an instruction in the futility of putting any dependence upon our hopes or designs, in the necessity of being *conscious* of this futility. At that time Marina replies to the Doge that "I do not think of such things,/So I be left with [Jacopo]" (II, i, 375–76). When he dies Marina throws the Doge's wisdom back in his face in a fit of despair. "Where is now/The stoic of the state?" she cries at him. He accepts the rebuke as just, for not until Jacopo's death does he experience himself complete human emptiness. When he makes his stoic speech to Marina, for example, he is still confident that some hopes are sure, that Marina and Jacopo will, if exiled, at least have each other: "Thus much they cannot well deny." But events finally do take away all his surety on life and the truth of his own wisdom is proved upon himself. He stands the final test, but Marina continues to torment herself with her sense of injustice: "Oh, for vengeance! . . . Well, well; I have sons, who shall be men" (V, i, 99 and 101–2).

When the Doge dies, however, Marina seems so struck by the enormity of this history, or perhaps by its radical absurdity, that she yields up her demand to force her will upon such an existence. The defect lies not in the malice of Loredano but in the ignorance of those who are his dupes, and of those who made Loredano what he is. Her consciousness of the need for consciousness makes her turn to Barbarigo and the other nobles to urge their awareness of what a self-reproach will be a splendid funeral for the Doge. They do not listen, of course, but neither does she berate them. She exposes the horror of their lives as clearly as she can, and for the rest: "Well, sirs, your will be done! as

---

[16] Again, a constant theme in Byron. Compare *Childe Harold's Pilgrimage IV*, stanza 127.

one day, I trust, Heaven's will be done too!" (V, i, 360–64). Heretofore Marina's passion has been no more than the expression of her sense of ineffectualness. She was "distracted," but now her understanding becomes a concentrate and her personality self-possessed. The education in self-knowledge which Barbarigo misses at the end Marina gains. After she has made their hypocrisy plain to the councilors she is warned by the Chief of the Ten:

> Know ye, Lady,
> To whom ye speak, and perils of such speech?

Her reply:

> I know the former better than yourselves;
> The latter, like yourselves; and can face both.
> Wish you more funerals?

and Barbarigo's:

> *Heed not her rash words;*
> Her circumstances must excuse her bearing.
>
> (v, i, 362–67, my italics)

are the exact measure of what she has won and what he has lost.

Readers of Byron have argued for a long time about his attempt to "reform" the theater. He called his plays a dramatic "experiment" and he said that his models were the classics, the Greeks. He said the plays were not political, that the unities were his "great object of research," and that "they might as well act the Prometheus of Aeschylus" as try to put *Marino Faliero* on the stage.[17] But Byron never explained why the unities appealed to his aesthetic sense, or why he turned to the Greeks, or what specifically he expected a mental theater to achieve. In fact, the whole question of Byron's intentions in this matter remains obscure, and—worse luck—suggestively obscure. We know what he did not like—melodrama and excessive sentiment; we know at least the direction that his likes took—toward the Greeks, Alfieri, and certain things in a few modern dramatists; but we do not know what his purposes were other than to get people to *think* while at the theater.

Some people have simply thrown over the subject as another example of Byron's deliberate obscurantism. His respect for the "older" dramatists is deemed merely another example of his sentimentality about the classics and the past, and his admiration for Alfieri's *Mirra*

[17] *LJ* 5:67, 84, 229, 313.

is regarded as no more than a psychological response to the incest theme (Byron said he wept at a performance of the play). Some of this may be true, but how much we will never know, anymore than we will ever be able to resolve once for all Byron's thoughts on the entire affair. It is nonetheless clear, from all his harping on the matter and all the work he put into the plays, that he was quite serious about his efforts and had something (at any rate) in mind.

To understand Byron's purposes we might usefully draw a distinction between his theatrical and poetic ends. His work with the Drury Lane theater committee seems to have stimulated his desire to reform the stage, to produce a theater that was free of the melodrama so prevalent in his own day (and often exemplified in his own work *Manfred*). Bring back the unities, bring back a less spasmodic dramatic spectacle; let passion be dramatized not by ever more extravagant displays but by the very restraint in its display. These are theatrical ends. Poetically, Byron sought—particularly in his Venetian plays—to write about the same kinds of themes that we find in his tales: the nature of a sick or doomed society, the dilemma of a man caught in such a milieu. The two purposes merge very nicely, however, for his Venetian plays are not concerned with the issue of events but with their meaning. The plays do not aim to arouse suspense about the outcome of a plot development, as melodrama so frequently does; on the contrary, they are intended to make the audience thoughtful and self-conscious, to force an understanding of the nature and causes of the fatality which the plays dramatize. *Marino Faliero* and *The Two Foscari* certainly have a parable-like quality to them, and it is not at all unlikely that Byron's term "mental theatre" was meant to have a significance somewhat beyond its specialized meaning of simple "closet drama."[18]

[18] The general Byronic theme of the need for self-consciousness tends to suggest this. Moreover, the term "mental theatre" seems to be another of Byron's verbal equivocations intended to mean both "drama of self-consciousness" and "closet drama." David V. Erdman ("Byron's Stage Fright: The History of his Ambition and Fear of Writing for the Stage," *ELH* 6 (1939): 219–43) has shown quite conclusively that Byron did indeed have hopes that his plays might be successfully performed, and that his many disclaimers were intended to absolve him from blame if his plays should have failed on the stage.

The King of Peace

"Attempting to become more than Man We become less," said Luvah
As he rose from the bright feast, drunk with the wine of ages.
                                          WILLIAM BLAKE, *The Four Zoas*

On January 13, 1821, Byron noted in his *Ravenna Journal* that he had
"Sketched the outline and Drams. Pers. of an intended tragedy of
Sardanapalus, which I have for some time meditated."[1] After dinner
that same evening he went to see La Guiccioli and brought her an Italian
translation of Grillparzer's *Sappho*. A small quarrel broke out during
their conversation which was to have a considerable influence upon
Byron's new play. "I said that love was *not the loftiest* theme for true
tragedy," but Teresa disagreed, "and, having the advantage of her
native language, and natural female eloquence, she overcame my fewer
arguments. I believe she was right. I must put more love into *Sardanapalus* than I intended."[2] Teresa took something of a proprietary interest
in Byron and his works—she even got him to promise not to continue
with *Don Juan*, which she heartily disapproved—so that it is not surprising to find how proud she was in the *Sardanapalus* affair. As she
wrote in her unpublished *La Vie de Lord Byron en Italie*, "The sublime
love of Myrrha was conceived that evening."[3]

Most later readers of the play have recognized Teresa as Byron's
life-model for Myrrha just as they have agreed that Byron sat for his
own portrait in Sardanapalus. If Teresa was aware of this—as she no
doubt was—her idealization of Myrrha would be quite understandable,
especially in view of her notoriously idealized account of her relations
with Lord Byron, which she published in her *Lord Byron jugé par les
témoins de sa vie* (Paris, 1868). It is strange, however, particularly in
these later days, that commentators have not been more attentive to
the Myrrha of Byron's play, or, failing that, to Teresa as Byron knew

[1] *BSP* 2:565–66.
[2] *Ibid.*, p. 566.
[3] Quoted by Irish Origo, *The Last Attachment* (New York, 1949), p. 240.

228

and loved her. Both are distinctive and equivocal personalities, and both bear little resemblance to Teresa's simplified (and prejudiced) account of them. To a large extent Myrrha probably did grow out of Byron's experience of Teresa, but it is neither likely nor true that Byron's idea of Teresa was quite the same as Teresa's. Professor Bonamy Dobrée has said that Myrrha demands "our homage," and Samuel Chew regards her as "the finest, as she is the most individual, of Byron's women." Having said this he goes on to equate her with other famous Byron heroines: Angiolina from *Marino Faliero*, Haidée from *Don Juan*, and Marina from *The Two Foscari*.[4] Now Myrrha may be the "finest" of Byron's heroines, but if she is the reason is not so simple as has been suggested. If, for example, Myrrha is like Marina, she cannot possibly be like Angiolina or Haidée, for the latter women are submissive and unworldly feminine ideals, whereas Marina is portrayed realistically as a passionate and extremely self-willed individual.

This uncomplicated understanding of Myrrha's character in *Sardanapalus* seems a measure of the traditional attitudes toward the play as a whole. It is, for the most part, a highly praised work—justly so, I think. But criticism of Byron's plays is usually most disappointing, mainly because readers do not treat them as plays but as documents in which one can rummage about for Byronic ideas and themes. Paul West has written what is in many ways an interesting essay on Byron's dramas, but his general argument is that they represent rather simplified treatments of complicated human problems. But the simplification process is, I think, Mr. West's. He remarks incidentally, for example, that *Marino Faliero* and *The Two Foscari* are almost wholly without an imagistic substructure, and the factual error in this case seems to me indicative of the kind of neglect which Byron's plays have suffered from.[5]

Byron himself thought very highly of his dramas, put much thought and labor into their conception and execution, and predicted that they would one day be regarded among the most important things he had written. Goethe thought they epitomized Byron's best work, but Gifford's opinion—that they were his worst—has been, historically, more influential. In any case, these sharp differences of opinion are not at all characteristic of current attitudes, for the plays are not often analyzed

---

[4] Bonamy Dobrée, "Byron's Dramas," *Byron Foundation Lecture* (University of Nottingham, 1962), p. 17; Samuel C. Chew, *The Dramas of Lord Byron* (reprinted, New York, 1964), p. 114.

[5] See Paul West, *Byron and the Spoiler's Art* (London, 1960), p. 118.

any more for their specifically aesthetic qualities. Fundamental questions—like the nature of Myrrha's characterization in *Sardanapalus*—are simply not raised because it is generally taken for granted that the plays are not worth such questions. It seems to me, however, that neither the meaning nor the merit of the plays should have to depend upon our inherited judgments; they deserve a close rereading which will test traditional opinions against the texts themselves and the relevant biographical documents which shed light upon Byron's intentions. In the discussion that follows, then, I want to reconsider first the whole question of the meaning of *Sardanapalus* itself, and then return to the problem I initially raised of how both Byron and Teresa imposed themselves upon the play as it was finally conceived.

II

The basic dramatic action of *Sardanapalus* indicates why the traditional descriptions of Myrrha are misleading. She is indeed one of Byron's finest female characters, but the reason is that she lives an independent life in the world of the play. She is complexly motivated, and the play dramatizes the growth of her character to the point where she is completely worthy of the apotheosis at the conclusion. But she does have to grow to that *Liebestod*. At the beginning of the play she is caught between her love for Sardanapalus and her sense of shame for loving him. She wants to achieve what Salemenes also wants: the reawakening of his "latent energies" (I, i, 11) in order that he might appear manly and heroic, "To sway his nations" and "To head an army" (I, i, 22–23). Salemenes works for this end not only because, at bottom, he esteems Sardanapalus, but even more because he would "not see/The blood of Nimrod and Semiramis/Sink in the earth" and the Assryian empire finally end (I, i, 5–7). Myrrha, however, does not care about the empire—indeed, one of the thoughts she indulges is that a powerful Sardanapalus would "tread down the barbarous crowds" of the now discontented Assyrians and thus make suffer "The natural foes of all the blood of Greece" (I, i, 703, 707). Myrrha is too "sanguinary" and Sardanapalus knows it (II, i, 574). Her temperament is part of her warlike Greek heritage, as she herself points out (V, i, 100–103). But neither Byron nor Sardanapalus esteems the love of the exercise of power and force. Salemenes is honest and brave, but "too severe" (II, i, 521), and Byron frequently points his resemblance to Myrrha. At the end of the second act, for example, Myrrha—like Salemenes—suggests that Sardanapalus ought to have executed Arbaces and Beleses.

Sard.   This is strange;
    The gentle and the austere are both against me,
    And urge me to revenge.
                                'T is a Greek virtue.
Sard.
    But not a kingly one—I'll none on 't; or
    If ever I indulge in 't, it shall be
    With kings—my equals.
Myr.   These men sought to be so.
Sard.
    Myrrha, this is too feminine, and springs
    From fear—
Myr.   For you.
    Sard.   No matter, still 't is fear.
    I have observed your sex, once roused to wrath,
    Are timidly vindictive to a pitch
    Of perseverance which I would not copy.
    I thought you were exempt from this, as from
    The childish helplessness of Asian women.   (II, i, 578–90)

Though Myrrha is free of feminine "helplessness," her character is
flawed at the other extreme. In this respect she does indeed resemble
Byron's Teresa, whom he characterized as an Italian, and slightly moderated, version of Caroline Lamb. Thinking of Myrrha, Sardanapalus
says that "all passions in excess are female" (III, i, 381), and he goes on
to describe her fierce address during the battle. Her resemblance to the
warrior-empress Semiramis is all but impossible to overlook and Byron
enforces the parallel in the next scene when Sardanapalus has his nightmare. In this brilliantly conceived incident Sardanapalus tells Myrrha
how he dreamed that he was "Here—here—even where we are" (IV, i,
79). Nimrod and Semiramis come to him with a terrible greeting, and
seem to be seeking his life, or enforcing their claims of kinship upon
him. He tells Myrrha how Nimrod reached out for him, and how
Semiramis "flew upon me/And burnt my lips up with her noisome
kisses" (IV, i, 149–50). When Sardanapalus awakes, the Semiramis of
his dream-vision fades out and is suddenly replaced by the real apparition of his Ionian lover. A likeness between the two women is thus
dramatically enforced. At the same time, Byron is careful to emphasize
here Myrrha's more tender virtues, so that while the Semiramis-parallel
is offered, it is immediately qualified in the context. Myrrha is not the
moral equivalent of Semiramis, but she does resemble her in some important ways, and it is the function of the play to show both her com-

plex nature and the way in which she overcomes what Byron (like Sardanapalus) regards as her less admirable qualities.

Byron was always fascinated by passionate characters, and he often admired them. Napoleon was his fallen hero and he praised Rousseau. But he criticized both men in *Childe Harold's Pilgrimage III* because— like the Ali Pasha of Canto II—their passions turned destructive. Byron had a profound understanding of man's tragic desire to force his will upon the circumstances of life precisely because he himself suffered from the same impulsion. As he matured the conviction grew upon him that such a desire often had its origin in fear and personal insecurity. Thus, the explicit condemnation of "the lust to shine or rule" in *Childe Harold's Pilgrimage III* is a clear foreshadowing of many similar remarks by Sardanapalus, and of a major theme in *Don Juan*. But is was not until Byron had settled down in Italy that he applied his understanding of this problem to women (and, by extension, to the relations between the sexes). Gulbeyaz is a comic version of Semiramis, while Myrrha and Marina Foscari are both women of deep devotion who incline to vengefulness and emotional excess. All four have a certain passionate willfulness, but only Myrrha and Marina undergo a process whereby their emotional instabilities are corrected in the dramatized actions of their lives. They become not less passionate, but less willful.

Byron's analysis of the passionate personality is more acute in *Sardanapalus* than perhaps anywhere else in his work. Myrrha's position in the play is, to a great extent, the reason for this complexity, for she is at once the drama's heroine and an important representative of the fundamental evil which is anatomized in the play. She is Sardanapalus' lover but she is also his moral antagonist. In the first act Sardanapalus argues with Salemenes about treasonous plots and the exercise of regal power. His main point is exactly the same as that which he makes in his later exchange with Myrrha (quoted above).

> Must I consume my life—this little life—
> In guarding against all may make it less?
> It is not worth so much! It were to die
> Before my hour, to live in dread of death,
> Tracing revolt; suspecting all about me,
> Because they are near; and all who are remote,
> Because they are far. . . .   (I, i, 391–97)

It is this kind of fear for life that produces sanguinary heroes and heroines, and that renders impossible the simple living and enjoyment of life itself. Moreover, fear of this sort is an implicit accusation of self, a revelation that a person doubts the integrity and self-sufficiency of his own resources.

Such a doubt is the basic weakness in Myrrha's character, and it is well dramatized in the play's first important dialogue between Myrrha and Sardanapalus. She urges him to heed the cautionary advice of Salemenes and he is surprised to find her in agreement with her erstwhile antagonist. He asks her if she is afraid. She vehemently denies this and says that she only wants to save the man she loves, make him a better king, and help him to preserve his realms from the civil war. On the surface, then, her motivations seem quite selfless. But when Sardanapalus finally leaves her at the end of the act she utters a soliloquy that illuminates a number of problematical remarks in the earlier dialogue. "Why do I love this man?" she begins, and again we see the struggle in her mind between her love and her contempt for Sardanapalus.

> Could I save him
> I should not love *him* better, but myself;
> And I have need of the last, for I have fallen
> In my own thoughts, by loving this soft stranger. . . .
>
> (I, i, 650–53)

She says she does not respect him, but the truth is—as she herself declares—that she does not respect herself. Indeed, if Sardanapalus has a fault it is that he is too good for a world that loves war, glory, and the exercise of power. Like the Byron of *Don Juan*, Sardanapalus mercilessly exposes the folly of such ideas, and counters with his own political philosophy.

> Oh, thou wouldst have me doubtless set up edicts—
> "Obey the king—contribute to his treasure—
> Recruit his phalanx—spill your blood at bidding—
> Fall down and worship, or get up and toil."
> Or thus—"Sardanapalus on this spot
> Slew fifty thousand of his enemies.
> These are their sepulchres, and this his trophy."
> I leave such things to conquerors; enough
> For me, if I can make my subjects feel
> The weight of human misery less, and glide
> Ungroaning to the tomb; I take no license
> Which I deny to them. We are all men. (I, i, 255–66)

It is no coincidence that the conclusion of this speech echoes some famous verses from Byron's declamatory manifesto "Prometheus":

Thy Godlike crime was to be kind,
To render with thy precepts less
The sum of human wretchedness. . . .   (ll. 35–37)

These lines could have been an epigraph for *Sardanapalus*. "We are all men," the king says, and Byron's prose is littered with similar attitudes. At the time he was writing the play he wrote in his *Ravenna Journal:* "There must be a universal republic,—and ought to be." It was an idea he always cherished. During his first pilgrimage to the East he wrote to his mother that "a man is not intended for a despot or a machine, but as an individual of a community, and fit for the society of kings."[6]

But Salemenes, like Myrrha in the first part of the play, keeps arguing for glory and authoritarian rule. Salemenes holds up the bloody but renowned Semiramis as a model for his king, and Myrrha would have him trample his restive subjects. "For a king/'T is sometimes better to be fear'd than loved," she says, else a kingdom cannot maintain its power (I, i, 533 ff.). She goes on to say that a true king must foster self-love in himself, and that he must do this politically, by putting his people in awe of him. Some sort of oppression is necessary. But because Sardanapalus will have none of it Myrrha thinks he is unkingly. She despises herself for maintaining her apparently foolish passion, and rationalizes her position by trying to make him into a more worthy object of love. Sardanapalus, however, does not need fame or an empire or "popular love" to give him a sense of his own integrity. Unlike Myrrha, he does not need "*self*-love" for he is already completely self-possessed. As a result, his reign has been a devoted attempt to enjoy life and to give others the opportunity for enjoying it as well.

Myrrha rightly sees that Sardanapalus is in imminent danger of losing his empire and she is sincere in wanting to help him. Her error lies in judging that Sardanapalus ought to be more concerned with the preservation of the political structure than with maintaining the moral empire for which he proselytizes, and over which he rules. "I love thee far—far more/Than either the brief life or the wide realm,/Which, it may be, are menaced," he tells her, but she argues that his unconcern about politics and the rule of power is extravagant: "Kingdoms and lives are not to be lost" (I, i, 488). Unlike Salemenes, she is not interested in the welfare of the Assyrian empire as such. This we have already seen. Rather, she wants Sardanapalus to prove himself manly and regal, and she mistakenly believes that these virtues can only be

6 BSP 2:555; LJ 1:284.

present in a man who exerts his power over others, and in a king who rules by force. She has been "Degraded" by her love, she says (I, i, 502), but it is clear that her sense of shame does not stem from deficiencies in Sardanapalus but from her misunderstanding of his essential character, and of the significance of his apocalyptic message.

From this derives her passion to make Sardanapalus over again—to teach him how to live like a man, rule like a king, and, if necessary, die like a hero. Her plans are mocked by the plot of the drama, however, since he is ahead of her in all these things, and teaches her what integrity, love, and kingship really entail. He does not like war and fighting, but no one has to instruct him in courage when the circumstances demand it. He not only fights well, but his handling of the dispute between Salemenes and the chief conspirators (II, i, 175 ff.) is both human and diplomatic. His actions in this instance would have prevented the success of the insurrection had he not later acceded to Salemenes' suggestion to send the plotters to the frontier (a gesture that implies fear). Like Myrrha, Salemenes wants to instruct the king in how to live and how to rule, but his advice is always directed at making Sardanapalus a less benevolent king, and in this instance it precipitates the downfall of the empire. Toward the end of the play Myrrha hopes to convince Sardanapalus that they should each take poison rather than fall into the hands of the revolutionaries. Once again, however, Sardanapalus overgoes her intentions, for while she is planning a double suicide, he is looking forward to the glorious immolation scene on which the play concludes. The death he purposes is both a fulfillment of his own life and a prophecy to future ages.

Myrrha's doubt of Sardanapalus' greatness, and her self-doubt, begin to break down in the third act when she sees his firmness in the face of insurrection. "How I do love thee!" she exclaims, and when he says "I ne'er doubted it" she replies: "But now I know thee" (III, i, 108–9). That she needs signs of this sort is part of her weakness, however. Abandoning at last her wish to change him, she also loses her need for "*self*-love." "Now let them take my realm and life!" Sardanapalus says at the end of Act IV, and this time Myrrha agrees that such things have no value beside their love. Accepting implicitly the morality of the established order, Myrrha argues in Act I that "Kingdoms and lives" are to be preserved since they are the measure of one's self-love: and the basis of all love is self-love. But the integrity of Sardanapalus is of his essence and not of his existence, and hence does not depend upon life, or realms, or glory. Thus he does not seek after self-love as Myrrha does. By Act IV, however, Sardanapalus has so "wound about [her] heart" (III, i, 177–78) that she embraces the principle of essential integrity which he epitomizes, and can finally offer him "a heart/That loves without self-love! 'T is here—now prove it." (IV, i, 527–28).

The character of Sardanapalus is one of Byron's greatest triumphs because he survives his idealized status to live as a distinct and human personality. Most other idealized characters in Byron's works have not fared so well. Jacopo Foscari is wholly unconvincing, while Angolina Faliero and Adah, Cain's wife, are little more than active Byronic ideas. Only Haidée and Sardanapalus keep their full humanity in the process of their glorification, and the reason is that both live in a Don Juanesque world: they represent forms of the human sublime, and do not achieve their ideality because they are beyond the natural and the human but because they *are* mortal. Their glory is precisely their humanness, and their sublimity depends upon our melancholy understanding of the impermanence of the wonder that is the human person. *Sardanapalus* is a tragedy not because the king loses his throne and the Assyrian empire seals its doom, but because in the defeat of Sardanapalus is imaged the permanent loss of the earthly paradise. Sardanapalus and Myrrha go to live, it may be, with the gods, but we are left feeling that a paradise has been lost with them.

> I thought to have made mine inoffensive rule
> An era of sweet peace 'midst bloody annals,
> A green spot amidst desert centuries,
> On which the future would turn back and smile,
> And cultivate, or sigh when it could not
> Recall Sardanapalus' golden reign.
> I thought to have made my realm a paradise,
> And every moon an epoch of new pleasures.   (IV, i, 511–18)

John Galt long ago remarked upon "the graciousness in the conception of the character of Sardanapalus."[7] He is a voluptuary, but he is neither gross nor weak nor indifferent. All his efforts are directed toward making his kingdom a garden for men's enjoyment. His concern is for mortal men (to "lessen,/By mild reciprocal alleviation,/The fatal penalties imposed on life," I, i, 399–401) and his imagination is earth-centered. Nearly all those around him, however, want him to act the part of a god by inspiring terror and awe in his people. Semiramis and Nimrod "have been revered as gods," Salemenes tells him (I, i, 267), but Sardanapalus says "Those gods were merely men. . . ./I feel a

---

[7] John Galt, *The Life of Lord Byron* (New York, 1833), p. 228.

thousand mortal things about me,/But nothing godlike" (I, i, 272–74). The traditional forms of address irk him because such language "makes life itself a lie./Flattering dust with eternity" (I, i, 565–66). By insisting on the ultimate value of "life itself" he incurs the displeasure of Beleses particularly, for the priest fears that Sardanapalus' attitudes will destroy the divine order which Assyria's glorious history represents. For Sardanapalus, as for Byron himself, the gods are most admirable when they "become as mortals" (*Childe Harold's Pilgrimage* IV, 52). This fact is well dramatized when the king and Salemenes discuss the significance of Bacchus. After presenting the history of Bacchus Sardanapalus argues that he became godlike only after he became humanized.

> But here, here in this goblet is his title
> To immortality—the immortal grape
> From which he first express'd the soul, and gave
> To gladden that of man, as some atonement
> For the victorious mischiefs he had done.
> Had it not been for this, he would have been
> A mortal still in name as in his grave;
> And, like my ancestor Semiramis,
> A sort of semi-glorious human monster.
> Here's that which deified him—let it now
> Humanise thee: my surly, chiding brother,
> Pledge me to the Greek god!   (I, ii, 173–84)

This kind of "impiety" shocks not only Salemenes and Beleses but even Myrrha. At the banquet Altada raises a pledge to "the god Sardanapalus" because he is "The king of peace, who holds a world in jubilee" (III, i, 18 and 28). The gesture recapitulates Sardanapalus' toward Bacchus, and as Salemenes is scandalized in the earlier scene so Myrrha is here: "King, wilt thou bear this mad impiety?" In the exchange that follows Sardanapalus tells Myrrha that human kings are better than divine ones precisely because they intend good for men even if they have not the power to carry out their intentions. The gods are no better, and may be something worse if they really are able to amend the human condition and do not exercise their power. But Sardanapalus does not accuse the gods of this for he seems to think them little different, morally speaking, from men. The human and divine orders are alike fully natural and it is man's part to worship and seek to imitate not the destructive power of the gods but their human graciousness.

But Sardanapalus' attempt to restore a kind of Saturnian Age fails

because men reject the earthly paradise in favor of a heavenly waste-
land. Sardanapalus wants to emulate "The shepherd kings of patriarchal times,/Who knew no brighter gems than summer wreaths,/And
none but tearless triumphs" (I, ii, 560–62). The nature metaphor here,
predominant throughout, suggests the bases of all of Sardanapalus'
attitudes. Beleses worships Nature, and particularly the stars, because
they are a cosmic iconograph of the divine order (see II, i, 1 ff.). The
priest calls upon Sardanapalus to "respect" the "starry mysteries" of
their traditional religion, and the king's answer is not a denial of respect
but an assertion of a very different sort of Nature worship.

> Oh, for that—I love them:
> I love to watch them in the deep blue vault,
> And to compare them with my Myrrha's eyes:
> I love to see their rays redoubled in
> The tremulous silver of Euphrates' wave,
> As the light breeze of midnight crisps the broad
> And rolling water, sighing through the sedges
> Which fringe his banks: but whether they may be
> Gods, as some say, or the abodes of gods,
> As others hold, or simply lamps of night,
> Worlds, or the lights of worlds, I know nor care not.
> There's something sweet in my uncertainty
> I would not change for your Chaldean lore. . . .   (II, i, 252–64)

Sardanapalus' reaction to the stars is immediately to involve them in
more earthly contexts. He cannot think of them "in lone splendour
hung aloft the night," but must (like Keats) bring them close to man
and make them relevant to his emotional life. He does not worship a
Nature that has a fixed religious significance but one that is beautiful
and infinitely various. Sardanapalus' Nature answers to the gods of any
man's affective longings, and to the indefinite capabilities of each
man's imaginations.

But the natural orientation of Sardanapalus' attitudes has a tragic
aspect when the life of Nature is made normative for the community
of man. The king exposes the problem himself very early in the play.

> If then they hate me, 't is because I hate not;
> If they rebel, 't is because I oppress not.
> Oh, men! ye must be ruled with scythes, not sceptres,
> And mow'd down like the grass, else all we reap
> Is rank abundance, and a rotten harvest
> Of discontents infecting the fair soil,
> Making a desert of fertility.—   (I, ii, 412–18)

Salemenes' principal argument against the king's way of life is that the "abundance" which he wants is only possible if the garden is carefully tended: the scythe and authoritarian rule are needed if the fertility is not .to run wild. Sardanapalus' natural dream is thus an "unreach'd Paradise of our despair" (*Childe Harold's Pilgrimage* IV, 122) since its realization seems impossible except in a community raised and supported by political control, even though such controls inevitably destroy the especial value that the paradisal garden has. The human god Bacchus is both a warrior and a reveler, and his equivocal character seems a measure of the unresolvable conflict in the ordinary human person, and in all human institutions.

But Sardanapalus is not an ordinary man and is not personally subject to this tragic flaw. The conflict between power and pleasure has been resolved in his character. He does not need imposed controls to secure his life, not even controls imposed by his own active self-consciousness, and he seeks to persuade men to follow his example of perfect self-possession just as he follows the example of Nature. Nevertheless, the death of Sardanapalus is inevitable because he makes a public value out of his private life at a time when men are not prepared to understand his message, are not capable of living the way he lives. He uses his regal office not to perpetuate the traditional ideas about empire and kingship but to break them down, and he sets up his position in Assyria as a new kind of kingly life which all men can live. Like the Christ of our Western mythology, he speaks a prophecy that contradicts the traditions and institutions which have raised him to his office. He denounces the very bases of Assyria's past and present life and in so doing he denies the only kingship which the ordinary citizen or governmental functionary could understand. Thus he forfeits the very means by which his message must be communicated. Though he is a king, Sardanapalus cannot sanction the truth he embodies by an appeal to the symbols of his office. This would be to deny his own message, for he has come to institute a different kind of kingship. His authority is from himself since his message is the integrity of the individual. Not understanding such an authority, his people (for the most part) refuse to hear him. Thus his word must die with him and await a reconstitution of the social order before it can have anything more than an individual efficacy.

We should see, then, that Salemenes speaks a more profound truth than he realizes when he tells Sardanapalus "Thou art guarded by thy foes" (I, ii, 281). Salemenes is thinking of Beleses, Arbaces, and their adherents, the men who represent the old order and who oppose the king because he flouts it. But Salemenes, who is the trusted defender of the king and who dies in his service, also wants to preserve the old ways and is equally a "foe" to Sardanapalus' moral values. He wants to change Sardanapalus, but if he were to succeed the king would cease to be a hero. Circumstances nearly bring about the victory of this friendly enemy, for the insurrection drives Sardanapalus to take arms and to shed the blood of his people for the first time. After the battle Sardanapalus falls asleep and experiences the nightmare visitation of his ancestors.

> I felt life in them,
> And life in me: there was a horrid kind
> Of sympathy between us, as if they
> Had lost a part of death to come to me,
> And I the half of life to sit by them.   (IV, i, 123–27)

Later he tells Salemenes that, in his dream, "all the predecessors of our line/Rose up, methought, to drag me down to them" (IV, i, 175–76). The nightmare is the manifestation of Sardanapalus' fear that his recent career in battle may have reestablished old and discarded ties. This is the interpretation that Salemenes himself puts on it, for when Sardanapalus tells him that he was especially menaced by the ghost of Semiramis, "her, the homicide . . . whom you call glorious," Salemenes retorts: "So I term you also,/Now you have shown a spirit like hers" (IV, i, 180–82).

As the play draws to its conclusion Sardanapalus becomes increasingly skeptical about himself, his hopes for Assyria, and his present circumstances. He hates warfare but has been forced to fight, and even finds himself going to it with a will. He has tried to make people happy but finds all but a few rebellious. The whole situation is "monstrous," he declares. "Misplaced upon the throne, misplaced in life," he asserts nevertheless that his life had a grand purpose which was thwarted only by circumstance: "I know not what I could have been, but feel/I am not what I should be" (IV, i, 332–34). The wish is an appropriate one, for as affairs stand at this point it will matter very little whether he wins or loses in the struggle for political power. The war has destroyed everything he has lived for. Thus it happens that Sardanapalus turns to his death in order to justify his life. His purposes annulled by his enemies, he determines to wrest success out of failure by "making Death a Victory."

It is his consciousness of his political failure that guides all his actions in the last great scene of the play. When his military defeat becomes clear he sets about the preparations for his death. Everything is ar-

ranged to make it a prophetic act. He orders, first, that the funeral pyre
be built upon and around the throne.

> Let the throne form the *core* of it; I would not
> Leave that, save fraught with fire unquenchable,
> To the new comers. Frame the whole as if
> 'T were to enkindle the strong tower of our
> Inveterate enemies.   (v, i, 362–66)

The throne—symbol of a king's society rather than a "society of kings"
—has been the chief obstacle preventing the establishment of Sardanapalus' paradisal realm. He directs that it be wrapped in "fire unquench-
able" that the "inveterate enemies" of the humanized community may
never again assume its power. "There must be a universal republic—
and ought to be."

Secondly, Sardanapalus sends Pania away with the command to
"turn back" to the fiery sign in Nineveh as he sails up the Euphrates.
When he reaches Paphlagonia he is further directed to tell everyone
there "what you *saw* at parting" (V, i, 390 ff.) in order that the meaning of this prophetic flame may be spread abroad.

> and the light of this
> Most royal of funeral pyres shall be
> Not a mere pillar form'd of cloud and flame,
> A beacon in the horizon for a day,
> And then a mount of ashes, but a light
> To lesson ages, rebel nations, and
> Voluptuous princes.   (v, i, 436–42)

The biblical comparison underlines the enormous significance which
the voluptuary Sardanapalus attaches to this act. Just before he dies he
recalls the paradise he attempted to found in his country: "I sated thee
with peace and joys; and this/Is my reward" (V, i, 495–96). The declaration clarifies once again the significance of the immolation and the
lesson it carries to all succeeding ages. Assyria perished because she
turned from the man who offered her new and more abundant life.
Sardanapalus is the martyr of the new dispensation which he himself
introduces; indeed, he is its Messiah. His death will be the beacon of the
future, however, and his faithful retainer Pania will be his first evan-
gelist. The highly romantic theme of this conclusion and the grand
manner in which it is carried out are both typically Byronic. Though
we are used to such gestures in Byron, few are brought off so well as

this one here. The theme of the drama demands it, and the sophistication of Byron's art has in this case earned it.

III

Being what she was, Teresa Guiccioli would probably not have been pleased to know that Myrrha's "nobility" and love were more complicated values to Byron than she had imagined; or that it is Sardana-palus (Byron) and not Myrrha (Teresa) who is the play's chief norm of value; or, finally, that it is the integrity of the king which redeems and finally perfects the love of his mistress. Lesser matters than this precipitated quarrels between Byron and his "Italian wife." But Byron was no less devoted to Teresa than Sardanapalus was to Myrrha, and her influence upon the play is, in the end, quite pronounced. The real woman whom Iris Origo has described as a person "of quite exceptional vitality and strength of will"[8] is the manifest "original" of Myrrha. Iris Origo's penetrating summary of her character deserves to be quoted at length because it suggests how Byron used his play to alleviate some of the anxieties which this clever and passionate woman caused him.

> Teresa was in some ways—like Caroline Lamb and Augusta—a *silly* woman; but she was not a stupid one; and she had all the strength of a one-track mind. From the moment that her passion for Byron held her, she knew what she wanted, and it was a fore-gone conclusion that she would get it. She persuaded her father . . . that nothing was wrong in her relations with Byron. . . . She defeated the complicated manoeuvers . . . of her husband. She im-posed an acceptance of the situation . . . on the whole tight little society of Ravenna. . . . And, finally, she imposed her will upon Byron himself. He struggled, he grumbled, he tried to laugh at her; but in the end, he did what she wanted. . . . Moreover she succeeded in shaping this relationship according to *her* standards, *her* view of life. For in such cases it is always the narrower, but more positive, purpose that wins.[9]

Byron was no less volatile and self-willed than Teresa, but the evidence is clear that his *dama* did control the affair, and her lover, exceedingly well. It is also clear that Byron was frequently annoyed and more fre-quently frustrated by Teresa's success in managing him to please her-self. In real life it may be "the narrower, but more positive, purpose that wins," but in *Sardanapalus* Byron would work his own will un-

[8] Origo, *Last Attachment*, p. 9.
[9] *Ibid.*, pp. 11–12.

hindered, and set matters the way *he* knew they ought to be. Sardanapalus loves Myrrha, and he is capacious, benevolent, and candid; Myrrha loves Sardanapalus, but she is—at least initially—more narrow and designing. Sardanapalus does not lecture Myrrha on her imperfections, but in the course of the play he corrects them by simply living up to his inherently noble and generous nature. Now why hadn't Teresa learned to behave better, more like Byron, for example! That tone is shot through letter after frustrated letter which Byron sent to Teresa during their many disputes and love-entanglements.

But if Teresa was the occasion for Byron's act of compensation, she also—along with Italy in general—had a strong influence upon the attitudes of mind which are Sardanapalus' chief glory. Before he met Teresa Byron was wayward, moody, and undisciplined, but his liaison, and especially his role as *cavalier servente*, forced him to curb these tendencies in himself. Teresa writes in her unpublished *Life* of Byron that

> Lord Byron began to play his role of Cavalier Servente with pleasure, indeed, but not without laughing at it a little. . . . One would almost have thought that he was a little ashamed—that in showing himself kind he was making an avowal of weakness and being deficient in that virility of soul which he admired so much. . . . This was a great fault of Lord Byron's.[10]

For all his complaints, Byron not only loved Teresa but respected her, and it is not unlikely that she lectured him frequently, in her sometimes maddening way, about this "great fault." The poet of "Prometheus" declares a code of kindliness as well as a moral of eternal defiance of evil. Sardanapalus drops altogether the attitude of passionate rebellion and speaks constantly of more humane and benevolent virtues in a voice that is sometimes deeply sincere and sometimes jocose. The tone in both cases fits Teresa's picture of Byron learning the life of the *cavalier servente*. Moreover, Sardanapalus has completely assimilated the idea that "virility of soul" is by no means incompatible with a softer disposition, and that kindliness is not to be equated with weakness. It is true that Byron respected and embraced such notions well before he met Teresa or lived a member of Italian society, but it is equally true that he had neither the chance nor the inclination beforehand to exercise these ideas with any regularity. The first year of their liaison was rather a stormy one, but during 1821–22 they became quite domesticated.

If the routine into which he fell with Teresa palled occasionally, at

---

[10] *Ibid.*, p. 147.

least he had the Carbonari to keep himself on edge. Besides, the routine
of the affair seems to have triggered some thoughts on indolence which
were to occupy an important place in *Sardanapalus*. Shortly after Byron
began writing the play, well before he finished the first act, he found
himself without any inclination to continue. It is just indolence, "lazi-
ness," he thinks, and he pursues the notion in his diary:

> Rochefoucalt says that "laziness often masters them all"—speak-
> ing of the *passions*. If this were true it could hardly be said that
> "idleness is the root of all evil", since this is supposed to spring
> from the passions only: *ergo*, that which masters all the passions
> (laziness, to wit) would in so much be a good. Who knows?[11]

Salemenes (like Myrrha!) urges Sardanapalus to a more active life but
the king will have none of it. He is all for ease, and explicitly declares
that the most active people, like Semiramis and Nimrod, are also the
most evil. "Eat, drink, and love; the rest's not worth a fillip" (I, ii, 299).
Thus Sardanapalus dedicates the two cities he has founded, and Teresa
might have been pleased to know that she, more than any other single
person, was responsible for reawakening in Byron his feeling for the
apocalyptic ideas implicit in the epigram. Then again she may not have,
for Sardanapalus' verse is laced with an earthiness and sophisticated
irony that were not part of Teresa's makeup. She did not appreciate
at all well Byron's ironic temperament; love for her—if very earthly
indeed—had always to be publicly represented as having a supermundane quality. Sardanapalus' love ideal, on the other hand, is godlike
precisely because it is so human, even gently laughable. This is pure
Byron. But La Guiccioli has her influence here too, for as the relationship continued Byron came more and more to regard his mistress as a
fascinating and almost childlike creature, full of peccadillos, annoying
habits, even outrageous faults, but always, in her way, true, and completely devoted. This is not exactly Myrrha, but the stamp is unmistakably there.[12]

[11] *BSP* 2:580.
[12] Zarina, Sardanapalus' queen, does not resemble Lady Byron very closely—except
in her unfaithful husband. Nevertheless, it is clear that the scene involving Zarina and
Sardanapalus (IV, i, 232 ff.) is biographically oriented, with the King and Queen
standing for the estranged Lord and Lady Byron. Byron seems to have used the scene
to express his sincere regrets about the failure of his own marriage.

Contentious Worlds

> Then addressing me, He spoke and said; Hear, neither be afraid,
> O righteous Enoch, thou scribe of righteousness . . . : Go, say to
> the Watchers of heaven, who have sent thee to pray for them;
> you ought to pray for men, and not men for you.
> Wherefore have you forsaken the lofty and holy heaven, which
> endures for ever, and have lain with women; have defiled your-
> selves with the daughters of men; have taken to yourselves wives;
> have acted like the sons of the earth, and have begotten an im-
> pious offspring?   *The Book of Enoch*, XV

"*Cain*," Shelley said, "is apocalyptic; it is a revelation never before communicated to man." Goethe, scarcely less enthusiastic, had extremely high praise for Byron's other mystery play as well, *Heaven and Earth*.[1] But whereas *Cain* has always kept a distinguished place in the Byron canon, *Heaven and Earth* is hardly read anymore. This is somewhat unfortunate, for though *Cain* is clearly a much superior work of art, the two plays have a good deal in common, thematically and otherwise. Together they represent Byron's most coordinated attempt to dramatize the fundamental cosmic premises of man's situation on earth and his relation to the gods.

That the two plays were closely associated in Byron's mind seems clear. For example, *Cain* tells the beginning and *Heaven and Earth* the end of a doomed race. Had the second part of Byron's last mystery play been completed we would have witnessed this end. As it is, we have at least Byron's detailed outline of his intentions for the second part.[2] The two plays are also allied in a less obvious though, I think, no less significant way. The central angelic figure in *Cain*, Lucifer, is a Cherub, while in *Heaven and Earth* Azaziel and Samiasa are Seraphs. This distinction is an important one, as Byron points out in *Cain* (I, 417–23): the Cherubim are the angels associated with knowledge, the Seraphim with love, and the focal problem in *Cain* is the limits of human knowledge just as the focal problem in *Heaven and Earth* is the limits of love.

[1] See *P* 5:199–204, 281–82.
[2] *Medwin*, pp. 156–57.

Shelley's remarks on *Cain* intimate the allegorical character of the play. Byron, however, rarely discussed his works in terms that would admit allegorical intentions, though he did say that *Cain* was written on "a metaphysical subject."[3] He was well aware of mythic and allegorical interpretations of scripture, but his critical observations, even on his mystery plays, are almost invariably made from a psychological point of view. The state of Cain's or Manfred's mind interests Byron, as do those passionate outbursts (like Eve's curse) which tend to expose the heart and its complicated makeup. In this respect Byron is closer to Goethe than to Shelley. The latter is an allegorist in the tradition of Pico della Mirandola, whereas Goethe and Byron look back to Tasso (who treated allegory more in a psychological than a cosmological framework). Byron's own psychological criticism compares with much of Goethe's. Writing on *Cain*, for example, Goethe says that "his burning spiritual vision penetrates, beyond all conception, into the past and present, and in their train, also into the future." But when he goes on to explain Byron's "method" of conveying this wonderful vision, he resorts to a psychological rather than cosmological analysis. Or when he praises Calderon's *Daughter of the Air* he does so because Calderon's "story is based on motives purely human, and there is no more of the supernatural element than is necessary for the extraordinary and exceptional in human affairs to develop and proceed in a natural fashion."[4] Similarly, though Byron was well aware that *Cain* dealt with "the politics of Paradise,"[5] his practical analysis of the work is, like all his other criticism, psychologically oriented (see *LJ* 5:470, for example).

Byron and Goethe's criticism suggests that, while writing, both applied much of their conscious artistry to the evocation of "realistic" human drama. The allegories in *Faust, Cain, Manfred, Elective Affinities*, etc., are presented in a less self-conscious way than Shelley presented his in *Prometheus Unbound* or *The Witch of Atlas*. In this respect Shelley is to Byron what Spenser is to Milton. It is a question of emphasis, but the emphasis results in a radically different sort of writing in each case. Nevertheless, *The Cenci* suggests that Shelley was quite capable of writing allegories in a more realistic manner, just as

[3] *LJ* 5:189.
[4] Goethe's review of *Cain* is translated in J. G. Robertson's *Goethe and Byron* (London, 1925), pp. 73–76. I have used the translation of the Calderon review which is printed in *Goethe's Literary Essays*, ed. J. E. Spingarn (New York, 1921, 1964), pp. 208–11.
[5] *BSP* 2:671.

The Island and some of Byron's early tales reflect a more purely allegorical approach in his poetry.

Be that as it may, it behooves us to follow a Shelleyan rather than a Byronic direction in an analysis of the mystery plays. In the first place, some readers now tend to think that *Cain* is not so much apocalyptic as sensational, that Shelley's enthusiasm was merely a function of his milieu, which recorded a sort of world-wide astonishment at Byron's boldness. The ideas seem less daring today and the play might, as a result, seem more sensational than anything else. On the contrary, I think Shelley (like Goethe) was quite right about *Cain*, as I shall try to show in the following discussion. Moreover, the play is based upon a cosmic view which is developed further in *Heaven and Earth*. This view, which involves a remarkable interpretation of the fall of man, lies behind nearly all of Byron's poetry. In his mature work, especially *Don Juan*, Byron uses his myth of the fall to help organize his materials. George Ridenour[6] has pointed out the pervasiveness of the "fall" imagery in *Don Juan* but I do not think he always interprets his data correctly. This question I shall take up directly in the next chapter. For now I need only remark that if we understand Byron's peculiar version of the fall I think *Cain, Don Juan*, and much of his other work will be helpfully illuminated. The subject is a complicated one and we might best begin by examining Byron's general religious and philosophical views.

II

Brought up a Calvinist, Byron told Annabella before they were married that he subsequently experienced a strong reaction against the sect and that he became in his young manhood an atheist and materialist. His atheism was, however, a short-lived thing and for the rest of his life he remained a professed Deist, though it has never been made perfectly clear which form of this Proteus he chose to assume. An inquiry into Byron's religious opinions, however, turns up some surprising information. Take, for example, the question of his Calvinism. Recollecting her courtship and brief union with Byron, Annabella repeatedly refers to his gloomy Calvinism and sense of his moral predestination (to evil).[7] There is some truth in this, though less than might appear at first, for after returning from the East and prior to leaving England again in

---

[6] *Ridenour*, esp. pp. 19–88.
[7] *LBW*, e.g., pp. 270–71.

1816 Byron was indeed, though only sporadically, wrung by a sense of his spiritual doom. After the separation, however, he begins to move further and further away from this attitude. In fact, he works at the renovation of his attitudes with such a purpose that one infers in him a deeply felt *need* to do so, to justify himself. The separation was, in this respect, a religious necessity for Byron, and most of the poetry between 1816 and 1818 contains the record of this necessity and process of justification. So we find him constantly opposing the doctrine of the eternity of hell, asserting the primacy of the forgiveness of sins, and emphasizing the need for and the means of spiritual reformation. It does not require much study to see that both *Cain* and *Heaven and Earth* are decidedly anti-Calvinistic.[8]

Two of the most influential texts which have been used to allege his Calvinism are reported in Dr. James Kennedy's record of their conversations. Dr. Kennedy vigorously defends the doctrine of original sin: that "we are born, from the fall of our first parents, with inclinations contrary to the will of God, and grow up indulging these in defiance of his precepts," and that we have need of Christ's atonement as a result. Byron answers:

> Of the wickedness and depravity of human nature, I have no doubt . . . ; I have seen too much of it in all classes of society . . . ; but these doctrines, which you mention, lead us back into all the difficulties of original sin, and to the stories in the Old Testament, which many who call themselves Christians reject . . . the history of the creation and the fall is, by many doctors of the Church, believed to be a mythos, or at least an allegory.[9]

Neither here nor anywhere else in these conversations does Byron opt for the doctrine of original sin. It is not that he does not recognize the cruelty and evil in men and their acts, but that he does not ascribe that evil to a sin against God. Man's evil is not theological but ethical. It is this belief which leads him to make a flat denial of the doctrine of the Atonement, and to speak in the above context of the allegorical interpretations of the Genesis story. Fundamentalist attitudes toward evil lead one into the difficulties of the doctrine of original sin. As he makes

---

[8] Hoxie Neale Fairchild, in his fine *Religious Trends in English Poetry* (New York, 1949), has some illuminating, if religiously partisan, pages on Byron (volume 3, pp. 3?8–451). He heartily disapproves of what Byron stood for, but he understands him rather well; and Fairchild sees clearly that Byron's Calvinism has been overemphasized (pp. 393–97).

[9] *HVSV*, p. 437.

abundantly clear in numerous other contexts, moral equations must be made in terms of man and man, or man and himself, but not between man and God.

Another statement reported by Kennedy seems at first to establish Byron as a Calvinist predestinarian and thus to contradict his well-known advocacy of religious tolerance and the forgiveness of sins.

> On predestination . . . it appears to me, just from my own reflections and experiences, that I am influenced in a way which is incomprehensible, and am led to do things which I never intended. . . . But I have never entered into the depths of the subject, but contented myself with believing that there is a predestination of events, and that that predestination depends on the will of God.[10]

What Byron is affirming here is not moral predestination but necessitarianism, two notions which are, as Priestley had so eloquently demonstrated, radically different. Byron was a fatalist all his life, but—except possibly for a brief period during the Years of Fame—he was not a predestinarian. For Byron, fated events in a man's life do not acquire a moral aspect until after the fact, until we see what a man will do in response to those events. What man must beware is his "worst, his second fall," when he shows himself cunning in his own overthrow. Byron's view here is analogous to his theory of history, which he saw as a blind series of cycles, totally without morality as such. In this respect Shelley and Blake—both of whom, like Novalis, assert a distinctly moral view of history—are more properly predestinarians than Byron. One of Byron's remarks to Kennedy made shortly after the statement quoted above emphasizes his antipredestinarian views. Kennedy anathematizes "Arians, Socinians, Swedenborgians, and fanatics of all descriptions" from the Christian community and Byron chides him, particularly on the Socinians: "You seem to hate the Socinians." Kennedy says they can never become "real" Christians and Bryon answers: "But is this charitable? . . . why should you exclude a sincere Socinian from the hope of salvation?"[11] The remark recalls the famous stanzas 13–15 in *The Vision of Judgment* where Byron pleads against the idea of damnation.

The more Byron's views are examined, in fact, the more clear his position becomes. Kennedy goes on to attack the Socinians and Byron responds:

[10] *Ibid.*, pp. 446–47.
[11] *Ibid.*, p. 447.

"The Socinians [Kennedy says] reject such parts of the Scripture, as interpolations or corruptions, which do not suit their scheme; they turn literal things into metaphorical, and metaphorical into literal, until they succeed in representing original sin, the depravity of our nature, the necessity of atonement, and consequently the whole necessity of a revelation, as perfectly useless. According to their scheme, there was very little need of a Savior.

"Their religion," said his Lordship, "seems to be spreading very much. Lady B(yron) is a great one among them. . . . She and I used to have a great many discussions on religion, and some of our differences arose from this point; but on comparing all the points together, I found that her religion was very similar to mine."[12]

Doctrines like the eternity of hell and the Virgin Birth Byron rejected out of hand as at variance with the Bible. He fought for religious liberty and against those who "have sworn a bond against that charity which thinketh no evil."[13] He denied the divinity of Christ and insisted upon the unicity of God, the preeminence of "the great first cause, which we call Almighty God."

I am sure that no man reads the Bible with more pleasure than I do; I read a chapter every day, and in a short time shall be able to beat the Canters with their own weapons. Most of them are like Catholics, who place the Virgin Mary before Christ, and Christ before God; only they have substituted the Apostle Paul for the Virgin, and they place him above Jesus, and Jesus above the Almighty.[14]

For Byron, the worst results of these "superstitions" are ignorance, sectarian dogmatism, and ultimately uncharitableness. The last effect is especially pernicious in Byron's view, and it will not be eradicated "until the bulk of mankind think for themselves."[15] This last is a key Byronic idea. Finally, he denied the doctrine of Atonement[16] and insisted that the significance of Christ's life lay in its exemplary value. Not only were the ideas of Jesus worthy of imitation; he showed in his actual history that he had lived as he had said life ought to be lived.

Now all these ideas are distinctly Socinian in character. As he pointed out to Kennedy, however, Byron was not in total agreement

[12] *Ibid.*
[13] *Ibid.*, p. 568.
[14] *Ibid.*, p. 569.
[15] *Ibid.*, p. 568.
[16] See below.

either with Lady Byron or with (say) Priestley, the arch-Socinian of the eighteenth century in England.[17] His ideas about man's capacity for evil were a good deal darker than his wife's, Priestley's, or the usual Socinian's. He was a benevolist but preserved a strong element of skepticism in his makeup which prevented him from ever fully accepting the progressive meliorism of Lady Byron and Priestley. Nevertheless, though he was not sanguine in his hopes for society, he acted on the premise that men must be persuaded to "liberal sentiments"[18] even if the results were painfully slow in coming. The perception of this fact, and the sense (like Shelley's at the end of *Prometheus Unbound*) that, once gained, it might all be lost again and have to be regained, made Byron somewhat gloomy about it all. Still, he persisted with his addresses from the throne of virtue, and the two basic ideas that he constantly iterated were (*a*) tolerance and mutual sympathy, and (*b*) a determined intellectual freedom. As for religion specifically, his Socinian inclinations supported his belief in a single reigning deity—the Almighty God of Deism, the First Principle and Cause of all. Man, including that exemplum of the best man, Christ, dwells apart from the primordial seat of power, the energic source of the universe.

This loose set of principles existed alongside a markedly different group of convictions. The man who affirmed that "the great object of life is sensation—to feel that we exist, even though in pain," looks odd sporting the antimaterialist ideas that appear throughout his writings. One famous series of *Detached Thoughts* (nos. 95–101) is a declaration of Byron's "partiality for spirit." But if his statements are examined carefully, especially numbers 97–99, it will be clear how dependent Byron is upon his professed philosophic materialism when he wants to discuss the nature of the immortal Soul and the eternal Mind. The fact is that Byron sometimes would have liked to divorce man's so-called spiritual powers from his so-called physical, but he could never do it conclusively. God might be "up there," and man "down here," but in man the "dust" and "deity" (*Manfred* I, 301) were somehow inseparable. For all his partiality toward spirit, his thought is not Christian. Matter and spirit have their own absolute prerogatives. Indeed, matter is so vital that it acquires what a Christian would call a "spiritual" dimension. The story of this truth is most eloquently told in *Don Juan*, but Byron talks about it all his life. In 1813, for example, he tells us how Lord Holland's librarian loaned him

[17] See Basil Willey's essay "Joseph Priestley and the Socinian Moonlight," in *The Eighteenth Century Background* (London, 1949), pp. 168–204.
[18] *HVSV*, p. 568.

> a quantity of Burn's unpublished and never-to-be-published Letters. They are full of oaths and obscene songs. What an antithetical mind!—tenderness, roughness—delicacy, coarseness—sentiment, sensuality—soaring and grovelling, dirt and deity—all mixed up in that one compound of inspired clay!

Eight years later, at the end of another journal, he relates how he mixed his drinks at a party.

> All was pretty well till I got to bed, when I became somewhat swollen, and considerably vertiginous. I got out, and mixing some soda-powders, drank them off. This brought temporary relief. I returned to bed; but grew sick and sorry once and again. I took more soda-water. At last I fell into a dreary sleep. Woke, and was ill all day, till I had galloped a few miles. Query—was it the cockles, or what I took to correct them, that caused the commotion? I think both. I remarked in my illness the complete inertion, inaction, and destruction of my chief mental faculties. I tried to rouse them, and yet could not—and this is the *Soul*!!! I should believe it was married to the body, if they did not sympathize so much with each other. If the one rose, when the other fell, it would be a sign that they longed for the natural state of divorce. But as it is, they seem to draw together like post-horses.[19]

Try as he might, Byron was never able to elevate the claims of the "soul" above those of the "body." By the time he wrote *Don Juan* he had come to accept this strange marriage within man, and even to apotheosize the creature "formed of fiery dust" (*DJ* II, 212).

This fusion in man's nature is mirrored in Byron's paradoxical co-ordination of his liberal Socinian thought with his Catholicism. Byron elsewhere ridicules a number of very traditional, and particularly Catholic, doctrines, but just before writing his mystery plays (and his *Detached Thoughts* on the soul) he tells Richard Belgrave Hoppner of his determination to raise Allegra "a Roman Catholic, which I look upon as the best religion, as it is assuredly the oldest."[20] A year later he explains his attraction to Catholicism further.

> As I said before, I am really a great admirer of tangible religion; and am breeding one of my daughters a Catholic, that she may have her hands full. It is by far the most elegant worship, hardly excepting the Greek mythology. What with incense, pictures,

---

[19] *LJ* 2:376–77 and 5:211.
[20] *BSP* 2:599.

statues, altars, shrines, relics, and the real presence, confession, absolution,—there is something sensible to grasp at. Besides, it leaves no possibility of doubt. . . . I am afraid that this sounds flippant, but I don't mean it to be so. . . .[21]

This half-jocular treatment of ideas he is seriously interested in is characteristically Byronic. Indeed, the thought that a person ought to be prepared to believe *anything*, and the use of extreme Catholic doctrines and attitudes to illustrate the point in a slightly humorous way, are beautifully coordinated in some famous stanzas at the beginning of *Don Juan* XIV. But, as the quotation suggests, the most important aspect of his leanings toward Catholicism is its pagan (not irreligious) character. He compares it to "the Greek mythology" and greatly appreciates its sensuality. Here speaks the man for whom the object of life was sensation. Indeed, as Santayana and others have suggested, it is the sensualist who is most strongly attracted to eternal sleep and nonentity, which Byron so frequently wrote about. Byron explicitly relates death and sensualism in much of his poetry (*The Island*, for example), and at the end of *Mazeppa* he affirms the ability of the "sons of pleasure" to die more easily than most other people.

Byron was himself a man of strong passions and they seem to have been aroused, as he had said, at a very early age. His amours, casual and otherwise, real and fictional, are, of course, legendary. In fact, his attitude toward love seems to epitomize his paradoxical reactions toward flesh and spirit, toward the humanly concrete and the ideal. He told Annabella and Lady Melbourne both that he could not exist without some particular object of love,[22] but he also frequently spoke of the pain that these passionate attachments always caused him. "Stanzas to the Po" deals explicitly with his equivocal responses toward love. "Though my temperament was naturally burning," Byron says in his *Detached Thought*, "I could not share in . . . commonplace libertinism . . . without disgust." His habit is toward "fixing upon one (at a time)," he goes on to say—but with a certain amount of regret, for if he were a complete libertine instead of a passionate lover of one woman at a time a number of people would have been saved some trouble.[23] He cannot help himself, however, for he was born a "constant" lover (to use Byron's own pun: *DJ* II, 209). He is not a perfected sensualist, as the following extract from a letter to Teresa illustrates.

[21] *LJ* 6:38–39.
[22] *LBW*, pp. 166, 177.
[23] *BSP* 2:636.

> For some years I have been trying systematically to avoid strong
> passions, having suffered too much from the tyranny of Love.
> *Never to feel* admiration—and to enjoy myself without giving too
> much importance to the enjoyment in itself . . . this was the basis
> of my philosophy. I did not mean to love any more, nor did I hope
> to receive Love. You have put to flight all my resolutions; now I
> am all yours. . . .[24]

Despite his sporadic attempts to change, Byron needed love, passion,
and "enjoyment" constantly, but this need is always bound up with
his "search for the 'ideal'—the being to whom I would commit the
whole happiness of my future life."[25] Thus Byron's desire and pursuit
of the whole are necessarily bound up with his commitment to an earth-
centered existence. He can only carry out his spiritual quests in terms
of something sensible and particular that he can hold on to. As we have
just seen, this attitude is a crucial element in *Sardanapalus*, and we will
have occasion to look at it again in connection with *Beppo* and *Don
Juan*.

It is probably impossible to think of Byronism without also thinking of conflict. The strange marriage of Socinianism and Catholicism
in Byron's thought exemplifies this very well. Yet it is plain that, as he
matured, Byron moved away from some of his less essential Socinian
ideas. He always insisted upon the need for intellectual freedom and
personal responsibility (even though he was a fatalist), but his stay in
Italy seems to have proved to him that people could, for example, ad-
here to certain religious "superstitions" (like the Trinity) and still preserve a strongly independent spirit. Indeed, he came to see that such
ideas could, in fact, be extremely liberating intellectually. He was led
to this position by his own vigorous skepticism, which made it difficult for him to affirm or deny anything categorically (in the area of
ideas, that is: pragmatically, and especially politically, he was unambig-
uous and sure just as he was generally lucid and decisive in his understanding of personality).

Conflicted though he often was, Byron's attitudes moved in a noticeable direction—toward a position in which spirit and matter (or,
following a Byronic analogy, thought and love) became more and
more inseparably related in his mind. "I have often been inclined to
Materialism in philosophy," Byron said in that central group of his
Detached Thoughts, "but could never bear its introduction into *Chris-*

[24] *Ibid.*, pp. 446–47.
[25] *LBW*, p. 177.

tianity, which appears to me essentially founded upon the *Soul.*" This division in his thought was always in danger of breaking down because of his consciousness that man was a piece of "inspired clay." Often it had seemed to him that soul and body "longed for the natural state of divorce," but his residence in Italy convinced him otherwise: "they seem to draw together like post-horses." The change of attitude, perfectly evident in *Don Juan* and all the later work, is intimately related to his attraction to Italian Catholicism. The Christianity he had always known was an exclusively soul-oriented phenomenon, but Italy's Catholicism gave his ideal longings "something sensible to grasp at." Indeed, his newfound "tangible religion" was scarcely Christianity at all but something closer to "the Greek mythology." Being naturally fideistic, he even found its rigorous doctrinal demands attractive to his searching mind. Who knows what interpretations of the Virgin Birth he may have been driven to invent in his more inspired (or intoxicated) moments? However that may be, it is certain that if those last seven years did not settle Byron into the earthly paradise, they did lead him to a clear understanding of what was entailed in that idea.

III

Cain is much the more complex of the two works, so I will begin with it. Contrary to some traditional critical attitudes, Lucifer is not the play's norm of value, though he is *a* norm of value. He represents the "Eternal Spirit of the chainless Mind," and as such occupies a positive role in Byron's moral scheme. Enough has been said of this by critics that I need not go into it again here.[26] The moral norm in *Cain* is not embodied in any single character, but is implied in the dramatic relationships that develop between the various people. It is in their relationships that we can perceive Byron offering his own standards, and that we can see (for example) Lucifer falling short of those standards, or revealing his own negative qualities.

Let us look at some of Lucifer's more obvious deficiencies. In the first place he does not always tell the truth, in particular the truth about himself. He tells Cain that he knows all things (I, i, 300) but he himself elsewhere confesses that this is not so. "I know not death," he says just before his boast about omniscience (I, i, 289). Further, he has promised Cain that he will satisfy his thirst for truth, but at the crucial stage of their dialogue he rebukes Cain for aspiring to know too much:

[26] For a good brief survey of the criticism of *Cain* see W. Paul Elledge, "Imagery and Theme in Byron's *Cain*," *K-SJ* (Winter, 1966), p. 49, n. 2.

"Dust! limit thy ambition" (II, ii, 406). Lucifer, however, is not presented as a liar but as a creature whose powers of knowing are limited. He understands neither himself nor Cain fully. The fact is that Cain has the capacity for an even more far-reaching knowledge than Lucifer does precisely because he was born to die. As Lucifer himself surmises, "It may be death leads to the *highest* knowledge" (II, ii, 164).

Further, Lucifer denies that he has assumed the form of a serpent to tempt Adam and Eve.

> But we, who see the truth, must speak it. Thy
> Fond parents listen'd to a creeping thing,
> And fell. For what should spirits tempt them? What
> Was there to envy in the narrow bounds
> Of Paradise. . . .   (I, i, 240–44)

Given Byron's Preface and the lack of contradictory evidence in the text, we must assume that Lucifer is telling the truth about the serpent. But his statement exposes him in a different way. True to his characteristic snobbery toward the mere race of man, Lucifer suggests that angels would never have demeaned themselves by tempting man. But if there were nothing on earth to envy, as he says, why is he spending so much time with Cain? More importantly, if angels do not condescend to tempt man, why does Lucifer later tempt Cain to murderous thoughts about his brother? In each case the reasons are good ones, as we shall see, but the point is that in these situations Lucifer shows how far beyond his comprehension those reasons are, how much he does not understand about himself and his relationship to men.

His haughty attitude toward Cain suggests a further and more serious deficiency in Lucifer. He tells Cain that he wants to enlist him among his host of the defiant enemies of God because he sees in Cain a skeptical, enquiring mind that will not rest in the blind fideism of his parents. But this is no fellowship that Lucifer offers Cain. On the contrary, he treats Cain like the dirt he conceives him to be (morally speaking), and at one point demands that Cain bow down and worship him. When Cain declines Lucifer says that it does not matter, that Cain became his slave as soon as he refused to serve God. Thus the devil quotes scripture to his own purpose—but also to Byron's, for in this biblical echo Lucifer indicates his kinship with the God of an either/or morality, the God whom the dogmatic Kennedy defended and the latitudinarian Byron opposed. Cain says that he will serve neither God nor Lucifer, but the latter says it is impossible. In this situation Lucifer seems to have forgotten entirely his own most fundamental principle: never to yield dominion of his mind where he does not himself freely choose to do so. He honestly seeks to reinforce this principle in Cain, but does not seem to recognize his own dogmatism. Originally, because of God's imposition, Lucifer felt the need to create his own system or be enslaved by the other's. Having done so, however, he becomes like his dialectical antagonist, God, and seeks to impose upon the latest creature, man, who then becomes the victim of the war in heaven. Lucifer's demand that Cain choose sides, with Cain's refusal, is an important event in the drama as a whole, and I will return to it later.

Finally, Lucifer's most serious moral weakness is his inability to love. His general contempt for a corporeal existence proceeds by extension to a contempt for personal love, which Byron presents as the peculiar virtue of the human being. "I pity thee who lovest what must perish," Lucifer says to Cain, and the latter properly retorts: "And I thee who lov'st nothing" (II, ii, 337–38). These two lines highlight Cain's moral superiority to Lucifer and, appropriately, it is just at this point that Lucifer answers Cain's unanswerable retort with a temptation to murder. It is a wonderful example of smoke-screen tactics on Lucifer's part, and Cain, still unable to control his inherent powers at this point, ultimately succumbs. Later we find that Cain's intelligence is potentially the equal of Lucifer's and when this occurs the moral relationships in the play are definitively laid out. Cain's larger capabilities, however, should not be taken to mean that he is the play's norm of value. Byron's standard is not Cain but the ideal, the possible Man. Cain's greatest fault is thus not his positive evil but his lack of self-knowledge. But his ignorance differs from Lucifer's. Lucifer (as spirit) cannot rise to a greater moral accomplishment in his present condition, but Cain (as human being) can. Any moral advance for Lucifer is contingent upon a change in his state, a change much like that achieved by the angels in *Heaven and Earth*.

All of Lucifer's weaknesses spring ultimately from his incorporeality. A pure spirit, certain areas of experience are forever beyond his understanding. On meeting Lucifer, Cain says that he never met anyone before who sympathized with him so completely, but Lucifer really does not sympathize with Cain. His tone makes this quite clear, among other things. What he sympathizes with is Cain's mind, and in general with spirits who will pledge themselves to eternal enmity with the god of this world. But there is a sense in which he also sympathizes with Cain's corporeality: the sense of need, which becomes a kind of envy masking itself as contempt. *Heaven and Earth*, for example, is partly the story of gods longing for mortality, of angels who break away from Jehovah not, like Lucifer, out of a need to establish their primal integrity, but out of a desire to fulfill themselves with the virtues that are peculiar to corporeality. Knowledge is a marvelous thing to Byron but as early as *Manfred* he points out its deficiencies (e.g., II, iv, 430–33). What a pure intelligence like Lucifer's cannot grasp is the deep mystery of the visible. Lucifer prefers to see things "from afar" when he wants to have a sense of their beauty (II, ii, 246–47), but Cain says that things seen close are even more beautiful. "The loveliest thing I know is loveliest nearest" he tells Lucifer, and when the angel challenges him to reveal what this loveliness is Cain delivers a fine monologue praising the beauty of Adah and the natural earth (255–69). But Lucifer's "brotherhood" is "with those who have no children" (II, ii, 275), and his all but puritanical reaction against materiality (cf., e.g., II, i, 50–60) contrasts sharply with the Seraphs' reaction in *Heaven and Earth*. Lucifer, however, is a Cherub and committed to the world of Intelligences whereas Samiasa and Azaziel are angels for whom love is their *modus essendi*. Thus Lucifer is telling the truth, albeit an unconsciously ironic one, when he says that had *he* made Adam and Eve he would have made them pure spirit (I, i, 204 ff.). What Lucifer does not understand is that this apparent benefit would actually have been a limitation.

William Marshall has quite rightly pointed out that "the central dichotomy" in the play is Manichaean in form "but reverses the terms of the Manichaean thesis: Lucifer represents the intellectual and ideal Principle, and the Godhead the material Principle."[27] But he does not go on to examine the significance of this important transference of values—one, in fact, which is reflected in a similar reversal not only in *Sardanapalus*, but even more radically in *Beppo* and *Don Juan*. Cain is told by Lucifer that he must choose between heaven and hell, or matter and spirit, but he refuses to make such a choice for the very good reason that to do so would be to deny half of his own person. He evades a similar either/or imperative when Lucifer tells him that he must "choose betwixt love and knowledge" (I, i, 426). Adah tells him to choose love, but Cain answers that he cannot make a choice. Enoch and Adah represent that in the material world which is mysterious and valuable, and his attachment to them, and the values they stand for, is, as he says, born with him. But he loves nothing else, he says, and proceeds to an alliance with Lucifer in order to gain that knowledge which

[27] *Marshall*, pp. 150–51.

he lacks: an awareness of his intellectual powers. Thus Cain in his own person represents the dichotomy laid out on the cosmic level between Jehovah and Lucifer. They represent the warfare between the material and spiritual Principles, and Cain is likewise torn by this strife.

Cain's problem involves being able to keep his (correlative) values of love and corporeality while he is striving toward the apparently antagonistic values of intellect and spirituality. In this he succeeds, but just barely. Lucifer preaches a doctrine of eternal conflict, and the scorn he exhibits for everyone except himself shows up that essential lack of sympathy for mankind. As a younger man, Byron had shown a similar inclination, but during his *Don Juan* years he developed a strong sense of social sympathy and constantly praised men who had it (like Shelley) and attacked men who did not (like Castlereagh). He even saved George III in his *Vision of Judgment*, and in *Heaven and Earth* it is clearly Japhet's desire for the salvation of all men that is the play's moral standard. Lucifer wants his war in heaven, however, and his temptation of Cain is the sign that he desires to perpetuate that warfare on the earth as well. Much of Byron's poetry, as we have seen, is a testament to the success of Lucifer's designs.

Cain is subject to feelings of jealousy toward Abel, and Lucifer begins his temptation by appealing to, and exposing, those hidden feelings. But Cain truly loves his brother and he successfully resists this initial temptation, if we can judge by later events. As Marshall has pointed out, when the whirlwind scatters Cain's offering Abel regards it as a judgment upon Cain's impiety. But Cain is simply happy that in his case Nature has not been violated (III, 282 ff.). The murder that follows does not merely represent Cain's fulfillment of Lucifer's hatred of Jehovah. Cain kills Abel because Abel says "I love God far more/Than life" (III, 315–16). Abel's attitude seems to Cain (and in this he judges correctly) a violation of the corporeal aspect of existence. Indeed, for Abel to say that he loves Jehovah more than life amounts to an admission of his paradisal ignorance (II, ii, 306) of the true nature of God, the creator of all life. Yet Abel's god does demand blood sacrifice, and we seem to be faced with a contradiction in the play.

I will return to this problem in a moment. The immediate point is that when Cain kills Abel he acts like Lucifer, the despiser of material existence and the enemy of Adam's god, but also not like Lucifer insofar as he wishes to defend the claims of the created order of man. By his act Cain has not so much brought death into the world—Adam and Eve already did that—as he has brought violence. This violence is the evil that his association with Lucifer has brought him, for Lucifer is committed to eternal strife. But the act is, as Cain says, an awakening for him. He now sees what violence means, and his immediate sense of regret and sorrow at his rashness is a certain sign that he is no minion of Lucifer's hatred. Thus, ironically, Lucifer does in the end lead Cain to a higher knowledge, but that knowledge includes the rejection of any exclusively Luciferian position. Cain regrets his act and returns to Enoch and Adah.

What we witness in this important scene is Cain's attempt to balance the godlike and the Luciferian elements in his own person and his discovery that the god whom Lucifer despises is in some way very like Lucifer. Both use man to preserve the dialectic and to manifest their respective powers. Lucifer does not have the "highest knowledge" because he is pure spirit, however, and Abel's god, though the creator of all corporeal existence as it is presently constituted, has no more sympathy with hypostatic man than Lucifer does. He brutalizes creation (and circumscribes himself) with his demand for blood sacrifice. Further, Abel's god is, like Lucifer, a being of categories, fostering strife through the doctrines of election and sinfulness. Again, Japhet in *Heaven and Earth* is the readiest norm against which we can measure the evil represented by Jehovah.

Lucifer is right to oppose this being, and the contemporary outcry against the play was (in this sense) justified. If we look more closely, however, we will see why Goethe thought Byron's mystery plays fundamentally orthodox, and why Byron vigorously defended their morality. I have not yet had occasion to discuss Byron's decision to introduce Cuvier's theories into *Cain*. Those theories are the means by which Byron resolves his allegorical difficulties (specifically, the problem of Abel's bloodthirsty god). Cuvier provided Byron with a historical scheme for making Jehovah a sort of local deity rather than Byron's revered and immutable Almighty Lord who is the source of all Life. Lucifer says that other creatures inhabited man's world before Adam's time. The earth has gone through a series of convulsions in which different orders of beings have succeeded each other in sovereignty over the material world. (The transference of power from the Saturnians to the Olympians is a comparable event). The present earth "Is but the wreck" of a previous world.

> *Cain.*
> What! is it not then new?

Lucifer.

> No more than life is; and that was ere thou
> Or *I* were, or the things which seem to us
> Greater than either. Many things will have
> No end; and some, which would pretend to have
> Had no beginning, have had one as mean
> As thou. . . .

(ii, i, 153–59)

This is a rather remarkable piece of information, for if Jehovah—who pretends to have existed from all time—is in truth a relative upstart deity, then our understanding of the play must take account of it. What has existed from the beginning, Lucifer says, is "Life" along with some form of corporeality. This accords with Byron's view expressed in his *Detached Thoughts*. The world that Cain sees is the latest form that Life has urged upon matter through the agency of the god Jehovah. In fact, Jehovah's attitude toward sacrifice supports Lucifer's view of his historical character. Similarly, when Lucifer points out the relativity of sin and all moral codes to Cain and Adah (i, i, 358–80) he supports his later assertion about god's circumstantial nature.

Thus, *Cain* lays out a series of crucial relationships between men, angels, and their gods. The One True God is the source of all life, a totally amoral Entity which presides over and perdures through the various convulsions that the earth and its inhabitants suffer. Adam's god, Jehovah, is a temporary power—very like Shelley's Jupiter. Byron makes no suggestion as to when he will be superseded. Jehovah has formed the present state of the world. (Though immaterial himself, his province is over matter.) Lucifer is the intellectual power of man's world. Finally, man stands in the center coordinating in himself the cosmic duality imaged by Jehovah and Lucifer. Their opposition is the allegorical representation of man's dual nature (mind and body). Being a composite of these two powers, man alone has the power to love truly (Lucifer cannot love, and Jehovah can only establish restricted, codified, and unfree relationships). This power is a function of his corporeality, his spiritual faculties, and his social nature. Lucifer and Jehovah "reign/Together; but our dwelling are asunder" (II, ii, 375–76), and the extreme solitude of each—a fact emphasized throughout the play—is the measure both of their respective desires for absolute power and their respective inabilities to love truly. Lucifer reigns over a confederacy of anarchists bent upon hatred and opposition only, while Jehovah reigns over a union of ignorant worshipers. Only Cain and

Adah, who as male and female represent an opposition analogous to Lucifer and Jehovah,[28] are able to establish and maintain a true love union. Their love is, however—and by Cain's choice—too exclusive, and Cain's violent rejection of Abel is the sign and the result of this fact. The communal earthly paradise dreamed of by Sardanapalus and Japhet, and achieved by Torquil and Neuha in the world of Toobonai, is not gained by Cain and his race. His experience, however, points the way toward it.

IV

The importance of love in this mythic scheme is underlined by a play like *Heaven and Earth*. Byron had an impulse to write upon the theme of the fall of the Seraphim as early as 1814, and he told Annabella several times that he sometimes believed he was himself a fallen angel.[29] He clearly saw himself in the role of fallen Cherub many times, but on these particular occasions his mind took a Seraphic turn: he was one of those "sons of God" who left heaven and the love of God for earth and the love of woman. (He often suggested that the exchange, if not exactly a bad one, was certainly troublesome.)

Running through all of *Heaven and Earth* is the image of the "All beauteous world" that is this earth. Japhet is particularly eloquent on the subject (I, iii, 1 ff.), but Anah and the Seraphim defectors also attest to it. The beauty of the two women, especially Anah, is an analogous phenomenon, as it is in most of Byron's works. Japhet is in agony that the earth and Anah are both to be destroyed by the deluge.

> All beauteous world! . . .
> I cannot save thee, cannot save even her
> Whose love had made me love thee more. . . .   (I, iii, 47, 51–2)

Byron told Medwin that, in the sequel, he had

> once thought of conveying the lovers to the moon, or one of the planets; but it is not easy for the imagination to make any unknown world more beautiful than this. . . .[30]

Thus speaks one fallen angel, and his attitude carries over into Samiasa and Azaziel. "Stung," as Raphael says, "with strange passions, and de-

---

28 We have already seen that Byron often associated male with spirit and female with earth. Not always, however, as the examples of Aholibimah and Marina Foscari attest.

29 *LBW*, pp. 263, 271.

30 *Medwin*, p. 157.

based/By mortal feelings for a mortal maid" (iii, 543–44), the errant Seraphim choose to give up immortality rather than their love for the earth and its beautiful creatures. As angels they "should be, passionless and pure" (715), but they prefer the "strange" and mysterious world of corporeal desires and Byron clearly sanctions their inclinations. The angels propose to bridge the gap between earth and heaven, and their aim is matched by that of their lovers. The godlike angels long to "become as mortals" (*CHP* IV, 52), and mortality aspires to a state of divinity.

But Noah sets out the inhibiting force in the play when he says:

> Woe, woe, woe to such communion!
> Has not God made a barrier between earth
> And heaven, and limited each, kind to kind? (iii, 473–75)

Japhet is much too orthodox to reject such a decree outright, but he protests constantly against the evident evil which it produces. His protests generally take the form of requests for mercy, baffled questions about the nature of his god, or declamations that he will share the fate of the sinful lovers. He cannot secure mercy or share their doom, however, nor can he solve the riddle of Jehovah. He is left at the end "condemn'd" to ponder the significance of it all. This is what he must "remain" for. As such, Japhet stands for the well-intentioned, relatively liberal Christian of Byron's day. Reading Byron's play, such a man will be led to question the fundamentals of his orthodoxy as Japhet does.

Much of *Heaven and Earth* is superficial, and the allegory is flimsy compared with the richness of *Cain*. But the play helps us to understand what *Cain* is about. The importance of the earth in any "divine" scheme is clearly stated, as is the idea that the upper and the lower worlds in some way need each other, and that each constantly gravitates toward the other despite Jehovah's decree. As Raphael says of the angelic hosts:

> oh! why
> Cannot this earth be made, or be destroy'd
> Without involving ever some vast void
> In the immortal ranks? (iii, 562–65)

They cannot because the earth is as beautiful as the love of woman (who is, in so many of Byron's works, the genius loci in the world of nature): "but she will draw/A second host from heaven, to break heaven's law" (592–93).

Further, the play sets out, more clearly than *Cain*, a redemptive program. Japhet represents the first stage in that process. Early in the play a chorus of Luciferian spirits chants to Japhet a hymn about the future doom of man. In the midst of it he interrupts them to say that a time will come when all the evils they have prophesied will cease: hell will be abolished, earth transfigured, and all creatures will live in peace.

> *Spirits.*
>> And when shall take effect this wondrous spell?
>
> *Japh.*
>> When the Redeemer cometh; first in pain.
>> And then in glory.
>
> *Spirit.*
>> Meantime still struggle in the mortal chain,
>> Till earth wax hoary;
>> War with yourselves, and hell, and heaven, in vain,
>> Until the clouds look gory
>> With the blood reeking from each battle plain.
>> New times, new climes, new arts, new men; but still,
>> The same old tears, old crimes, and oldest ill. . . .   (iii, 204–13)

At first it seems as if Byron (through Japhet) were being perfectly orthodox in his Christianity: the millennium will be established after Christ's second coming, and man will suffer as usual in the meantime. But the gloomy prospect which the play appears to hold out for man in the "meantime" suggests Byron's unorthodox attitudes. From a traditional point of view, Christ's first coming ("in pain") reconstituted the moral world. He saved man by that coming, by that atonement. But the Spirit echoes Byron's own pessimism when he prophesies the general persistence of evil, a fact which we all (with Byron) recognize even after the coming of Jesus. The Christian Redeemer seems not to have succeeded in saving man from sin by his death.

As I mentioned earlier, however, Byron did not believe in the Atonement. What he is doing in this passage is analogous to what he does in *Childe Harold's Pilgrimage IV*, and elsewhere, when he eulogizes "Spirits which soar from ruin" (IV, 55); or what Foscolo does in "De' Sepolcri," a poem which may have influenced Byron's Italian canto. Both poets resurrect and praise the heroic spirits of the past because their particular examples can inspire men now. Jesus is not *the* Redeemer to Byron but *a* Redeemer, or an embodiment of the meaning of redemption. Shelley's *Defence* is written from a similar vantage. Byron's Jesus is a specific man who represented the larger humanistic ideal.

Pragmatically, what Jesus achieved for himself all men have also to achieve for themselves; and the time that this takes to be effected is the time of "pain." Byron suggests much the same thing in an early letter to his friend Francis Hodgson, who was trying to lead him back to an orthodox Christianity.

> I won't dispute with you on the Arcana of your new calling; they are Bagatelles like the King of Poland's rosary. One remark, and I have done; the basis of your religion is *injustice*; the *Son* of *God*, the *pure*, the *immaculate*, the *innocent*, is sacrificed for the *Guilty*. This proved *His* heroism; but no more does away *man's* guilt than a schoolboy's volunteering to be flogged for another would exculpate the dunce from negligence, or preserve him from the Rod.[31]

In this view, Jesus becomes the example of the man who *consciously* suffered all this life's "pain" and achieved "glory" as a result. Byron's redeemed earth will be a communion of such saints. To Byron, Jesus is significant in a classical (and pagan) sense: he is a model for others, more sublime, perhaps, than men like Sylla, Tasso, or Alexander, but not essentially different. Similarly, the convulsions in human history are for him images of the redemptive agonies which each particular man has to undergo. In other words, Byron is always primarily interested in the individual rather than the collective man. Man as "humanity" is inconceivable except as a diverse group of specific persons; and humanity is not redeemable as a whole but only (so to speak) piece by piece. Thus, the St. Peter's stanzas do not simply lay out the fundamental Byronic *aesthetic* at the end of *Childe Harold's Pilgrimage*. They intimate his pluralistic ethic as well when they urge a "piece-meal" salvation, an advance to a univocal end through "mighty graduations, part by part" (IV, 157).

Given the terms of his analogy in the *Heaven and Earth* passage, however, Byron had to postulate an eventual millennium in order to assert the possibility of individual fulfillment. He fought shy of all optimistic, evolutionary theories of history, and his skeptical mind naturally found Cuvier's ideas most congenial. In the mystery plays Byron chose to use Cuvier as a guide to more ancient patterns of historical thought, and he sets out a regressive theory of history to usher in the necessary millennial event. Cuvier's theories appealed to Byron because they asserted a series of cataclysms in which the earth proceeded from her Golden Age, her youth, to her less and less splendid

[31] *LJ* 2:35.

periods. His own was the Age of Bronze, or worse, and the future certainly seemed a bleak one. But in terms of the theory of redemption set out above (and the book of Revelation would support Byron), such increasing horrors and advancing age were the means to the return of paradise. The regressive myth of history is ancient and quite classical, of course, and Shelley's Count Maddalo (Byron) indicates the psychological aspect of it when he tells Julian:

> Most wretched men
> Are cradled into poetry by wrong,
> They learn in suffering what they teach in song.   (544–46)

For Byron, this myth is epitomized in the repeated "falls" which center in the book of Genesis particularly, and which Byron (with some help from the book of Enoch) reiterates in his two mystery plays. In Byron's view, every "fall" occasions a convulsion of some sort and though the event seems to signal a recession in one sense, its truest function is to provide an occasion for further blessedness. Falls are evil only if they are not capitalized upon. More surely they are the gifts of life, for, as Byron told Augusta during his great fall, "not in vain,/Even for its own sake do we purchase pain." Samiasa and Azaziel fall away from heaven, but in so doing they become more admirable, indeed, more capable morally than the god whom they desert. Their "lower" state of being is presented as really more full. Similarly, Japhet defects from his father's orthodoxy in the end and the play clearly argues that his retrograde behavior is actually a gain.

Cain presents a whole pattern of falls that constitute a remarkable interpretation of Genesis. The Socinian God reigns supreme over the forces of life which he originally set in motion. Byron conceives of him as a kind of Shelleyan Demogorgon—a deterministic but basically providential being who has given his creation the capability of developing life forms. He does not meddle in the relative world of morality and value, however, but leaves the choice of forms up to his creation. He provides the gift of life, and all subsequent life forms are the result of the particular efforts of local deities or demigods like Jehovah. Thus the primordial fall in Byron's scheme is one that has existed from eternity. It is the fall into corporeality and establishes the first great cosmic imperative: material existence, or Life. The only demand upon the life-process is that it should eventually return whence it came: "All things remount to a fountain, though they may flow to an Ocean."[32] The point

---

[32] *LJ* 5:459.

behind this is, in one sense, that the story of life is everywhere the story of God, and that when the end of the story comes God will be revealed. As we shall see, however, that revelation requires a series of cosmic falls which establishes man as the center and norm of all life.

At the beginning of the story God is equivalent to a Life Force which maintains and exercises its energies in a series of material transformations. This God has no consciousness, however. All his activities are self-conscious, and because he is undivided he is unable to reflect upon himself. The second primordial event, the fall of Lucifer, changes this state of affairs entirely. The original unified God now splits into two reigning but antagonistic principles. Lucifer falls in order to give life a consciousness, and his action establishes the second cosmic imperative: Thought.

After his fall, however, the cosmos is divided into unreproductive consciousness and reproductive corporeality. These are the two principles of which Lucifer speaks. Lucifer accuses Jehovah of being a despot, a power incapable of true communion. Lucifer's fall establishes the first example of relationship in the universe, but that relationship is founded upon antagonism and opposition. To offset it Jehovah creates man and thereby establishes a community that is wholly benevolent. Man is made in the image and likeness of Jehovah and thus, being without Lucifer's type of knowledge, can live in complete accord with his creator. But Jehovah's society is, as Lucifer and Cain both point out, a kind of ant hill in which everybody acts like everybody else. Like the automated Nature which Jehovah rules, Jehovah's unfallen man is without integrity. Not until man gets Lucifer's kind of knowledge will he be capable of a meaningful relationship.

But Jehovah's creation of man is the third great fall, and it secures the third cosmic imperative: Love. Lucifer divides, establishes integrity, and creates opposition; Jehovah unifies, establishes society, and creates bonds (as well as bondage). Adah and the defected Seraphim both indicate that Jehovah was moved to sink his power and establish his image in the material world out of a desire to exhibit his love and diffuse joy (*Cain* I, i, 478 ff., *Heaven and Earth*, iii, 477 ff.). "Who could be happy alone," Adah rightly asks, and her question defines the reason for Jehovah's creation. God and creature acquire a communion which is the paradigm for the Love imperative. All subsequent relationships and acts of creation within Jehovah's material world are exercised after the love-paradigm that he initially establishes (e.g., Cain and Adah). But human love relationships eventually acquire an additional dimension through the fourth great cataclysm. It should be noted in passing that from Lucifer's point of view man's creation is not an act of love but an act of enslavement since all community must impinge upon the prerogatives of the individual. Lucifer is, as Cain says, unable to love—a member of an order that would remain forever childless.

Individual and society, thought and love, mind and matter, Lucifer and Jehovah, are the divided aspects of a primordial unity. The original man Adam, however, is made in the image of Jehovah only. He cannot be the image of the true God without Intellect and consciousness, without incarnating the Lucifer/Jehovah duality in his single person. Adam and Eve gain a Luciferian knowledge when they eat of the forbidden tree. The fourth cosmic fall occurs immediately afterward when Adam and Eve discover that their act has gained them an unlooked-for result —Death, the fourth great imperative.

This is the crucial event as far as *Cain* is concerned. In Byron's presentation, Cain's history is not itself a cosmic fall but a variant upon Adam's fall. Cain's story dramatizes the meaning of Adam's fall by repeating it at a higher level of consciousness. When man first becomes aware that he supports a war within his members, as the fallen Adam (i.e., Cain) does, he suffers the insecurity, guilt, and agonies of one who is mastered by, and not master of, his own complex personality. He is the victim of the enmity between Jehovah and Lucifer. But Adam is also their victim, although in a different way. Adam is to Cain what Bonnivard is to Christian. After Adam eats of the tree of knowledge and is chastened by Jehovah with death, he renounces his conscious connection with his Luciferian principle and becomes, in Byron's play, a meek and ignorant worshiper of a despotic deity. He is a classic example of what we call repression. Cain then comes along to reacquire Luciferian knowledge, and by doing so he exposes once again the death imperative which Jehovah had declared to Adam and Eve but which they have since chosen not to think about.

Cain, then, asks the reader also to become conscious of the problems involved with life, thought, love, and especially death. The play ends without offering any systematic solution to the problems mainly because the key idea—death—remains mysterious and terrifying. The fifth, and last, cosmic fall occurs when death is recognized for the gift that it is. Such a recognition is no part of the drama in *Cain*, however. The play closes after a relationship has been established between death and violence, and Cain is understandably perplexed at the end. Implicit in the work, however, is a different, and redemptive, understanding of death. The first three falls culminate in the creation of man, and as such they represent a process in which the primordial God seems to be shrinking *à la Cuvier*. As each new fall occurs, however, it becomes more and more clear that God's apparent diminishment is really his way of dying into life, as Keats puts it. The "lower" God falls the more capable he becomes, until in the end he falls to the position where the notions of "upper" and "lower" are finally wiped out. No longer separated according to the decree that Noah obeys, Heaven and Earth collapse into a single order of reality. For this to happen, however, death is necessary, i.e., man must suffer the "pain" of which Japhet speaks and which Cain discovers. That pain is the knowledge that all things have their contradictories, and that existence itself is not fully conceivable (or livable) without death, or the terminus of existence.

Byron does not make this an explicit theme of *Cain*, as I have noted, but a number of things in the play distinctly point to it. First is the theory of successive falls: the example of Samiasa and Azaziel indicates that spirit is not fully capable until it has perished in life, until it has opted for mortality. Moreover, both plays show that beings born for death, like Cain and Adah, are the moral superiors of both Lucifer and Jehovah. Byron's humans are by no means perfect, but it is clear that they are headed in the right direction. In both of these examples death and mortality define, paradoxically, a moral advance in existence. Byron's presentation of the temptation in the garden underlines this fact as well. Lucifer insists that Adam and Eve were tempted by a snake, not by a spirit, and if we accept the truth of this (as we must in the context) we will be led to a fresh understanding of man's first "sin." The great Cherub thinks it both choice and appropriate that men should have been tempted by a snake. Such an event indicates how grossly material man is that he should be subject to the wiles of the lowest of creeping things. Yet that very temptation by a lowly snake is a striking allegorical statement that even the meanest parts of material existence possess startling powers and urgencies. By drawing man further into his corporeality, the snake leads man to the gift of death. As Lucifer himself admits, had he made man he would never have done such a thing. Thus, by yielding to the temptation man advances God's self-realization by dragging him down still further.

Thus it is that the first imperative, life itself, is not fulfilled without death. Death is the consummation of life, for only when life can die are we assured that it has reached its most exquisite condition. The ani-

mal and vegetable orders are caught in endless cycles of reproduction
and hence are not subject to death. Only man will die, and it is this
extreme mystery which establishes his divinity conclusively. Death also
"leads to the highest knowledge," as Lucifer tentatively suggests, for
when man becomes aware that death is for him a personal event his
whole understanding of life must be altered. Once again, the animal and
vegetable orders lack this higher knowledge, and so do the beings of
every spiritual order. Death puts man beyond all three orders in both
state of being and knowledge. Finally, death alone fulfills that third
great imperative. Death is the term of love both in the benevolent social
sense ("Greater love than this," etc.) and in the passionate subjective
sense (e.g., Tristan and Isolde).

All of these ideas are prevalent in Byron's work, especially during
the *Don Juan* years. Cain, however, is not personally conscious of them,
for to be so is to have undergone that fifth cosmic fall. In biblical mythology this conclusive fall is epitomzed in the life and death of Christ,
and Byron indicates his awareness of the pattern when he has Japhet
refer to "the Redeemer." In the biblical version of the story God *consciously* becomes man, and by doing so falls for the last time and dramatizes in that fall the final imperative: conscious acceptance of the four
basic existential demands. When the redeemer finally comes "in pain"
to live, love, think, and finally die he ensures the eventual glorification of
this world. Byron did not believe in atonement, of course. What he
means by Japhet's assertion is more classical. Jesus is the exemplum of
the man born for paradise, and his fulfillment of that consummating
norm is the prophecy of a future that, now once realized, at last seems
possible. Byron's perception that all things which flow out to an Ocean
remount at last to their fountain-source is another way of imaging the
paradoxically reversed journey that must be made if one would be
harmonized. A person becomes himself fully only by successive falls
away from an original condition, or—to use another of Byron's favorite
images—by traveling, by constantly going somewhere and becoming
something else. In each separation, in each fall, one can look for an increase in consciousness.

Instead of using the Christian mythology to tell this final act of the
story, however, Byron chose to use himself. Byron never wholly stilled,
or completely harmonized, the conflicting principles in himself (essentially, love and thought, or desire and consciousness)—not that anyone
else has done so either. But by 1817, when *Beppo* and *Childe Harold's
Pilgrimage IV* were being written, an air of self-assurance becomes
more noticeable in his poetry. He would continue to have strong emo-

tional fluctuations, but the period of *Don Juan* is marked by a decided sense of confidence in himself and his personal world. Existence is not less painful, particularly—certainly love continued to pour out its mixed blessings—but, like himself, his work is unmarred by any serious emotional instabilities. The beauty of the earth becomes a noticeable theme in his poetry and prose alike. Previously nature had often served him only as a sounding board, but during the last seven years he showed a strong inclination to "love Earth only for its earthly sake" (*CHP* III, 71). In addition, though sometimes acutely subject to the war within his members, Byron grew more and more assured of an essential harmony between his corporeal and spiritual, his passionate and intellectual, powers. In one sense *Don Juan* is the full story of that assurance. The passage from the end of his *Ravenna Journal*, quoted earlier, registers the pleased surprise that he felt upon discovering that soul and body do not really long "for the natural state of divorce." How charming to find at last that "they seem to draw together like post-horses." In sickness and in health, and until death. If the marriage was made in heaven, Byron made sure of its consummation on the earth.

It is in this context of ideas that Byron iterates his understanding of what death means. To take some passages we are already familiar with, both Mazeppa's concluding soliloquy and Byron's lament over the Princess Charlotte epitomize what he had to say about death. In those passages death is seen as rest and consolation for the pain of life, the proper fulfillment of those energies in life that man must exercise and suffer. A marvelous letter from Bologna in 1819 makes this point perfectly and deserves lengthy quotation.

> I . . . went to the beautiful Cimetery of Bologna . . . and found . . . an original of a *Custode*, who reminded me of the grave-digger in Hamlet. He has a collection of Capuchins' skulls, labelled on the forehead, and taking down one of them, said: "This was Brother Desiderio Berro, who died at forty—one of my best friends. I begged his head of his brethren after his decease, and they gave it me. I put it in lime and then boiled it. Here it is, teeth and all, in excellent preservation. He was the merriest, cleverest fellow I ever knew. Wherever he went, he brought joy; and when any one was melancholy, the sight of him was enough to make him cheerful again. He walked so actively you might have taken him for a dancer—he joked—he laughed—oh! he was such a Frate as I never saw before, nor ever shall again!"

To analyze this passage here would be gratuitous, but it is surely obvious that the sentence rhythm and the selection of details is extraordinarily brilliant. Acknowledging Shakespeare as his model, Byron equals him in a different form. The letter continues.

> In showing some older monuments, there was that of a Roman girl of twenty, with a bust by Bernini. She was a Princess Barberini, dead two centuries ago: he said that, on opening her grave, they had found her hair complete, and "as yellow as gold." Some of the epitaphs at Ferrara pleased me more than the more splendid monuments of Bologna; for instance:—
>
> > "Martini Luigi
> > Implora pace."
>
> > "Lucrezia Picini
> > Implora eterna quiete."
>
> Can any thing be more full of pathos? Those few words say all that can be said or sought: the dead have had enough of life; all they wanted was rest, and this they *"implore."* There is all the helplessness, and humble hope, and deathlike prayer, that can ever arise from the grave—*"implora pace"*. I hope, whoever may survive me, and shall see me put in the foreigners' burying-ground at the Lido, within the fortress by the Adriatic, will see those two words, and no more, put over me. I trust they won't think of "Pickling, and bringing me home to Clod or Blunderbuss Hall". . . . I believe the thought would drive me mad on my deathbed, could I suppose that any of my friends would be base enough to convey my carcase back to your soil.[33]

With his uncanny knack for quotation, Byron concludes his little sketch by quoting Carlyle's words on the dead Mowbray (*Richard II* IV, i, 95–100), who died at Venice. The letter reveals Byron's attitudes with a sharp, dramatic exactness.[34] Like his "original of a *Custode*" whose irrepressible spirits seem perfectly in place at the cemetery, Byron too manages to convey his sense of the necessary and beautiful connection between life and death. Brother Desiderio Berro, the *Custode*, and Byron form a natural company of men who have known how to live. That Byron could have done them such perfect justice with his pen is the sign of his own consummate humanness. His sense of equilibrium is perfect throughout the letter. Though the "pathos" he speaks of is an emotion proper to both life and death, Byron pro-

---

[33] *BSP* 2:456–58.
[34] G. Wilson Knight has a brilliant little essay (originally a lecture) on "Byron's Dramatic Prose" in which he analyzes a number of Byron's best letters (Nottingham, Byron Foundation Lecture, 1953).

poses to go gently, if somewhat spiritedly, into that good night just as, while visiting the cemetery (and later writing about it) he manages to be gay and reverent at the same time. Like so much in *Don Juan*, Byron's style here is a brilliant, human achievement. All the imperatives of being seem incarnated in his person, and death—like life—rises up as a profound and deeply to be reverenced gift. For not only does death bring eternal rest. It is also that without which life would not be the exquisite thing that it is. Death defines transience, and it is this very quality of evanescence which gives to an earthly existence its spiritual dimensions. This Byronic fact is most clearly manifest in the poems now to be considered—*Beppo* and *Don Juan*, those delicate, human, and culminate triumphs of his genius.

Fulfillment

The Broken Dandy

Beppo begat *Don Juan* and *Whistlecraft* begat *Beppo*. This genealogy holds good at least for proximate causes, as Byron said ("Whistlecraft was my immediate *model!*" *LJ* 4:217). Scholars have sometimes suggested other influences, but what Andrew Rutherford has written on this subject seems to me definitive.

> There is . . . no evidence to suggest that he had any first-hand knowledge of the poetry of Berni or of Pulci in September 1817, and though he had read Ariosto and Boiardo, they are rather different in effect and tone. He had, on the other hand, enjoyed the works of Casti, but neither these nor any of his other readings in Italian had so far affected his poetic practise. *Whistlecraft* revolutionized it, by showing how the form and manner of these poets could be adapted to the English language, and by suggesting a technique by which he could express himself in verse with the same freedom, wit, urbanity and ease as he did in his letters and conversation.[1]

In its way Frere's poem is a charming thing, and at times (e.g., stanzas 38–41 of the second canto) shows a brilliance that rivals many of the best comic passages in *Beppo* and *Don Juan*. Never does it manifest Byron's genius for the seriocomic, however, and the remarkable tonal variety of Byron's poems remains outside its range. This difference has been noted before. But *Whistlecraft* stands apart from Byron's *Don Juan* manner in a related though, I think, even more significant way. Except for brief asides, Frere never indulges in digression. His work begins with a chatty proem, and similar stanzas begin or finish off other cantos. But when he gets going he never stops, is not lured from the

---

[1] *Rutherford*, pp. 109–10.

story as Byron so often is into general or personal remarks on virtually any subject. Yet digression is, for Byron, the point of it all. As a versing wit in *Blackwood's* put it at the time.

> The story that's in it
> May be told in a minute;
> But *par parenthèse* chatting,
> On this thing and that thing,
> Keeps the shuttlecock flying,
> And attention from dying.[2]

(This was written of *Beppo* particularly, and for the remainder of this chapter I direct my remarks to that poem, though with occasional references to *Don Juan*. I follow this procedure partly for convenience—the material in *Beppo* is limited and more easily managed—and partly to indicate how completely Byron realized the style and themes of *Don Juan* in the shorter and earlier work.)

The matter of digression is the key to Byron's method, and its implications are far reaching. Digression, more than anything else, produces the famous "conversational" manner, makes the work, as Rutherford suggests above, a poetic equivalent of Byron's intimate letters and journals. But it differs from the letters and journals in its rhetorical bases, for the prose does not presuppose the vast audience of *Beppo* and *Don Juan.* Byron can be intimate with his friends, but it is quite another thing to be intimate with an entire country, not to say the whole Western community. Sensing this difference, M. K. Joseph has emphasized Byron's assumption of the role of poet-raconteur.[3] A poem written about itself, Hazlitt called *Don Juan*, and Joseph properly emphasizes its narrated quality. Byron performs before the world in *Beppo*, shows off, lets us know what being a poet means. Fascinated by his own artistic powers and the immediate act of composition, Byron writes about these matters. He throws off a remark or an image, thinks about it (in public), tells us how it makes him think of something else, goes on to talk about that, and so on.

> speculating as I cast my eye
> On what may suit or may not suit my story.   (*Don Juan* xv, 19)

Throughout we are with him making it all up as he goes along.

> To turn,—and to return;—the devil take it!
> This story slips for ever through my fingers. . . .   (*Beppo*, 63)

---

[2] Quoted at *P* 4:157.
[3] *Joseph*, esp. pp. 194–211.

The coast—I think it was the coast that I
Was just describing—Yes, it *was* the coast. . . . (*Don Juan* II, 181)

W. W. Robson has called this the art of the improviser,[4] and in so
doing he has recovered an important term. Shortly after Byron's death,
Medwin offered this summary of his poetic genius and its relation to his
personal manner.

> It may be asked *when* Lord Byron writes. . . . I am often with him
> from the time he gets up till two or three o'clock in the morning,
> and after sitting up so late he must require rest; but he produces,
> the next morning, proofs that he has not been idle. . . . He seems to
> be able to resume the thread of his subject at all times, and to
> weave it of an equal texture. Such talent is that of an *improvisa-
> tore.* . . . I never met with any man who shines so much in con-
> versation. He shines the more, perhaps, for not seeking to shine.
> His ideas flow without effort, without his having occasion to
> think . . . there are no concealments in him, no injunctions to
> secresy. He tells every thing that he has thought or done without
> the least reserve, and as if he wished the whole world to know
> it. . . .[5]

Byron was himself quite taken with the whole idea of improvisation.
"Why should we not be able to improvise in hexameters, as the Italians
do," he once said to Medwin.[6] Sgricci fascinated him: "But Sgricci!
To extemporize a whole tragedy seems a miraculous gift." Continuing,
he explains what the art of the *improvisatore* means to him.

> The inspiration of the improviser is quite a separate talent [from
> that of the poet who writes]:—a consciousness of his own powers,
> his own elocution—the wondering and applauding audience,—all
> conspire to give him confidence; but the deity forsakes him when
> he coldly sits down to think. Sgricci is not only a fine poet but a
> fine actor.[7]

Clearly, this is the same man who set a high value upon work produced
"in *red-hot* earnest." Byron loved to talk, act, and orate, and his pro-
ficiency in these arts was considered remarkable. They all involve both
spontaneity and self-dramatization, and of course so does improvised
poetry. I have shown in an earlier chapter that Byron was interested
in the phenomenon of oral poetry from the time of his first trip to the

[4] W. W. Robson, "Byron as Improviser," *Essays*, pp. 88-95.
[5] *Medwin*, p. 265.
[6] *Ibid.*, p. 136.
[7] *Ibid.*, p. 138.

East, and that in *The Giaour* he attempted an imitation (or, rather, a printed codification and reminder) of the form. Indeed, *The Giaour* manifests Byron projecting himself into the role not only of his first Byronic hero, but of the oral storyteller as well.

Byron did not try an experiment of that precise sort again, though all of *Childe Harold's Pilgrimage* is self-dramatizing. Moreover, poems like *Manfred*, *The Lament of Tasso*, *The Prophecy of Dante* and *The Dream* are clear examples of his using verse as a vehicle for self-projection. Even *Mazeppa* and *Sardanapalus*, as we have seen, contain elements of this sort. In fact, none of Byron's poetry ever escapes completely from this manner. All poetry, no doubt, exemplifies this quality to some degree, but in Byron's case self-projection is integral, since the corpus as a whole continually, and deliberately, provides us with biographical facts that make up the form of a story about his own life. In all these works Byron presents himself, to a greater or lesser degree, before his "wondering and applauding audience." He wants us to be aware of himself as well as the story. In some cases (like *Childe Harold's Pilgrimage*) his life and personality are his story; in others an objective tale takes the more prominent, but by no means exclusive, position (*Sardanapalus*); and in a few (*The Dream*) his own history and psychology determine nearly the entire meaning and form of an apparently objective narrative.

Beppo, and Byron's *Don Juan* manner as a whole, seem to represent a synthesis of direct self-revelation, objective storytelling, and the art of the poet-raconteur. The form is the art of the *improvisatore*, but with a difference: that Byron as a specific individual is part of its substance. He is not just a performer, like Sgricci, whose skill we admire. This important distinction is nicely epitomized in Mme de Staël's *Corinne, ou L'Italie*, a book familiar to Byron and which, we know, directly influenced *Childe Harold's Pilgrimage IV*, and perhaps earlier portions of the work as well. In the novel Corinne is presented as Italy's greatest *improvisatore*, and we are treated to a number of discussions of this art early on. Her close friend, the Prince Castel-Forte, speaks glowingly of Corinne's improvising powers as well as of her

> talents in painting, in music, in elocution, in dancing. He said that, in everything she did, Corinne herself was always the focus of one's attention. . . .[8]

---

[8] A. I. G. de Staël, *Corinne, ou L'Italie*, Nouvelle Édition (New York, 1853), p. 26 (Book II, ch. ii). My translation. George Ridenour has also called attention to the theory of improvisation outlined in *Corinne* as an analogue to Byron's practice, but his approach is somewhat different from mine. See *Ridenour*, Appendix B.

Later, Corinne gives a long explanation of improvised poetry, and of herself as an *improvisatore*. Lord Nelvil asks her if she prefers her reflective poems to her spontaneous effusions. She answers that

> improvisation seems to me a sort of animated conversation. I do not permit myself to be confined to this or that subject; I abandon myself to the impression which the interest of my audience produces in me . . . sometimes that interest raises me above myself and enables me to discover in nature or my own heart daring truths and vital expressions which solitary reflection could not have produced. Then I think I experience a supernatural enthusiasm. . . . I feel myself a poet . . . when my soul is uplifted, when it disdains from above all egoism and base thoughts; in short, when a fine act would be easier for me to do. . . . I am a poet when I admire, when I despise, when I hate, not from personal feelings, not in my own behalf, but because I am moved by the dignity of humanity and the glory of the world.

Noticing that Lord Nelvil has been watching her in a rapt enthusiasm, Corinne breaks off and begs his pardon for getting carried away: "Pardon me, my Lord, although a woman like myself does not resemble those who are esteemed in your country." But he answers: "Who could resemble you? . . . And can anyone make rules of behavior for a unique person?"[9] From Corinne's point of view her improvisation seems a gift of the gods. She is a *vates* who speaks not of herself personally but what the spirit, which has temporarily infused her, seems to command. But Lord Nelvil and the Prince define the effect she has upon her audience, and that is strictly personal: it is Corinne the individual whom they see and hear.

The theory of *improvisatore* set out by Corinne would perhaps be more appropriately applied to *Childe Harold's Pilgrimage*, where Byron is not quite so self-conscious about his bardic skills as he is in *Beppo*. On the other hand, if we emphasized her audience's viewpoint we would focus upon the common element in both works: they project an image of a very specific human being. This difference suggests a pattern for Byron's poetic development. His themes never really changed, nor did the personal tone of his works. Nevertheless, a change did gradually take place. To use Mme de Staël's dramatic counters: Byron is always Corinne, but as he develops he appropriates more and more of Lord Nelvil to himself, becomes more and more self-conscious about his own powers. As his remark to Medwin suggests, and as we

[9] De Staël, *Corinne*, pp. 46–47 (Book III, ch. iii).

have seen elsewhere, Byron tended to compose poetry in which he could demonstrate his personal "magnetism, or devilism, or what *You* please" (*Don Juan* VI, 38). An oral poet was living proof of the possibility of such power in a man, and Byron's poetry is proof as well. But it also exemplifies his need to express himself so, and his desire to manifest this power of drawing, like the Giaour, our "gaze of wonder." In *Beppo* and *Don Juan* Byron replaces Mme. de Staël's unconscious *vates* (his dramatized self). *The Giaour, Hours of Idleness*, and *Childe Harold's Pilgrimage* differ in this respect from Byron's *Don Juan* manner, for they do not make Byron's self-dramatizing intentions a substantive part of the poetry. Nevertheless, they are all works of a piece since each emphasizes the teller in the tale, the man behind the work. They differ in the degrees of their emphasis, in the level of their self-consciousness.

II

Readers have always remarked upon the narrated style of *Beppo* and *Don Juan*, so it will suffice here merely to summarize what has already been often and well said. Robson and Joseph are in basic agreement in pointing to the role of *improvisatore*, or poet-raconteur, that Byron assumes while writing *Beppo* and *Don Juan*. Laura's Count "patronised the Improvisatori" (33), indeed, could himself extemporize if he chose, and his character in this respect is an explicit reminder to the reader of what Byron the narrator is doing. This parallel is enforced through Byron's evident sympathy with the Venetians and the "seat of all dissoluteness." His worldly-wise manner is the equivalent of the Count's, and as for improvisation:

> This form of verse begun, I can't well break it,
> But must keep time and tune like public singers. . . .   (63)

Examples of Byron playing the role of public performer abound. Sometimes he reflects upon his own act of composing:

> It was the Carnival, as I have said
> Some six and thirty stanzas back. . . .   (56)

Sometimes he addresses his audience directly:

> And then he was a Count, and then he knew
> Music, and dancing, fiddling, French and Tuscan;
> This last not easy, be it known to you,
> For few Italians speak the right Etruscan.   (31)

He has a firm sense of his public, which is, most immediately, English.

> In this they're like our coachmen, and the cause
> Is much the same—the crowd, and pulling, hauling,
> With blasphemies enough to break their jaws,
> They make a never intermitting bawling.
> At home, our Bow-street gemmen keep the laws,
> And here a sentry stands within your calling;
> But for all that there is a deal of swearing,
> And nauseous words past mentioning or bearing. (86)

Verses like these, however—with their explicit English references and brilliant dialect accomplishment—also establish the poet's own general personal character and thus provide a basis for his mockery of things English. He plays the role of the genial expatriate and citizen of the world, and by so doing he expands the range of his digressive capabilities. He is not just a raconteur, not simply "an author that's *all author*" (75), but comes before us with a persona that suggests his more human qualities. By donning the mask of the English cosmopolite he can more easily act out the part of the specific human being delivering a very specific poetic performance.

> They went to the Ridotto ('t is a place
> To which I mean to go myself to-morrow,
> Just to divert my thoughts a little space,
> Because I'm rather hippish. . . .) (64)

In fact, Byron is a good deal less interested in the story, especially the drama of the story, than he is in the possibilities it offers to his digressive imagination. Considered strictly as a tale its main point is didactic rather than dramatic: Byron wants to show his tight little islanders a pattern of civilized behavior. His Venetians show up the narrowness and ill-bred prudery of England. But the Venetians are not Byron's *norm* for the civilized man. Though they are better than the English, and much more charming, they too have their follies.

> Now Laura moves along the joyous crowd,
> Smiles in her eyes, and simpers on her lips;
> To some she whispers, others speaks aloud;
> To some she curtsies, and to some she dips,
> Complains of warmth, and, this complaint avow'd,
> Her lover brings the lemonade, she sips;
> She then surveys, condemns, but pities still
> Her dearest friends for being dress'd so ill. (65)

But, as he says of England, he loves the country and its people still. In fact, his tolerance, his ability to appreciate and benefit by different life styles, his wide ranging talents: all these things establish Byron the narrator as our norm of the civilized man. Moving somewhere between the North and the South, he continually draws upon both and lives in the best of his possible worlds.

This consciousness of his own sanity and comprehensiveness changes his oral style from that of the unconscious *vates* to the self-conscious improviser. As Byron said of Sgricci, the *improvisatore* is always aware of his own powers and of his audience's admiration. *Beppo* is exceedingly self-conscious in just this way, and the result is that we do not respond to the anecdote as such but to the brilliance with which it is retailed.

> Now Laura, much recover'd, or less loth
> To speak, cries "Beppo! what's your pagan name?
> Bless me! your beard is of amazing growth!
> And how came you to keep away so long?
> Are you not sensible 't was very wrong?

> "And are you really, truly, now a Turk?
> With any other women did you wive?
> Is 't true they use their fingers for a fork?
> Well, that's the prettiest shawl—as I'm alive!
> You'll give it me? They say you eat no pork.
> And how so many years did you contrive
> To—bless me! did I ever? No, I never
> Saw a man grown so yellow! How's your liver?

> "Beppo! that beard of yours becomes you not;
> It shall be shaved before you're a day older:
> Why do you wear it? Oh, I had forgot—
> Pray don't you think the weather here is colder?
> How do I look? . . .   (91–93)

This is not so much "Laura" speaking as it is Byron parodying woman in general through a highly stylized portrait of a Venetian beauty. The details are brilliantly selected to convey a charming mixture of officiousness, naiveté, selfishness, and conventionality. She is not real as a human being, but the values which Byron makes her dramatize are extremely realistic. The important thing is that we should recognize how everything in the story depends upon the way it is told, depends upon our watching Byron the raconteur. Even the most "objective" parts of the narration, like the stanzas above, cannot escape the presence of the teller's artistic style.

That style itself, as I have already hinted, depends upon the style of life which he dramatizes as his own. His role as improviser depends upon his role as expatriate Englishman and cosmopolite. But as we examine the poem even more closely we see that these two roles, or personae, themselves depend upon something yet more fundamental.

> Oh that I had the art of easy writing
> What should be easy reading! could I scale
> Parnassus, where the Muses sit inditing
> Those pretty poems never known to fail,
> How quickly would I print (the world delighting)
> A Grecian, Syrian, or Assyrian tale;
> And sell you, mix'd with western sentimentalism,
> Some samples of the finest Orientalism.
>
> But I am but a nameless sort of person
> (A broken dandy lately on my travels),
> And take for rhyme, to hook my rambling verse on,
> The first that Walker's Lexicon unravels. . . .   (51–52)

Verses like these contain an additional biographical element which is not only *not* extraneous to the work, but the key element in it. The brilliantly subtle moralizing in line 5 of stanza 51—amused self-depreciation, scorn of vulgar taste—and the fine offhand irony in the opening lines of stanza 52 depend upon our recognizing the speaker as Lord Byron, a person about as "nameless" to his age or ours as Napoleon. He writes the passage with the expectation that the audience will recognize who the author is. Indeed, without that recognition the verse is charming, like Frere's, but with it it reaches for greatness. Whether or not a reader catches the personal allusions is beside the point, for the rhetorical intention of the verse is clear: if we would appreciate it not only fully, but properly, we must be familiar with Byron's life.[10]

In writing poetry of this sort Byron was merely showing himself aware of his own position as an artist. His poetry was read because it was his, was appreciated because it was his. Byron had suspected as early as *Hours of Idleness* that his own personality might be interesting to society at large, and in *Childe Harold's Pilgrimage* he had judged this

---

[10] The fact that Byron's name did not at first appear on the title page is not especially important. He never intended that the book should remain anonymous, which would have been impossible anyway. Moreover, the constitution of the poem defies anonymity.

to be the case. Such poetry is written on the assumption that people are interested in the individual Byron as he is revealed in it, and such a judgment has, of course, been fully substantiated. So, when he would dissertate on Fortune, for example, he may not go to literature or mythology for an exemplum but to this own life.

> She rules the present, past, and all to be yet,
> She gives us luck in lotteries, love, and marriage;
> I cannot say that she's done much for me yet;
> Not that I mean her bounties to disparage,
> We've not yet closed accounts, and we shall see yet
> How much she'll make amends for past miscarriage. . . .   (62)

Basically the stanza employs a very conventional device: history as moral example. What drastically alters the conventional character of the figure is its personal basis.[11] The assumption made here is that the poet's own personal life—which he merely alludes to—is as historically prominent, and significant even, as the Battle of Agincourt, or (better) Waterloo.

Such an assumption was correct, and it permitted Byron to go so far as to speak of intimate things in his life which only a few close friends (or enemies) knew about. In the following lines he is praising Turkish women at the expense of their English counterparts:

> No chemistry for them unfolds her gases,
> No metaphysics are let loose in lectures,
> No circulating library amasses
> Religious novels, moral tales, and strictures
> Upon the living manners, as they pass us;
> No exhibition glares with annual pictures;
> They stare not on the stars from out their attics,
> Nor deal (thank God for that!) in mathematics.
>
> Why I thank God for that is no great matter,
> I have my reasons, you no doubt suppose,
> And as, perhaps, they would not highly flatter,
> I'll keep them for my life (to come) in prose. . . .   (78–79)

The key allusions here are to Lady Byron—his "Princess of Parallelograms"—and to his Memoirs, which were later destroyed. Now it is

---

[11] Byron did not invent the personal use of a conventional figure, as the example of Boethius, among others, attests. Byron is interesting because he rarely more than hints at events in his life. He treats personal events as if they were already common knowledge and could be alluded to.

clear that Byron does not expect most of his audience to understand the precise import of his remark. He lets them know, however, that the reference is quite personal and that they will all find out about it by and by. Again the assumption is that the reader will always be aware not only of Byron as poet-raconteur but of Byron the man as well. That Byron took his audience's interest in himself for granted is mirrored in the ease of the verse, the perfect manners with which he engages in personal discussion.

These implications are important. Earlier we spoke of his assumption of the roles of improviser and citizen of the world. These personae, however, depend for their effect upon the more strictly personal character of the speaker. The *Don Juan* manner develops out of our understanding that personae are being assumed and manipulated, that somebody ("a nameless sort of person") is having fun at playing roles and treating his reader to the fun by letting him watch it all. But this "nameless sort of person" can be seen as a persona only if we strip all useful meaning from the term. The "person" is the historical Byron, as everyone is made to know while reading the poem, and the persona at the bottom of everything is Byron himself.

Byron in propria persona sometimes looks like a persona in his poems because of the universal, in a sense impersonal, quality that hangs about his projected image. The self-dramatized Byron is not a persona, however, but a myth, for although the details of his life have a historical basis, the meaning of those details is also, and simultaneously, moralized. Byron's "real life" has assumed a mythic form, and this curious phenomenon seems partly the result of Byron's deliberate choice—his desire for greatness and personal fame—and partly the result of his audience—what has been made of him from his time to our own. Biographical interpretations of his works, therefore, need not be "extrapoetic" in his case, especially if the critic—like so many in the nineteenth century—casts his interpretation into a moralizing form. By *moralizing* I do not necessarily mean passing an ethical judgment on Byron's personal character. I intend the word in its larger sense: a story with a moral is one that evidences a pattern of meaning, a cooperation of its elements that issues in some specific or general conclusions about the nature of man.

Seen in this way, Byron's life has become a kind of modern hagiography. Working from "primary documents," contemporary and subsequent chroniclers have been forced to advance the myth; nor has it much mattered from what point of view they have chosen to tell his story. Charles Williams has written of both "The Figure of Beatrice" and "The Figure of Arthur," and his term "figure" was meant to convey the mythic stature which these particular individuals acquired. The concept is applicable in Byron's case as well. Nor have we only inherited "The Figure of Byron"; he *was*, in his own day and to many of his most intimate friends, such a figure. Moreover, Byron himself took an active part in the creation of the myth, and this is what makes his case so especially interesting. I suppose it is G. Wilson Knight's sense of this fact which has led him to compare Byron with Christ, and to say (in his most recent book) that Byron personally lived out the universe which Shakespeare created in his art.[12]

This basic aspect of Byron's poetry suggests a further and more general meaning that attaches to his art, particularly in a poem like *Beppo*. The very style of Byron's poetry defines what individuality means. All poets do this to a greater or lesser extent—we speak of Popian or Miltonic style, for example—but in Byron we come upon a polarity so extreme that the notion becomes clarified. Everything in *Beppo* orbits around Byron; it is the figure of Byron, both as an artist and (more importantly) as a human being, which determines both the form and significance of the details. Ultimately, then, the poem defines the nature of personality, demonstrates what it means to be sui generis. Lord Nelvil is rapt when he hears Corinne. He tells her that she is herself alone and that, having known her, he understands finally why laws cannot be made for an individual. Corinne exists to demonstrate this truth to Nelvil, and Byron does to us. The difference is that Byron the poet actually existed as an "author not all author" and that he poured into his poetry the image of a man who, in the end, did not become a style or any group of styles, a persona or personae. *Beppo* and *Don Juan* epitomize this fact about Byron's poetry: the man portrayed in it is one who has apotheosized personality, has escaped conventional definition (despite so much in his own work that is conventional) for something much more specific. We leave his poetry with the understanding that we have been in contact with a very particular man. Nor is this merely some vague general notion. As I have tried to show already, we can trace the artistic construction of his mythic personality in the study of his style and themes alike.

One final remark on the general form and style of *Beppo* before I turn to a discussion of its themes. Classical aesthetic theory holds that writers adapt their styles to their tales: the matter determines the man-

[12] G. Wilson Knight, *Byron and Shakespeare* (London, 1966).

ner. In the case of *Beppo* this aesthetic is reversed. If we retreat slightly from the poem we can, for example, see the autobiographical relevance of the story very easily. Like *Othello*, it is a tale about marriage and jealousy, and it gains an added dimension by being viewed against the background of Byron's own domestic affairs. Beppo, Laura, and the Count behave remarkably well in their circumstances,

> Because in Christian countries 't is a rule
> To view their little slips with eyes more lenient. (24)

The point hits equally at Christian England and a certain unnamed connection of Byron's. What is more significant, however, is that the story, like the digressions, depends primarily upon the biographical substructure. Read without the biographical framework, the story will still suggest certain insights into domestic relations and societal conventions. But the poem would be radically altered without the biographical element, and not only with respect to value. It would be a different poem altogether, for the speaker would have been denatured to a persona and the story would have lost its pointedly didactic aspect. As in *Sardanapalus, Mazeppa, The Lament of Tasso*, and *The Prophecy of Dante*, Byron is using the story in *Beppo* not so much as a mirror for certain truths but as a mirror of a mirror. The determining exemplum, or story, is always in the canon of the Byron Myth, and all other stories —like the anecdote in *Beppo*—are written as variants and analogues which, though having a certain point in their own right, are more especially intended to remind us of the original story. Like so much in Byron's *oeuvre*, *Beppo* is a version of the basic myth, or, rather, of a part of that myth (in the same way that the Gawain stories are versions of the larger myth of Arthur).

III

The image of himself that Byron creates in poems like *Beppo* is perfectly individuated. He demands self-definition and, like an angel, seems to exhaust a species. But he does this by "falling," as it were. He surrounds himself with specific details and makes his mythologized character depend upon the accumulated trivia, habits, scandals, and general notoriety of his life. Byron is an "ideal" being, is unique, but he is so as much by virtue of his most mundane characteristics as by his more sublime gifts. The two interact to make him an incarnate spirit, or an angelic man. He fills out the human form divine because, as we should see, his human form is very mortal indeed.

This aspect of his dramatized personality is mirrored in the themes which he favors in his works. He liked to keep his poetry factually accurate, disdained "imagination," and in his later years grew more and more gossipy. Mr. West has judged that he had an "ingenious disregard" for "the world of things," but I confess I see quite the reverse in his poetry. From the very beginning he tried, like all Romantics, to wed the divine and the natural orders, and eventually he decided that the two could only be fused if this world were regarded as a paradise. To achieve a state of infinite capability we must not move beyond the natural but into it. Materiality, the physical man, is the ideal, and his spiritually distinguishing element—paradoxical as it may seem—is precisely his physicality. At one point in *Beppo*, for example, he addresses the Italy that he loves.

> Eve of the land which still is Paradise!
> Italian beauty! didst thou not inspire
> Raphael, who died in thy embrace, and vies
> With all we know of heaven, or can desire,
> In what he hath bequeath'd us?   (46)

At first glance it appears that "all we know of heaven" is embodied in Raphael's art. This is true, however, only in the sense that Raphael's art participates in a prior, and more comprehensive, spiritual value (cf. "vies"). His art is an imitation of the real thing, that which originally "inspired" Raphael: "Italian beauty." Again at first glance we seem to be looking at a verbal definition of the conventional *beau idéal*, i.e., at a Platonic concept or "idea." It is not so, however, for in these verses, and especially in the phrase "Italian beauty," Byron is deliberately summarizing the specific accumulation of mortal beauties and delights which he has been praising in the previous five stanzas. "All we know of heaven" is right here, as Sardanapalus also says in another context.

This, Byron's curious reinterpretation of an originally Platonic aesthetic, is made the basis of *Beppo* and *Don Juan*. According to Byron, art imitates an original ideal image. The original is not, however, a supermundane reality but something "real," something from the natural or human world. Raphael's art shows forth the glory of all those very specific and mundane things itemized in stanzas 41–45. Byron defines this view even more graphically earlier in the poem.

> They've pretty faces yet, those same Venetians,
> Black eyes, arch'd brows, and sweet expressions still;
> Such as of old were copied from the Grecians,

In ancient arts by moderns mimick'd ill;
And like so many Venuses of Titian's
(The best's at Florence, see it if ye will),
They look when leaning over the balcony,
Or stepp'd from out a picture by Giorgione,

Whose tints are truth and beauty at their best;
And when you to Manfrini's palace go,
That picture (howsoever fine the rest)
Is loveliest to my mind of all the show;
It may perhaps be also to your zest,
And that's the cause I rhyme upon it so:
'T is but a portrait of his son, and wife,
And self; but *such* a woman! love in life!

Love in full life and length, not love ideal,
No, nor ideal beauty, that fine name,
But something better still, so very real,
That the sweet model must have been the same;
A thing that you would purchase, beg, or steal,
Wer't not impossible, besides a shame.
The face recalls some face, as 't were with pain,
You once have seen, but ne'er will see again;

One of those forms which flit by us, when we
Are young, and fix our eyes on every face;
And, oh! the loveliness at times we see
In momentary gliding, the soft grace,
The youth, the bloom, the beauty which agree,
In many a nameless being we retrace,
Whose course and home we know not, nor shall know,
Like the lost Pleiad seen no more below.   (11–14)

The stanzas succeed to a brilliant fusion of the upper and lower worlds. Venetian women are so beautiful that they seem just stepped from the canvases of Titian and Giorgione, Byron says first, and goes on to explain how one particular picture of one particular woman attracted him extraordinarily. This "Venus" could only have been so beautiful, Byron says, if she were *not* "ideal beauty," if she were "something better still, so very real" that the model for such beauty—the standard of it—must have been a real lady. Constantly the poem forces us to define terms and ideas like "paradise," "beauty," and "love" in the specifics of a mortal order, for to Byron it is their corporeality which imparts a spiritual value to these things. "All the fashions of the flesh stick long/By people in the next world," Byron says in *The Vision of Judgment* (st. 66), and the poet mirrors this fact: "I borrow my comparisons from clay,/Being clay myself" (54). Ordinarily such reversals would negate spiritual values for lesser, realistic ones, but in Byron's case the lower world is the norm and realization of what the upper world, to fallen men, has always stood for.

But we must examine the passage a bit further if we would understand why Byron finds ideal values in mortal things. He compared her to a girl whom a man might see briefly at a ball, be charmed by, and yet never see again. Byron's lost but remembered beauty is conceived as a specific individual yet she takes on the aspect of an Egeria: "the lost Pleiad seen no more below." The simple, almost trivial, fact that a man may fail to find out where a lady lives comes to assume enormous importance in the context. The lady is Venus, her address is paradise, and on the particular occasion detailed in the image we see a man losing both. To Byron she is divine because she is real. An actual lady, born to die, her reality makes her subject to time and circumstance. Her materiality makes her a perfect Egeria, the ideal with which Byron's "orphans of the heart" (*CHP* IV, 78) seek a permanent communion, but in vain. All we get are "interviews" (*CHP* IV, 178) with these beautiful, haunting "forms which flit by us." As Byron puts it in *Don Juan* (the context is frankly, though urbanely, sexual): "Love, constant love, has been my constant guest" (III, 209). In the passage from *Beppo* the phrase "momentary gliding" epitomizes her mortality and spirituality alike. The phrase suggests not only the insubstantiality of a beautiful wraith that "flits" by, but the very real picture of a young lady's elegant carriage. She is preeminently splendid even amid the dazzle of a Holland House ball (which is the sort of context evoked in the passage).

Such beings are born in a day to perish in a day. Their values, like those in *Der Rosenkavalier*, are only possible in an emphatically temporal milieu, where Time also destroys those values. Beauty fades and lovers part—or never even get a chance to meet. It is all very circumstantial. But the "momentary" quality of ideal values also suggests an answer to the pain of loss. Because all spiritual values are momentary and physical they are both irrevocably lost and necessarily found again. The girl at the ball *is* a heavenly being. When she passes out of Byron's immediate orbit her virtue is lost forever—carrying an image of her around in his heart would be of no use whatever, except to remind him of his loss, for her value depends upon her physicality, her immediate presence. But just because all value is only conceivable as incarnate it also remains forever. We lose it and find it again because each moment and each lady (or the successive apparitions of one lady) have an absolute value. What we find after loss is not the same as what we have lost—all loss is irrevocable—but it is equivalent to it in value, or perhaps even more valuable. Each particular is absolute to itself, and human life is a succession of such absolute moments. Time rules eternity, the gods, and paradise, and the result is that spiritual values, e.g., "very real" ladies or any other incarnations of beauty, are continually lost and found again. "Tomorrow to fresh woods, and pastures new." Passing Time insures the continual reappearance of visionary maidens, for in Byron's imparadised earth we "see the sun set, sure he'll rise tomorrow."

This view is not something that Byron suddenly achieved, though he was not steady in his conviction until the last seven years of his life or so. It appears everywhere in the poetry after the separation, and if we go back to *Hours of Idleness* we find it blatantly, if somewhat naively, asserted. Thomas Little's poems are based upon the same attitude. Through this way of thinking Byron possesses the cultural future as no other Romantic does, for he has cut himself off from the usual forms of Christian thought completely. He thinks about life like the ancients, like the Jews, or like certain of the Greeks (the Stoics especially). Though showing everywhere the imprint of Christianity, his thought has modified it radically, especially in the matter of transcendentalism. Take the idea of the Resurrection. In a traditional Christian frame of reference, the notion of the body's resurrection follows upon the spiritual nature of man. Because the spirit is transcendent the body will rise again. But in Byron's view the terms are reversed: "Matter is eternal, always changing, but reproduced, and, as far as we can comprehend Eternity, Eternal; and why not *Mind?*" In the same context he declares his "partiality for spirit," but—as the quotation above indicates—he arrives at his partiality because matter provides the norms. "Believe the resurrection of the body, if you will, but *not without a Soul*. The devil's in it, if, after having had a Soul in this world, we must part with it in the next, even for an Immortal Materiality."[13]

Blake serves as a useful contrast, for though he is a renegade Christian in many of his ideas, particularly his ideas about love, he always remains within the essential Christian frame of thought. For Blake, nature and the fleshly portion of man are lower than his more spiritual

[13] *Detached Thoughts* nos. 97–98 (*LJ* 5:458).

powers in both value and state of being.[14] Man will save himself when he finally can direct his life from the spirit alone, the "poetic genius" trapped, as Paul would say, in the body of this death. Blake often rejoices in the expression of passion and in the pleasures of the human world, but for him corporeality is a *means* of grace whereas for Byron it *is* grace and should never be treated as a means toward something supposedly better or more spiritual. Byron holds this view because to him the man of flesh and blood should not be divided into spiritual and physical. It is not enough to assert the union of body and soul. Whenever man is conceived as an amalgam of higher and lower powers a sense of internal division necessarily follows. Man is made to feel that he is not integrated. This feeling is common to most men, Byron believes, but it should not be regarded as "the last state of that man." Moreover, the attitude is a crippling one, and he suggests in all his work between 1817 and 1824 that men can escape it. Such a belief is the basis of his normative visions in *The Island, Sardanapalus*, and *Beppo* (in the latter he is himself the image of the restored man). Similarly, in *Don Juan* he ridicules Berkeley's pure idealism (*DJ* XI, 1 ff.) and asserts at every opportunity that corporeality is not a means to something else but is its own end.

It might be useful to examine Byron's ideas on this subject in *Don Juan* since the epic helps to explain its precursor *Beppo*. That knowledge and intellect "depend . . . upon the gastric juice" (*DJ* V, 32) is a minor motif in the poem, as is the fact that love and beauty are intimately, and necessarily, connected with sex. There is scarcely a passage in all of *Don Juan* where Byron talks about love without also bringing in sexuality, frequently by employing puns. Discussing "first and passionate love" in Canto I, for example, Byron goes on to talk about man's inventiveness, and about mechanical inventions especially. The passage had opened with the observation that

> I care not for new pleasures, as the old
> Are quite enough for me, so they but hold.   (118)

But inventive man is always dreaming up new ways to please himself.

---

[14] A good example of Blake's thought in this matter is provided in one of his annotations upon Reynolds' *Discourses*. Reynolds writes that "My notion of nature comprehends not only the forms which nature produces, but also the nature and internal fabrick and organization . . . of the human mind and imagination." Blake answers: "Here is a plain confession that he Thinks Mind & Imagination not to be above the Mortal & Perishing Nature. Such is the End of Epicurean or Newtonian Philosophy; it is Atheism." *Poetry and Prose of William Blake*, ed. Geoffrey Keynes (London, 1961), p. 807.

> Man's a strange animal, and makes strange use
> Of his own nature, and the various arts,
> And likes particularly to produce
> Some new experiment to show his parts. . . .   (128)

In the context "parts" can only be an erotic pun. The sexual motif continues as he speaks of the "real lues" come from America and the "pseudo-syphilis" (131) of England, the latter not being a frankly sexual disease but the sickness of an oppressive "civilisation." Finally, as he is winding up this discussion of man's passion for pleasure and varieties thereof—stanzas 122–27 itemize the many things that please man, including money, death, wine, revenge, and pillage—he again resorts to sexual innuendo. This time he is punning in the *Don Leon* manner upon "end" for what is, of course, an obscene (not ribald) joke.

> Man's a phenomenon, one knows not what,
> And wonderful beyond all wondrous measure;
> 'T is pity though, in this sublime world, that
> Pleasure's a sin, and sometimes sin's a pleasure;
> Few mortals know what end they would be at,
> But whether glory, power, or love, or treasure,
> The path is through perplexing ways. . . .   (133)

Being, like the Count in *Beppo*, "a lover of the good old school," Byron does not care especially for the more civilized varieties of pleasure, like revenge and pillage. He remains unperplexed by such goals, sticks to more innocent sexual aims—though the lines suggest that his sexual pleasures have a certain variety of their own. The phrase "perplexing ways," enshrining at once the unconventional character of the lovemaking which Byron seems to favor, and his sense of bewilderment that conventional man should be bothered by it, emphasizes the complexity of the poetry here. Indeed, the passage is a brilliant example of pornography translated to the highest reaches of art.

As George Ridenour has shown,[15] this sort of poetry depends upon Byron's use of the theme of the fall of man. The world of *Don Juan* is "both good and bad" because it is fallen, as Ridenour has argued, but certain people—like Byron, who narrates the poem—can acquire a stature and wisdom which set them apart from the ordinary man. Though fallen like his fellows, Byron in *Don Juan* shows that he accepts it, accepts the interdependence and equality of flesh and spirit. In this he differs from the objects of his satire. What he does not accept

---

[15] *Ridenour*, esp. pp. 19–88.

are the brutal uses to which both body and spirit can be put. Ridenour points out how in *Don Juan* love both elevates and debases man, is the cause of ecstasy and tragedy alike, of peace and war. Such contraries are a necessary part of a dualistic existence, Byron holds, but—*pace* Ridenour—he does not hold that they necessarily produce a corresponding disequilibrium in man. And yet it is only in man's moral life that salvation and paradise have any meaning as ideas. Byron the narrator, for example, seems perfectly equilibrized despite his subject matter and his personal experiences (which are much the same thing). His equilibrium is a function of his tolerance and forgiveness. Only Romilly, Castlereagh, and the spirit of tyranny remain unforgiven. Indeed, one of the themes of the poem is that it is man's psychic disharmony which makes his fallen condition an evil. Jealousy, a form of inner chaos, is allied to revenge, another form of chaos, and Byron's view is that one can only establish a sovereignty of the self by acknowledging the sovereignty of others. Thus tolerance and forgiveness remove the immoral elements in a painful dialectic, in a conflict of desires or persons or ideas, and also prevent the dialectical situation from becoming a cycle (e.g., a cycle of sex combat).

It is the cyclic nature of contraries, in fact, which generates evil. All elements in life, like different persons, or more particularly and symbolically, male and female, are set off against one another, but only when such elements seek to change simple opposition into cycles of warfare—only when men are, for example, "apostles of affliction"—does chaos become realized. This event is what Byron calls "man's worst, his second fall." Forgiveness prevents the dialectical cycle but it does not prevent dialectical encounters. Man and woman, for example, are forever opposed in the directions of their incarnate wills, but their opposition becomes "true love" when they acknowledge each other. The cycle of sex war is prevented by this "tolerance" (which is a form of self-consciousness), and a pattern of behavior is also provided for each future encounter between lovers. Further, by blunting the evil at its source—in man's heart—one also prevents it from assuming more complicated and difficult forms. Thus, evil in *The Two Foscari* and *Marino Faliero* has progressed too far, become too complicated. Or take the example of warfare. In *Don Juan* it is constantly allied to sexual problems, and the idea is enforced that if we could solve our sex problems—if Catherine of Russia could have done so—man would have been saved much agony. In a stanza like the following, then, we get a number of complicated ideas working at once.

Oh thou "*teterrima causa*" of all "*belli*"—
Thou gate of Life and Death—thou nondescript!
Whence is our exit and our entrance,—well I
May pause in pondering how all souls are dipped
In thy perennial fountain:—how man *fell* I
Know not, since Knowledge saw her branches stripped
Of her first fruit; but how he *falls* and rises
Since,—*thou* hast settled beyond all surmises.   (IX, 55)

Once again Byron is treating us to some clever sexual jokes. The Horatian allusion ("cunnus taeterrima belli causa," *Satires* I, iii, 107–8), besides explaining the word "nondescript," keynotes the eroticism that pervades the stanza. Love is the occasion of terrible wars, Byron suggests, but throughout the context it is clear that greed and frustration (which are much the same thing, whether sexual or otherwise) are the real causes of evil conflicts. Thus, in this stanza Byron also implies that the sexual act is redemptive. Indeed, his tone suggests that sexual love is definitively redemptive, though not necessarily so, for it can be corrupted by man. Catherine, for example, *uses* sex and therefore makes it an equivocal value. Byron's equivocal vision is different. On the one hand he sees how love can be a source of evil conflict, and on the other he sees that it is the manifestation of a paradisal conflict, of a heavenly combat. The latter is the poem's normative vision and serves as the validating standard for all of his critical perceptions on the misuse of love and life.

Byron's equilibrium, his self-possession, is proved by his morals, which, if unconventional in certain ways, are very conventional—indeed, classical—in others. Catherine, for example is presented as a kind of whore—she divides the flesh and the spirit and acknowledges only the former. Haidée and Juan's relationship fuses the spiritual and fleshly aspects of love perfectly. English moralists, however, refuse to embrace their corporeality—Southey and Wordsworth are their poetic equivalents—and hence they too miss their humanity. Byron seeks to mediate these attitudes with a more comprehensive view.

>   that which
> Men call inconstancy is nothing more
> Than admiration due where nature's rich
> Profusion with young beauty covers o'er
> Some favour'd object; and as in the niche
> A lovely statue we almost adore,
> This sort of adoration of the real

Is but a heightening of the "beau idéal."

'T is the perception of the beautiful,
A fine extension of the faculties,
Platonic, universal, wonderful,
Drawn from the stars, and filter'd through the skies,
Without which life would be extremely dull;
In short, it is the use of our own eyes,
With one or two small senses added, just
To hint that flesh is form'd of fiery dust.   (II, 111–12)

The stanzas recapitulate those in *Beppo* which deal with real and ideal beauty. Byron's basic position is a humanistic mean, but because his principal adversaries are moralists who denigrate the flesh for the spirit, his pronouncements generally emphasize the corporeality of the spirit. So he speaks of love and beauty as subject to the dominion of purely biological urges, or knowledge and intellect to good or bad meals, or drinks. But passages like the one just quoted remind us of the basic point, that flesh and spirit are inseparable. Nor are they inseparable in precisely a Christian sense. To a Christian, like Blake, the body and the soul are indeed united, but corporeality is a means of grace—it exists to serve the spirit. As I have already argued, such a view would not be acceptable to Byron: it destroys the equality of value between the two terms and produces disorder as a result. Byron was sometimes attracted by this Christian position in his more melancholy moods, but the ideal he celebrated was one that established an equality of value between flesh and spirit. *Beppo* and the fourth canto of *Childe Harold's Pilgrimage* are the first major poems in which this idea is made a forceful aspect of the assertion.

Thus, not only does the style of *Beppo* foreshadow that of *Don Juan*, the themes and fundamental outlook which we find elaborated on a grand scale in *Don Juan* are epitomized compactly in the shorter work. In *Beppo*, however, the image around which Byron tries to resolve the conflicting claims of "dust" and "deity" (*Manfred* I, 301) is that of Venice herself. Her decadent society seems "the seat of all dissoluteness" to the English moralist, but to Byron it is precisely her decadence which makes Venice capable of fostering the highest values that men strive for. *Beppo* may seem only a fascinating jeu d'esprit, but in fact it is a deadly serious attempt (in the way that hilarious comedy can be serious) to solve the problem of Eros. It seems to me a complete, and thoroughly pagan, success. Everything about Byron's Venice bespeaks the presence of Time. Man longs for a life in the Saturnian Age, in the "patriarchal times" of pastoral dream, and what keeps him from such a world is his bourgeois culture of getting and spending, of empire building, of the pursuit of the conventional life with its "cant political, cant poetical, cant religious, cant moral."[16] Decadent Venice suggests a means of redemption for morally crippled England, whose values are neither divine nor human. Like the paradise of childhood, Venice is good for nothing except living. It is merely a stately pleasure dome filled with exceedingly well-mannered people who, like Strauss's Marschallin, have the gift of immediate life.

> Oh, Mirth and Innocence! Oh, Milk and Water!
> Ye happy mixtures of more happy days!
> In these sad centuries of sin and slaughter,
> Abominable Man no more allays
> His thirst with such pure beverage. No matter,
> I love you both, and both shall have my praise:
> Oh, for old Saturn's reign of sugar-candy!—
> Meantime I drink to your return in brandy.   (80)

The Saturnian Age is rocovered in Byron's toast, for in a world where decadence is the image of innocence brandy will do as well as milk—better, in fact, for it will keep the terms of the imagery straight. In fact, decadence is in many ways a most suitable image for innocence since it is at once amoral, sensual, and strange. But Byron's Venice is an artificial world. He does not hold it up as a picture of a comprehensive morality. Rather, he uses it as an extension of his consciousness, like England. Byron stands between the two worlds and takes the best of each: from England, moral earnestness and a sense of reality, from Italy, beauty, sensuality, and a sense of innocence. Thus he becomes the norm of the fulfilled man—an Englishman who replaces his northern weaknesses with southern strengths. Moreover, his journey to the values of Italy and Venice was a journey to a kind of underworld, to a land where immorality was morality and where decadence presented a symbolic alternative to the hell of conventionality. In our own day we are told that the way up and the way down are the same, but in a bourgeois culture where the values of the upper world have been codified and denatured, it is the lower world, and the way down that will most readily appeal to man's moral imagination. Thus decadence became important to the nineteenth century, especially on the continent. In *Beppo* it is Byron's image for connecting heaven and earth, and later writers, especially the French, have enjoyed following Byron down this path of good intentions.

---

16 *LJ* 5:542.

Appendices

A

The Speaker in
Childe Harold's Pilgrimage

The difficulty in identifying the speaker stems from two basic technical decisions on Byron's part: (*a*) to forgo the use of quotation marks around Harold's words (except in the case of the songs);[1] and (*b*) to designate Harold as the speaker only after he has finished talking. Thus, as we begin reading Canto I we have no difficulty perceiving that stanzas 1–13 are in the voice of the narrator. The problem of attribution crops up only in relation to stanzas 14–93. The opening line of 27 indicates that the poet has resumed the speaker's role from Harold. If we trace back over the stanzas preceding 27 we find that no indication is given after stanza 14 that the poet is the speaker. Stanzas 15–26 constitute one coherent thought pattern, and must, therefore, be the referent of "So deemed the Childe" in 27. I except stanza 14 because its narrative/descriptive style differs markedly from the burst of direct address with which 15 opens. In 14, for example, the speaker's tone is noticeably objective, as if he considered himself primarily an observer on the trip. Stanzas 27–84 nowhere suggest that Harold is the speaker; on the contrary, the Parnassus digression (60 ff.), the opening lines of 28 and 45, and the reintroduction of Harold in 84 all indicate that this portion of the poem is wholly the utterance of the poet. Again, stanzas 85–93, after Harold's lyric "To Inez," must be attributed to the poet, given the direct address in 91 to the recently deceased "friend," along with Byron's note to that stanza. Further, the four canceled stanzas after 87 (replaced in the received text by stanzas 88–93) show clearly that Byron intended the speaking poet and not Harold to be the voice of this closing section of the Canto.

In Canto II Harold speaks directly to us even less frequently than he did in Canto I. The poet maintains the speaking position until the middle of stanza 30. Harold then addresses five lines to Florence, whereupon the poet immediately resumes his role as narrator. Stanzas 31–72 provide no notice

[1] This is a significant departure from the practice of those poets on whom Byron modeled his work. Compare, for example, *The Minstrel*, *Marmion*, *The Lay of the Last Minstrel*, and James Montgomery's *Wanderer of Switzerland*.

of Harold as the speaker; on the contrary, the presence of the poet is constantly thrown before us. The stanzas that conclude the canto after the Suliote song (73–98) are all of a piece and seem to be the mournful utterance of the poet as he returns to the subject with which he opened this canto. Of the critics who have addressed themselves to the problem only E. H. Coleridge has argued for Harold as speaker.[2] The external evidence is clear, however, that Byron intended the stanzas to be read as his own reflections.[3] Moreover, line 6 of stanza 96 is clearly a subjective reference intended to recall the personal lament in stanza 9 as well as the stanzas on Wingfield at the end of Canto I along with the prose note to those stanzas. Moreover, if the poet is not musing to himself in 94 then Harold the dramatic character must be addressing his creator—a situation not unparalleled in poetry or drama but one which is as pointless as it is unsanctioned in *Childe Harold's Pilgrimage*. Finally, in 79 the speaker refers directly to his poetic function and activity ("Alas! her woes will still pervade my strain!").

The narrating poet is fully as present in Canto III as in Cantos I–II. Harold is responsible for only five stanzas in the third canto, plus the lyric "The Castled Crag of Drachenfels." In stanza 52 we read: "Thus Harold inly said." Stanzas 1–46 are demonstrably the utterance of the poet in his own person. He finishes his meditative commentary in 45, and in 46 he turns to the objective scene before him and tells us that Harold too stands gazing at the natural setting. Lines 6–9 of 46 are the poet's brief general description of the landscape. Stanzas 47–51 are a single and continuous comment upon the significance of the scene for the speaker, and since nothing in these forty-five lines indicates that the poet is the speaker, we must—following the signal in line 1 of stanza 52—assign them to Harold. In 46 Byron prepares Harold for his short disquisition, and the poet's analysis of his hero's state of mind, put forth in 52–55, is an accurate description of Harold's sentiments expressed in 47–51 and in "The Castled Crag of Drachenfels." These are the last words that Harold speaks in the poem. *Childe Harold's Pilgrimage* sweeps to its conclusion in Canto IV as an uninterrupted first-person narrative in which the poet bears along to a personal resolution the theme symbolized by his poetic dream-creature Harold: the theme of *Angst*, an individual's doubt of his own moral efficacy.

[2] *P* 2:142. But compare: *Byron: Childe Harold*, ed. H. P. Tozer (Oxford, 1891), p. 247, note to line 693; Francis Jeffrey's review of the first two cantos, *Edinburgh Review*, 19 (June, 1812):474; and George Ellis' review, *Quarterly Review* 7 (March, 1812):189.
[3] See, for example, his remarks in letters to Dallas at *LJ* 2:66, 161, 162.

B

Tabular Collation of MS M and MS D of Cantos I–II with the First Edition

CANTO 1

I. Revisions to MS M

  a) Additional Stanzas

    [7] 8. "Yet oft-times in his maddest mirthful mood,"

    [8] 9. "And none did love him!—though to hall and bower,"

    [12] 13. "But when the sun was sinking in the sea"

    "Childe Harold's Good Night."

    "To Inez."

  b) Deleted Stanzas

    [7]. "Of all his train there was a henchman page,"

    [8]. "Him and one yeoman only did he take,"

    [21/22]. "Unhappy Vathek! in an evil hour,"

    "The Girl of Cadiz."

II. Revisions to MS D

  a) Additional Stanzas

    1. "Oh, Thou! in Hellas deemed of heavenly birth,"

    43. "Oh, Albuera! glorious field of grief,"

    85. "Adieu, fair Cadiz! yea, a long adieu!"

    86. "Such be the sons of Spain, and strange her Fate,"

    88. "Flows there a tear of pity for the dead?"

    89. "Nor yet, alas! the dreadful work is done,"

    90. "Not all the blood at Talavera shed,"

    91. "And thou, my friend!—since unavailing woe,"

    92. "Oh, known the earliest, and esteemed the most,"

  b) Deleted Stanzas

    [24]. "In golden characters right well designed,"

    [26]. "But when Convention sent his handy work,"

    [27]. "Thus unto Heaven appealed the people: Heaven,"

    [87]. "There may you read with spectacles on eyes,"

    [88]. "There may you read—Oh, Phoebus, save Sir John,"

    [89]. "Yet here of Vulpes mention may be made,"

  c) Reworked Stanzas

    [25] 25. "Convention is the dwarfish demon styled,"

    [86] 87. "Ye, who would more of Spain and Spaniards know,"

CANTO II

I. Revisions to MS M

  a) Additional Stanzas

    [14]15. "Cold is the heart, fair Greece! that looks on Thee,"

    [52/53]52(53). "Oh! where, Dodona! is thine aged Grove?"

    [79/81]80(88). "Where'er we tread 'tis haunted, holy ground,"

II. Revisions to MS D

  a) Additional Stanzas

    8. "Yet if, as holiest men have deemed, there be,"

    9. "There, Thou! whose Love and Life together fled,"

    83(93). "Let such approach this consecrated Land,"

    84(94). "For thee, who thus in too protracted song,"

    85(95). "Thou too art gone, thou loved and lovely one,"

    86(96). "Oh! ever loving, lovely, and beloved!"

    87(97). "Then must I plunge again into the crowd,"

    88(98). "What is the worst of woes that wait on Age?"

  b) Deleted Stanzas

    [8]. "Frown not upon me, churlish Priest! that I,"

    [15]. "Come, then, ye classic Thieves of each degree,"

    [16]. "Or will the gentle Dilettanti crew,"

  c) Reworked Stanzas

    [12]13. "What! shall it e'er be said by British tongue,"

    [64]63(64). " 'Mid many things most new to ear and eye,"

C

The Composition and Revision of
Childe Harold's Pilgrimage III

We are given, or can deduce with certainty, specific dates for each of the three versions of the poem, as well as for a number of particular stanzas and passages. Concrete details provided on the manuscripts or from other sources are the following:

> *May 4:* Byron wrote twenty-six stanzas for his poem, including "some on Waterloo." Stanzas 17–18 were definitely among them.[1]
>
> *May 11:* Byron wrote his lyric "The Castled Crag of Drachenfels."[2]
>
> *May, date unspecified:* Stanzas [74] 77 and 110.[3]

---

[1] See *The Diary of John William Polidori*, ed. William Rossetti (London, 1911), p. 66; Pryse Lockhart Gordon, *Personal Memoirs*, 2 vols. (London, 1830), 2:325.

[2] P 2:249, n. 1.

[3] A MS leaf containing these two stanzas and the general date "May, 1816" is bound up in MS R. See discussion below.

June 3: Stanza 67.[4]

June 13: Stanzas 92–97.[5]

June 23: Byron writes to Hobhouse saying he has finished a new canto for *Childe Harold's Pilgrimage* which numbers 111 stanzas.[6]

June 27: In a letter to Murray Byron states that he has finished Canto III to a total of 117 stanzas.[7]

July 4 and 10: Two separate dates written at the end of MS C in Byron's hand to indicate the completion of the poem.[8]

Using these facts as a base, we can give a fairly specific chronological reconstruction of the poem's stages of composition. The discussion of the composition of the original one hundred-stanza poem will be left to the last since the problems with regard to it are somewhat complicated.

It seems certain that Byron finished the first version of the canto sometime after June 3, when he wrote stanza 67 (which was part of it), and before June 13, when he wrote stanzas 92–97 (which were not part of it). Between June 13, the date of the storm sequence, and June 22, when he left with Shelley on a ten-day sailing tour to some of the more famous sites around Lake Geneva,[9] Byron added eleven stanzas to his poem (88; 92–98; 110; 113–14). Of these, only stanza 110 seems to have been written before June 13.[10] Byron's lost fair copy must have been made at this time as well, for Claire Clairmont wrote out her transcript from this manuscript while Byron was away with Shelley. Stanzas 99–104 were written sometime between June 23–27; probably on the 25th or 26th when Byron and Shelley were at Clarens and Vevey respectively (*Biography* 2:631–32). After the two poets returned to Montalegre on July 1 Byron incorporated his six new stanzas into MS C from the loose sheets on which he had written them while he was away. He must have revised his fair copy and MS C into a unit of 117 stanzas by July 4, the first date written at the end of MS C. Afterward, while he was adding some notes to the poem, he composed stanza 33 on a small scrap of paper to be found in MS R and incorporated it into the canto as the final edition.

Heretofore a lack of information about the condition of MS R has led to some confusion about the early stages of the poem's composition. The profound influence that Shelley had upon Byron's mind during their stay in

---

[4] *P* 2:299, n. 16.

[5] *P* 2:303, n. 20. The leaves in MS R containing these stanzas are dated June 12, 1816, by Byron. The discrepancy is explained by Byron's statement that the storm occurred "at midnight." He must have written the stanzas while the storm was actually raging.

[6] *Correspondence* 2:11.

[7] *LJ* 3:336–37.

[8] *P* 2:214, 289.

[9] *Biography* 2:630.

[10] It was written in May, as I have already indicated, but was not given a place in the original one hundred-stanza poem. It is possible that Byron's renumbering of stanza [96] 109 twice is an indication that he was trying to find a place for stanza 110. We cannot be certain, however, since the stanza is given no number by Byron in MS R.

Switzerland together is a matter of general knowledge, but it has never been altogether clear just how much of the canto was written after Byron met Shelley, or precisely when the order of the stanzas was decided upon. Coleridge, for example, appends the following note to stanza 6:

> At this stage in his poetic growth, in part converted by Shelley, in part by Wordsworth as preached by Shelley, Byron, so to speak, "got religion," went over for a while to the Church of the mystics. *(P 2:219, n. 1)*

But while Shelley's characteristic thoughts and attitudes are unmistakable in the later portions of the poem, the manuscript evidence will not sanction the discovery of a similar influence in any of the first fifty-seven stanzas, and it argues strongly (though not conclusively) against Shelley's influence upon any of the first seventy-one stanzas as well. The only exceptions are stanzas 33 and 67. As I have already suggested, Canto III in its original form was written much as Cantos I–II:[11] he began at the beginning and numbered the stanzas sequentially at the time of their composition. Byron did not even meet Shelley until May 27, but by May 25 he had probably already written stanzas 1–62 and may have even got as far as stanza 71 by May 26. Some care must be taken, then, when we look for specific instances of Shelley's influence. From passages in the first half of the canto like stanzas 5–6 we cannot avoid the conclusion that Byron must have come to Lake Geneva in a state of mind that was already more than just susceptible to Shelley's enthusiasms and ideas.

The composition of MS R began some time in late April or early May, and its one hundred stanzas were completed sometime between June 3 and 12. The schedule of dates for the various stages of its composition is as follows:

> *April 25—May 3:* Stanzas 1–3
> *May 4:* [4–29] 4–25, 27–30
> *May 5–10:* 26; 31–32; [33–38] 34–39; [39, 41–43] 40, 42–44
> *May 11:* "The Castled Crag of Drachenfels"
> *May 11–13:* [40] 41, [44–56] 45–57
> *May 20–31:* [57–61] 58–62
> *May 26–31:* [62–69] 63–66, 68–71
> *May 27–31:* [70–73] 72–74, 76; [74] 77; and 110
> *May 27—June 3:* [75–78] 78–81; 67; 75
> *June 4–12:* [81–96] 82–91, 105–9, 111–12; [97–100] 115–18[12]

Byron left England on April 25, with his traveling companion Dr. John Polidori. They visited Waterloo on May 4, and Polidori noted in his diary that

---

[11] This pattern is repeated in the case of Canto IV as well, and it reflects his general practice of composition.
[12] *Biography* 2:607–8.

We rode back together through Soignies forest. . . . On reaching home we found the coach was jogged; so much so that it would not allow us to put confidence in it, etc. At last we gave it into Mr. Gordon's hands. My friend has written twenty six (?) stanzas today —some on Waterloo.[13]

Rossetti conjectured (p. 67) that these twenty-six stanzas might be the first twenty-six in the received poem. But the manuscript shows this to be impossible, for stanza 26 was not written until after stanza 30 was completed. Stanzas [4–29], an integral sequence of twenty-six manuscript stanzas, are undoubtedly the lines to which Polidori refers. Stanza 26 appears in MS R after this sequence—written in pencil on the back of the leaf which contains stanza [29] 30. Stanzas [4–29] are all written in ink[14] and are numbered consecutively at the time of their composition. From this we can also be sure that stanzas 1–3 already existed, though we cannot date them any more precisely than April 25–May 3.[15]

The first state of stanza [54] 55 shows that Byron intended the stanza to introduce the Drachenfels lyric in the canto.[16] The question is, when was stanza [54] 55 written? An entry in Polidori's diary seems to give us a definite answer. On May 13 he mentions the lyric for the first time: that it was composed two days earlier and sent then to Byron's sister. Polidori then adds: "See *Childe Harold*, from 'The Castled Crag of Drachenfels' to 'Still sweeten more these banks of Rhine'."[17] This reference to *Childe Harold* establishes May 13 as the latest date possible for the composition of stanza [54] 55. Further, since the stanzas before stanza [54] 55 are consecutively numbered in MS R at the time of their composition, it seems certain that Byron wrote stanzas 26, 31–32, and [33–54] 34–55 all between May 5 and 13.

Byron's travel itinerary for the period corroborates this view, and also helps us to determine even more exactly when Byron was writing specific groups of stanzas. He left Brussels with Polidori on May 6, passed through St. Trond and Aix la Chapelle, and arrived in Cologne at 11 P.M. on May 8.

[13] Polidori, *Diary*, p. 66. The question mark in parentheses in the text is Rossetti's. In a footnote to the passage he writes: "The entry, as written by Charlotte Polidori, stands thus–'26 st,' which I apprehend can only mean 'stanzas' " (p. 67).

[14] After writing stanza 26 in pencil he later numbered it "26" in ink, and renumbered stanzas [26–29] to 27–30.

[15] They are written on a single piece of MS, as a sequence, and were numbered 1–3 at the time of their composition.

[16] See the variants for the stanza printed by Coleridge at *P* 2:248. He does not list all of them, but the variants for the last line are complete and they indicate that the lyric was intended to follow stanza 55 from the time that the latter was written.

[17] Polidori, *Diary*, p. 87. Rossetti adds a misleading note to this entry in his edition of the diary: "it is to be presumed that Dr. Polidori wrote his entry some while after May 13, 1816." He gives no reason for this presumption, and it is difficult to understand what it might have been. Possibly Rossetti thought that Polidori could not have known the lyric was to be part of the canto unless he had seen the whole of it in its final form. But MS R shows, of course, that Byron was composing Canto III in sequence during his journey with Polidori to Switzerland. There seems no reason to doubt the validity of Polidori's entry.

They departed Cologne on the 10th for Bonn, left Bonn on the 11th, and arrived at Coblenz later that day. They saw both Ehrenbreitstein and Marceau's tomb (stanzas 56–58) on the same day, but did not inspect either at close range until the 12th. They arrived at St. Goar late on the 12th and at Mainz late on the 13th. Polidori became ill on the 14th when they arrived at Mannheim, so that after they got to Karlsruhe on the 15th their progress was held up until May 18, when Polidori was sufficiently recovered to resume the journey (*Diary* 71–90).

The condition of MS R substantiates the presumption that stanzas 26 and 31–32 were written earlier than stanzas [33–54] 34–55. Stanzas 31–32 appear by themselves on a single leaf of manuscript, a good portion of which is left blank below them; stanza [33] 34 continues the poem at the top of a fresh page. Further, the handwriting of stanzas 31–32 shows a slight but noticeable difference from what immediately follows. The manuscript also indicates that stanzas [33–38] 34–39 were not written at the same time as any portion of stanzas [39–54] 40–55. Once again there is a slight gap in the manuscript, a noticeable difference in the speed of the writing and the letter formation, and a change in the paper. Since all of stanzas 26, 31–32, and [33–38] 34–39 remain focused upon Waterloo and its significance, the likelihood is that they were written before the Rhine Valley began to exert its influence upon him around May 11–13.

In order to date stanzas [39–54] 40–55 we must get a precise idea of how these stanzas were written. The process of their composition is rather interesting in itself. Byron begins by writing four stanzas which he numbers [39–42] and which correspond to stanzas 40, 42–44 in the received text. At this point Byron has not yet worked himself out of the Waterloo phase of his poem. The manuscript shows another interruption in the composition process after stanzas [39–42]. When he returns to the poem Byron immediately begins writing about the Rhine Valley. He drafts a new stanza [40] (received text: st. 41), changes the numeration of stanza [42] 44 to [43] 44 in order to accommodate the insertion, and then writes stanzas [44–45] 45–46 to continue the sequence of the poem. The new stanza [40] 41 is well conceived, for it provides the poem with a fine transition from the Waterloo/Napoleon section to the Rhine Valley sequence: the Rhine castles exist in the new landscape of quiescent fecundity, but they represent in themselves the same kind of dangerous *hubris* which possessed Napoleon. Byron then writes stanzas [46–48] 47–48, 51 and begins stanza [49] 52. The latter is crossed out after two lines are written, however, and Byron goes back to add a new stanza [48] (received text: st. 50). This is no sooner done than he composes yet another stanza [48] (received text: st. 49), after which he goes back over what he has written and corrects the numeration. Stanza 52, begun earlier but crossed out, is now drafted again immediately after stanza [48] 49. It is now numbered stanza 51, which is its correct position relative to the sequence of the canto in the first form of the poem. Again there is an interruption in the composition of the canto. When Byron resumes his poem he writes in sequence stanzas [52–56] 53–57, after which he again pauses.

Thus it is probable that stanzas [40] 41 and [44–51] 45–52, all of which were composed together, were written between May 11 and 13. They are the first stanzas that deal with the Rhine Valley, and although Byron entered it on May 9 at Cologne, he could not have got a look at "a tower upon a headlong rock" (st. [40] 41) until he left Bonn on May 11. Most of the castles are near Coblenz, and the northernmost are still a good deal south of Bonn along the route that Byron took. Stanza [46] 47 begins, "And there they stand, as stands a lofty mind." On May 12 Byron and Polidori arrived at St. Goar, which is surrounded by lofty fortresses and directly faces a line of them across the river. It is not impossible that stanzas [40] 41 and [44–51] 45–52 were all written in that town. The two men arrived at Mainz on the 13th, at which point they would have been past all the magnificent old castles and on their way out of the valley toward Carlsruhe. Finally, stanzas [39, 41–43] 40, 42–44, which were written as a unit before stanzas [40] 41 and [44–51], 45–52, were probably composed before Byron and Polidori came to Coblenz and their first sight of the Rhine fortresses (*Diary*, 81). The stanzas continue the earlier Waterloo themes, but they register no impressions at all of the Rhine Valley.

The next significant date that we have is a notation on a leaf of foolscap manuscript in MS R which contains stanzas [74] 77 and 110.[18] The two stanzas are headed "Detached stanzas to be inserted in the progress of the poem—May, 1816." MS R also shows that the following three sequences were written as integral units, at separate times: stanzas [57–61] 58–62; [62–69] 63–66, 68–71; and [70–73] 72–74, 76. Knowing as we do Byron's predilection for writing about scenes only if he had actually seen them, we can be fairly sure that stanzas 58–62 were not composed before May 20 (when he had a good view of the Swiss Alps from a hill just outside Krolzingen, and when he got a last look at the Rhine just before he crossed into Switzerland—*Diary*, 90–91); that stanzas 63–66 and 68–71 were not written before May 26 (the day Byron first saw "the blue rushing of the arrowy Rhone" from the Villa Diodati near Geneva;[19] and that stanzas 72–74 and 76 must have been written between May 27 and 31, or some time before stanza [74] 77 and sometime after stanzas 63–66 and 68–71. The exact date for stanza [74] 77 has to be very late in the month, certainly not before May 27, which is the earliest possible date for stanzas 72–74 and 76. This whole group of stanzas *may* have been written between May 27 and 31, but it is more likely that the dates of composition were spread out between May 20 and 31. We are probably justified in concluding that stanzas 58–62

[18] The leaf contains also stanzas [75–78] 78–81, but they were clearly not written at the same time as stanza [74]77, though they too may have been written in May. See discussion below.

[19] *Biography* 2:621. See also stanza 71 and Byron's notes to it.

were written between May 20 and 23, or before Byron saw Morat and Aventicum (May 24) (*Diary*, 96); that stanzas 63–66 and 68–71 were written on or shortly after May 26–27; and that stanzas 72–74 and 76 were composed within a day or two of Byron's first acquaintance with Shelley.

We know from Byron's note to stanza 67 that it was written on June 3. The stanza is not part of the original sequence [62–69], nor does it appear anywhere in MS R. Its date, however, helps us to fix the chronology of stanzas [75–100]. MS R shows the sequence of the canto proceeding regularly up to stanzas [75–78] 78–81. These four stanzas appear on the same leaf as stanza [74] 77, but they were not written at the same time as the latter, nor were they numbered when they were first written. Stanza 75 is not numbered in MS R; it is written into the manuscript across stanza [70] 72. After the inserted leaf containing stanzas [74] 77 and [75–78] 78–81, the canto picks up again at stanza [81] 82 and continues uninterruptedly to its conclusion. All of these last twenty stanzas were numbered at the time of their composition. This final sequence could only have been numbered [81–100] if Byron had written two new stanzas for his poem after stanzas [75–78]. These two stanzas would be 67 and 75. The outside limits for dating stanzas [75–78] 78–81 and 75 would be, then, May 27—June 3.

Finally, the last twenty stanzas of the original poem must have been written between June 3 and 13. On the latter date Byron wrote his storm sequence (st. 92–97) which appears as an integral set of stanzas among the additions at the end of MS R. The storm sequence is not numbered in the manuscript, however, nor is any attempt made to incorporate it into the original "finished" form of the poem.

Tabular Collation of MS R and MS C, Canto III

FIRST FORM OF CANTO (MS R)	SECOND FORM OF CANTO (MS C, FIRST FORM)	FINAL FORM OF CANTO (MS C, COMPLETED FORM)
1–32	1–32	1–32
		33
[33–86]	33–86	34–87
	87	88
[87–89]	88–90	89–91
	91–96	92–97
	97	98
		99–104
[90–93]	98–101	105–8
[96]	102	109
	103	110
[94–95]	104–5	111–12
	106–7	113–14
[97–100]	108–11	115–18

D

The Composition and Revision of
Childe Harold's Pilgrimage IV

In his Introduction to the fourth canto of *Childe Harold's Pilgrimage*, E. H. Coleridge collated the MSS of the poem and discussed its growth during the process of composition. The canto was begun on June 26, 1817—only nine days after Byron had written to Murray stating that he had no intention of continuing his famous work—and it was not completed until the beginning of 1818.[1] Drawing from Byron's letters during that period, Coleridge gave the following chronology for the poem's numerous additional stanzas.

> . . . on June 26 he made a beginning. Thirty stanzas were "roughened off" on the 1st of July, fifty-six were accomplished by the 9th, "ninety and eight" by the 15th, and on July 20th he announces "the completion of the fourth and ultimate canto of *Childe Harold*. It consists of 126 stanzas." One stanza (xl) was appended to the fair copy.

> Byron had no sooner completed this "fourth and ultimate canto," than he began to throw off additional stanzas. His letters to Murray during the autumn of 1817 announce these successive lengthenings; but it is impossible to trace the exact order of their composition. On the 7th of August the canto stood at 130 stanzas, on the 21st at 133; on the 4th of September at 144, on the 17th at 150; and by November 15th it had reached 167 stanzas.

> Of nineteen stanzas which were still to be added, six—on the death of the Princess Charlotte . . . —were written at the beginning of December, and two stanzas (clxxvii., clxxviii) were forwarded to Murray in the early spring of 1818.

> Sometime during the month of December, 1817, Byron wrote out a fair copy of the entire canto, numbering 184 stanzas (MS D): and on January 7, 1818, Hobhouse left Venice for England, with "the whole of the MSS.". . . .[2]

All of Coleridge's facts here are correct, except that the "fair copy [of] 184 stanzas" was not transcribed wholly in December. It was originally written out as a poem of 144 stanzas, at the end of which Byron wrote "Laus

[1] P 2:311–19, 327, n. 1. See also *LJ* 4:139.
[2] P 2:311, 313.

Deo! Byron. La Mira, near Venice, Sept. 3, 1817." Between September 3 and January 7 Byron added 41 new stanzas to this fair copy.

As Coleridge states, the difficulties in dating accurately the many additions to Canto IV are very great. Nevertheless, a substantial amount of new and more specific information than Coleridge assembled can be obtained through a careful examination of the extant MSS and a comparison of them with the available biographical data.

Two integral MSS of the poem exist, both of which are fair copies. The first (MS B)[3] consists of 126 stanzas, the composition of which was completed in rough form on July 20, as Coleridge indicates. The rough drafts of this MS are not forthcoming, however; MS B is a fair copy made from them, and was completed on July 29, 1817.[4] The second integral MS of the canto is MS H[5] which Hobhouse took with him to England on January 7th, 1818 as a poem of 184 stanzas. The original form of this MS, however, was completed on September 3, 1817, and was a fair copy poem of 144 stanzas made up from the 126 stanzas in MS B and eighteen new stanzas written between July 29 and September 3. Between September 3 and January 7 Byron made 41 additional insertions in MS H.[6] Also extant is a large group of loose MS leaves (MS BA bound up together at the end of MS B.) MS BA contains the rough drafts for 51 of Byron's 60 additions to the canto made after July 29.[7] One other of these additions is written on the back of the last leaf of MS B, as Coleridge has noted. A fair copy of two others—stanzas 177–78 —can be found on a single foolscap sheet bound up at the end of MS H. Finally, the rough draft of stanza 98 also exists on a single scrap of MS in the Berg Collection of the New York Public Library. Five other stanzas were added to MS H but of these no rough drafts seem to exist. They appear only in MS H as fair copy insertions; stanzas 41, 120, 121, 122, and 124.[8]

---

[3] This is Coleridge's MS M. I have changed the designation because the symbol M was already used, both by Coleridge and myself, for one of the MSS of Cantos I–II.

[4] This is written on the MS at the end of stanza 126 (cf. P 2:463, n. 1). On the back of the last leaf of MS B is received stanza 40, with a note in Byron's hand directing that it be inserted "after stanza 30th" in MS B.

[5] This is Coleridge's MS D. Again I have changed the designation because I have already referred to a MS D in relation to Cantos I–II.

[6] It seems clear from MS H that Byron expected to make extensive additions to the poem after he completed the fair copy on September 3. The MS is made up entirely of foolscap sheets on each of which only one stanza was originally written—at the very top of the front side. Thus, each of the 144 sheets had ample space on front and back for additional stanzas, and Byron did in fact write his additions in those spaces.

[7] It includes one stanza that did not appear in the poem ("If to forgive be 'heaping coals of fire' ": see P 2:429, variant i). The other fifty stanzas are the following: 2; 12; 13–14 and 47 (on one leaf); 16–17; 27–29; 51–52; 54–55 and 109 (on one leaf); 56–60; 80–82; 85–86; 93–97; 112–14; 123, 152, and 182 (on one leaf); 125–27; 135–37 (the dropped stanza is on this leaf as well); 167–72; 173–74.

[8] Coleridge states, incorrectly, that there is no rough draft of stanza 97 in the loose MSS bound up with MS B (P 2:319).

Since the rough drafts of the 126 stanzas in MS B are not available, it is not possible to determine the precise order in which the stanzas for the first stage of the poem were written.[9] Between July 29, when the transcription of MS B was completed, and September 3, when the first form of MS H was copied out, Byron added 18 stanzas. A comparison of MS B with the first form of MS H shows that these 18 stanzas included the following: stanzas 27–29; 40; 54–55; 109; 120–24; 135–37; 152; 182; and the stanza that was later dropped from the poem ("If to forgive be 'heaping coals of fire' "). Even more precise dates for the composition of these stanzas can be established, however. From Byron's letters to John Murray of August 7, August 21, and September 4 we know that, of the 18 new stanzas added during that period, 4 were added before August 7, 3 between August 7 and August 21, and 11 between August 21 and September 3. It seems fairly certain that the additions were made in the following order.

a) July 20—August 7: stanzas 40 and 135–37.
b) August 7–August 21: stanzas 27–29.
c) August 21—September 3: stanzas 54–55; 109; 120–24; 152; 182; and the dropped stanza.

Stanzas 27–29 were composed on or shortly after August 18; Hobhouse and Byron both testify to this fact.[10] That stanza 40 belongs to the period of July 29—August 7 is clear not only from its position on the last leaf of MS B, but also from Byron's letter to Murray of August 7.[11] On August, 12, he wrote to Murray and mentioned that he had just heard of the death of Mme de Staël; it seems likely, therefore, that stanzas 54–55—with their note commemorating the memory of that lady—belong to the period of August 21—September 3.[12] Stanza 109 is written below stanzas 54–55 on the same loose MS leaf in MS BA, so that it was probably composed sometime after September 21 as well. Stanzas 120–24 are written in MS H as an integral sequence; being five stanzas, they must also have been added after September 21. Only one of these stanzas exists in rough draft, stanza 123. This is written on a single leaf which also contains rough drafts of stanzas 152 and 182. These two stanzas, then, were also probably added to the poem after September 21. Four undated stanzas remain: stanzas 135–37 and the dropped stanza. All four appear on one loose MS leaf in MS BA. Stanzas 135–37 are written there as a single sequence, but the dropped stanza—which appears

[9] The contents of MS B are given by Coleridge at *P* 2:316–17.
[10] See *P* 2:348, n. 2, and Lord Broughton [John Cam Hobhouse], *Recollections of a Long Life*, ed. Lady Dorchester (London, 1909–11), 2:77.
[11] *LJ* 4:155–56.
[12] "I have been very sorry to hear of the death of Me de Stael, not only because she had been very kind to me at Copet, but because now I can never requite her. In a general point of view, she will leave a great gap in Society and literature" (*LJ* 4:156). For the long and sympathetic note on Mme de Staël see *P* 2:490–91.

last on the MS leaf—was clearly written at a later date altogether. Since we know that Byron wrote four new stanzas between July 29 and August 7, stanzas 135–37 were probably added at that time (thus, with stanza 40, making a total of four), while the dropped stanza must have been written after August 21, and added to MS H while Byron was incorporating his additions into his new fair copy.

Between September 3, 1817, and January 7, 1818, Byron added 41 stanzas to the canto and deleted one.[13] Except in two instances, we have no precise and certain dates for these stanzas; nevertheless, highly probable dates can be fixed upon for a good many of these additions on the basis of their relation to certain reference points whose dates have been objectively established. A number of other stanzas have only an indirect relation to these points of reference, however, so that we must rely upon a certain amount of indirect evidence to determine their dates.

We know that the poem numbered 184 stanzas on January 7, and we also know—from two of Byron's letters—that the canto had grown to 150 stanzas between September 4 and 15, and had further increased to 167 stanzas by November 15.[14] Using these dates for our frame of reference, we can set up the following schedule for the rest of Byron's additions to MS H.

> a) September 4—September 15: stanzas 93–98 (six additions).
>
> b) September 15—November 15: stanzas 12–14; 47; 56–60; 80–82; 85–86; 112–14 (seventeen additions).
>
> c) November 15—January 7: stanzas 2; 16–17; 41; 51–52; 125–27; 167–72; 173–74; 181 (eighteen additions).

We can establish authoritative dates for three of these groups (a total of fourteen stanzas) from certain pieces of factual chronological evidence. The passage on the Princess Charlotte (stanzas 167–72) was composed late in November just after Byron had learned of it.[15] A calculation made by Byron on the foolscap leaf containing the rough draft of stanzas 56–60 fixes their date some time between September 15 and November 15.[16] Finally, MS H

---

[13] The decision to drop the stanza was made very late. The stanza is crossed out in MS H and followed by this note: "Omit this stanza. Byron. Jy. 6th 1818."

[14] *LJ* 4:168, 182.

[15] Byron learned of her death on November 23. See Hobhouse, *Recollections*, 2: 84–85.

[16] Byron indicated that these five stanzas increased the total number in the canto to 162 (on November 15 he had completed 167). Byron kept rather careful track of the number of his additions, as his letters of the period show. On this piece of MS he calculated the number of lines in the poem on the basis of 162 stanzas. We find a similar calculation on the leaf containing stanzas 177–78: there he not only figures the number of lines and stanzas in the canto, but the total number in the other cantos and in the poem as a whole. He seems to have been pleased that the total came to an even five hundred, and he may even have been moved to add the last two stanzas partly by the desire to bring the total to that round number. Stanzas 56–60 were probably added late in October or early in November, when Byron was inserting some new stanzas at Hobhouse's suggestion. See my discussion below.

shows that stanzas 12–14 were all inserted at the same time, and the rough draft containing stanza 12 is dated by Byron "November 10th 1817."

Reliable dates can be obtained for a number of other stanzas on the basis of Byron's methods of stanza numeration in MS H. It is sometimes possible to tell, for example, whether a certain stanza or group of stanzas was added before or after one of the three dated groups. A brief introductory note on this matter of stanza numbering (and renumbering) will help to orient the reader to the following discussion. When Byron completed his fair copy of MS H on September 3 the poem totaled 144 stanzas, and all were numbered in sequence accordingly. As Byron made his additions to this MS during the fall and winter, he would indicate their relative position in the developing text by numbering the new stanzas in relation to the existing ones that surrounded them.[17] He did not renumber the whole poem after each addition, nor even a large section of the poem, but just one or two stanzas immediately following the new insertion. At some late date he must have thought he had completed all his additions, for he renumbered the canto to a total of 183 stanzas. Shortly afterward, however, he renumbered every stanza from stanza 42 onward to a total of 184.

That final renumbering of the whole canto, then, indicates that stanza 41 was the last added to the poem before Hobhouse took it with him to England in January.[18] Because stanzas 173–74 were originally numbered 144–45 on MS H, we can be fairly sure that they were added some time after the Princess Charlotte sequence.[19] Similarly, the numbering in the MS shows that stanzas 16–17 must have been inserted in the poem sometime after stanzas 12–14.[20] Finally, stanza 47 appears in rough form on the same MS leaf that contains stanzas 13–14; thus it was probably placed in the poem on or about November 10, when stanzas 12–14 were added.

We cannot establish the chronology of any more of Byron's additions on the basis of MS evidence alone. Thus, although MS H shows that stanzas 85–86 were added shortly after stanzas 80–82, we have no way of determining from the MS when stanzas 80–82 were added. Nevertheless, we know enough about Byron's mode of living during the period when his additions were made to arrive at some reasonable conclusions about the chronology of some other additions. Hobhouse joined Byron at La Mira on July 31 after he had completed some traveling around Italy. During his journeys he had been compiling a large stock of historical information on Italy and her liter-

---

[17] See tabular collation.

[18] It was probably added on January 5 or 6. See Hobhouse, *Recollections*, 2: 88, 90.

[19] Probably very soon after. They were inserted right below two stanzas numbered 136–37 in MS H and consequently ought to have been numbered 138–39. The Princess Charlotte sequence was inserted immediately before stanzas 136–37, however, and was originally numbered 136–41. Thus Byron must have numbered his new insertions 144–45 with the knowledge that the Princess Charlotte sequence already existed in the poem. See tabular collation.

[20] See tabular collation. It should be noted that these two stanzas must also have been added after stanza 2.

ature. He was greatly pleased with the new canto when he read it in August, and Byron was so impressed with his knowledge of Italian history that he asked him to do the notes for the canto.[21] Hobhouse recorded later that he had been instrumental in getting Byron to write a good many of the additions for the poem.

> When I rejoined Lord Byron . . . I found him employed upon the Fourth Canto of *Childe Harold*, and, later in the autumn he showed me the first sketch of the poem. It was much shorter than it afterwards became, and it did not remark on several objects which appeared to me peculiarly worthy of notice. I made a list of these objects, and in conversation with him gave him reasons for the selection. The result was the poem as it now appears, and he then engaged me to write the notes.[22]

If we examine Hobhouse's *Historical Illustrations*, as well as his other notes published with the poem, we can determine pretty well what Hobhouse's "list" contained,[23] and what stanzas in Canto IV were added at his suggestion. They would include, at the most, stanzas 12–14; 54–55; 56–60; 80–82; 85–86; 112–14; and 173–74.[24] Stanzas 54–55 and 152 we have already dated sometime in late August or early September. But stanzas 12–14, 56–60, and 173–74 all belong to the period November–December, and it is most likely—as Hobhouse suggested in his statement just quoted—that stanzas 80–82, 85–86, and 112–14 were also added "later in the autumn" when he was working diligently on his historical notes and illustrations. Like stanzas 12–14 and 56–60, in fact, most, if not all, of these further "Hobhouse" additions were probably added sometime in late October or early November when Byron and Hobhouse were living together at La Mira—each working in his own way on further additions for the poem.

We are left with thirteen undated stanzas: 2; 51–52; 93–98; 125–27; and 181. The dates that I have assigned to them are based upon certain pieces of circumstantial evidence and a process of elimination.[25] Stanzas 125–27 seem to have been written about the same time as, or shortly after, the Princess Charlotte sequence. Not only do the themes coincide very closely; the same pas-

---

21 *LJ* 4:164–65.

22 Quoted at *P* 2:315.

23 John Cam Hobhouse, *Historical Illustrations of the Fourth Canto of Childe Harold* (London, 1818). See especially pp. 58–200; 224–63; 327–45; 510–53.

24 Over 60 per cent of the *Historical Illustrations* is taken up by notes on only eight stanzas (80–82, 112–14, and 173–74). The number of "Hobhouse additions" could, at the most, amount to twenty-one stanzas, or just over 10 per cent of the whole poem. These facts ought to be remembered when we estimate Hobhouse's influence upon the canto. See also Andrew Rutherford, "The Influence of Hobhouse on *Childe Harold's Pilgrimage, Canto IV,*" *RES* n.s. 12 (1961):391–97.

25 Byron indicated in his letters that six stanzas were added between September 4 and 15, seventeen between September 15 and November 15, and eighteen between November 15 and January 7. Thus we have still to determine the six stanzas for September 4–15 and seven stanzas for November 15—January 7.

sage from Milton is echoed in both stanza 126 and stanza 167, and in each case the allusion is made in the same way and to the same effect. A late date is to be expected for an isolated insertion like stanza 181 near the end of the poem, which seems to be a relatively spontaneous expansion of the Hymn to Ocean. The numeration in MS H suggests that stanza 2 was added when Byron was renumbering the whole canto for the first time—some time in December, and shortly before stanzas 16–17 were added.[26] Finally, the numbering in MS H also indicates that stanzas 51–52 were added after stanzas 56–60, and that stanzas 93–98 were added before the related sequence 80–82 and 85–86.[27]

Tabular Collation of MS B and MS H

Note: The bracketed numbers are numeration changes added
by Byron temporarily in order to locate his additions to MS H

MS B	MS H (FIRST FORM)	INSERTIONS IN MS H	MS H (FINAL FORM)
1	1		1
		2	2
2–10	2–10		3–11
		11–13	12–14
11	11 [14]		15
		16–17	16–17
12–20	12–20		18–26
	21–23		27–29
21–30	24–33		30–39
	34		40
		35	41
31–35	35–39		42–46
		40	47
36–38	40 [41], 41, 42		48–50
		43–44	51–52

[26] See tabular collation. Stanzas 16–17 must have been added very late, for their numeration coincides with that of the published poem from the time of their insertion in the MS.

[27] This seems to be a valid inference based upon Byron's usual practice of temporary renumbering for his additions to MS H. If two insertions stand in close proximity to each other in the MS, Byron regularly renumbered the second in relation to his temporary renumbering of the first *if* the second was added after the first (i.e., if it followed it in time). I have already called attention to this practice in the case of stanzas 80–82, 85–86, and 173–74. Stanzas 56–60 were originally numbered 46–50 in MS H. But if Byron followed his usual renumbering practice in this instance, and if stanzas 51–52 had been added to the MS before 56–60, then the latter group would have been initially renumbered 48–52, not 46–50. Similarly, stanzas 93–98 are initially numbered 73–78, but Byron would have numbered them 78–83 if they had been added after stanzas 80–82 and 85–86.

MS B	MS H (FIRST FORM)	INSERTIONS IN MS H	MS H (FINAL FORM)
39	43 [45]		53
	44–45		54–55
		46–50	56–60
40–47	46 [47]-53		61–68*
48–52	54–58		73–77
53–56	59–62		69–72
57–58	63–64		78–79
		65–67	80–82
59–60	65 [68], 66 [69]		83–84
		70-71	85–86
61–66	67 [72] – 72		87–92
		73–78	93–98
67–76	73 [79] – 82		99–108
	83		109
77–78	84–85		110–11
		86–88	112–14
79–83	86[89] – 90		115–19
	91–95		120–24
		96–98	125–27
84–90	96 [99], 97 [100]		
	98 [101], 99–102		128–34
	103–6**		135–37
91–104	107–20		138–51
	121		152
105–18	122–35		153–66
		136–41	167–72
119–20	136–37		175–76
		144–45	173–74
121–22	138–39		177–78
	140		180
123–26	141–44		181–84
			177–78***

* The four stanzas on the Falls of Terni originally followed stanzas 73–77 in MS H. Their position was changed to the present one when Byron renumbered MS H to a total of 183 stanzas.

** In the first form of MS H the dropped stanza ("If to forgive be 'heaping coals of fire' ") was numbered 104.

*** These two stanzas were added in March, 1818. As a result, the last eight stanzas in MS H (final form) were renumbered from 177–84 to 179–86 in the published poem.

Index

319